Emerging Market Economies and Financial Globalization

ANTHEM FRONTIERS OF GLOBAL POLITICAL ECONOMY

The **Anthem Frontiers of Global Political Economy** series seeks to trigger and attract new thinking in global political economy, with particular reference to the prospects of emerging markets and developing countries. Written by renowned scholars from different parts of the world, books in this series provide historical, analytical and empirical perspectives on national economic strategies and processes, the implications of global and regional economic integration, the changing nature of the development project, and the diverse global-to-local forces that drive change. Scholars featured in the series extend earlier economic insights to provide fresh interpretations that allow new understandings of contemporary economic processes.

Emerging Market Economies and Financial Globalization

Argentina, Brazil, China, India and South Korea

Leonardo E. Stanley

ANTHEM PRESS

Anthem Press
An imprint of Wimbledon Publishing Company
www.anthempress.com

This edition first published in UK and USA 2018
by ANTHEM PRESS
75–76 Blackfriars Road, London SE1 8HA, UK
or PO Box 9779, London SW19 7ZG, UK
and
244 Madison Ave #116, New York, NY 10016, USA

British Library Cataloguing-in-Publication Data
A catalogue record for this book is available from the British Library.

Library of Congress Cataloging-in-Publication Data
Names: Stanley, Leonardo E., author.
Title: Emerging market economies and financial globalization : argentina, brazil, china, india and south korea / Leonardo E. Stanley.
Description: New York : Anthem Press, 2018. | Series: Anthem frontiers of global political economy | Includes bibliographical references and index.
Identifiers: LCCN 2018004291| ISBN 9781783086740 (hardback) | ISBN 1783086742 (hardback)
Subjects: LCSH: Finance – Developing countries – Case studies. | Capital movements – Developing countries – Case studies. | Investments, Foreign – Developing countries – Case studies. | BISAC: POLITICAL SCIENCE / Economic Conditions. | BUSINESS & ECONOMICS / Economics / Comparative. | BUSINESS & ECONOMICS / International / Economics.
Classification: LCC HG195.S83 2018 | DDC 330.9172/4–dc23
LC record available at https://lccn.loc.gov/2018004291

ISBN-13: 978-1-78308-674-0 (Hbk)
ISBN-10: 1-78308-674-2 (Hbk)

This title is also available as an e-book.

CONTENTS

ILLUSTRATIONS

Boxes

Figures

Tables

PREFACE

In one of his latest books, Colombian writer Gabriel Vazquez quotes Napoleon Bonaparte, 'To understand the man you have to know what was happening in the world when he was twenty' (Vazquez, 2015). In my case, this period of my life turned out to be during the 1980s, the politically impassioned years when democracy was just returning to my country: Argentina. Discussions were wise but particularly highly emotional, and my interest in political economy was something innate but which suddenly blossomed during those years. In any case, politics was more about excitement than just reason. For the neoclassical school (the approach taken in most undergraduate courses), the market mechanism was the only mechanism which insured ultimate economic efficiency, and government intervention would bring about market failure and diminish economic efficiency. A more open economy and shock therapy would bring to an end all these vices. In view of that, I began to search for alternative explanations given Argentina's cyclical boom-and-bust behaviour. In other words, looking for alternative explanations, I became trapped in some sort of paranoia, like Carlos Carballo, one of the main characters in a Vazquez novel.

In the search for an answer, I was confronted with two contesting visions. On the one hand, there were those associated with the so-called mercantilist tradition attributed to Jean-Baptiste Colbert, for whom the state should play a decisive role in national development and international economic relations. Trade, investments and economic relations are always dealing with distributional issues and, hence, are subject to conflict. International negotiations (such as those involving the global financial architecture and related issues) might resemble a 'zero-sum game'. The liberal interpretation associated with Adam Smith's ideas, on the other hand, highlights agents' rationality and the importance of free markets. Certainly followers of Smith have been longer recognizing the relevance of market failures and why a proper regulatory framework is often needed. Consequently, harmonious relations make international economic relations a 'positive-sum game': all we need are a free trade environment and proper regulation, and, henceforth, economic development will follow.

But I consider myself a fervent eclectic and enjoy reading from both traditions. A Colbertian perspective might be helpful in order to understand the effects of the Opium Wars on China's approach to globalization. Smithian lenses, however, might be helpful in describing the long-term benefits generated by Chinese leaders' decision to open their economy in the late 1970s.

Thus, this brings me to the general question posed in the book: why do some countries enjoy success, while others are condemned to fail? Is it possible to find a clear-cut explanation of this divide? What remains clear is that failure goes with those dogmatically attached to one school, but who do not recognize the shortcomings associated with it.

In looking for an answer to the above question, I employ an international political economy framework and compare the different political courses adopted by a group of emerging markets in their journey towards financial globalization. In order to accomplish this goal, I make use of a series of theoretical models, each of which focuses on a set of constraints observed during the journey. I hope the framework will be helpful in understanding our present times.

A final thought on scenarios and settings. The world is now, more than ever, exposed to uncertainties (the unknown unknowns or black swans), not just to measurable risk (the know unknowns). The future is becoming more difficult to predict, and in such a scenario politicians should be rewarding more flexibility.

ACKNOWLEDGEMENTS

I would first like to acknowledge Kevin P. Gallagher, a distinguished colleague and leading expert on international political economy with whom I have had the privilege of working on a series of projects, including the coordination of an international seminar on capital account regulation and trade agreements, hosted at the Centro de Estudios de Estado y Sociedad (CEDES), in July 2012. He invited me to write this book, and to him all my gratitude.

I wish also to express my gratitude to Michael Mortimore, former chief officer at the United Nations Economic Commission for Latin America and the Caribbean (ECLAC), but, fundamentally, a passionate scholar in Latin America development studies with whom I have had the benefit of working.

In the process of writing this book, my parents were important sources of inspiration. To both my gratitude.

But, for the most part, I am eternally grateful to my family, Martina, Santiago and Alejandro, for their patience and the enthusiasm they bring into my life.

Chapter One

INTRODUCTION

In the past, foreign shocks to emerging economies (EMEs) spread out mainly through the trade channel, and transmissions to local economies took time to come into effect. This could certainly be considered a by-product of the international financial setting designed at the Bretton Woods Conference, where capital flows remained mostly local. As sovereign states benefited from more policy room, they were less constrained when fixing monetary and fiscal policies. The availability of policy options did not shield them, however, from macroeconomic instability and recurrent gaps on both the external and the fiscal front, and particularly affecting (by the time categorized as) developing Latin American and Asian economies. Yet this relatively harmonious world was predestined to alter, as cross-border flows began to erupt in the late 1960s, pushing local financial markets towards *unchartered waters*. Thus, we can trace the origins of the 2008 global turmoil to the collapse of the Bretton Woods system in the early 1970s, when leading developed nations agreed to a progressive dismantling of the former controls on capital flows and when the banks' transnationalization journey began. Overflowing with liquidity, thanks to large, readily available deposits (Eurodollars) and strongly rising petroleum prices (petrodollars), US (basically) transnational banks set out to find new clients everywhere – including those living in distant and less developed countries. A new era for global banks began. Small (and now open) economies were suddenly at the mercy of the constraints imposed by the so-called monetary trilemma.

The shift towards free markets was accelerated after Margaret Thatcher in the United Kingdom and Ronald Reagan in the United States came to power in 1979 and 1980 respectively. The dominant (neo-liberal) view perceived increased financial activity as beneficial for development, and Keynesian–Myskian caveats were suddenly set aside by policymakers and disregarded by mainstream economists around the world. By the same token, the efficient market hypothesis gained space and substituted Keynes's beauty contest parabola in trying to explain how financial markets actually behave. That was the central message that emanated from international financial institutions (IFIs) through the instructions and the recommendations laid out by the Washington Consensus. From then on, developing countries were urged to liberalize their capital account and deregulate their financial sector.

Capital returned to the developing world in the early 1990s, but now under a new format: bonds were replacing (syndicated) bank loans, a popular financial scheme during the 1970s. Capital inflows were not free of cyclical downturns and sudden stops, however, the consequences of which were observed elsewhere. In some cases, the crisis responded to internal factors as macroeconomic imbalances originated at public or private dislocations that made unsustainable the peg being adopted. In most cases, however, the crisis followed external factors.

Irrespective of the country fundamentals, officials at the International Monetary Fund (IMF) replicated the same (orthodox) recommendation: sustain the macroeconomic adjustment and announce important structural changes. Among the changes requested by IMF staff, maintaining the capital account liberalization process remained key for those expecting its financial help – although the Fund was now willing to debate whether sequencing should overtake shock therapy. Furthermore, and even after the collapse in Asia, the leading nations of the IMF, headed by the United States, attempted to amend the Articles of Agreement to extend the Fund's jurisdiction to capital movements, associating them to members' current obligations under the current account chapter.

Thereafter, the crisis would affect the Fund as few emerging market economies (EMEs) remained interested in being part of its loan programmes – 'Not Even a Cat to Rescue' ran a headline in *The Economist*.[1] In any case, conscious of the constraints that were imposed in the past and their failures, EMEs' leaders began to abandon the neo-liberal template offered by Washington, DC. Governments in emerging markets and developing countries decided to better accumulate foreign reserves in an attempt 'to immunize themselves' against a hypothetical sudden stop. Other countries went even further and reintroduced capital controls. In one way or another, all of them were clearly trying to enhance their financial resilience and to expand their policy space. All these changes were signalling the beginning of a new era, although few were aware of it.

In the North, few were ready to acknowledge either the procyclicality of the financial system or the destructive power of financial innovations (sometime later described as 'weapons of mass destruction' by Warren ('Buffett Warns on Investment "Time Bomb" ', BBC News, 4 March 2003)). They were just enjoying life under the 'great moderation' years (Ben Bernanke, 'The Great Moderation', 20 February 2004, federalreserve.gov). Monetary policy was primarily centred on price stability, and it disregarded the mounting credit balloon and asset price booms being generated by market liquidity. Mainstream economists, in contrast, were hardly attracted to the idea of integrating financial factors into their models.

Despite this *business as usual* picture on mainstream minds, a new financial boom mounted, which was now associated with the arrival of new funding sources (non-core financing), including derivatives and other non-traditional products. Independently of the original sources, global liquidity would be transmitted to EMEs through transnational banks. The arrival of this non-core banking funding (foreign creditors) permitted local banks to support the entry of new borrowers at home – formerly exclusively backed by domestic savers. But a financial system based on cross-border banking tends to raise risks at home as external liabilities (wholesale funding) prove more volatile than normal retail funding (domestic depositors). Additionally, in most cases financial flows remained

1. *The Economist*, 20 April 2006.

weakly regulated as monetary authorities pursued banks' self-regulation and financial micro-prudential measures.

External pressures were not eliminated after the 2008 global financial crisis, however. Initially economic authorities accurately responded to the challenge, but unconventional monetary policies in the United States and other developed countries rapidly created important spillovers in EMEs. The prospects of an increasing path for US interest rates generated a reversal of expectations and a sudden flight to quality, implying increasing foreign exchange (FX) volatility among EMEs. This new scenario would call for additional coordination at the multilateral level, alongside the activation of non-traditional weapons by policymakers in the developed world and also among EMEs. Unfortunately, this has not happened, as Raghuram Rajan, the former governor of India's central bank, recently affirmed: 'International monetary cooperation has broken down.'

The first section of the book introduces the theoretical scheme, which lays the foundation for the comparative analysis to be entered in the second part. Explicitly, it proposes three sets of constraints (macro, micro and institutional) as to evaluate the policy space left to policymakers. When considering each of them, the book offers a particular theoretical framework highlighting the specific collection of constraint sovereign states face after deciding to open its capital account and become global. Surprisingly, all the topics under consideration are subject to a particular trilemma: a trilateral space, whose resolution calls for a dual policy configuration. All of these concepts would be observed by EMEs in their globalization journey, a context (apparently) limiting sovereign states' choices.

International Capital Flows and Macroeconomic Dilemmas

Chapter 2 briefly introduces the constraints on a sovereign state's policy space which are imposed by capital flow mobility to traditional monetary and exchange rate policies. In such a context, the national government can either fix the exchange rate (at the cost of sacrifice their monetary policy autonomy) or maintain a flexible a flexible exchange rate (to preserve the central bank's policy space). This is the basic trade-off originally described by Robert Mundell in the early sixties, the famous monetary trilemma: international transmission of monetary (and fiscal) policy depends on the exchange rate regime. In particular, when capitals are free to move, policymakers can either opt for fixing the exchange rate or delineating the monetary policy, but not both. In the early nineties, all bets were on fixing, for example but the Mexican crisis led to dismissing *this* option to lose weight and a new consensus was arrived at. Now flexible exchange rates were favoured. From a monetary perspective, the model was centred on the presence of two concepts: central bank independence (CBI) and inflation targeting (IT). Sooner rather than later, however, the scheme proved not to be a solution for EMEs. After the Asian financial crisis, EME policymakers began to move away from corner solutions, applying mixed strategies instead. Fearful of keeping an artificial exchange rate and the presence of a highly volatile nominal exchange rate, officials were ready to intervene in FOREX markets. Simultaneously, aware of the timid financial cooperation coming from advanced nations and the considerable restrictions imposed by IFIs in the aftermath of the crisis, they initiated a massive build-up of international reserves. Another group of countries avoided the constraints by regulating capital flows. Ironically, after 50 years of financial deregulation, more and more professionals were considering this latest alternative as a unique solution to tame unfettered capital and to avoid extreme financial volatility.

Financial Deepening and the New Microeconomic Dilemmas

Chapter 3 traces an evolutionary view of all financial issues and political restrictions imposed following the deregulation of financial markets. The provision of financial services in EMEs has undergone a transformative expansion in recent decades, moving from a largely domestic market to an increasingly internationalized space. This process has so often involved the passing from a state-directed to a market-driven system, by means of a privatization process, that, in most cases, it has ended with the denationalization of the banking industry.

One of the latest explanations for the financial crisis is the presence of a financial trilemma, as recently introduced by Dirk Schoenmaker, as national regulators could not manage to attain financial stability when the local economy was being opened to international capital markets. In order to solve the problem, policymakers should either deregulate the market (the status quo scenario), propose a multilateral agreement (to solve the coordination problem) or ring-fence global banks' activities within national borders (to avoid costly bankruptcies). The first and third alternatives do not technically solve the trilemma but involve either accepting financial instability or maintaining financial autarky. Regulatory coordination is neither easy nor impossible. Starting in the early seventies, developed countries' central banking authorities and finance ministers began to gather at the Basel Committee on Banking and Supervision (BCBS) forum. As time passed and new crises erupted, new tasks were undertaken. The latest global financial crisis (GFC) gave a new impetus to this forum, expanding their membership in order to include a group of EMEs. In any event, international cooperation remains a difficult game, as leading nations are not interested in restricting foreign operations of their local banks, although they have firmly decided to regulate foreigners at home. So, in order to delineate a new regulatory scheme at the global level, some developed nations are pushing for financial defragmentation.

Financial Globalization and Capital Account Management: An Institutional View

Chapter 4 introduces the interrelationship between international financial markets and institutions. The Bretton Woods Conference basically centred on macro-imbalances, monetary issues and how to coordinate them. Financial issues, in contrast, were left behind as financial markets (and banks, in particular) were national 'at both life and death' (Bank of England Governor Mervyn King and economist Charles Goodhart), and financial services were regulated by sovereign states. The collapse of the post–Second

World War consensus implied the advance of a new financial pattern in which institutional deregulation became a central chapter.

Market deregulation has easily mutated into banking underregulation, particularly benefiting global banks – a dangerous trend which influences both multilateral and bilateral schemes. Unfortunately, this unregulated vision has impinged on financial regulators, while they have remained silent on the problems posed by cross-border funding and related systemic risks. The GFC would come to challenge this vision, with both global leaders and IFIs now advocating for re-regulating them locally. A similar deregulation trend was followed in the derivative market, a tendency that remained practically untouched after the GFC. Prudential regulation, however, might still be challenged by a series of legal commitments being settled at the multilateral (General Agreement on Trade and Services; GATS) or the bilateral (free trade agreement (FTA)–bilateral investment treaty (BIT)) level. This push will be analysed in detail, particularly as it has gone further and has particularly affected those without negotiating power. Similarly, some AEs are now pushing, both multilaterally and bilaterally, to condemn exchange rate undervaluation practices.

A Comparative Analysis

The second part of the book introduces the preceding debate from a comparative perspective, in particular by observing the recent experience of a group of emerging countries from Latin America (Argentina and Brazil) and Asia (China, South Korea and India).

Following the financial crisis of the 1930s and the depression that followed, Latin American countries began to introduce a battery of policies in order to industrialize their societies, which was a policy response to massive unemployment, and was also directed at curbing technological progress and avoiding a recurring balance-of-payments crisis. From the start, a heterodox exchange rate and monetary policies accompanied industrialism in order to bring the necessary funds to articulate structural change. To favour local production, governments in the region promoted dual exchange-rate regimes. Meanwhile financial repression became a widely used tool for redirecting savings from consumers and primary sectors to nascent industry. All this happened in a context in which there was little cross-border movement of capital, with Argentina and Brazil among the earliest adopters of this repressive approach. The import substitution industrialization (ISI) process initiated a process of economic progress and sustained growth but also induced increasing tensions as many governments made use (and abuse) of inflationary financing tools. All of these measures pushed Latin American countries to recurrently confront a balance-of-payments crisis, whose complexity mounted in scale as local savings were exhausted. This, in turn, prevented them from maintaining a stable and competitive real exchange rate (SCRER) necessary to bolster industrialization and sustainable growth.

Asia, meanwhile, remained a lagged agrarian society trying to escape from extreme poverty and colonial rule – mostly Japanese, though British in the case of India. Paradoxically, the pro-development path adopted by Japan in the aftermath of the Second World War came to be followed by those neighbouring sovereign states dreaming of industrialization and economic progress. In order to advance with industrialization, authorities subscribed to heterodox macroeconomic policies meanwhile the presence of important trade barriers permitted them to isolate their markets from external competition. In contrast to the Latin American experience, Asian policymakers adverted to the relevance of improving industrial competitiveness in order to compete globally. Inheriting a highly backward economy, South Korean authorities decided to set up a large industrialization process. As previously observed in Japan and later in China, South Korean global insertion responded to a gradualist approach. Forty years later, South Korea would become a leading post-industrial society. Under China's Mao Zedong, industrialization was pursued under a highly centralized regime to be modified after his death. Whereas Chinese elites adopted an export-led growth model, it came with variations as the government enthusiastically open their doors to foreign capitals – although they prevented them from entering the financial sector. At South Asia, India remained an exception to the export-led growth pattern, showing a more inward-oriented economy during the post-war period.

This book does not advance further in discussing this shock–gradual dichotomy, as today most academics and policymakers have recognized the virtues of sequencing. Nor does the book discuss the appropriateness of the export-led growth model, although it certainly highlights the differences both groups still observe in terms of exchange rate policy (recall the centre role played by the real exchange rate in an open economy framework). In this respect, both groups must (and still reflect) follow very different paths: Asian countries were successfully maintained a stable and competitive real exchange rate, whereas Latin American ones have cyclically suffered from either the traditional or the so-called financial Dutch disease problem.

Latin America: Argentina and Brazil

Historically, Latin American countries adopted a more amicable attitude towards the arrival of global capital flows, whereas Asian countries observed a prudential stance towards international investors and financial deregulation. A more nuanced picture emerged later, particularly when observing the de facto capital account openness indexes or when analysing emerging countries' institutional attitude towards cross-border financing. The picture turns even blurrier when observing the cautious attitude emerging from Latin America after the financial crisis of the 1990s, and the corresponding resilience evidenced by the banking industry in most countries in the region in the aftermath of the GFC. In particular, monetary authorities in Latin America adopted a cautious attitude towards global liquidity surplus, preventing the eruption of credit booms.

Nevertheless macroeconomic soundness has not favoured all countries on a similar basis. The last 40 years might show that financial globalization certainly became riskier for those maintaining unsustainable populist policies, as their economies began more exposed to the unexpected swings of capital flow. Populist macroeconomics basically neglects the role of internal factors in unravelling a crisis; unsustainable policies are never questioned, but external factors are always to blame. Thus, challenged by globalization (populist regimes) soon reverted to old autarkic macro policies. Argentina and Venezuela transformed into textbook examples of macro populism, both being forced to reintroduce repressive financial policies and controls to deter massive capital flights. But populist attitudes are also observed among those that, in order attract foreign investors, end granting them too many benefits – a policy observed during the nineties in Argentina. Once capital began to flood into the country, the real exchange rate plummeted and, with it, economic competitiveness. Populist regimes are not necessarily opposed to the entrance of foreign investors (they might be often attracting them). What differentiates them is their infantile attitude towards (accompanying) risks: either neglecting them or assuming all the costs.

The commodity boom put the Brazilian economy into a more relaxed place to be altered by the GFC. Although economic authorities accurately responded to the challenge, unconventional monetary policies in the United States created important spillovers in EMEs, which particularly affected the Brazilian economy after 2013. Turbulence arrived sooner than expected, including increased political pressure for the incumbent leftist government. Unfortunately, nobody knows when the slump will finally end nor the social and political consequences of it.

In sum, Argentina and Brazil are both once again experiencing a series of old well-known challenges on the macroeconomic front. In order to tame (hyper)inflation, authorities in both countries decided to make an extreme bet: use their exchange rate as an anchor. Initially successful, an inflationary surge in both cases caused the approach to be abandoned. Thereafter, and in order to gain monetary policy space, Brazilian authorities decided to rely on a flexible exchange rate (ER) regime. The scheme was continued under the Lula administration, but, fuelled by the commodity boom, the government advanced towards a nuanced regime – accumulating a huge amount of FX reserves. Argentina, for its part, adopted a more pragmatic regime in the early 2000s. The collapse of the convertibility plan, certainly, was central in this search. After the GFC, both began to suffer what new developmentalism would define as macro populism of a new era (Bresser Pereira, Oreiro and Marconi, 2015). Since then, ER appreciation has still been affecting competitiveness of the industrial sector in both countries.

Asia: China, South Korea and India

Asian countries, in contrast, give us a different picture of financial globalization and national insertion. In particular, they appear to have a more strategic attitude towards the subject – at least, initially. It seems that economic development is embedded in Asian leaders' agenda, as they are basically aiming to avoid social disruption. But it is also indisputable that policymakers in Asia are well aware of the constraint imposed by hyperglobalization.

Once the long journey towards development was announced in 1978, the People's Republic of China (PRC, Lin and Wang, 2008) qualified as a backward developing society, with a feeble real economy and an almost non-existent financial system. Forty years later, China has become a global superpower, backed by a growing economy (the world's second largest, just behind the United States), whereas their national banks are ranked at the top of the world rankings. A proper sequencing became central in achieving this structural transformation, as a way of preserving the national economy from financial turmoil. Until recently, the financial system remained highly repressed and almost closed to foreigners. Policymakers' pragmatic approach was also a hallmark of the Chinese success, including an accurate institutionalist development path. The Chinese national currency (renminbi; RMB) remains internationally underdeveloped, but the government is trying to alter this. RMB internationalization has become a strategic policy for China. One of the more enthusiastic advocates in advancing this is the People's Bank of China (PBoC), which envisages internationalization as pivotal and as favouring the foundation of a market-oriented financial system. The 'go-global' strategy, coupled with the increasing financial presence of China, is certainly pushing the process forward. On the institutional front, authorities are less enthusiastic, refraining from advancing further with opening up or making exaggerated promises to foreigners in the local financial sector. In any case, China is moving fast to a new growth model where internal consumption will become more relevant than external markets.

India is another vibrant example of a backward developing society which over time has been transmuting into a global leader. Practically since it achieved national independence India implemented a highly interventionist industrialization model, which it began to phase out in the eighties. As in China, and in contrast to the Latin American experience, Indian authorities introduced a proper sequencing policy. As for the capital account, sequencing implied first permitting the arrival of long-term investments, subsequently promoting the opening in equity to finally liberalize debt flows. Nevertheless, and despite advances in the opening, the capital account still remains closed and foreign competitors are prevented from entering several sectors, particularly those qualified as strategic. Furthermore, most Indian banks remains basically local. The government is also highly active in the multilateral realm, basically oriented towards maintaining a pro-development stance in international negotiations – including those related to finance and investment issues.

The last chapter analyses the financial liberalization experience in South Korea, a country historically characterized by financial repression and capital controls. In the nineties, authorities decided to embrace a market liberalization process, which ended in a massive crisis in 1997. Despite the financial crash, economic authorities further advanced with financial liberalization, in deepening the use of the market's instruments and decided to open their financial sector to international banks. From an institutional perspective, Korea also definitively embraced bilateralism, with authorities enthusiastically advocating for a more closed approach to the United States. The latest financial crisis led to questions about the convenience of some reforms, inducing Korean authorities to initiate a more pragmatic approach towards financial globalization.

A Final Message and a Caveat

The book explores EMEs' long journey to become more open economies and how them have reacted to the many (economic, financial and institutional) constraints they have encountered during the journey. The book attempts to analyse from a multidimensional perspective the problems and challenges faced by EMEs on their path towards economic development. Three are the angles used in the analysis: macroeconomic, financial and institutional. As previously mentioned, I use Mundell framework for the first, the Schoenmaker scheme for the second and the Rodrik democratic conundrum to observe the assertiveness of the third problem. Certainly, the different schemes used to describe all these constraints present important drawbacks in observing all those models and trying to describe a multidimensional problem. In short, the idea of the book is to profit from these three theoretical frameworks as building blocks in describing the different problems and challenges faced by those emerging countries aiming to advance with their global insertion.

Part 1

The Financial Globalization Journey: The General Framework

Chapter Two

INTERNATIONAL CAPITAL FLOWS AND MACROECONOMIC DILEMMAS

Introduction

After the collapse of the Bretton Woods system a wide-ranging consensus emerged among academics and policymakers in the North, to adopt a floating exchange rate system. Few countries opted for an extreme floating device; however, even developed economies decided to move towards a managed or dirty floating scheme in order to reduce the market's volatility trends. EMEs, however, attempted to match their local currency to some base country currency (basically the US dollar, but also with the French franc or the British pound).

In any event, besides the abandonment of US dollar parity, the new model implied a wide process of capital account openness. Henceforth, and unsurprisingly, the new setting was pushing economic authorities towards the constraints dictated by the so-called monetary trilemma.

The term refers to the impossibility of simultaneously achieving the triple contradictory, but desirable, goals of sustaining an independent monetary policy (to achieve domestic monetary policy goals) and a fixed exchange rate (to foster stabilization of trade and growth), while simultaneously freeing its capital flow (for an optimal allocation of resources). According to the trilemma, a small, open economy cannot achieve all three of these policy goals at the same time: in pursuing any two of these goals, it must forgo the third.[1] Theory, however, does not preclude national governments operating in the middle ground, as empirically observed since the 1970s. During the last decade most EMEs have been converging towards this middle focal point as policymakers 'maintained moderate levels of monetary policy space and financial openness while maintaining higher levels of exchange rate stability' (Chin, 2014, p. 6).

Assuming unfettered capital flows, policymakers were somewhat pushed to decide between two rigid alternatives: either 'pegging' the exchange rate and leaving interest

1. In order to evaluate the position of the national economy in respect to the trilemma, a series of indexes might be worth considering. Relative monetary independence could be evaluated through an index (M1) based on the inverse of the correlation of a country's interest rates with the base country's interest rate. The index for exchange rate stability (ERS), in turn, is the inverse of the exchange rate volatility, measured as the standard deviations of the monthly rate of depreciation (based on the exchange rate between the home and base economies). And, finally, the degree of financial integration can be approximated by the Chinn-Ito capital control index (KAOPEN).

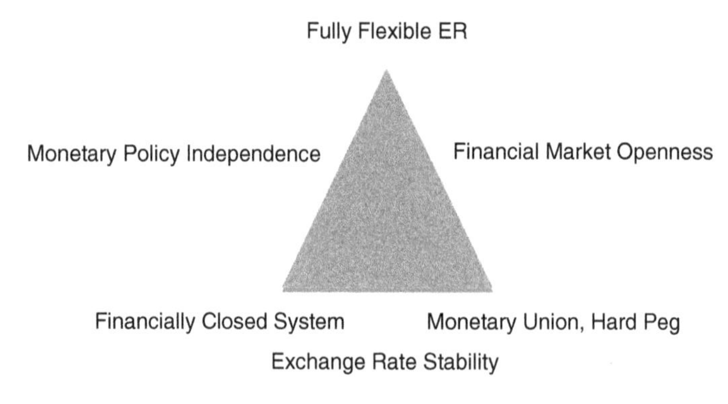

Figure 2.1 The monetary trilemma, or the 'impossible trinity'
Source: Aizenman, Chin and Ito (2015)

rates to be fixed by the market, or gaining in monetary autonomy, although leaving the exchange rate to be freely determined by market forces. Theoretically, fixed exchange rate regimes are better fitted if shocks are nominal, whereas floating regimes are superior when the shock necessary to confront presents a real character.

Yet both schemes have shown their drawbacks, and none of the settings can be considered as ideal for EMEs. Nevertheless, back in the late eighties to early nineties the fixed scheme became enthusiastically defended in academic circles, such as by the IMF. In the mid-nineties, however, the passion suddenly vanished, and policymakers were directed towards flex regimes – being charmingly seduced by the IMF to do that.[2] Two other tools accompanied the new recipe: CBI and IT. Certainly, the IT scheme generally disregarded balance-of-payments problems – an essential and sensitive issue for most policymakers in EMEs. Henceforth, it was normal to observe political pressures and they altered central bankers' original preferences, forcing floaters to intervene in the FX market.

In addition to the constraints imposed by the monetary trilemma, two different but complementary effects in EMEs were reducing central bankers' policy space: financial deepening and financial globalization. Unfortunately, this new scenario is still waiting to be comprehended as practitioners have elegantly avoided the inclusion of financial factors in their models (Borio, 2012). Governments need to simultaneously work on the financial, fiscal and monetary sides, if they are attempting to construct a solid and stable macroeconomic regime. The system being finally chosen, however, might pose ultimate and particular effects on the country's economic volatility. Furthermore, and despite the particular ER scheme which was chosen and the presence of (apparently) solid macroeconomic policies, the system may still be subject to important challenges – particularly, when market liquidity assumes a global character and financial instability problems become more acute (a topic analysed in Chapter 3).

2. The so-called Tequila crisis that took place in Mexico in 1994 can, without any doubt, be considered determinative in explaining this reversal. After 1989, and in order to alienate agents' expectations, the Mexican government decided to fix the value of the Mexican peso to the US dollar.

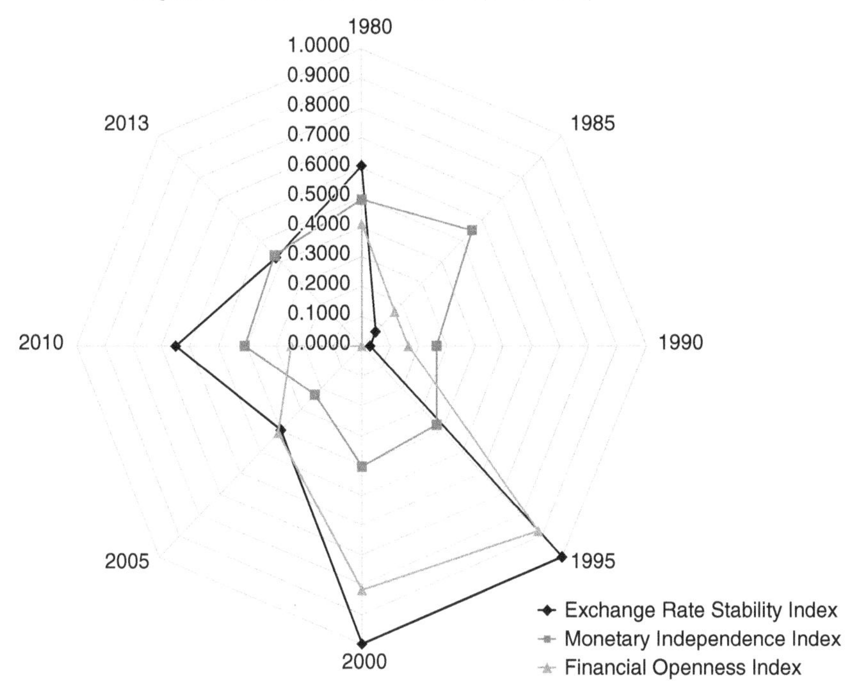

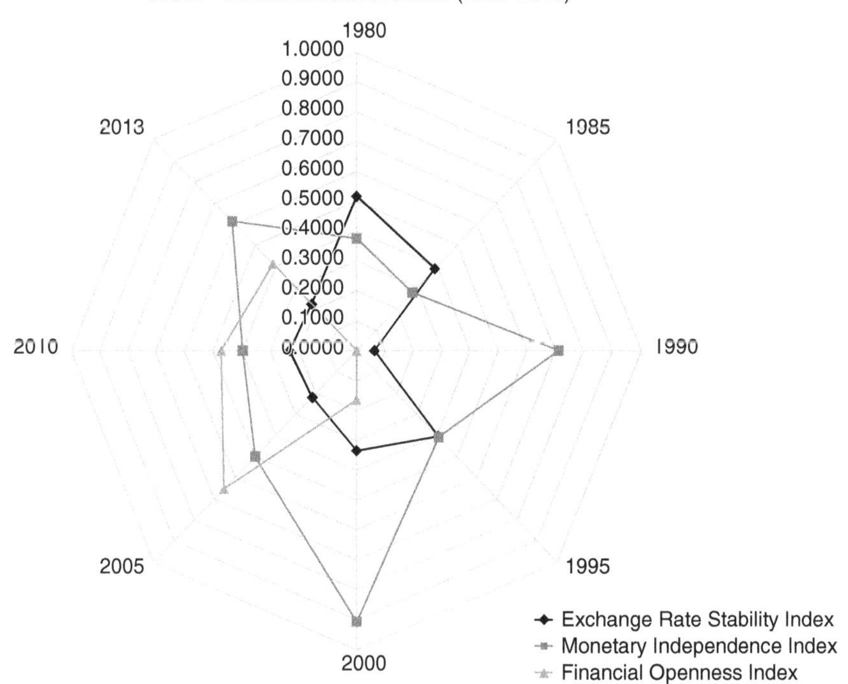

Figure 2.2 Trilemma index evolution for selected EMEs (5 graphs)
Source: Based on Aizenman, Chin and Ito indexes

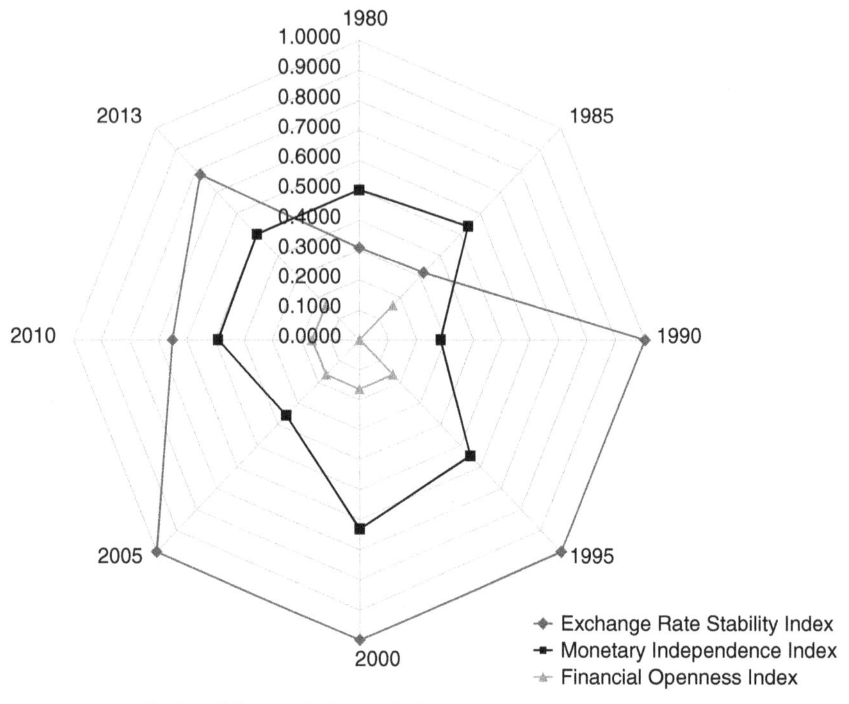

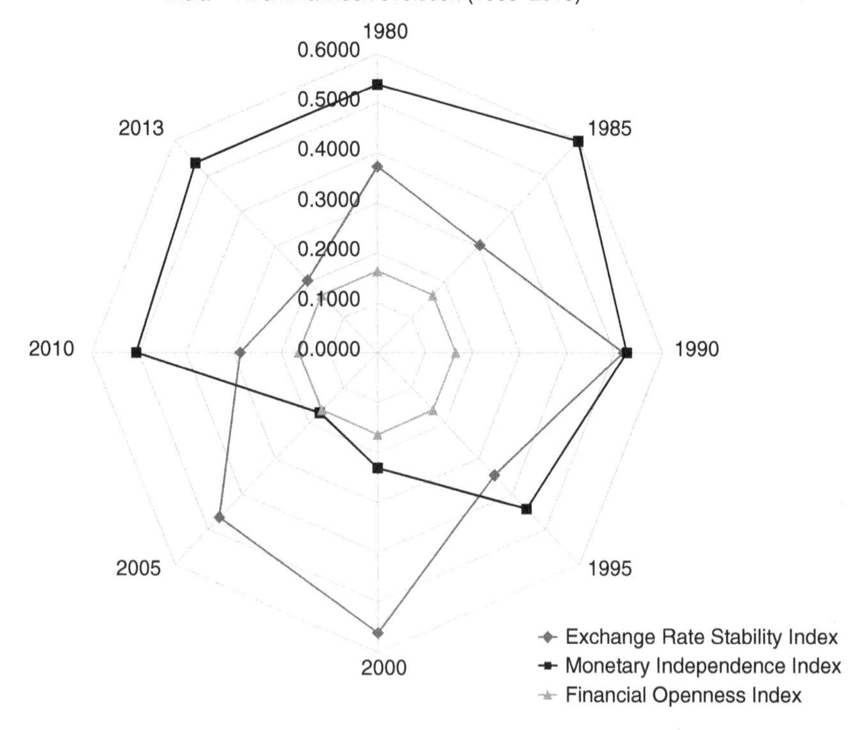

Figure 2.2 *(cont.)*

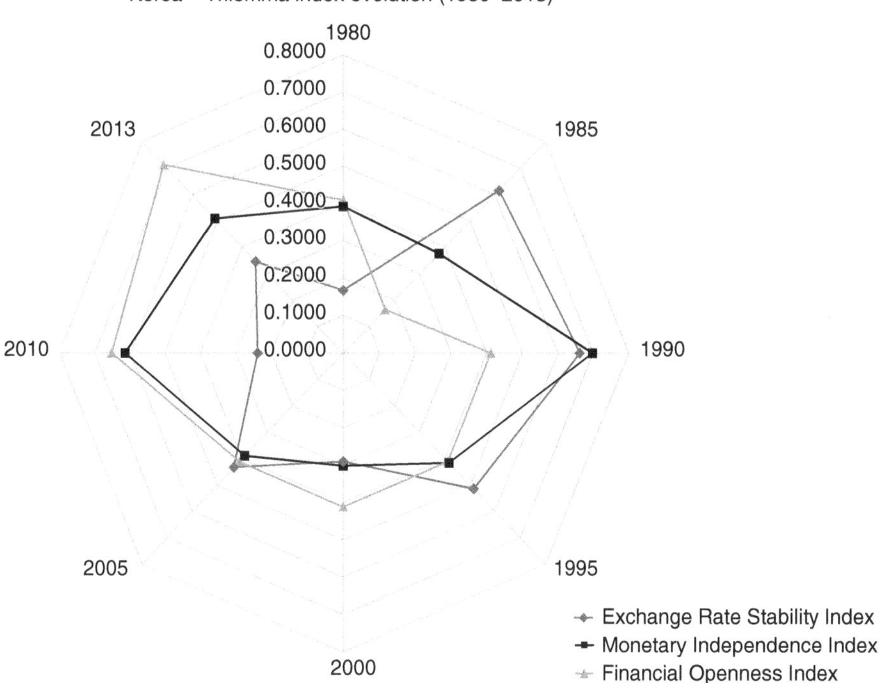

Figure 2.2 *(cont.)*

The new financial scenario might also claim some sort of regulation over the capital account (a topic analysed in Chapter 4). Certainly, another caveat seems appropriate: (capital) controls should be thought as a complement to sound macroeconomic policies, not a substitute for them. Nevertheless, whereas mainstream economists in the North remained silent regarding problems posed by financial globalization, challenges were observed early on in the South.

The paragraphs that follow delineate the basic constraints being faced by a small economy in an open macro framework, and the negative effects unfettered capital flow might pose for them. In particular, policymakers in EMEs are basically oriented towards guaranteeing a stable and competitive real exchange rate. How different ER regimes help in achieving that is what this chapter intends to delineate.

EMEs' Exchange Rate Policy in an Open Macro Framework

Theoretically, an array of exchange rate schemes coexists, but three different regimes (fixed or pegged, intermediate and floating) are predominant – whose pros and cons are succinctly analysed in the following paragraphs.[3]

3. Regimes differentiate along a de jure or de facto basis. The former classifies ER according to what each country claimed to be fixed. On a de facto basis, in contrast, several classifications are available (such as the one proposed by the IMF, or those introduced by Levy-Yeyati and Sturzenneger (2005), Reinhart and Rogoff (2004), or by Shambaugh (2004)).

One of the principal benefits associated with 'fixing' relates to the certitude it brings to economic agents, particularly to those producing tradable goods (Mill effect). It might also be of relief for borrowers exposed to foreign liabilities, as fixed schemes reduce the likelihood of a currency mismatch (Fischer financial effect). Finally, a fixed scheme might also be used to anchor inflationary expectations (as a price signal). In order to keep inflationary pressures under control, however, pegged countries should follow a base country interest rate more closely than floaters[4] – monetary authorities under a floating regime are less exposed to this movement (although they cannot ignore it) when setting interest rates.[5] As McKinnon and Schnabl (2004) once remarked, the close link between exchange rate and price stability observed in East Asian countries was key to the relative success of the dollar anchor in curbing inflationary pressures during the nineties.

A fixed regime shows a number of important caveats, however. Regime vulnerabilities are closely related with fiscal deficits, real exchange rate (RER) overvaluation bias and current account deficits. Traditional monetary policy tools become powerless (to affect the money supply or output) as the home country passively follows the monetary policy of the anchor country. Henceforth, a fixed exchange rate leaves policymakers with fewer degrees of freedom to face external shocks – which turns into null for those under a hard peg scheme. A crisis of confidence might be considered as another reason for fear, particularly when the exchange rate regime plays a stability policy role and the government is forced to maintain the peg although it is unable to sustain it indefinitely. The implicit guarantee granted by the government changes risk perceptions, encouraging excessive borrowing in foreign currency, which might end up becoming unsustainable – as observed under the convertibility plan in Argentina.[6]

Considering all the above-mentioned disadvantages and bearing in mind the loss of monetary tools for macro stabilization policies, academic consensus starting in the mid-nineties began to favour flex regimes. In brief, flexibility to absorb external shocks is considered one of the regime's main advantages. Central bankers are generally among the most fervent supporters of this approach as it brings them greater policy space, a valuable attribute for those seeking economic stability – particularly when price movements mainly respond to internal factors. Flexibility might also be helpful in mitigating unexpected capital surges (particularly tailored to low-volatility environments; otherwise, local

4. Theoretically, in order to maintain the ER, the parity local interest rate should equal the foreign one, and a riskless asset should be paid at exactly the same price in country A as in country B. The parity assumes unfettered capital movement and the fact that domestic and foreign bonds are perfect substitutes (i.e. when expected returns on domestic and foreign currency bonds are the same). If the substitutability condition is left aside, there is no chance that we can expect equality (in interest rates) unless we add a risk premium component to the formulae.
5. If the country is under a floating exchange rate, the interest rate differential reflects the expected growth rate of the exchange rate, or: $r = r^* + [(E^e - E)/ E]$, where r and r^* are local and foreign interest rates, E^e expected exchange rate and E exchange rate.
6. In analysing the effects of inflow-driven credit booms, a group of recent papers (Furceri, Guichard and Rusticelli (2011); Magud, Reinhart and Vesperoni (2012); Lane (2013); and Magud and Vesperoni (2014)) have all found that credit denominated in foreign currency is likely to increase more rapidly when less flexible ER regimes are in place.

agents might be exposed to increasing uncertainty). Thus, the more flexible the regime, the more rigidity it imposes on the rest of a government's policies.

Yet pure floating regimes also display important drawbacks (Klein and Shambaugh, 2010). First, a pure floating scheme is likely to exhibit a high degree of pass-through on local prices. Consequently, it places inflationary pressures on the real economy – despite the fact that more credible monetary arrangements might be reducing the degree of pass-through (Taylor, 2000; Aron, Farrell, Muellbauer and Sinclair, 2014; Cheikh and Louchini, 2014).[7] Second, this scheme can induce an excess of volatility, which adversely impacts on local firms' exporting behaviour (Nurkse's effect).[8] Third, unexpected price movements might also increase economic uncertainty. This affects economic agent decisions and long-term growth, certainly more among least developed countries (LDCs) and EMEs (Aghion et al., 2009).

EMEs' currency markets are even more exposed to volatility. To begin with, regarding the last point in the previous list, financial markets are small and less liquid in those markets. Consequently, policymakers have less experience in dealing with market forces, and the presence of 'Friedmanite speculators' remains atypical among them (McCauley, 2003; Aghion et al., 2009).[9] Lower credibility in a government's policies exacerbates the uncertainty normally associated with floats – while placing local citizens' savings on foreign currencies (e.g. dollarization in Argentina) protects them from an unexpected devaluation. A floating scheme might also intensify debt-related problems associated with financial markets' incompleteness – a problem particularly affecting EMEs as they are prevented from borrowing in local currencies (original sin bias) (Eichengreen and Hausmann, 1999).[10] If this happens, floaters might become unprotected against both currency and maturity mismatch problems emerging from widespread financial contagion and subsequently abrupt exchange rate depreciation.[11] Additionally, volatility might be particularly acute among raw materials and commodities exporters in contrast to

7. Some authors have demonstrated a relationship between inflationary regimes and the level of exchange rate pass-through (ERPT): lower (higher) levels are observed in lower (higher) inflation regimes.
8. For R. Nurkse, a floating ER creates an element of risk, which tends to discourage international trade.
9. According to Milton Friedman, the presence of speculators can helpful in order to stabilize the exchange rate: the possibility of hedging exchange-rate risk reduces the negative effects associated with the presence of volatility. Countries with mature, long-term domestic capital markets are, henceforth, the only capable of adopting a truly floating scheme: agents have more hedging possibilities (Calvo and Reinhart, 2002). In the same direction, Aghion, et al. (2009) highlight the importance of the country's financial deepening in order to opt for a particular exchange rate system: the more developed, the less problematic the volatility problem becomes.
10. The authors' 'original sin' hypothesis relates to a situation in which domestic currency cannot be used to borrow long term, even domestically. Henceforth, locals are (to some extent) forced to take external debt but are afraid to became indebted in foreign currency.
11. Note that, in contrast to conventional wisdom, ER depreciation might be associated with contractionary effects. Although it benefits aggregate demand (boosts exports), devaluation might affect economic agents balance sheets – which is particularly harmful for debtors.

those exporting industrial goods.[12] This Hicksian effect reflects their incapability to adjust quantities (fix producers), and the more volatile exports' earnings become, the more it highlights the advantages of a smooth ER policy.

Box 2.1 FX regimes, Latin America and Asia compared

When comparing Asian and Latin American EMEs' experiences, a diversified picture emerges. Asian EMEs have historically relied on either a fixed peg or a managed exchange rate policy (although they also maintain capital controls and financial repression for longer), in order to sustain an undervalued RER to advance in economic development. Beginning with Japan in the aftermath of the Second World War, this tool was later use by other East Asian economies (South Korea, Indonesia, Thailand, Taiwan and, more recently, by the People's Republic of China (PRC)). All of them pegged (de jure or de facto) the local currency to the US dollar, maintaining nominal values unaltered for a long time span. Closely associated with the export-led growth model, this strategy permitted them to upgrade their international competitiveness – but the peg ended in destabilizing the RER as their economies became more regionally integrated and, henceforth, highly exposed to the influence of the Japanese yen.

In comparison, ER policy among Latin American EMEs has been more erratic. Prior to the seventies, most countries in the region embraced a particular ER scheme, the so-called fixed but adjust rate (FBAR) regime (Corden, 2001). During the eighties they began to introduce some type of managed ER regime (soft pegs, bands, crawls and so on), to go towards some sort of (hard or soft) pegging regime in the early nineties. Beginning in the late 1970s, they embraced more open macro policies (financial deregulation and capital account liberalization), which push them towards the trilemma constraints sooner than Asian countries. Confronting important macro imbalances, the Latin Americans' ER policy was directed towards anchoring economic agents' inflationary expectations. Argentina's currency board (the convertibility plan) become the extreme version of this new trend, and Brazil also introduced a hard peg scheme (Plano Real) in order to curb inflationary expectations. In the attempt to peg their currencies to the US dollar (a nominal anchor), they recreated a mechanism of exchange rate overvaluation as the parity stimulated the massive influx of foreign capital alongside the economic costs associated with it (Dutch disease scenario) (Rodrik, 2008;[a] Bresser-Pereira, 2008).

For example, consider B. Eichengreen's support for this approach:

> Hence, the IMF needs to more forcefully encourage its member to move to policies of greater exchange rate flexibility, and the sooner the better. With

12. Trade-related drawbacks are also enlarged among EMEs as their external trade is mostly conducted in foreign currency – independently of the country's trade ties. For them, large ER swings affect the costs associated with trade invoicing.

few exceptions it should pressure its members, in the context of Article IV consultations and program discussions, to abandon simple pegs, crawling pegs, narrow bands and other mechanisms for limiting exchange rate flexibility before they are forced to do so by the markets.

Despite dissimilarities, both group of countries suffered a series of chaotic experiences with pegs and managed regimes, and a new consensus emerged by the end of the nineties – but floating schemes prevailed.[b]

---

[a] Rodrik (2008) explains the negative consequences of an overvalued currency. From a macroeconomic perspective, overvaluation harms growth as it spawns unsustainable current account deficits, balance-of-payments crises and stop-and-go scenarios. From a microeconomic perspective, overvaluation reshapes economic agents' behaviour and might induce FX shortages, rent seeking and corruption. Those concerns are common to Latin American policymakers, as the economy's exchange rates recurrently become overvalued. From a political economy perspective, this reflects the consumption bias associated with most stabilizing programmes installed in the region.

[b] In the aftermath of the Asian financial crisis, debtor countries, including Korea, Malaysia, the Philippines and Thailand, were forced by the IMF to float. Afraid of the negative effects commonly associated with pure floating schemes, and despite pressures, a group of countries reverted to the previous ER mechanism: Singapore moved from a one-currency peg to a basket peg, whereas Malaysia and Thailand both moved back from a managed float to a fixed exchange rate – the former with the additional support generated by the introduction of capital controls.

As interest in the fixed ER regime waned, a flex-regime-cum-IT-framework was converted into the preferred policy instrument to stabilize the economy: a monetary anchor replaced the former foreign exchange one.[13] Additionally, and in order to reinforce the power of central bankers, governments put in place a series of institutional changes which brought formal independence to monetary authorities (CBI dictum). Consequently, the new scheme became characterized by the simultaneous presence of an announcement of an inflation target, a major role to inflation forecast targeting and a high degree of transparency and accountability (Svensson, 2007).[14] The conversion to the floating-cum-IT group was now capturing mainstream economists' 'souls' (Epstein and Yeldan, 2009), as it simultaneously (theoretically) might help stabilize both inflationary

---

13. As articulated by Stan Fischer (*IMF Managing Director 1994–2001*) a new consensus emerged among academics. In an address to the American Economic Association, he stated, 'In the last decade, there has been a hollowing out of the middle of the distribution of exchange rate regimes in a bipolar direction, with the share of both hard pegs and floating gaining at the expense of soft pegs. This is true not only for economies active in international capital markets, but among all countries. A look ahead suggests this trend will continue, certainly among the emerging market countries. The main reason for this change, among countries with open capital accounts, is that soft pegs are crisis-prone and not viable over long period' (Fischer, 2001, p. 22).
14. Although the inflation rate became the main target, some authorities set a more flexible ruling permitting the pursuing of other real activity indicators such as output gap or unemployment rate.

and output gaps, a coincidence to be later popularized as being 'divine' (Blanchard and Gali, 2005).[15]

A series of heterodox economists came to challenge the likelihood of this outcome, contrasting their hypothetical benefits against the costs it imposed on EMEs. First, the regime ignored the disruptive effects of market forces– remaining silent on FX volatility. Additionally, they found that an IT scheme might induce an ER appreciation bias – particularly when a low inflation target is being installed (Epstein and Yeldan, 2009; Galindo and Ros, 2008; Barbosa-Filho, 2008),[16] negatively affecting the country's tradable sectors performance (Frenkel, 2006)[17] and definitively driving the economy towards a Dutch disease trap (Bresser Pereira, 2008). If carry trade operations are operating, this appreciation bias might be enlarged,[18] a phenomenon observed in Brazil (Rossi, 2015).[19] Last but not least, when inflation remains attached to international commodity prices, (an ambitious) target will not just fail to stabilize but also might even cause a recession (Stiglitz, 2008). In sum, and consequently, few governments will graciously leave the ER at the mercy of market forces, which explains why most floaters intervene (Calvo and Reinhart, 2002; Levy-Yeyatti and Sturzenegger, 2002).

After the global financial crisis, new critical voices emerged, as the regime narrowly focused on controlling near-term inflation, which induces monetary authorities to ignore 'the need to tighten policy when financial booms take hold against the backdrop of low and stable inflation' (Borio, 2012). In particular, Borio's comment implies that either financial markets are imperfect or economic agents are not fully rational (or being subject to information asymmetries), causes that might call for an active exchange rate policy.

From Fears to Market Intervention

Theoretically, a more flexible ER is better prepared to absorb adverse impacts of external shocks (Obstfeld and Rogoff, 1995). This attribute, however, was rarely present among EMEs. Pure flexible countries, in contrast, commonly exhibit a U-shaped relationship between real ER volatility and output volatility as (large values of) ER volatility becomes

15. Notice that this property does not hold when wage rigidity is introduced into the model (Blanchard and Galli, 2005).
16. An appreciation of the real exchange rate relates to the simultaneous presence of an ambitious IT and a rapid degree of convergence, which, in the medium run, could end in increasing financial fragility (Barbosa-Filho, 2008).
17. In such a case, and in order to maintain a competitive real exchange rate, the central bank's main challenge is to prevent appreciation but also to de-incentivize short-term speculative capital flow (Frenkel, 2006, p. 12).
18. A simple carry trade involves an investor selling a certain currency (US$ dollars), with a lower interest rate, and using this fund to purchase another currency yielding a higher interest rate (BRL). The investor´s objective is to capture the difference between the rates. This type of operation can be financed either locally or by foreign funds, with only the later implying a movement in capital flow.
19. In particular, IT regimes rely on tight monetary policy. In EMEs, an increase in interest rate induces carry trade operations, and, henceforth, it induces local currency to appreciate.

a source of real volatility.[20] This unfavourable pattern might justify why, independently of the selected policy option, policymakers remained apprehensive towards the challenges imposed by excessive ER volatility and why they experienced a 'fear of floating' (Calvo and Reinhart, 2002; Levy Yeyati and Sturzenneger, 2007).[21]

But policymakers' reluctance towards floating might also be observed under favourable circumstances if extreme appreciation follows (Reinhart, 2000). Certainly, this 'fear of appreciation' feeling has become entrenched with the massive entrance of capital inflows observed in recent years, when policymakers in EMEs became alarmed by the increasing revalorization of their local currencies (Levy Yeyati and Sturzenneger, 2007). As a result, and in order to smooth volatility (either to constrain local currency appreciation), an important number of countries decided to intervene the ER market.

The prior bipolar prescription was suddenly out of fashion, and a new academic consensus emerged towards the adoption of a new type of ER regime: a soft IT regime, tying the Taylor rule with a *managed* float scheme.[22] Government intervention is associated with several motives: reducing foreign exchange volatility, impeding sudden movements in the exchange rate, building up foreign reserves, smoothing the impact of commodity price fluctuations, maintaining or enhancing competitiveness.[23] In particular, 'Latin American central banks have explicitly claimed a right to intervene in the foreign exchange market under some circumstances, most often related to instability in the foreign exchange market and the financial system' (Bruno, 2008, p. 269). The relative strength evidenced by this new scheme (IT plus FX) reflected the concomitant work of two concurrent policies: the massive intervention in the foreign exchange market and also the impressive accumulation of foreign reserves initiated in the aftermath of the Asian financial crisis.

20. A sudden and unexpected depreciation might generate detrimental effects on trade and on aggregate demand (Keynesian channel), and, eventually, it might also have adverse consequences on financial markets (Fisherian channel).
21. In order to evaluate whether market forces under a floating regime really independently fix exchange rates, Calvo and Reinhart (2002) collected data on exchange rates, interest rates and reserves. Although all declaimed the presence of flexible regimes, few countries were finally allowing the ER to be strictly determined by the market.
22. Under a hard IT regime an inflationary surge induces central banks to raise interest rates, encouraging foreign investors to enter (pull effect). Capital inflows, in turn, induce local currency to appreciate, fuelling inflationary pressures. In short, the events being described here reflect the strong interrelation between monetary and exchange rate dynamics, and why EMEs remain sceptical of the convenience of floats.
23. Bofinger and Wollmershäuer (2001) introduced an index to classify market intervention in two main categories: ER smoothing or ER targeting. According to the first motive, intervention is undertaken to prevent short-term volatility. Intervention in the second case is motivated to establish a level or path for the exchange rate. Chang (2008), on their side, made an extensively analysis of four declared floaters in Latin America (Peru, Chile, Colombia and Brazil), demonstrating that intervention was widely expanded among them.

Domestic Monetary Policy and ER Intervention: Sterilization

In order to manage capital flow, authorities are often required to simultaneously operate both ER and interest rates. Intervention in the former occurs when authorities sell or buy foreign currencies against their own currency. Whether this intervention proves successful has been always subject to controversy. In a general (non-sterilized) scenario, when capital inflows arrive (exit), it raises (lowers) the local money supply. But capital movements could be sterilized. By bringing into service open market operations (OMO), the government sterilizes capital inflows (outflows): absorbing capital inflows (foreign assets) by selling its holdings of domestic bonds (domestic assets). Sterilization movements occur on the asset side of the central bank balance sheet (modifying its structure), but leave the monetary base unchanged. It might be stressed that FOREX interventions in EMEs exhibit a different nature than those undertaken in developed nations (Berganza and Broto, 2012), and presumably could be more effective in the former (Disyatat and Galatti, 2007; Koshlscheen, 2013).

Sterilization movements present both monetary and fiscal effects. The monetary channel associates with interest rate movements, either seducing investors or rejecting the arrival of new funds. Fiscal impacts, in turn, are related to the relation between foreign reserves and domestic government debt (including Treasury deposits).[24] In terms of the assertiveness of this policy, whereas originally it was dismissed as ineffective, recent studies have demonstrated their short- to medium-term effectiveness (Levy Yeyati and Sturzenerger, 2007; Frenkel, 2007).

Box 2.2 Sterilization policies in EMEs

In China, sterilization are routinely conducted through treasury bonds but are complemented by swaps and repurchase agreement (REPO) operations. Additionally, monetary authorities maintain special reserve requirements (RRs). The tool was originally directed to sustain the fixed rate against the US dollar, later transmuting to maintain the crawling peg regime – a competitive exchange rate to foster its export-led growth strategy. In the case of India, sterilization occurred through the selling of governmental securities, a mechanism later replaced by the market stabilization scheme (MSS), which is generally complemented by open market operations and the presence of RRs. Intervention operates through either the spot or the forward market. As India observes a structural current account

24. Central banks' costs increase when authorities are forced to increase the differential between the interest rate on domestic government debt (i_{local}) and returns granted by maintaining international reserves in their portfolio – normally equated to the return on a low-risk asset (US bond) (i_{USbond}). The government might be able to eliminate sterilization costs if the central bank targets a devaluation path (for the FX) that equals the difference between the domestic interest rate and a foreign portfolio's returns ($FX_{dev} = il_{ocal -} i_{USbond} = 0$). This ideal 'condition of zero cost for sterilized interventions' requires active government participation in both the exchange rate and the monetary market (Bofinger and Wollmershäuser, 2003, p. 11).

deficit, intervention has particularly been directed towards reducing ER volatility. The monetary authority in Korea (BOK) uses its own monetary stabilization bonds (MSBs), although transactions at the REPO market are also being used to sterilize funds. Brazil made wide use of this tool, too, with most of the operations taking place at the spot market.

Monetary authorities might also try to shape their balance sheet structure through the use of non-conventional (or quantitative) measures. In particular, by introducing some sort of RRs, they can discriminate among different types of investors, as for example, by fixing a higher ratio to non-resident investors or by introducing a differential ratio on FX operations.[25] RRs might be further differentiated according to be remunerated or unremunerated, whether applied to new deposits from a reference period (marginal RRs) or introduced to distinguish between a bank's core funding and other liabilities.[26] Obviously, requirements can also be reversed – as observed during the recent GFC when authorities decided to lower the rate (or, simply, to eliminate them) in order to seduce investors. In terms of its effectiveness, it becomes clear when bank credit remains 'king' – a fact that explains its widespread use among policymakers in banking-based societies (Federico, Vegh and Vuletin, 2013).[27] This requirement, in sum, which acts in relation to bank deposits and other bank liabilities in a countercyclical manner, had been used as a liquidity or credit policy tool but also exhibited a macro-prudential purpose (Glocker and Towbin, 2011; Montoro and Romero, 2011; IMF, 2012).

International Reserves and EMEs' Policy Space

After the Asian crisis, authorities in EMEs decided to rely on foreign reserve accumulation to buffer certain exchange rate parity, whereas some other countries continued to rely on capital controls.

Box 2.3 Foreign reserves accumulation in EMEs

The magnitude of the increase can be analysed by observing the balance-of-payment progress. Prior to the Southeast Asian financial crisis, current account deficits were matched with net capital inflows, a pattern particularly present in

25. Differentiating RRs according the currency of origin might prevent the financial system from experiencing the eruption of a currency mismatch problem
26. A recent working paper introduces an exhaustive list of non-conventional instruments which have been utilized by Latin American countries (IMF, 2012).
27. Authors differentiate RRs along two axes, including four different categories (single, maturity, currency and maturity + currency) and two groups of countries (developing and developed countries). One of the key results of the paper is the relevance the tool obtains at good times (fear of appreciation), while diminishing during bad times (fear of free falling).

Latin America. At the beginning of the 2000s, however, EMEs began to exhibit important surpluses on the current account alongside the arrival of net capital flow. Then, the massive hoarding of external reserves began. Reserves increased by a yearly rate of 20 per cent: from US$ 202 billion in 1990, to US$ 3,371 billion in 2008. China explains more than 50 per cent of this increase as reserves – actually up to US$ 4 trillion. Although the GFC forced EMEs to disburse an important share of them, most countries were quickly rebuilding reserves – but the pace of hoarding lessened with respect to the pre-GFC years.

Whereas hoarding was originally directed towards ensuring imports expenses and shelter debt repayments (gunpowder), some countries have accumulated enormous amounts of reserves whose existence suffices to deter greedy investors' most voracious appetite (nuclear weapon). As a consequence, the hoarding somewhat lessened the constraints being imposed by the monetary trilemma.

In trying to reduce volatility or in order to prevent financial distress, other groups of countries went still further, such as by introducing (or maintaining) different types of controls on the capital account. Obviously, the presence of controls reduces (or even eliminates) the constraints imposed by the monetary trilemma. Capital account regulations (CARs) are by no means supplementary to reserve accumulation but can certainly complement it (Bussière, Cheng, Chinn and Lisack, 2014). All countries in this sample were considering both: IR and CARs. The widespread use of both instruments can also demonstrate the culmination of the neo-liberal consensus initiated in the 1970s. Whereas in the late 1990s the exchange rate debate centred at the extremes, few were discussing the convenience of maintaining the free movement of capital.

The trade or transactional channel requires monetary authorities to hold a quantity of FX reserves equivalent to three months of imports. The relevance of trade-related reserves was profoundly analysed in the post–Second World War world, a period when international capital flows were mainly related to commerce.[28] But, since the early seventies, and following the (re-)emergence of the sovereign debt market, financial flows increased in importance among EMEs and new measures were now being required. After the Latin America debt crisis, in particular, market analysts' attention began to focus on the reserve-to-debt ratio. In considering the funds needed to repay external debt compromises, so as to avoid a financial distress scenario in the short term, 'Greenspan–Guidotti' suggested a sort of rule of thumb: just fix a level of reserves above government short-term (one-year) debt.[29] Although illuminating, this rule might become useless in

28. Heller (1966) analysed the demand for international reserves, observing a negative correlation with the marginal propensity to import: a higher propensity implies a smaller cost of balance-of-payments adjustment and, thereby, a lower demand for international reserves.
29. As observed by Obstfeld et al. (2010), this motive was originally described by Keynes in the *Treatise on Money* (1930), when commenting on the appropriate amount of reserves a country

Table 2.1 Reserve ratios, examples

Indicator	Factor	Ratios (in logs)	Objective
Reserve to GDP	Macroeconomic	[Reserves / GDP] x 100	Country size
Reserve to Trade		[Reserves / Imports] x 12	Purchase capacity
Reserve to Debt	Financial	[Reserves /S-T Debt] x 100	Service debt capacity
Reserve to financial deepening		[Reserves / M2] x 100	Stabilization role on domestic financial market

preventing capital account shocks and their effects on a population's assets. That is because financial liberalization has massively amplified local agents' financial options – including borrowing in foreign currency. Consequently, the more open the economy, the more unprotected it becomes to sudden stops, capital flights and volatility, and, henceforth, the more interested (EMEs' policymakers) in preventing this. This helps to explain why the ratio relating reserves to a broad monetary aggregate (M2) has turned relevant.[30]

The accumulation of foreign reserves might be associated with insurance purposes, although this is not the single available option nor is it classified as the more appropriate one.[31] Hoarding might be better explained by EMEs' limited access to international liquidity markets, alongside the limited scope for collective action observed at the multilateral level. For the same reason, authorities might be interested either to participate in credible reserve-sharing regional arrangements[32] or to be protected by some kind of swap

should meet after calculating the 'magnitude of the drain which India might have to meet through the sudden withdrawal of foreign funds, or through a sudden stop in the value of Indian exports (particularly jute and, secondarily, wheat) as a result of bad harvests or poor prices.'

30. A paper by Cheung and Ito (2008) describes different models which introduce money in explaining reserve hoarding. They mention Johnson's (1958) paper as the earliest one, followed a decade later by a paper of Courchene and Youseff (1967). The latest paper introduces money as an explanation for reserve hoarding under a monetarist balance-of-payments model. Finally, Cheung and Ito refer to Beaufort, Wijnholds and Kapteyn's (2001) paper, which also considered money stock as a proxy for potential capital flight (in their intent to measure the intensity of the 'internal drain').
31. Alternatives to hoarding are associated with the costs it entails and are obtained from the spread between the private sector's cost of short-term borrowing abroad and the yield that the central bank earns on its liquid foreign assets (Rodrik, 2006). Hoarding can also generate some benefits, in particular, as a complementary device providing short-term resources to governments. Costs and benefits are measured in terms of local bond yields versus US interest rates.
32. The Chiang Mai Initiative is well recognized in this respect, introducing a network of bilateral trade agreements that bring together a group of Southeast Asian countries (ASEAN (Association of Southeast Asian Nations) Plus Three Japan, Korea and China).

deal agreements.[33] Self-insurance options are also available, such as the countercyclical fund installed in Chile or the sovereign wealth funds (SWFs) introduced by some Asian countries.[34] Last but not least, and in order to prevent the eruption of a large financial crisis or to minimize its negative effects once it has started, the home country can also opt for introducing capital controls (CARs).[35] In brief, the previous list is by no means exhaustive nor is it intended to pick one option over another (although some among them might be more suitable).

Box 2.4 Foreign reserves accumulation and exchange rate manipulation

For some observers, the operation of these two concurrent policies (sterilized-intervention-cum-reserve-hoarding) is mainly introduced to maintain an undervalued currency: the mercantilist channel.[a] This explanation goes in hand with the 'revised Bretton Woods system', a macro framework supposedly anchored in emerging Asia and particularly helpful for explaining China's development model (Dooley, Folkerts-Landau, and Garber, 2009).

In the same direction, a significant number of academics and policymakers blamed the excess savings originating in China,[b] and a group of oil-exporting countries for the problems facing the United States (the savings glut hypothesis). In any case, and independently of the assertiveness of the accusation, a growing concern regarding currency manipulation practices is emerging in the United States. The issue is not new in the literature, nor it is the first time the United States has blamed third countries' incorrect behaviour, as seems to actually be the case (Frankel, 2015; Blustein, 2015).

[a] According to some academics and policymakers in the United States, Japan, Singapore, Malaysia, Korea and other Asian countries were pursuing this mercantilist strategy. Consequently, there is a growing interest among US legislators in including an exchange rate manipulation clause in FTAs (for more details, see chapter 4).

[b] By maintaining a highly repressive financial model and sustaining a largely undervalued RMB, China could accumulate an enormous current account surplus, particularly up to 2005–6, when Chinese authorities were fixing the RMB against the US dollar. Although a more flexible exchange rate system was later introduced, pressure remained (see chapter 4).

33. Providing liquidity swaps can be seen as substituting hoarding, although these agreements can complement a government's foreign reserves helping authorities restore market confidence.
34. As examples of sovereign wealth funds, consider the China Investment Company (CIC) or the Korean Investment Company (KIC)
35. Additionally, local authorities can ease controls on capital outflows in order to prevent ER from appreciating.

Capital Flows, Monetary Policy and the Global Financial Cycle

In recent years, the effectiveness of monetary policy has been contested, as financial globalization has confronted policymakers with new and more challenging constraints. Restrictions on policymakers' policy space have tightened even for those following a flexible regime, contradicting the original dictate of Mundell's trilemma. In the case of emerging market economies, two different but complementary effects have been active in reducing central bankers' policy space.

On the one hand, local financial markets have gained in complexity, progressing from an initial simple configuration to increasingly complex structures (Ocampo, Rada and Taylor, 2009). Back in the seventies or eighties, most EMEs were characterized by a financial repressed model, which offered few (financial) options to private agents and where funds were mainly intermediated through the banking sector. Under such a scenario, monetary authorities enjoyed a greater degree of freedom, with monetary policy relying on an eclectic mix of money and credit stock targeting and being mostly conducted through quantitative instruments (credit quotas, regulated interest rates, reserve requirement ratios).[36] Later, non-banking institutions entered the picture, but the financial sector remained closed to foreigners, whereas local agents were still prevented from borrowing in foreign currencies. System evolution implied the introduction of complex policy tools towards money supply management, including the use of OMO or the issuance of government bonds ($Bonds^G$).[37] The presence of hedge funds, broker dealers and new financial actors (such as shadow banking entities) added new sources of financing for EMEs. As the financial market becomes more complex and deepens, it incorporates new regulatory challenges too.

On the other hand, financial intermediation also transformed after the massive eruption of cross-border capital flows – and global funds behind them (Bruno and Shin, 2013). These jumbo global banks came to explain the enlarging levels of both foreign assets and liabilities observed in EMEs' banking systems (Gorton and Metrick, 2009 and 2010; CIEPR, 2012). Local citizens were now entitled to take loans in foreign currency either to invest abroad, structural change leading to new problems and macro difficulties – economic agents were now confronted with both exchange rate and maturity mismatch risks. Additionally, financial flows remained weakly regulated as most monetary authorities were accepting a soft approach based on banks' self-regulation and financial micro-prudential measures.

36. Alternatively, authorities can rely on monetary aggregates (M2/PBI). This 'monetarist' vision assumes that monetary policy objectives are best met by targeting the growth rate of the money supply. The monetarist view is based on the quantitative theory of money ($MV = PT$), an accounting identity. Empirically, the velocity of money (V) remains a highly controversial item.
37. In a previous stage, monetary authorities imposed banks' holdings of government debt. In this new stage, the market mediates between the government and the financial system.

Box 2.5 EMEs and financial globalization

As previously observed, Asian and Latin American countries have become increasingly integrated into the global financial system. Accordingly, citizens of both regions are now entitled to borrow in foreign currencies or abroad, and local corporations are permitted to issue debt in offshore markets, whereas foreign investors are becoming important players in the local financial markets. In the last decade Latin American countries remained more cautious than their counterparts in Asia and, consequently, less vulnerable to a sudden stop in foreign banks' financing (Kamil and Rai, 2010). Comparing the composition of foreign claims, 60 per cent are local among Latin American countries, whereas the fraction reduces to 40 per cent among countries in the Asian group. The specific nature of foreign banks' operations in the region together with the institutional configuration of the local banking system was key in obtaining this result. In Latin America (local subsidiaries of), international banks mostly channelled their funds into domestic currency.[a] Furthermore, domestic deposits were behind the funding of (international banks) local affiliates' lending practices.[b] In contrast, off-balance sheet financing became common practice among several Asian countries – particularly in South Korea.

After all, the internationalization process is by no means linear, as observed in some EMEs' attitude. Profiting from investors' confidence in emerging economies, policymakers switched local debt towards local sourcing (domestic currency denomination), and a deleveraging policy that helped them reduce the original sin. In particular, both Asian and Latin American countries have also experienced an increase in local currencies' (local) claims, reflecting the increasing importance of local currency bond markets and foreign investors' participation in these markets.

---

[a] The average of bank financing denominated in local currency was above 50%, a percentage that exceeds 70% in the case of Mexico (Kamil and Ray, 2010). Certainly, the financial system become more resilient to external shocks as lending was mainly extended in local currency.

[b] This was in sharp contrast to the situation in emerging Europe, where cross-border flows from parent banks were backing the credit boom.

The rise of non-core banking and its impact on domestic liquidity further increases the challenges for EMEs' policymakers – including the inadequacy of traditional monetary instruments. Some authors still consider that small and open economies can profit from international capital flows if they can guarantee coherent and credible macro policies. For those favouring monetary policy independence, a macro resolution remains feasible, and particularly attached to price (or output) stability and inflation-targeting policies (Woodford, 2010). Financial instability is seen as a micro-related phenomenon and is left to the market. But low inflation rates do not guarantee financial stability, as the mainstream pretended to demonstrate during the 'great moderation' years.[38] After the GFC, authorities were keen to simultaneously attain both monetary and financial stabilization objectives.[39]

Global financial markets intensify credit pro-cyclicality, as the movement of gross capital flows exhibits a strong commonality around the world (Calvo, Leiderman and Reinhart, 1993; 1996). Although pro-cyclicality has been largely demonstrated, recent research has come to show that both inflows and outflows are observed to co-move with the VIX – an index of market risk aversion and uncertainty.[40] When the VIX moves down, low interest rates push gross capital flows towards emerging markets and a boom is installed – an opposing pattern erupts when the VIX goes up.[41] Therefore, as EMEs become closely tied to the global financial cycle, their capacity to moderate the impact (of global finance and price movements) through their own monetary policy is reduced: the transmission mechanism of monetary policy loses its effectiveness. In this sense, financial globalization makes the monetary trilemma irrelevant (Rey, 2013).

In order to explain monetary policy irrelevance, a recent characterization turns out to be essential in highlighting global banks' increasing relevance in raising and rerouting funds around the world. To this H. Rey adds the expanded role of capital markets in most EMEs, whose returns are closely correlated to those observed at AE, which gives more pre-eminence to long-term interest rates in policymaking. In brief, she askes, 'how valid is the trilemma in a world of large cross-border capital flows and financial integration?' (Rey, 2014). As a consequence, and despite the possible independence in short-term interest rates, in the long term, home and base countries' rates tend to correlate. As financially integration deepens, traditional monetary responses lose their original potency, and policymakers have fewer options but to introduce capital controls – although sovereign states might be legally prevented from doing that, which is a topic analysed in Chapter 4.

Obstfeld (2014) gives monetary policy a chance, although recognizing the impossibility of isolating the local economy from exogenous financial and monetary distortions. Two channels transmit the effects of the financial cycle on EMEs. On the one hand, the classical *interest rate linkage*, reflecting the traditional forces of cross-border arbitrage between different rates of return, and over which the local monetary authority can take

38. Advanced economies' inflation records combined with output stability were not sufficient to restrain the emergence of important financial imbalances, as low levels of interest rates animate investor's riskier attitude. From a regulatory perspective, financial risks were perceived as a micro phenomenon and, eventually, left to a bank's self-regulation.
39. Borio (2014) explains that the low inflation–high financial instability dilemma was also observed under the gold standard, when liberalized financial markets coexisted with passive monetary policies.
40. The CBOE Volatility Index® (VIX®) is a key measure of market expectations of near-term volatility conveyed by S&P 500 stock index option prices. Since its introduction in 1993, the VIX has been considered by many to be the world's premier barometer of investor sentiment and market volatility (https://www.cboe.com/micro/vix/vixintro.aspx)
41. As investors observe low (high) levels of VIXs, credit continues to grow (stalls), and so does leverage (a sudden deleveraging process begins).

action (monetary-traditional stabilization policies).[42] On the other hand, there is a *credit channel*, associated with cross-border flows, which (unfortunately) are beyond monetary authorities' control (financial-regulatory policies). In this sense, changes in credit volumes at a global level can have strong effects across national borders. As stated by Cetorelli and Goldberg (2012), 'global operations and global liquidity management are traits that can make loan supply effectively insulated from domestic monetary policy'.[43] Global operations and global liquidity management, however, also came to augment the systemic risk faced by the local financial system (Schoenmaker, 2013). In sum, and as the latest GFC demonstrated, the presence of global banks can easily transform into a destabilizing mechanism for the host country. In brief, M. Obstfeld's (2014) paper takes a middle ground between more extreme positions in the debate about monetary independence in open economies. On the one side, Woodford (2010, p. 14) concludes, 'I find it difficult to construct scenarios under which globalization would interfere in any substantial way with the ability of domestic monetary policy to maintain control over the dynamics of inflation'. His pre-GFC analysis, however, leaves aside financial-market imperfections and views inflation targeting as the only objective of monetary control. On the other side, Rey (2013) argues that the monetary trilemma really is a dilemma, because EMEs can exercise no monetary autonomy from United States policy (or the global financial cycle) unless they impose capital controls'. In sum, according to Obstfeld (2014) the monetary policy dilemma is complemented (or further complicated) by the presence of a financial trilemma: the impossibility of coordinating financial policy at the national level to achieve financial stability when the country is being integrated to the international financial system. Under such circumstances, some kind of market segmentation between domestic and international capital markets will prevail – a topic analysed in Chapter 3.

42. The more financially integrated, the more relevant the interest parity relation became, particularly as domestic interest rates began to be closely tied to foreign interest rates. This differential is not exactly matched but adjusted for expected changes affecting the local exchange rate valuation alongside the risks of default and political turmoil that might affect the local economy and, henceforth, the theoretical (interest rate) parity.
43. Non-banking financial globalization can also alter monetary policy relevance, as observed in Brazil. In order to limit this, authorities can prevent or limit local firms from raising debt or issuing debt in foreign markets.

Chapter Three

UNFETTERED FINANCE AND THE PERSISTENCE OF INSTABILITY

The financial collapse created by the 1930 crisis pushed national banks into a corner, a highly regulated space in order to limit banks' operations and avoid their former excess greed. Banking regulation expanded worldwide, generalizing a highly restrictive financial scheme – which was later popularized by R. McKinnon as a 'financial repressive' model.

Thirty years later the deregulation movement ended with years of highly regulated but, on average, highly stable financial markets. Beginning in the late seventies, financial innovation matched market deregulation to generate a new but highly unstable environment. The traditional banks were being transformed into financial supermarkets, whereas the engineering of pooling and securitizing loans was beginning to transform banks' balance sheets, the effectiveness of industry regulation, and the dictates of conventional monetary policy. This huge transformation in financial services intermediation also comprised the moving away from a largely domestic market to an increasingly internationalized space. The next paragraphs describe all the measures and instruments, and also all the regulatory challenges imposed by this new financial model. In the second part, the chapter explores the recent trend towards deregulation and the more recent aim to re-regulate financial markets. In particular, and basically aimed at understanding the problem posed by the financial trilemma, this subsection evaluates the challenges being imposed by the recent expansion in cross-border funding.

From Financial Repression to Global and Deregulated Markets

The neo liberal wave coming after the arrival of Ronald Reagan and Margaret Thatcher resulted in the erosion of the financial regulatory model institutionalized in the aftermath of the Second World War. Countries in Latin America and Asia will soon embrace this dictate and dismantle the 'repressive model'.[1] Deregulatory measures were aimed at increasing the role of market forces in interest rate fixing and credit allocation.[2]

---

1. The term 'financial repression' (FR) was originally introduced by McKinnon (1973) and Shaw (1973) when describing governmental policies directed at 'capturing' or 'underpaying' domestic savers. Under such a framework, monetary authorities often fixed interest rates (price) and allocated credit (quantities). Although largely criticized by the mainstream, other scholars (Stiglitz (1994)) assigned a positive role to FR if market imperfections are observed that could lead to improved financial stability.
2. The removing of the interest rate ceiling (regulation Q) in the United States in 1980 by the Carter administration signalled the beginning of a new financial era. Introduced by the 1933

Suddenly, the financial repressive model that was implemented became outdated, and developing countries were pushed to dismantle it. The slogan was certainly powerful among Latin American policymakers, with pundits along with IFIs recommending the immediate liberalization of interest rates along with advocating a greater role for markets in credit allocation. As elegantly observed by C. Diaz Alejandro (1984), they considered financial markets as comparable to other markets (*butcher shops*), and, henceforth, not eligible for any special treatment.[3] Unfortunately, in the late seventies a group of Southern Cone countries in Latin America took their advice, deregulating (denationalizing) the local banking industry[4] and advancing in liberalizing its capital account. As the process was poorly managed and regulation relaxed, some countries passed from repression to crash without scale. South Korea would observe a similar deregulation experiment, but few analysts considered it (financial liberalization) relevant as it did not hit developed countries' financial system.

Financial transformation, thus, bring with it the triumph of the universal banking model (in particular, after the repeal of the Glass–Steagall Act during the Clinton administration[5]). Institutional convergence would help introduce a new business model, universal banking, which was financially more aggressive than the prevailing one based on a commercial–investment split. This new banking model would not only affect the effectiveness of traditional financial policies (and the regulator's role), in particular, but it would also install an unstable financial environment. Furthermore, as cross-border flows expanded, financial instability expanded worldwide.

Financial innovation, in particular, implied the continuous introduction of new products and instruments, such as, among others, repurchase agreements (repo), securitization, synthetic securitization, residential mortgage backed securities (RMBSs), credit default swaps (CDSs), collateralized debt obligations (CDOs, also named asset-backed securities or ABSs) and collateralized loan obligations (CLOs). Briefly explained, securitization comprises the transformation of illiquid loans (for example, mortgage loans) into a security – a new liquid asset. ABSs could be partitioned into different tranches or seniority, ordered decreasingly in terms of risks (from BBBs, to As, to AAs to AAAs).

Banking Act, regulation Q limited interest rates on time deposits and saving accounts, basically to prevent banks' abusive behaviour. But ceilings become outdated as inflation advances, forcing the government to raise (or directly eliminate) ceilings. In this context, President Jimmy Carter signed the Depositary Institutions Deregulation and Monetary Control Act (DIDMCA), which fixed a complete phase-out of interest rate ceilings within a six-year period.

3. They implemented 'a special version of the monetary approach to the balance of payments, plus the hypothesis that financial markets, domestic and international, were no different from the market for apples and meat' (Diaz Alejandro, 1995, p. 9).
4. In many developing countries and emerging economies, the transformation process implied the passing from a state-directed to a market-driven system.
5. Until this movement, US legislation prohibited commercial (retail) banks from operating in the investment (wholesale) segment. Universal banking, by contrast, was widely expanded in Continental Europe. The purpose of the Glass–Steagall Act was to prevent a conflict of interest within the bank, because, under an universal banking system, the same institution could be both granting (lending) and using credit (investing).

In exchange for loans, banks obtain securitized (and pooled) bonds, which they offer to investors (including institutional investors and money-market-mutual-funds;[6] MMMFs), although the bank makes an agreement with the investor to repurchase the same asset later (the so-called repo agreement). REPOs are like demand deposits, but often are associated with short-period maturity (overnight).[7] In sum, as a result of all this engineering, banks in the United States entered into the 'securitized' business,[8] packaging and reselling loans, with REPO agreements as the main source of funds (Gorton and Metrick, 2009; 2010).[9]

The arrival of all these new products transformed the traditional balance sheet (deposits by securities). But, whereas the entrance of ABSs into a bank's liabilities was theoretically considered as granting more guarantees, by transforming deposits into securities, bank's risks were mounting to unprecedented levels. What is worse, all of these new products, instruments and institutions remained beyond the regulator's burden, uninsured by the government (Sheng, 2009; D'Arista and Griffith-Jones, 2011). In short, as a result the 'shadow banking' industry was born.[10] Operations expanded in size, and in order to maintain returns, financial agents increased their leverage, and risk moved from regulated banks to the shadow unregulated banking system. Rather than monitoring and restricting these sorts of practices, regulators approved this trend: 'the US FED developed a systematic bias for easing liquidity, which, after all was assumed to be a free good in prevailing economic theory' (Pistor, 2012; p. 7).[11]

But global banks were also highly active in the derivatives trade, including the (largely unregulated) trading over-the-counter (OTC) segment. Hedging derivative products have a long history, being basically traded at stock markets and subject to a set of institutional rules governing their trading and information flow (Dodd, 2012). Derivatives, as

---

6. MMMFs are a by-product of the regulation Q. Institutional investors, in turn, have become outstanding actors but also pension funds, mutual funds and so on.
7. Repo is described as the difference between the price being paid by the financial entity at t+1 ($Y) to an institutional investor that deposits at t (and receives $X on that date) and receives some asset (for example, the weakly regulated CDS) from the bank as collateral (i.e., repo: (y – x) / x), being the 'haircut', or the difference between the amount deposited, with the value of the asset used as collateral (Gorton and Metrick, 2010).
8. Global banks that were established in the United States, including, among others, American and German banks, were highly active in this market, both as sellers and buyers of ABSs.
9. Although the REPO market could be tough as a deposit market, participants rapidly expanded their use to hedge derivative positions and similar transformations, changing it into a mechanism to obtain leverage. But when agents' panic increased, it raised the demand for cash, and, henceforth, it pushed for an increase in REPOs' haircut. Consequently, a deleveraging process ensued and a crisis will follows – as observed in the subprime one's (Gorton and Metrick, 2010).
10. For the Financial Stability Board (FSB), the presence of shadow banking is described as 'credit intermediation involving entities and activities outside the regular banking system' ('Transforming Shadow Banking into Resilient Market-Based Finance', FSB, 27 October 2011, http://www.fsb.org/what-we-do/policy-development/shadow-banking/).
11. According to the 'institutional autopsy' approach taken by Katherine Pistor, the specific design finally adopted 'was neither natural nor inevitable; it was the product of a set of institutional choices that in conjunction created this outcome' (Pistor, 2012, p. 8).

for instance those hedging against FX movements, are a great tool for firms involved in global trade. But this 'old financial product' suddenly transformed into a highly speculative tool – a phenomenon observed worldwide (Dodd, 2009; Zeidan and Rodrigues, 2013). For this reason, some scholars found in the OTC market one of the main channels for financial crisis dissemination – from the AEs (particularly from the United States and Europe) to the EMEs[12] (Dodd, 2009).[13] In this sense, this channel severely affected firms from Korea and Brazil, which would be among the most affected (for more details, see Chapters 6 and 9).

Derivative products and securitized debt were now representing 90 per cent of global liquidity, with the remaining 9 per cent being represented by broad money and an insignificant 1 per cent by traditional high-powered money: an unstable and inverted pyramid was now characterizing the global financial system as observed by Independent Strategy analyst David Roche in his liquidity pyramid.[14]

Global banks suddenly became the main actors in transferring (off-balance) funds to developed countries and EMEs. As stated by Coley (2015), (developed countries') regulators were not only aware of the phenomenon but also actively supported it: 'In the decades prior to the crisis, cooperation between central bankers and bank supervisors in major financial jurisdictions, including the United States, set the conditions for globalized finance to flourish'. Financial flows remained weakly regulated, with monetary authorities pursuing banks' self-regulation and financial micro-prudential measures. And the more deregulated the sector, the more risky the collateral. As risks mounted, the crisis became a pre-announced phenomenon. The crisis, however, affected developing countries and EMEs against their will.[15] Is contagion what explains the financial turmoil in these and other emerging markets (Pistor, 2012), and are cross-border funds the channel transmitting it?

In sum, financial deregulation has induced the entrance of foreign banks and, with them, the rise of cross-border funds. The following paragraphs discuss how these flows evolved in recent years, the effects such a raise caused and how authorities around the world have dealt with these challenges.

---

12. According to Dodd (2009), during the 2008–9 period, non-financial firms experienced losses of around US$ 500 billion
13. As observed by Randall Dodd, beyond being differently named (for instance, Korea's KIKO or Brazil's Sell Target Forward), all of them share a basic (and complex) structure. Other derivative markets are certainly more important than the FX, take for example the interest rate derivative one, but EMEs are highly active in the former as their currencies are more prone to volatility.
14. For the year before the GFC, the pyramid was structured as follows: at the base lay power money (M1 and M2) with 1%. Broad money represented another 9%, whereas securities debt added another 10%. Amazingly, 80% of total liquidity was represented (rising to $ 607 trillion or 12.5 times global GDP) by derivatives (Independent Strategy, 2007).
15. As for several countries in Central and East Europe, which would become severely affected by financial liberalization and the arrival of cross-border flows, despite the far-reaching reforms, most of them banned the use of sophisticated financial products.

Box 3.1 Shadow banking in China

Whereas financial innovation was behind the shadow banking revolution in the United States, the increasing relevance of shadow banking in China has been driven by a highly restrictive or 'repressive' regulatory scheme that ended in pushing private firms and investors away from traditional banks. But, in contrast to what has been observed in the North, the Chinese shadow banking sector remains a locally encapsulated phenomenon.

Although informal finance has a long history in China (Lan, 2015), the share of shadow banking was unimportant until recently and still remains around 50 per cent of the country's gross domestic product (GDP) (Elliot et al., 2015). From a political economy perspective, shadow banking reflects bottom-up development originating in the private sector (Lan, 2015). The government's regulatory behaviour, however, has certainly helped in explaining their recent expansion.[a]

For instance the government has imposed tight conditions on the real estate sector or restricted local government financing (Li and Hsu, 2013; Elliot et al., 2015).[b] More broadly, households, but also corporations, are increasingly being tempted by shadow banking's larger returns. In any case, despite the costs cyclically imposed, this informal activity is not necessarily prohibited nor encouraged by the government.

Obviously, shadow-banking operations are beyond PBOC scrutiny and, until recently, have been poorly regulated.[c] Shadow banking practices in China present important differences with the US case, both in term of techniques and instruments used in transactions.Among the most important tools observed in China, are wealth management products (WMPs), trust beneficiary rights (TBRs), entrusted loans, loans and leases by trust companies, Quasi-real estate investment trusts (or Q-REITS) and local government funding vehicles (LGFVs). Commercial banks (through off-balance-sheet operations) and trust companies are considered among the market's main actors, collecting funds from private firms and individuals and investing in a range of credit instruments more risky but bearing a higher interest rate than normal loans. Commercial bank deposits, in turn, are transferred into

Table 3.1 China's shadow banking, composition, size and rate of growth (RMB 1 billion)

Product	2007	2010	2013
Entrusted loans	CNY 1.44	CNY 3.42	CNY 8.55
Trust loans	CNY 342.00	CNY 1.48	CNY 4.81
Banker's acceptances	CNY 1.25	CNY 4.15	CNY 7.00
Interbank entrusted loan payments	CNY 558.00	CNY 1.68	CNY 3.00
Financial leasing		CNY 270.00	CNY 766.00
Small loan companies		CNY 198.00	CNY 819.00
Total	**CNY 3.50**	**CNY 11.11**	**CNY 24,952.00**

Source: Elliot et. al. (2015)

management products, obtaining funds in exchange, which are then lent to project developers.[d] The strict credit policy in force, however, has driven the recent spread in TBRs as this instrument permits the circumventing of prohibitions on banks' lending limits (Lan, 2015). The entrusted loan scheme is also being increasingly used, which permits non-banking entities to bypass PBoC regulation and enter into the lending market.[e] The stimulus package introduced by the Chinese government in the aftermath of the GFC has indirectly induced the implosion of LGFVs (used by local authorities to circumvent budget constraints).[f] Informal financing also arose at the regional level and involved a wide variety of firms, such as the Yangziijiang case certificates.[g] Q-REITS are associated with government-linked real estate investment, and generally are observed in the form of a trust (Li and Hsu, 2013). Finally, there are WMPs, an investment product sold to investors. This instrument has been attracting investors' attention but also financial regulators' zeal as they transformed it into 'the latest growing investment vehicle'.[h] Despite the relevance recently achieved by the shadow banking system and the emergence of new financial tools, securitization remains limited and strictly regulated by authorities.[i]

---

[a] According to the PBoC, shadow banking should be considered as 'credit intermediation involving entities and activities outside the regular banking system' that serves to provide 'liquidity and credit transformation' and 'which could potentially' be a source of 'systematic risk or regulatory arbitrage' (Elliot, Kroeber and Qiao, 2016, p. 4).

[b] Economic recovery after the crisis induced a boom in the real estate sector, which the government tried to turn back. In order to accomplish that, authorities introduced a series of macro controls (including home-buying restrictions). Tight financial conditions on developers pushed them to alternative sources of financing, a role to be played by non-banking institutions – and affecting the Q-REITS trusts. Similarly, as the rescue package introduced by the central government in the aftermath of the crisis showed signs of overheating, authorities decided to cut loans to local projects. In order to avoid a disruption in public works, municipalities made the decision to search for new sources of financing and introduced the LVFGs deal.

[c] Through a series of documents, Chinese authorities tightened their regulatory effort since 2013. In January 2013, the State Council introduced the document 107 'Notice on Some Issues of Strengthening the Regulation of Shadow Banks'. In May 2014, the document 127 'Notice on Regulating Financial Institutions' Interbank Business', and the CBRC´s document N 140 'Notice on Regulating Commercial Banking Interbank Activities'.

[d] The increasing involvement of traditional banks in this practice reflects a problem of (weak) enforcement, not the lack of regulation (Li and Hsu, 2013).

[e] Under this scheme the bank acts as an intermediary (and receives a fee for this), although it does not assume any risk. Investors, including state-owned enterprises (SOEs) with *excessive* liquidity, bring funds.

[f] As the use of this scheme increased (totalling US$ 1.7 trillion by 2012), default risks began to augment – with risk assumed to be around 30% to 40% by some market experts (Elliot Wilson, 'LGFVs: China's $ 1.7 Trillion Hangover', *Euromoney*, April 2012).

[g] A worldwide leader in shipbuilding, Yangzijinag has also transformed into a 'shadow-banking' entity. The firm generated an entrusted loan in order to lend its excess funds to other companies. Yangzijinag is not alone. Several SOEs are competing in the money-lending market with it (*The Economist*, 'Battling the Darkness', 10 May, 2014.

[h] The sectorial regulator (CRBC) has recently began to examine WMPs in more detail. Until recently this instrument remained weakly regulated.

[i] See Clifford Chance, 'Shadow Banking and Recent Regulatory Developments in China', CliffordChance.com, January 2015.

Financial Globalization and the Rise of Global Banks

The interest equalization tax (IET), legislation preventing foreign borrowers from entering the US market, is often mentioned as a key factor in explaining the roots of the modern process of globalization.[16] This regulation which was introduced during the Kennedy administration induced US banks to move abroad (in particular to the United Kingdom) in order to circumvent the law and be able to lend to foreigners: the Eurodollar market was born. The movement somewhat pushed US authorities to reconsider financial regulation. The market unification process in the European Union (EU) could be seen as triggering another process of transformation, as the new legislation forced members to open their financial system and European banks to compete – at least regionally. For them, *going global* became the logical response to increasing competition at home and by the prospect of obtaining economies of scale abroad.

Banking globalization resulted in the appearance of a new funding model. A financial system based in cross-border banking, however, tends to raise risks at home as external liabilities (wholesale funding) reveal more volatile than normal retail funding (domestic depositors).[17] As previously observed, the intermediation of funds could be made internally, with liquidity flowing between headquarters and subsidiaries of the same, globalized bank, either indirectly, as when a bank located in country A (home country) lends to another unconnected bank located in country B (host country).[18] Obviously, with the exception of European banks redirecting funds within their branches operating in the EU (monetary union members), cross-border funding would naturally convey exchange rate risk – whose costs are associated with a bank's failure, as the state should provide an implicit guarantee. As the GFC demonstrated, an external shock affecting the global bank balance sheet could suddenly alter the cross-border funding logic, with headquarters abruptly reducing their loans to EMEs but simultaneously demanding their local subsidiaries bring funds back (Cetorelli and Goldberg, 2010). Under such a scenario a currency and maturity mismatch problem could easily be present and, thus, an exogenous shock would transform a bank solvency problem into a macroeconomic and financial crisis. From a macro perspective, cross-border activities are key to explaining gross flow expansion as global banks increase the levels of both foreign assets and foreign liabilities.[19] After being largely omitted, institutional issues like the organizational financial structure or the legal form being adopted by global banks were suddenly back on the agenda after the GFC – a debate which is introduced in the following paragraphs.

---

16. Banking internationalization was also present during the so-called 'first globalization' (from 1870 to 1914) with London and Paris as the world's most prominent financial centres.
17. Non-core banking funding (foreign creditors) permitted local banks (nationally owned entities or subsidiaries of foreign banks) to support the entry of new borrowers at home – formerly exclusively backed by domestic savers (deposits or other host market sources).
18. Another dimension of cross-border flows relates to (non-banking) financial offshoring, which involves the use of offshore equity markets by local firms (or government) for funding.
19. A widely documented example is the role played by European banks in expanding credit in the United States, although net flows between both partners were minimal. The already mentioned MMMFs along with other institutional investors were an important source of funds for European banks operating in the United States.

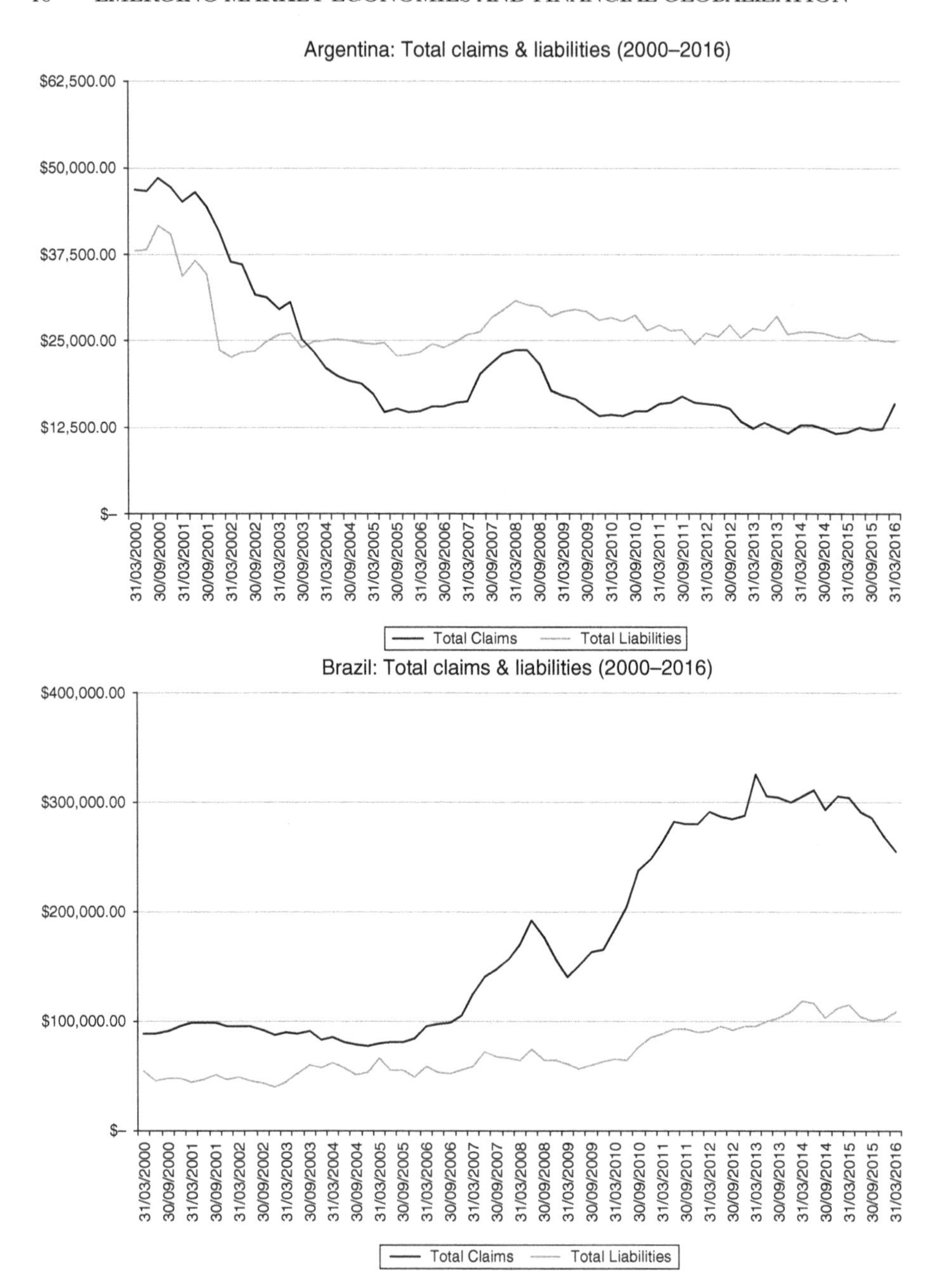

Figure 3.1 Cross-border claims and liabilities by each of the analysed countries (5 graphs)
Source: BIS

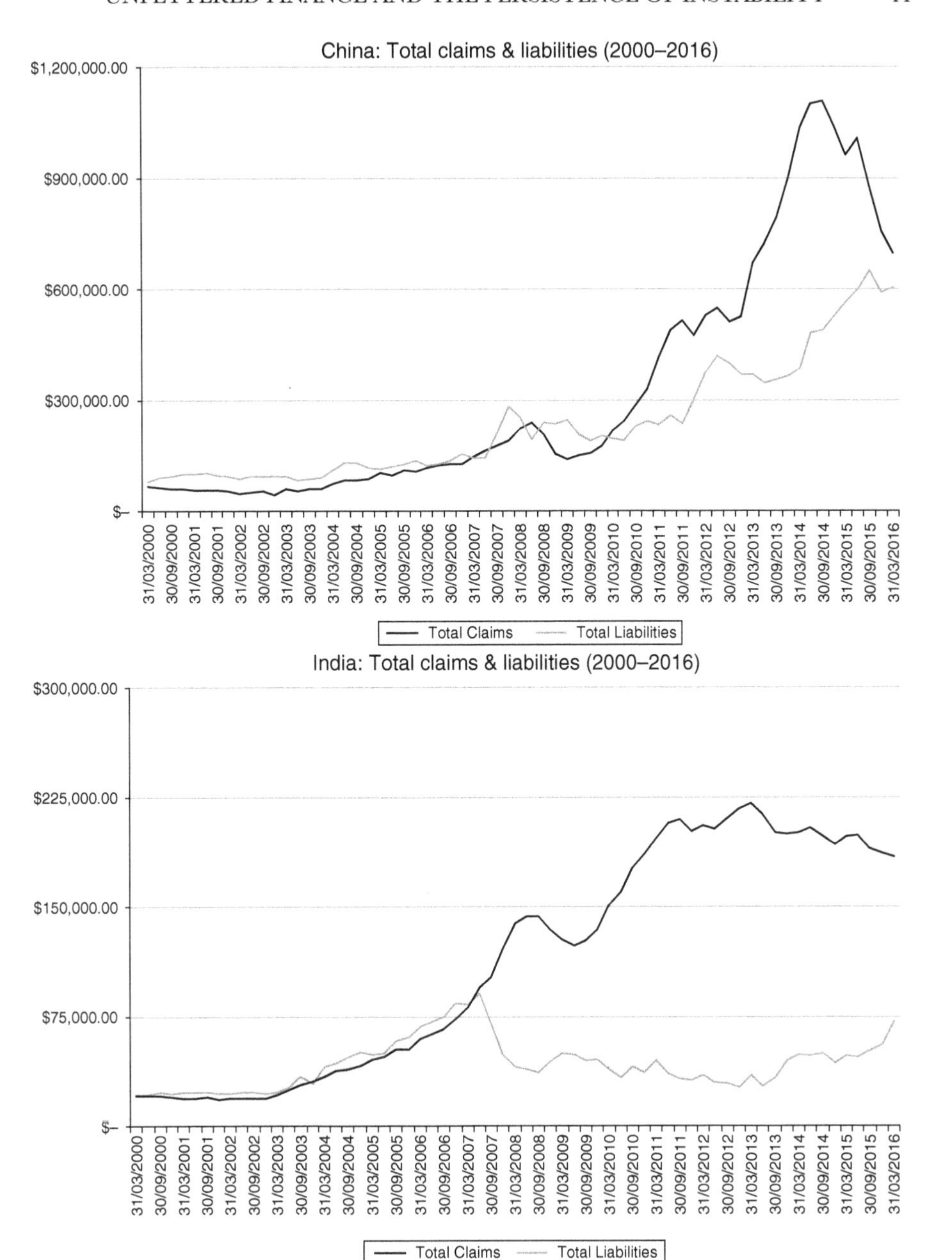

Figure 3.1 *(cont.)*

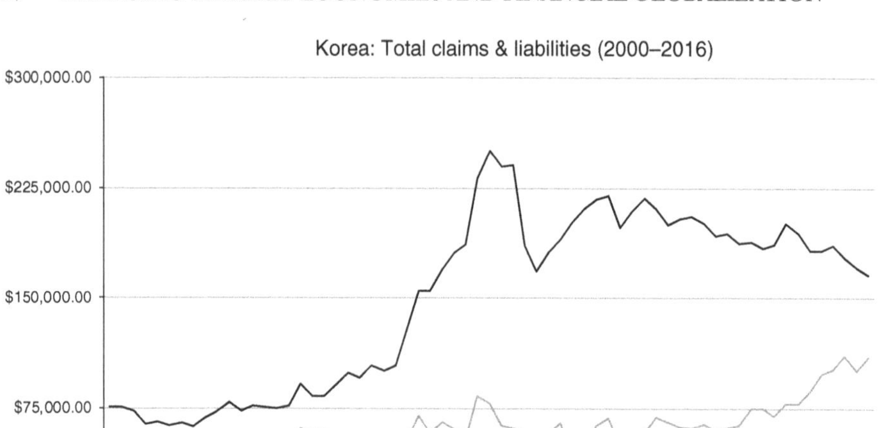

Figure 3.1 *(cont.)*

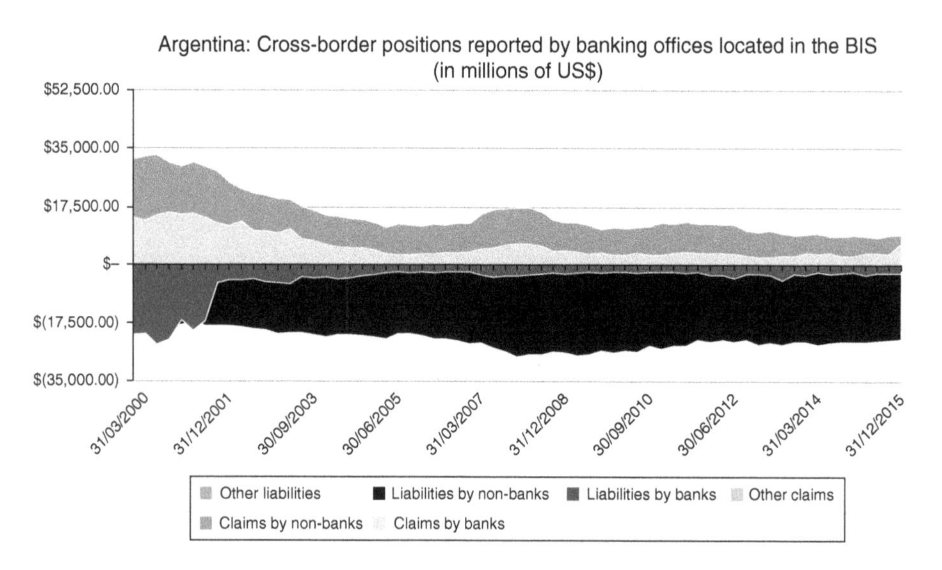

Figure 3.2 Cross-border positions by each of the analysed countries (5 graphs)
Source: BIS

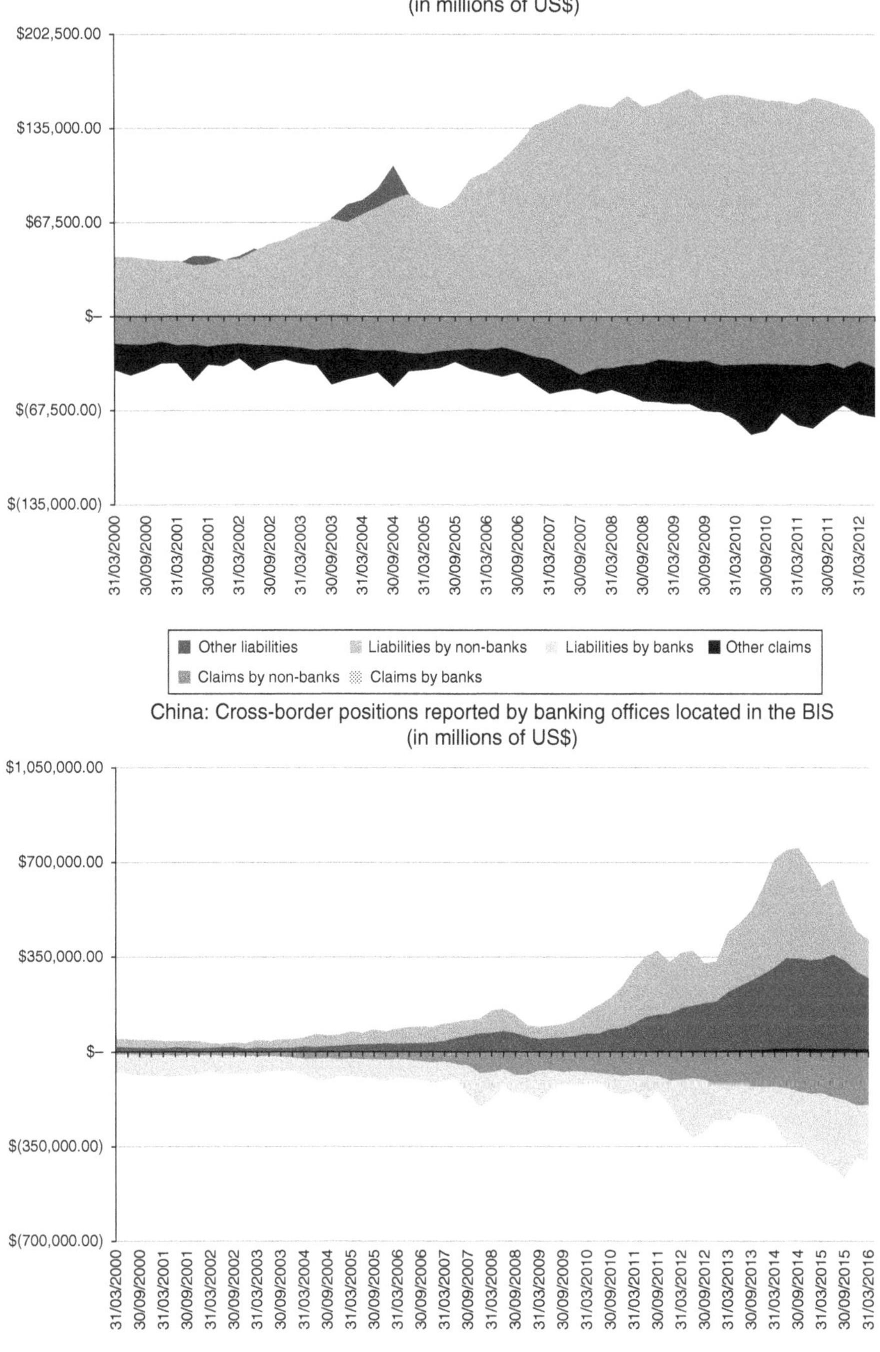

Figure 3.2 *(cont.)*

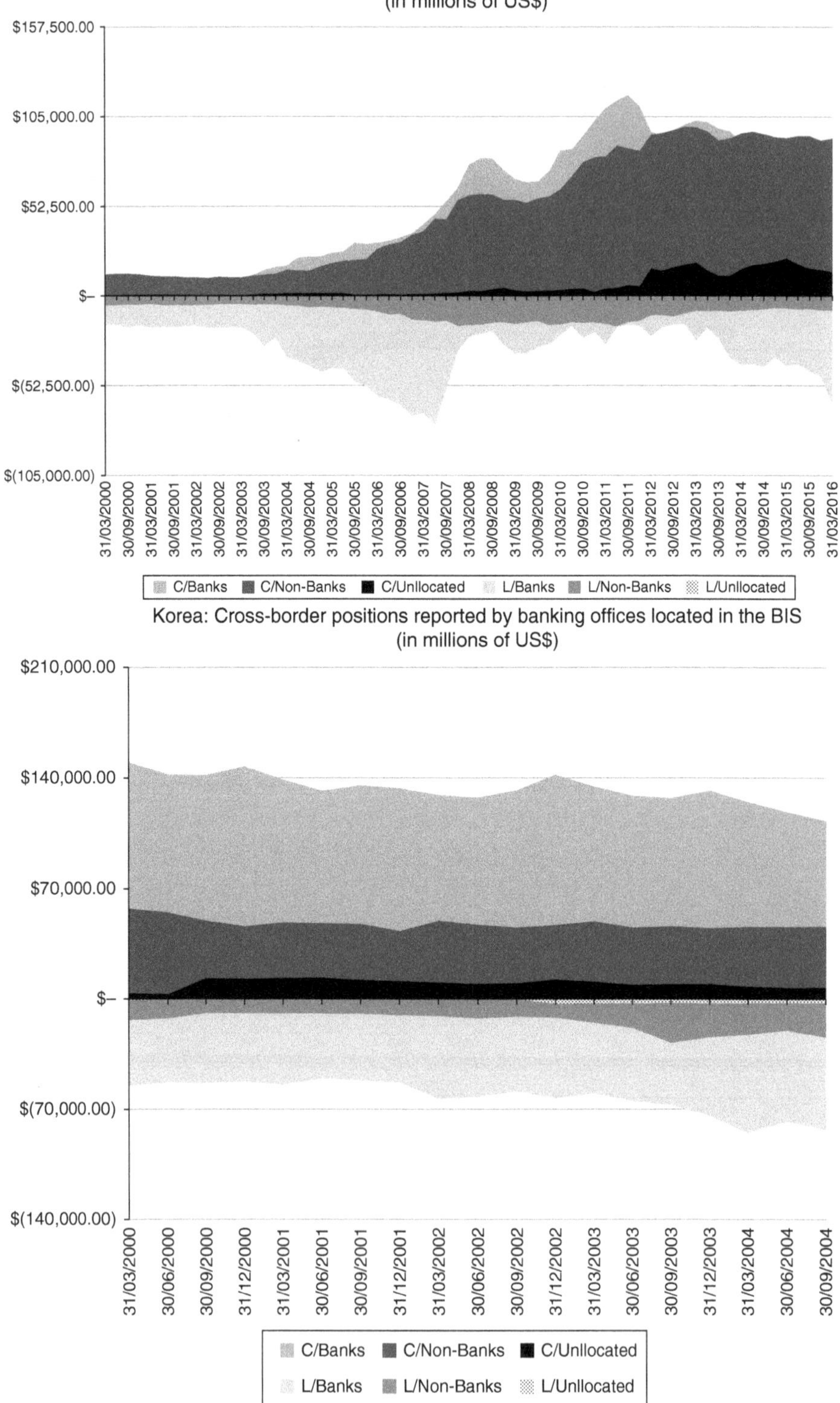

Figure 3.2 *(cont.)*

Global Banks' Funding Practices and Legal Status

Banking internationalization was originally considered beneficial to growth, and as posing no risk to hosting countries: developed countries' banks were now arriving in developing countries.[20] This did not preclude Bank for International Settlements (BIS) authorities from consider supervision of foreign banks, however, which actually began in the mid-1970s and was articulated in the report 'Principles for the Supervision of Banks' Foreign Establishments' (the so-called 'Concordat').[21] Under certain circumstances, the presence of cross-border flows introduces more stress, not less, as regulators lose control over transactions, while bankers' appetite for risk soars – a tragic dual pattern observed in the recent past.

Whereas funding and liquidity vary from bank to bank, cross-border flows are managed by a battery of business practices, financial strategies and legal schemes, implemented either on a stand-alone basis of complementary. Funding practices might originate either inside (intra-group) or outside (financial intermediate) the bank's arms. Funding and liquidity vary from bank to bank, although a pattern emerged in the pre-crisis years from more centralized to extreme decentralized experiences.[22] For example, after the Argentina's convertibility crisis European banks operating in Latin America (mainly Spanish multinational banks) decided to rely on local funds and manage liquidity on a country basis.[23] In other latitudes a more centralized model continued, with global banks pooling deposits which originated at their different foreign branches. Centrally managed funds are subsequently downstream to the various operational units, a practice widely observed among US and Swiss global banks (CGFS, 2010). Certainly, centralizing the management of liquidity might be an optimal decision from a micro perspective, as banks gain in economies of scale (in risk management). The GFC came to show the challenges this model conveys, however. As cross-border flows plunged, the credit squeeze severely affected the level of activity.[24] From this perspective, Latin American countries outperformed those operating in Asia as they relied on local funds and, consequently, became less vulnerable to a *sudden stop* in foreign banks' financing. The specific

20. Global banks were considered to be a sort of stabilizing mechanism, and as generally leading to institutional and regulatory improvements as they promote 'strong property rights' and permit installation of 'a financial system that directs capital to its most productive uses' (Mishkin, 2009).
21. The principles exposed in the 'Concordat' were originally designed to prevent foreign banks from bypassing supervision: a regulatory mandate should be fulfilled either by the host or the home country depending on the legal entity adopted by the bank (branch or subsidiary). In any case, and beyond the relevance of this, other proposed standards were characterized by their (legal) informality (i.e. sovereigns were not bound to follow their commitments nor banned from freely exiting).
22. From a microeconomic perspective, both options show pros and cons. Among the advantages of a centralized model, one should count the presence of funding costs and diversification, coherence, economies of scales and overhead costs. In contrast, a decentralized model induces greater diversification in funding sources, contagion prevention, enhancement of transparency, market discipline and, finally, the value of local presence.
23. Other international banks operating in the region replicated the 'Spanish' bank pattern'.
24. Cross-border funding plunged in each emerging economy from 40% to about −20% in the wake of the collapse of Lehman Brothers (CGFS, 2010, p. 17).

nature of foreign banks' operations in the region together with the institutional configuration of the local banking system was key in obtaining this result, as they funded 'from an expanding deposit base rather than from parent banks' resources (or from wholesale funding)' (Kamil and Rai, 2010).[25]

A subsidiary question relates to the type of fund being collected by the bank. On this point a clear pattern emerged, with Spanish transnational banks (TNBs) relying on retail funding (as traditional banks), whereas Anglo-Saxon financial entities basically funded the (mostly unregulated off-balance-sheet) wholesale market.

Institutional design can also influence the relevance of cross-border financing, as some types of legal insertion are more prone to financial instability than others: branches versus subsidiaries. From a business perspective, the first legal framework is associated with a centralized model, displaying an intra-group pattern of capital and liquidity management. The latter corresponds to a decentralized model, in which each unit of business (in each of the specific countries where the bank is being established) finances and manages its own risks. From a business perspective, it seems to be the case that global universal banks prefer a branch to a subsidiary, whereas the opposite might be true for those performing in retailing. Of course, each of the options presents both benefits and drawbacks, with branches permitting a better allocation of funds, whereas subsidiaries exhibit lower risks of contagion.

From a legal standpoint, a subsidiary represents a different legal entity, whereas branches are not (legally) separated from the group. Those organized as subsidiaries are entitled to periodically present a balance sheet to the host country regulatory authorities, whereas the home country remains in charge of the supervision of the balance sheets associated with the foreign branches of their locally born (but globally installed) banks. In other words, regulatory authorities in the host country are legally empowered to supervise and license subsidiaries but not branches (a not-always convenient division as the Icelandic banking crisis recently showed).[26] Branch operations, in contrast, remain under the holding firm's balance sheet – and, henceforth, they can avoid being scrutinized by the local regulator.[27] Beyond legal obligations, however, reputational issues should be considered if banks are interested in remaining in global markets. Under such circumstances no legal scheme outperforms another as some banks prioritize reputational risks over short-term gains (Fiechter, 2011).[28] In any event, as a matter of fact, branches remained the

25. Two-thirds of all foreign banks′ lending in 2008 was disbursed through local affiliates, i.e. not involving cross-border funds. The share of local funding was even greater in Ecuador, Argentina and Brazil (Kamil and Rai, 2010, p. 6).
26. During the 2000s, Icelandic bankers' expanded their risky business abroad, particularly to the City of London. As the crisis came, the government of Iceland proved incapable of protecting the insured depositors of overseas branches.
27. Yet regulatory bypass is not complete. According to the above-mentioned Basel Concordat, the host country remains able to monitor branches' solvency.
28. Latin American countries tend to support subsidiaries over branches, although this does not preclude the appearance of different attitudes. In this sense, we observed competitive behaviour during the financial crisis of the late 1990s–early 2000s in Latin America. During the Argentina crisis, the US Citibank, one of the leading foreign banks at the time, preferred to sell one of its subsidiaries in a country (Bansud), whereas the Portuguese Banco Espiritu

most accepted legal form between developed America and Western Europe, although this entity is also present in other regions – such as the Middle East. Emerging countries' regulatory authorities, however, have historically opted for subsidiaries (as observed in Latin America, Mexico or Brazil), although this form is also present in countries like New Zealand, France or Switzerland. In a nutshell, branches are under the scrutiny of the home country's regulators, whereas subsidiaries are monitored by the host country's regulators. Thus, local authorities could still allow foreign banks to operate under a branch legal figure, but forced them to ring-fence their operations in the country, and, henceforth, this resulted in transforming the branch into something close to a subsidiary.[29]

From a macro perspective, whereas both types rely on national savings, subsidiaries are more likely to do so. And, thus, as banks are less exposed to cross-border funding, the system is more resilient to the effects of exogenous shocks and financial instability. Although protecting the economy from exogenous shocks, however, this model entails a lower availability of funds – which is a problem for countries short of savings.

Independently of the organizational form, guaranteeing financial stability remains key for local (host country) authorities, either by regulating itself or by delegating the task to the home country regulators if an 'effective mechanism to oversee and resolve cross-border banking groups' is available (Fietcher et al., 2011, p. 6). From a theoretical viewpoint, international coordination of supervision and resolution of cross-border groups and burden-sharing arrangements might represent the best solution. Unfortunately, the post-GFC scenario showed how difficult cooperation remains and why countries are turning towards second-best solutions.

A related question needs to be answered: who bears the cost of distressed financial institutions? Should a bail-in be considered?[30] Should we instead think in the way of a traditional bailout process?[31] Or should bankers be left at the mercy of the courts and firms be permitted to enter into bankruptcy? Independently of the restructuring scheme finally adopted, a regulatory challenge emerges when financial entities have a global presence: which authorities would be entitled to initiate the process? If coordination is not feasible, who dictates that bank's shareholders and creditors should bear the costs? If a bail-in is not feasible, who bears the costs of a bailout process?

Santo, by contrast, opted to inject capital into its Brazilian subsidiary after the devaluation of 1999 (Banco Boavista). Some European banks adopted another attitude. Swedish banks, which accepted responsibility for supporting their branches and subsidiaries operating in the Baltic region, and similarly Austrian and Italian banks granted their support to their subsidiaries operating in Central and Eastern European countries.

29. This attitude became adopted by regulators in the United States who forced foreign branches to maintain a certain amount of assets in the country.
30. A bail-in tool empowers regulators to write down a bank's liabilities to absorb losses and, thus, to absorb losses and, thus, to avoid (or reduce) the use of public funds. In contrast to bailout procedures, under this scheme bank creditors rather than taxpayers are carrying the costs of failing banks. Bail-in proposals are certainly a by-product of the GFC, and an issue extensively discussed in the multilateral space (at both Financial Stability Board (FSB) and Group of Twenty (G20) meetings) but also at the national level (for example, the UK Independent Commission on Banking).
31. When the rescuing (of the bank) is made through the use of public funds.

Table 3.2 Banking regulation: main differences, binary choices

Funding	Source	Intra-group	Financial intermediation
	Fund's management	Local	Global
	Funds / Clients	Retail / traditional banking	Wholesale / Offshore
Institutional	Organizational type	Subsidiaries	Branches
	Bank in distress	SPE	MPE
Regulation	Scope	Ring-fencing	Global

Source: Own elaboration

As widely known, the issue re-emerged after the GFC, and became a hardly debated topic, as regulators in the EU,[32] the United States[33] and some other developed countries were called to assist financially distressed (global) banks. Theoretically, some had argued for the parent company to be the legal entity bearing distressed subsidiaries' related costs. This sort of 'solidarity call', however, might remain unanswered, as the Iceland case illustrates, because either the financial entity or the (home) regulatory authority lacks the resources to rescue the foreign branch.[34]

Two different resolution strategies for distressed banks could be envisioned: the single point of entry (SPE) and the multiple point of entry (MPE) (IMF, 2014; Faia and di Mauro, 2015).[35] Resolution is undertaken by home country authorities under the first scheme and, thus, they are in charge of restructuring the global bank[36] (IMF, 2012; IMF 2014). Nevertheless, and despite the fact that the home country is legally entitled to govern the process, the effectiveness of this so-called SPE scheme would depend on the willingness of national supervisors to cooperate in the assignment of cross-border losses (IMF, 2012; Faia and di Mauro, 2015). In the presence of an MPE scheme, by contrast, local regulators in each of the host countries (where the global bank operates) were entitled to solve the problem – and global banks would assign losses to the each of the different subsidiaries or branches being affected, avoiding the transfer of resources from the headquarters.

32. Several European financial institutions were hardly affected by the crisis, as they profited from weak regulations and showed a widespread use of innovative but highly risky financial tools (derivatives, CDS and so on). As a result, entities like Dexia, Fortis, ING, Hypo Alpe Adria or KBC were highly affected by the crisis, forcing authorities to rescue them in order to sustain market stability.
33. The crisis hardly hit the financial system, both local and foreign banks operating in the country – for example, take the case of Deutsche Bank, which the US Federal Reserve had to rescue.
34. Starting in 1999, a reduced group of local banks decided to go abroad, particularly attracted by the business opportunities granted by the London financial district. Traditional Icelandic banks' balance sheets were suddenly transformed, as they relied now taking international deposits and on short-term repos.
35. Hybrid strategies are also possible (IMF, 2014).
36. They are entitled to push banks into a bail-in process, forcing shareholders and creditors to absorb the losses of the entire group.

The crisis came to demonstrate, however, how regulatory policies differentiate between prior and expected responses, observing an increasing unilateral trend. This is because the (local) regulator's main responsibility is now considered as 'to protect domestic financial stability and minimize any risk of public funds' (IMF, 2014). We observe, on the one hand, developed countries' authorities moving towards 'unilateral ring-fencing' regulation (explained below). And, on the other hand, developing countries (small hosts) would certainly be less affected (more protected from financial instability) if they undertook this 'unilateral bias' (ring-fencing) or subsidizing global banks; operations), as they could not guarantee to achieve a cooperative agreement ex-ante (IMF, 2014, p, 23). In any case, and independently of the particular response being implemented, a new regulatory pattern seems to privilege financial stability at home: disregarding assistance to foreign banks. Sometimes the presence of foreign financial entities augments risks (as well as the likelihood of failure).

Derivatives, OTC and Regulation: ET Is Back

When the US government finally declared it would bail out the American Insurance Group (AIG), a US multinational insurance firm with a presence in more than 130 countries and employing more than 64,000 people in 90 countries, a new acronym appeared on the late evening news: OTC derivatives.[37] This company operated in 'opaque and unregulated OTC derivatives markets, neither AIG nor its counterparts required the other to post margin as collateral for their obligations' (Coffee, 2014). A liquidity crisis that started on 16 September 2008 would push AIG into technical bankruptcy, but the federal government came to the rescue and took control of the firm – after the largest private bailout in the US history: $180 billion. In sum, despite the *destructive power* of these 'weapons of massive destruction' (Warren Buffett) remained hidden for most mortals before 2008, to become famous worldwide thereafter.

A derivative is 'a financial contract whose value is derived from an underlying asset or commodity price, an index, rate or event. They commonly go by names such as forward, future, option, and swap, and they are often embedded in hybrid or structured securities' (Dodd and Griffith-Jones, 2007, p. 13). By virtue of this type of contract, economic agents could negotiate, in the present, the future value of an asset.

---

37. In January 2011, the Financial Crisis Inquiring Commission (FCIC) concluded, 'The Commission concludes AIG failed and was rescued by the government primarily because its enormous sales of credit default swaps were made without putting up the initial collateral, setting aside capital reserves, or hedging its exposure – a profound failure in corporate governance, particularly its risk management practices. AIG's failure was possible because of the sweeping deregulation of over-the-counter (OTC) derivatives, including credit default swaps, which effectively eliminated federal and state regulation of these products, including capital and margin requirements that would have lessened the likelihood of AIG's failure' (The Financial Crisis Inquiry Report. *Final Report of the National Commission on the Causes of the Financial and Economic Crisis in the United States.* Submitted by The Financial Crisis Inquiry Commission Pursuant to Public Law 111-21 January 2011, p. 352).

Table 3.3 Global OTC derivative markets (amounts outstanding, in trillions of US dollars)

	Notional Amounts Outstanding	
	June 2010	H2 2014
Grand Total	$ 582.70	$ 629.10
Foreign Exchange Contracts	$ 53.10	$ 75.80
Interest Rate Contracts	$ 451.80	$ 505.40
Equity-linked Contracts	$ 6.30	$ 6.90
Commodity Contracts	$ 2.90	$ 1.80
Credit-Default Swaps	$ 30.30	$ 16.40

Source: BIS

The global OTC derivative market comprises different types of swaps, but interest-rate contracts predominate (see table above).[38] Banks, hedge funds, pension funds, government entities and corporations are the main players, although the market concentrates around a limited number of dealers.[39] Certainly, and despite the fact that OTC derivatives take place in a larger number of countries, the bulk of operations are concentrated in a few financial places in the United States and Europe. Thus, independently of the geographical origin and the predominant role assumed by US banks, derivatives risks spread around the world almost instantly – although their effects were (initially) unnoticed by regulators.[40]

As previously mentioned, financial innovation implied the appearance of new tools, but what differentiates OTC derivatives from other financial instruments is their private character,[41] their misaligned incentives and inadequate liquidity requirements. In theory, OTC derivative markets might be beneficial to the national economy as they permit improvement in the pricing and managing of risk. Instead of improving market resilience (risk management tool), however, OTCs have contributed to increasing market turbulence (risk-taking tool) (Oldani, 2015; Rossi, 2015). In the case of Brazil, the presence of deep and liquid derivatives markets transformed the process of exchange rate determination (Rossi, 2015).[42] Farhi and Zanchetta Borghi (2009) document how FX future contracts transformed from being a risk management tool into a highly risk-taking one, into speculative bets that seriously affected the financial integrity of exporters firms

38. Almost all interest rate derivative contracts are denominated in a small number of currencies: US dollar, the euro, sterling or the Japanese yen (CGFS, 2011).
39. Within each class, around 5 to 15 dealers dominate OTC market turnover (CGFS, 2011).
40. The US Federal Reserve and the US Treasury Department, for instance, lacked information about which institutions were exposed and the size of those exposures (Jackson and Miller, 2013).
41. At the time of the crisis, the market was highly decentralized and most of the contracts were bilateral.
42. In particular, if derivatives are being used as a hedge, the operation of risk coverage is matched by an opposite position to the one assumed in the spot market. If no coverage in the opposite position is being observed, derivatives are being held for speculative purposes (Farhi, 2009)

around the world (including numerous EMEs) but also generated important macroeconomic effects.[43]

In addition, OTC derivative markets span national borders and national regulators. As transactions mainly take place across borders, this might call for the creation of a robust and consistent framework – at least in theory. As a consequence, G20 leaders began discussions on how to regulate the OTC market, agreeing that changes should be directed to the following: (1) standard derivatives must be traded on exchanges or electronic platforms and settled through central counterparts (CCPs) entities (clearing houses);[44] (2) OTC derivatives must be registered and reported to trade repositories (TRs); and (3) international standards and policies for capital requirements should be developed and implemented, although OTC derivatives traded with no central counterpart must face higher ratios of capital requirements.[45] The underlying goals of G20 proposals were directed towards increasing the market's transparency, to mitigate systemic risk and to protect against the market's abuse (Carney, 2013). Furthermore, G20 leaders were also interested in developing a set of international rules and standards, and, particularly, in permitting OTC derivatives to be centrally cleared[46] – a commitment originally expected to be met by the end of 2012. Based on recommendations prepared by a collective of international organizations (Bank for International Settlements; BIS, the International Organization of Securities Commission; ISOCO, and the Committee on Payments and Settlement Systems; CPSS), the BIS proposed a set of standards including the convenience to install a central counter-parties (CCP) figure. This new figure would be entitled to clear standardized OTC derivatives contracts (BIS, 2014).[47] From a legal

43. A group of Brazilian firms were exposed to heavy losses in derivatives associated to the dollar increase, including Aracruz (cellulose), Votrantim Group (diversified), Sadia (processed foods). Also from China (China Cosco Holdings – shipbuilding; Air China Ltd. – airline). Korean firms were also affected, with some among them forced to file for bankruptcy as they operated in FX derivatives (KIKOs options) against the appreciation of the local currency (Farhi and Zanchetta Borghi, 2009).
44. There are a reduced number of CCPs already operating, and located in major financial districts in Europe and the United States. For instance, the London-based LCH Clearnet's SwapClear dealing (interest rate swaps) or ICE Clear, also located in this financial district, and specialized in CDSs. BM&F Bovespa (Brazil) specializes in equity index and currency options clearing, whereas the Clearing Corporation of India specializes in FX swaps. In the case of China, authorities proposed the establishment of the Shanghai Clearing House.
45. These changes were proposed in 2009 at the G20 leaders' summit in Pittsburgh, Pennsylvania, to be later reaffirmed at the Toronto summit (2010), at Cannes (2011) and at Los Cabos (2012), although the issue was already evaluated at the Washington meeting in November 2008.
46. According to the Committee on the Global Financial System (CGFS), access to CCPs could be either direct or indirect (clearing at the regional level). In both cases, interconnection becomes crucial, because links might help in reducing collateral requirements – which could be beneficial but risky, as it could become a channel of transmission of systemic stress (CGFS, 2011).
47. For the FSB, the presence of standards 'seek[s] to enhance safety and efficiency in payment, clearing, settlement and recording arrangements and, more broadly, to limit systemic risk and foster transparency and financial stability' (FSB, 'Key Standards for Sound Financial Systems', http://www.fsb.org/what-we-do/about-the-compendium-of-standards/key_standards/).

standpoint, the CCP is an independent entity intermediating between buyers and sellers, and, henceforth, helps in managing market risks (Cecchetti, Gyntelberg and Hollanders, 2009).[48] But the existence of multiple CCPs makes regulatory consistency mandatory; otherwise, arbitrage, would prevail.[49]

Unfortunately, G20 leaders failed to consider the tensions posed by the emergence of legal inconsistencies when regulating, a phenomenon that could lead to market fragmentation. Consequently, the impasse at the multilateral level pushed the bargain at the bilateral level: US regulators and the EU commission.

US authorities decided to advance unilaterally, and on several fronts as for them (absent extra-territoriality; ET) 'major financial institutions could simply park their higher-risk operations outside the United States and thereby effectively escape the principal reforms intended by the Dodd-Frank Act' (Coffee, 2014, p. 1263). The Volcker Rule disallowed banks from short-term proprietary trading of securities, derivatives, commodity futures and options, as these instruments did not benefit their customers.[50] In particular, and considering the recent experience, US banking authorities' objectives were directed to disincentive systematically important financial institutions (SIFIs) from taking large risks. Tittle VII of the Dodd–Frank Act addresses G20 commitments, including the regulation of (previously unregulated) derivative operations. OTC regulation also attracted the interest of two other agencies, the US Securities and Exchange Commission (SEC) and Commodities Futures Trading Commission (CFTC). According to the new legislation, dealers should now be registered with the SEC or the CFTC, which now applies not only to those domiciled in the United States but also to foreigners.[51]

European authorities also advanced on their own, installing a series of directives and regulations to curb inconsistencies. A central clearinghouse for OTC derivatives was installed through the European Market Infrastructure Regulation (EMIR) and capital requirements regulations and directives (CRR/CRD IV) implemented to make the transition from the Basel III framework to domestic directives. The EMIR (partially in force since August 2012) has five major objectives: (1) establish clearing obligations for certain classes of OTC derivatives; (2) establish risk mitigation techniques for non-centralized cleared OTC derivatives; (3) establish reporting obligations to trade repositories; (4) establish organizational, conduct of business and prudential requirements for

48. By virtue of this legal figure, the original single contract (linking buyer and seller) was replaced by two new contracts (one between the buyer and the CCP, and the other between the seller and the CCP) (Cecchetti, Gyntelberg and Hollanders, 2009).
49. The existence of multiple clearings might induce an increase in agents' costs as they need to post equity capital at an initial margin in each entity in which they participate. But market participants might also benefit if they prefer to operate in those which are weakly regulated. (Cecchetti, 2009, 54–56).
50. The definition of 'proprietary trading' is extremely broad, although some exceptions were originally included – and later ratified by the 'final rule' (Cervone, 2015).
51. Registration with the CFTC is mandatory for swap dealers (SD) or major swap participants (MSP), whereas security-based swap dealers must register with the SEC.

central clearing parties; and (5) establish requirements for trade repositories, including the duty to make certain data available to the public and to the relevant authorities.

EU and US negotiators failed at obtaining an agreement on cross-border transactions, particularly, the ET issue. Debate centred on whether the local authority recognizes third-country central counter-parties (CCPs) and trade repositories (TRs). In the case of Europe, extraterritoriality (to derivative contracts) is observed under the EMIR's mandatory clearing obligation if market dealers (both or one of them) are being established at the EU.[52] Nevertheless, in order to avoid conflicts (with foreign regulators) or to prevent an increase in costs, some contracts could remain outside the EU scope if implemented under an equivalent regime or mutual recognition rule.[53]

A different perspective was adopted in the United States. In order to decide whether a third-country resolution would be accepted, authorities decided to rely on the substituted compliance (SC) rule, a subjective criterion used to evaluate 'how the host country interprets, comply and enforce its different standards, and whether those standards achieve the outcomes they are designed to achieve' (Grenee and Potiha, 2013, p. 3). In order to advise market participants on the SC issue, both agencies bypassed a series of guidelines. On the one hand, the CFTC issued proposed guidance on *Cross-Border Application of Certain Swaps Provisions on the Commodity Exchange Market* on July 2012.[54] On the other hand, in May 2013 the SEC proposed *Rules and Interpretive Guidance on Extraterritoriality*, directed at addressing two basic questions – including the SC issue and when it comes into play. In contrast to the CTCF rules where properly defining the US person remains key to determining extraterritoriality, the SEC's application depends on where transactions take place. Nonetheless, the CS rule does not apply to OTC derivative (including margin and capital) requirements as regulation is under the Federal Reserve sphere. The Volcker Rule, finally, implemented the so-called solely, outside of the United States test under which foreign banking institutions are forced to follow a series of conditions, in order not to be affected by ET.[55]

52. Extraterritoriality might also apply when both are non-EU entities, but the contract has 'a direct, substantial and foreseeable effect within the EU or where such obligation is necessary or appropriate to prevent the evasion of any provision' of the EMIR (Consultation Paper, 'Draft Regulatory Technical Standards on Contracts Having a Direct, Substantial and Foreseeable Effect within the Union and Non-evasion of Provisions of EMIR', European Securities and Markets Authority; ESMA).
53. In this sense, according to Articles 4 and 27, foreign subsidiaries of EU banks and EU branches of foreign banks can be exempted if they are subject to measures that in the opinion of the Commission are deemed to have *equivalent effect* to those in the Regulation (Cervone, 2015).
54. Those guidelines were fundamentally aimed at setting out how requirements installed by Title VII may be transacted across national borders. The objective was to narrow the extraterritoriality scope of the registration provisions being previously established – although more stringent registration requirements were proposed at the 'transaction level' (Greene and Potiha, 2013; Coffee, 2014).
55. First, the banking entity may not be located in the United States. Second, the banking entity that makes the decision to purchase or sell may not be located in the United States or organized under the laws of the United States or any state. Third, the purchase or sale is not

As observed by Coffee (2014), the approach toward defining ET is not uniform, with banking regulators taking a broader perspective than the substituted compliance adopted by both the SEC and the CFTC.[56] For him, the differences might be in the fact that through ring-fencing regulation European countries prevented commercial banks from entering into proprietary trading, thereby forcing a broader ET rule to be put in place. In the end, US authorities disregarded the concept of substituted compliance, enacting (a slightly modified version of) the Volcker Rule instead. Thus, when a comparison is made with the equivalent EU approach, the ET rule that is part of the Volcker ('Final') Rule shows the strongest effects: whereas both jurisdictions have extraterritoriality effects, in the case of the United States, it acts unilaterally (Cervone, 2015).

The Financial Trilemma: From Deregulation to Financial Re-regulation

One of the latest explanations for the GFC, which can thought of as originating after the European financial crisis, lay in the presence of a financial trilemma. This new trilemma states that national financial policies could not manage to obtain financial stability[57] when the local economy was being opened up to international capital markets (Schoenmaker, 2011; 2013). In short, the trilemma might be helpful in answering the question of 'How […] can we successfully reduce the risk to financial stability posed by large, international active banks? (Tarullo, 2014, p. 2).

If we consider the trilemma as a triangle, financial stability, national financial policies and international banking would lie at each of their three different corners. Whereas nobody would discuss the relevance of financial stability, the latest crisis has certainly called into question global banks' contribution to it. Henceforth, and with few exceptions (i.e. financial havens) the status quo scenario (unregulated banking) is not being considered, as no country would accept financial instability as a response. The remaining question to be answered is who should regulate global banks, and whether this should be at the local level or subject to an international body.

As a first best option is being integrated into global markets (because market participants could profit from pooling funds at a global level), local authorities should support a multinational agreement – a supranational agency to deal with financial stability

accounted for, directly or on a consolidated basis, by any branch or affiliate that is located in the United States or organized under the laws of the United States or any state. Fourth, no financing for the transaction is provided by any branch or affiliate located in the United States or organized under the laws of the United States or any other state. Five, the purchase or sale is not conducted through any US entity.

56. In December 2013, five different federal agencies finally decided to adopt the Volcker Rule, thereby implementing the so-called Final Rule. According to Cervone (2015), this new rule expands the ET application but it also modifies the 'solely outside the US' (SOTUS) exemption by adopting a risk-based approach.
57. Financial stability is associated with the presence of systemic risk, a loss of confidence in a substantial portion of the financial system (Schoenmaker, 2013).

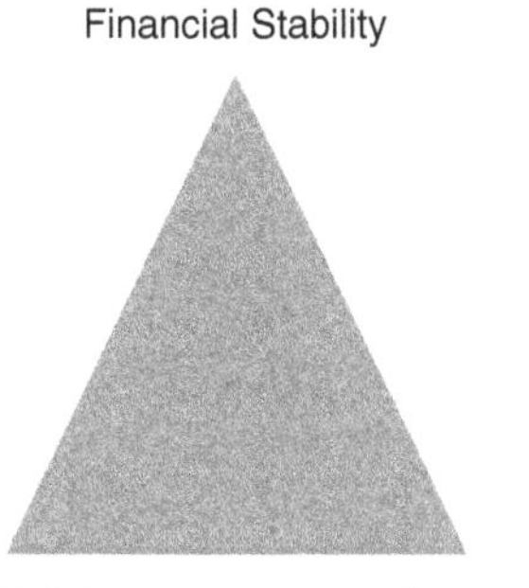

Figure 3.3 Schoenmaker's financial trilemma
Source: Schoenmaker (2013)

problems within national borders (CIEPR, 2012).[58] In other words, the problems posed by the trilemma would be alleviated throughout the pre-establishment of international agreements between the member countries, a sort of pre-accorded agreement stipulating how countries would share in the costs of an eventual banking run. Alternatively the sovereign states (home and host countries) could negotiate such a deal on a bilateral basis – a feasible outcome if both are considered to be equal partners (in terms of both economic development and markets), although not when disparity among participants remains important. Under this latest case, local authorities could be tempted to regulate by themselves.

As unexpected that could be, some policymakers in the North are devising such a scenario as convenient, whereas (financial industry) lobbies consider this trend as favouring banking fragmentation (see below). Maintaining the local market (somewhat) close to cross-border funding certainly resembles a Bretton Woods scenario, an option that gained new followers after the GFC. In any case, and despite the inefficiency being associated with it, as the next paragraphs show, there is a trend towards solving the problem at the local/national level. This sort of arrangement has remained in place among a reduced yet powerful group of EMEs, notably China and India. Both remain closed to cross-border flows, and have also maintained (and still preserve) important restrictions on foreign banks operations. Legally, regulators in China (as in Brazil) still obligate foreigners to operate through locally incorporated subsidiaries for all domestic banking activities (FSB, 2014). Furthermore, and despite some recent progress, important restrictions banning foreigners from acquiring an established financial institution remain in force. In other words, entering into the market does not guarantee (foreign banks) to become an important player in it.

58. The proposal also envisages monetary policy coordination at a global level. From a regulatory perspective, this collective is asking for the establishment of macro-prudential policies operating on both the asset and the liability side of the banks' balance sheet.

Financial regulation is intrinsically attached to the liberalization process initiated in the 1970s. As long as financial services go global, this reduces local regulators' policy space. As the next paragraphs explain, this new situation imposes either greater cooperation or market fragmentation.

International Cooperation in a Historical Perspective

According to Schoenmaker (2013), an integrated financial market remains a first best option.[59] In order to guarantee financial stability, participants' countries delegate the regulatory power to a central agency. Historical evidence has demonstrated how elusive international cooperation remains, however. The first attempts to create a supranational body came in 1974, with the establishment of the BCBS. The failure of the (German) Bankhaus Herstatt originated in losses from FX operations. A similar pattern was observed in the bankruptcy of the (US) Franklin National Bank a few months later. Both episodes would become central for the introduction of this committee (Tarullo, 2014; Blustein, 2015). The Basel Concordat would become a by-product of this body, an institutional setting introducing a series of standards towards the supervision of foreign branches and subsidiaries (Eatwell and Taylor, 2005; Schoenmaker, 2013).

In any case, responsibility for looking after foreign banks' solvency was originally shared between host and home countries: subsidiaries are under local scrutiny, whereas branches are not. Those operating on a branch basis are not subject to host country regulation. But along with power came the burden of providing assistance when necessary (Blustein, 2015). As such, two unrelated events altered this and revised the original scheme. The bankruptcy of the Italian Banco Ambrosiano in 1982 is one of them. The other one was Mexico's default declaration of 1982, which pushed US banks to the edge of bankruptcy. To solve this, but also to avoid the global rise of Japanese banks (Blustein, 2015),[60] the US Congress intended to increase the capital requirements for all international lenders but 'finally obtained a compromise with bankers and directed the Reagan administration to seek common international financial standards' (Levinson, 2010, p. 78).[61] Under the new document the jurisdictional gap was amended, introducing the possibility to consolidate banks' supervision on a transnational basis.[62]

---

59. Which, theoretically it is. Thus, Schoenmaker`s analysis remains central at the EU, which explains why central coordination remains a feasible first best.
60. Increasing capital ratios at home would leave US banks at a disadvantage vis-à-vis foreign (mainly Japanese) competitors; therefore, it was out of the question.
61. In charge of this issue was the Basel Committee, though agreement proved difficult to obtain until the US authorities joined the United Kingdom. The agreement implied alignment between the two leading financial centres of the world, forcing Japanese banks to accept the rules of the game. Once the three main actors agreed, the rest of the countries followed, and in 1988 the agreement would become known as the Basel Accord (Levinson, 2010).
62. The Bank of Credit and Commerce International, whose bankruptcy in 1991 resulted in a new global political scandal, would find the hole. This new national legislation would present US banks with disadvantages vis-à-vis non-US banks – as for example, Japanese ones.

As a result, US authorities began to promote a unique playing field for the global banking industry, pushing for revision of international standards. Thereafter, the Committee works oriented towards fixing capital ratios, leading to the Basel standard ratios. The first agreement, obtained in 1988 (Basel I), reflected the interest of the leading financial centres (London and Wall Street)[63] in introducing a legal common field that (theoretically) permitted them to simultaneously curb financial stability and competition at a global level.[64] The Asian financial crisis gave new impetus to those advocating greater international coordination, and several voices emerged to install a new financial architecture. A broader consensus was difficult to obtain at the supranational level after all, and IMF members agreed to create the financial stability forum (FSF) instead.[65] This 'highly exclusive club' based in Basel,[66] Switzerland, basically envisioned to foster policies and practices in developing countries, whose erratic financial systems were seen as the only source of instability (Blustein, 2012).[67] In looking after them, however, FSF authorities were incapable of anticipating the looming financial crisis at the north: for them, self-regulation was seen as guaranteeing a safe and stable global financial system.

A new version of the Basel agreement came into force in 2004, as Committee members were intending to address the banking crisis beyond credit risk.[68] This second agreement was based on three pillars: capital requirements, supervision and disclosure. This version, however, proved insufficient (as the GFC would come to demonstrate) and remained silent on the liquidity issue (Levinson, 2010).[69] The agreement also permitted global banks to use their own models to assess risks – a highly critical decision.

The crisis reaffirmed the relevance of international cooperation, and new efforts emerged – now among G20 members, a league of traditional superpowers and emerging

---

63. Claire Jones, 'The Basel Committee on Banking Supervision', *Financial Times*, 23 October 2011. These two big players were trying to prevent Japanese banks from free-riding, as they were subject to less strict capital requirement ratios than US global banks.
64. According to Daniel K. Tarullo, it was 'motivated by two interacting concerns, the risks posed to the stability and the competitive advantage accruing to banks subject to lower capital requirement' (2008, p. 45).
65. Among US officials the vision prevailed that the crisis basically originated at the local level, as most countries were perceived as having corrupt financial systems (Blustein, 2015, p. 35). Therefore, a radical transformation was needed, meaning more market deregulation and an increasing role for foreign banks.
66. FSF comprised a privileged group: Group of Seven (G7) finance ministry officials, G7 regulators and officials of international organizations (all controlled by G7 members), and G7 central bankers.
67. In this sense, the FSF's implicit message to them was 'transform your domestic systems in accord with these principles, and you can be rich like us' (Blustein, 2012, p. 11).
68. Basel II based banking regulation in three pillars: (expanded) minimum capital requirements, regulatory supervision and risk management, and harnessing market forces through effective disclosure to encourage sound banking practices.
69. Two other (highly) controversial issues were affecting the capital ratio – although they remained poorly regulated (Kay, 2015). On the one hand, banks were permitted to include some of their debt as part of its capital base. On the other hand, now most of the positions were associated with off-balance-sheet operations.

giants.[70] New tasks were granted to the FSB, an institution created at the 2009 London Summit and described by former US Treasury Secretary Tim Geithner as the 'fourth pillar of the architecture of cooperation'.[71] G20 leaders, meanwhile, reaffirmed that failures in financial regulation and supervision were 'fundamental causes of the crisis' (G20 London Summit: Official Communique, http://eu-un.europa.eu/g20-london-summit-official-communique/). At the 2011 Cannes Summit they endorsed the implementation of 'policy measures to address systematically important financial institutions'. Two years later, G20 leaders were asking the *triade* which integrated the FSB, the IMF and the Organization for Economic Cooperation and Development (OECD) 'to assess cross-border consistencies and global financial stability implications of structural banking reforms' (FSB, 2014). In order to improve financial stability, at the beginning of 2014 this collective proposed a structural banking reform, which centred on the return to the original division of traditional and investment banking – proposed measures could be initiated by (host or home) country initiative.[72] Yet despite all the initiatives being introduced to increase cooperation among members, the attempt came to nothing. As member countries failed to grant powers to the extensively promoted 'four pillars', nobody was entitled to enforce new international standards.

At the end of the day, coordination remained difficult to achieve, as leading nations remained uninterested in restrict their local banks' foreign operations yet advanced firmly in (re-)regulating foreigners at home – a highly contradictory policy observed in many developed countries like the United States. As the crisis moved stability to the centre of sovereign states' preference list, monetary authorities were now behind global banks behaviour.[73] Consequently, several (developed) countries have finally opted for constraints on foreign banks cross-border operations (limited internationalization, deglobalization or fragmentation scenario), putting national (or regional) regulation back into the picture (Buch et al., 2013; Lehman, 2014; Barnier, 2014; Carnier, 2014; Coley, 2015; Beck et al., 2015).

After the enactment of the Dodd–Frank Act and the Fed's later amendment on foreign banks operations,[74] foreign banks operating in the United States with $50 billion of US non-brand assets were being forced to restructure under a new legal figure: the

70. The membership of both the Basel Committee on Banking Supervision and the Financial Stability Forum was expanded in 2009, with the inclusion of Argentina, Australia, Brazil, China, Hong Kong SAR, India, Indonesia, Korea, Mexico, Russia, Saudi Arabia, South Africa and Turkey.
71. The G20 FSB would become the continuation of the former the Basel-based FSF.
72. Among the initiatives it requires (1) ring-fencing or separation of specific activities into different legal entities; (2) the imposition of activity restrictions; (3) the introduction of or materially strengthening of requirements related to capital, intra-group exposure limits, liquidity and funding sources to parts of a banking organization on a sub-consolidated basis, or (4) requirement or incentive for banks to operate through certain structures rather than others.
73. As Martin Wolf (2007) correctly asserted, we actually leave in a world of unfettered finance, which 'has many friends and foes, all concerned about the possibility of serious instability' (Sheng, 2012, p. 7).
74. The 'Enhanced Prudential Standards for Bank Holding Companies and Foreign Banking Organizations'.

intermediate holding company (IHC).[75] They were also required to establish a risk committee whose chief was a US national (Beck et al., 2015). Global banks,[76] financial organizations[77] and foreign regulators[78] immediately accused the United States of discriminatory treatment towards foreign banks – and of violation of the national treatment clause (Coley, 2015). Critics have also remarked on the pervasive effect that regulation could make on fragmenting the global banking industry (Barnier, 2013; Carnier, 2013).[79] Aware of the critics, US regulators defended their right to regulate foreign banks' activities in the country – particularly after observing the attitude adopted by foreign banks' branches and agencies during the pre-crisis years when they became net providers of funds to their non-US affiliates. As the crisis erupted and the Fed was forced to provide liquidity to them,[80] several voices interjected claiming injustice and reproving this behaviour, forcing local authorities to rethink how to prevent a new crisis from occurring.[81]

The new legislation also proved critical of the centralizing funding model applied by (an important group of) global banks. Academics and policymakers have recently rediscovered the benefits of a decentralized cash flow management, and accordingly began to draft important regulatory changes. Once an extreme deregulator, UK authorities were now turning back after the enactment of new rules aimed at ring-fencing

75. IHCs must meet liquidity risk-management standards and conduct an internal liquidity stress test. Furthermore, foreign entities must maintain a liquidity buffer for a 30-day liquidity stress test
76. Deutsche Bank, one of the leading players in the US banking system, took a stand against the fragmentation that would be triggered by the new regulation, stating that the Fed's attitude would lead to 'lack of cooperation and coordination among regulators will lead to unhealthy, fragmented, and nationalistic approaches'. The Bank of Canada also showed a strong fear of market fragmentation.
77. Among the several voices opposing the regulation, Coley (2015) mentions the Committee on Capital Markets Regulation (CCMR), which warned that 'the adoption of ring fencing measures [like the IHC requirement] would prevent parent banks from taking swift action to address financial shocks because of restrictions on moving liquidity and capital between its subsidiaries in different jurisdictions' (Coley, 2015, p. 17)
78. EU Commissioner Michael Barnier has openly defied the legislation. He even insinuated the possibility of retaliatory measures from European regulators.
79. Mark Carney (former governor at the Bank of Canada and currently at the Bank of England) warned, 'the costs are potentially enormous […] A global system that is nationally fragmented will lead to less efficient intermediation of savings and a deep misallocation of capital.' Barnier made a similar point, highlighting that the new legislation 'will send the wrong signal to markets and to the rest of the world. It would increase the cost of capital, and reduce growth prospects' (Coley, 2015, p. 19).
80. When the crisis erupted and the Fed was forced to help banks in trouble, foreign banks were among the largest borrowers of emergency loans.
81. For instance, consider former Fed chair Ben S. Bernanke's remarks on the issue: 'as became apparent after the financial crisis broke, many European financial institutions were funding their purchases of U.S. assets with short-term dollar-denominated liabilities like commercial paper or bank deposits, much of which attracted U.S. investors' (Bernanke et al., *International Capital Flows and the Returns to Safe Assets in the United States, 2003–2007*, 2011).

capital and liquidity inside their realm.[82] The Banking Reform Bill introduced after the *Vickers Report*, required major banks to separate their retail banking from the group's operations (retail-ring financing) and further strengthens the capital requirement.[83] By separating operations, authorities intended to delink retail banking services from universal services offered by global banks operating in the London financial district and, henceforth, limit the government's involvement [guarantee] in an eventual financial crisis (Lehmann, 2014; Osborne, 2015)[84] and[85] limit guarantees in an eventual financial crisis.

Similar legislation was passed in the United States, where the so-called Volcker Rule[86] prevented traditional banks from performing off-balance-sheet riskier operations – although not banning them from offering investment services.[87] In sum, and despite the universal model having been kept alive, it has also excluded banks from certain types of activities (Lehmann, 2014). The Rule's critics have argued that US legislation would lead the international financial system towards balkanization (Coley, 2015). The EU Commission's Liikanen Report[88] also inspired important institutional changes in Germany and France, limiting (although not prohibiting) proprietary trading and investment in hedge funds and other leveraged investment funds by deposit-taking institutions but excluding SIFIs. Furthermore, and according to evidence from EU surveys, between

---

82. Following the crisis, the UK government offered to Sir John Vickers to lead an Independent Commission on Banking (ICB), whose 2011 results would be popularly known as the *Vickers Report*. (The report considered ring-fencing appropriate to '(1) make it easier to sort out both ring-fenced banks and non-ring-fenced banks which get into trouble, without the provision of taxpayer-funded solvency support; (2) insulate vital banking services on which households and SMEs depend from problems elsewhere in the financial system; and (3) curtail government guarantees, reducing the risk to the public finances and making it less likely that banks will run excessive risks in the first place' (*Vickers Report*, 2011, p. 35) The proposed measures would 'reduce the probability and impact of systematic financial crises' (Independent Commission for Banking (ICB)/ *Vickers Report*. Final Report, Recommendations. September 2011).
83. The capital and liquidity requirements of a ring-fenced bank remain initially undetermined (*FT*, 'UK Regulators Seek to Squash Fears over Bank Ring Fencing Rules', 12 October 2015), although authorities permitted them to use dividends in order to transfer capital to other parts of their business (*FT*, 'Banks with Fresh Concession on Ring Fencing Rules', 15 October 2015).
84. UK Chancellor George Osborne supported the idea that reforms were aimed at resolving 'that British dilemma of being a host for global finance without exposing our taxpayers again to the calamitous costs of financial firms failing' (*FT*, 'Global Banks Fret over UK Ring Fencing Rules', 19 June 2015).
85. Additionally, the new Banking Reform Bill inspired by the *Vickers Report* granted local depositors a guarantee – an insurance practice that was previously absent in the UK legislation (Schwarcz, 2014).
86. The Volcker Rule prohibits banks from (1) engaging in proprietary trading or (2) acquiring any equity, partnership or other ownership interest in, or sponsoring a hedge fund or a private entity fund.
87. Proprietary trading in US government debt instruments, however, is exempted from the new regulation. In the same vein, FBEs operating in the US are permitted to engage in proprietary trading in their home country's government debt securities (FSB, 2014).
88. Erkki Liikanen, governor of the Finnish Central Bank, chaired the High Level Group of Experts (producing the above-mentioned report), although it was Commissioner Michel Barnier who established the group.

2008 and 2013 several new measures with ring-fencing effects were introduced with far-reaching consequences for an integrated European banking system (Beck et al, 2015). If finally approved, it might lead to the mandatory separation of banking groups (Lehmann, 2014).

By ring-fencing traditional operations, regulators avoid guaranteeing banks' riskier operations – limiting safeguards tools to bank's traditional operations (specifically retail deposits) and insulating them from other legal liabilities and further insolvency risks (Schwarcz, 2014). (Geographic) ring-fencing regulation implies, therefore, the imposition of new rules on cross-border capital and liquidity flows between banking groups' (Beck et al., 2015, p. 19). Regulation introduces some potential costs, yet it pushes banks to face important invest requirements associated with the transferring of assets (Schwarcz, 2014; Lehmann, 2014). This trade-off was certainly known when the Glass–Steagall Act was passed, with policymakers opting for stability. In sum, institutional changes were inspired by regulators' interest 'to shield depositors' assets from risky bank activities' (Lehmann, 2014, p. 2).

For some observers, all these measures might appear to be pushing the (actually highly globalized) banking system into a deglobalization process (Lehmann, 2014; Barnier, 2014; Carnier, 2014; Coley, 2015), even within the European context (Beck et al., 2015). New regulations would have 'broad extraterritorial effects', preventing the development of a multilateral solution, but might also block the development of a multilateral solution (Lehmann, 2014). Henceforth, as international coordination proved unviable and a 'not realistic prospect for having a global banking regulator' (Tarullo, 2014), regulation of banks at the local (local or regional) level became preferable.

Banking fragmentation is also being induced by 'financial nationalism' practices (or 'financial mercantilism'), a term used to describe the increasing regulatory bias benefiting local banks that was observed after the crisis (*The Economist*, 2009; Baldwin and Evenett, 2009; Evenett and Jenny, 2011; Rose and Wieladek, 2011; Beck, et al., 2015). In particular, scholars placed under scrutiny some government interventions (as, for example, bank recapitalization and bailout deals, nationalization, moral suasion, and all other norms affecting banks' lending strategy), because of their effect on cross-border capital flows.[89] Rose and Wieladek (2011) have analysed the British case, observing a 'nationalistic change in bank's lending behaviour as a result of public intervention, which led domestic banks to either lend less or at higher interest rate to foreigners (or both)'. According to the authors, bank nationalization has reduced foreign lending disproportionally, which, in turn, evidences the rise in financial protectionism. A similar conclusion has been observed by Buch et al. (2013), when analysing German banks' behaviour abroad: those receiving state support after the crisis have reduced their international assets.[90] Furthermore, as observed by the study of Beck and co-authors, banks benefiting

89. According to press, in the fourth quarter of 2008 UK banks had 'sharply cut lending to foreigners customers' (*The Economist*, 'Homeward Bound', 7 February. 2008).

90. The authors refer to an EU report (EU 2009) and a work by Zimmer and Blaschczok (2012), who denounced that government´s conditionality on banks (to those benefited by state aid): they were forced to close some of their foreign affiliates (Buch et al. 2013, p. 2).

from public support were explicitly asked to withdraw from their cross-border banking activities (Beck et al., 2015, p. 32–33).

The GFC, in sum, brought regulation back into the political debate. Although EMEs' voices were hardly active at the multilateral level since the early 1970s, developed countries are now ready to mitigate global banks' unlimited power at home. The main challenges faced by both monetary authorities and regulators relates to the negative effects posed by shadow-banking activities and cross-border funding. Both types of activities are taking place outside banks' traditional balance sheet and, henceforth, beyond the local regulator sphere. If the negative effects posed by an unregulated shadow-banking sector could be reversed (through re-regulating it), the power to limit global banks' cross-border activities once granted might not be maintained. This asseveration might prove not certain, with countries reinstalling the regulation despite the apparent high-efficiency costs attached to the decision. Aware of the costs imposed by cross-border funding, some regulators have began to re-regulate global banks – particularly in developed countries. Facing the same problem, others opted to not do that – in particular EMEs and developing countries' regulators, as they might be legally prevented from regulating them. This is the subject of the next chapter.

Chapter Four

FINANCIAL GLOBALIZATION, INSTITUTIONS AND GROWTH

Introduction

The Bretton Woods Conference delineated a new macroeconomic framework, which accompanied the embedded liberal framework that appeared at the end of the Second World War. This framework would become characterized by a system of fixed exchange rates and the regulation of capital flows permitting participating countries to maintain their monetary autonomy, whereas local financial markets remained highly restricted to foreigners. Somehow, but perhaps not unexpectedly, in the mid-1960s the consensus on the post-war economic system began to wane. And, by the early 1970s leading advanced countries began to call for the opening of capital accounts and financial liberalization.

After 40 years of continuous liberalization the world has become, no doubt, more financially integrated. Highly integrated financial markets, however, tend to lead to greater instability as a way of constraining sovereign states' policy options. As noted in Chapter 2, a highly integrated country can become subject to important restrictions on the macroeconomic front, leaving almost no policy room for those in charge of monetary issues. Chapter 3 discussed the vast array of common practices and restrictions a highly globalized financial system imposes on sovereign countries, as (cross-border) funds are intermediated by global banks. The present chapter introduces an institutional analysis of both sets of constraints imposed by this phenomenon: global financial markets are constantly confronting sovereign states with the constraints imposed by international legal norms, an institutional setting envisioned at both the multilateral (GATS commitments) and the bilateral level (FTAs or BITs).

This chapter discusses the rationality behind the introduction of both capital account regulations (CARs) and macro-prudential policies (MPPs), including those regulatory tools associated with OTC derivatives. In addition, it considers the rationale behind the presence of cross-border regulation, whose institutional setting can be thought as a third practical tool for regulating global capital flows. In sum, this chapter analyses the main institutional constraints impeding the regulation of international capital flows, either originating at the multilateral level (World Trade Organization; WTO) or being imposed by investment agreements (BITs and FTAs). In doing so, we distinguish between those constraints preventing the sovereign state from regulating cross-border financial flows ("mode 1" in WTO parlance) and those that reduce sovereign states' capability to regulate financial market structure – global banks' entrance or establishment phase ("mode 3" in WTO parlance). Additionally, we explore the ER manipulation debate, and the recent attempts to institutionalize the issue on the bilateral front. In a final section, we introduce the so-called globalization paradox. Originally introduced by Harvard economist Dani Rodrik, this paradox helps us in describing the political options and social tensions generated by this institutional push, to explain why some countries are leaving the *hyperglobalization* angle.

Capital Controls' Rationality

A 'regulatory (i.e. Keynesian) consensus' was floating around in academic circles after the Bretton Woods Conference, drawing wide-reaching attention from policymakers including the IMF's explicit recognition of the need to institute capital controls by member states. Partially isolated from international capital flows and profiting from the presence of fixed exchange parity to the US dollar, policymakers in the West enjoyed vast degrees of monetary autonomy, which was certainly valuable in promoting full employment and in accommodating social welfare benefits for their inhabitants. In academic circles this consensual scheme become known as the 'embedded liberalism compromise' (Ruggie, 1988).

Controls were then set, basically, in order to minimize volatility side effects generated by the cyclical pattern of capital flows. A regulated environment might permit to enhance monetary policy autonomy, increasing the effectiveness of short-term interest rates (limiting carry trade operations) (D'Arista and Griffith-Jones, 2011). In this sense, a proper regulation could also be convenient in reducing the pervasive effect of capital inflows on asset price bubbles or for altering the composition of flows (Epstein, 2011).[1] It might also be designed in order to maintain the exchange rate at a competitive and stable level (an SCRER policy).[2] The rationale for their inclusion, in sum, might be to respond to the presence of macro imbalances or to manage different macroeconomic objectives.[3]

The government's political goal would, therefore, dictate the temporal character of the regulation in place. Macro-prudential tools are targeted to guarantee financial stability and may have a temporal presence, whereas controls might have a permanent basis if responding to developmental goals (including those in response to competitiveness objectives or trade-related ends). Long-lasting controls would affect the RER and the current account balance, and, certainly, they evidence a Keynesian flavour.[4]

1. As for example, India's pecking order policy favouring long-term investments over short-term flows.
2. China has profited from permanent 'walls' (on cross-border flows) in order to keep the local currency secure from external pressure. This *wall effect* is losing consistency, however, as authorities continue to advance with the RMB internationalization process.
3. Controls might also be introduced to prevent capital flight (associated with corruption practices, tax evasion or other illegal activities) or, and fundamentally, to prevent failing economies from collapsing.
4. Keynes wrote, 'it is widely held that control of capital movements, both inward and outward, should be a permanent feature of the post-war system' ('Proposals for an International Currency (or Clearing) Union', 11 February 1942, reprinted in Horsefield, *International Monetary*

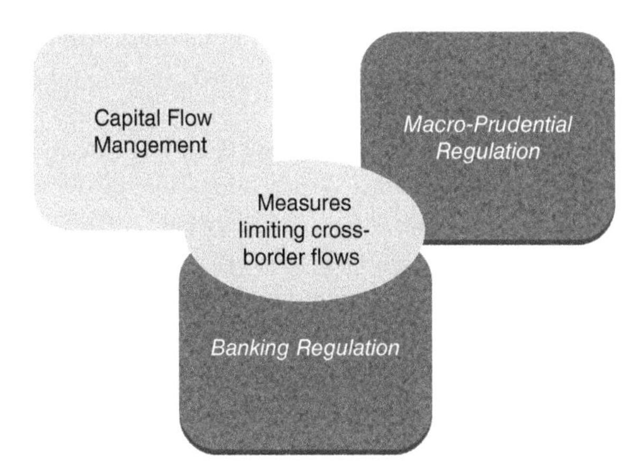

Figure 4.1 Measures limiting cross-border flows
Source: Own elaboration after Gosh et al. (2014) and Beck et al. (2015)

IMF economists Gosh, Quershi and Sagawara (2014) analyse these two broad categories of tools, but label them macro-prudential regulation (MPR) and capital flow management (CFM) techniques – categories encompassing traditional capital controls as well. Considering the source of funds, the latter might be appropriate if inflows are being channelled from foreign entities to domestic companies (when local firms are directly financing from external entities). Besides duration, CFMs' measures are always directed to limiting cross-border flows: controlling the amount of capital flowing into the country. MPRs, in contrast, are a better fit when capital flows are being intermediated by the banking system. This measure might be attached not only to limit capital flows but also to guarantee financial stability – which could have observed a local origin. This could be the case with the use of a particular regulatory tool to tackle a real estate boom (as for example, loan-to-value or debt-to-income as used in Korea). In sum, only a subgroup of MPRs is directed at limiting cross-border flows by altering the '*magnitude, composition and/or other characteristic*' of them (Beck, et al., 2015, p. 15). But it is worth mentioning that neither CARs nor MPRs were originally designed to tackle the challenges imposed by financial derivatives – at least not in all cases (Fritz and Prates, 2014; Prates and Farhi, 2015; Gallagher, 2015). This calls for the introduction of a third class of regulations, an issue where Brazil is leading the initiative (further discussed in Chapter 6).

Fund, 1945–65, Vol. 3, Documents, p. 13. (3rd Printing, May 1981). A similar statement was made in the British House of Lords, when Keynes explained the formal institutionalization of capital controls in the IMF Agreement: 'Not merely as a feature of the transition, but as a permanent arrangement, the plan accords to every member government the explicit right to control all capital movements. What used to be a heresy is now endorsed as orthodox' (quoted at Jeffrey M. Chwieroth 'Capital Ideas: The IMF and the Rise of Financial Liberalization'. Princeton: Princeton University Press, 2010, p. 109).

A final caveat: as observed at Beck et al. (2015), financial integration can also be challenged by a series of norms and rules not classified as macro-prudential by the literature nor considered as forming part of the CFM camp. Under this category fall regulations that, for instance, privilege certain legal figures for foreign banks' entry (e.g. subsidiaries over branches) or prevent local banks from some specific source of funding. Furthermore, the introduction of a ring-fencing scheme prevents cross-border flows (i.e. it limits capital flows). By virtue of this set of rules and norms (institutions), the government can prevent or weaken the presence of cross-border flows on a permanent basis. Similarly, the scope of OTC derivatives could be altered by regulatory measures enacted by local jurisdictions – as recent movements are showing.

The Global Commons: Multilateral and Bilateral Perspectives

The move from the General Agreement on Tariffs and Trade (GATT) to the WTO can be thought of as a milestone in the history of global trade in recent global trade history. Contrary to the singularity and informality of the GATT, the WTO would become a rules-based organization dealing with trade but also extending into other areas: performance requirements, trade in services (including finance-related issues), and traded inventions, creation and design (that is, intellectual property).

At the negotiations, the United States, the EU and other advanced economies were, from the very start, pushing for capital account liberalization (CAL) requirements and financial deregulation.[5] The objective was finally achieved with the signing of the GATS, which became a constitutive part of the newly constituted organization.[6] The developmental character contained at the preamble should be stressed, whereas the overall purpose and principle of the GATS are fixed.[7]

This multilateral agreement, which was reached after the Uruguay Round, would become the first to deal with trade in services (including financial services), and also the first to provide the principles and rules for government policies and regulation affecting trade in services. WTO financial commitments, in particular, are included at in the GATS Annexes on Financial Services (the Annex), which contain additional provisions relating solely to financial services; the Second and Fifth Protocols of the GATS (commonly referred to under the Financial Services Agreement; FSA); the Understanding on

5. US interest in liberalization in services was observed under the GATT. By virtue of the Trade Act of 1974, the US Congress instructed negotiators to promote an agreement on services at the Tokyo Round.
6. The GATS agreement is divided into six parts, including the scope (Article 1); the principles and obligations (Articles II–XV), market access and national treatment obligations for members (Articles XVI–XVIII); and three further technical sections (Articles XIX–XXIX). Additionally, the GATS has a series of annexes, including those covering the financial.
7. In particular, the GATS aimed: (1) trade expansion to promote economic development; (2) progressive trade liberalization; (3) preservation of member governments' right to regulate services sectors to meet national policy objectives; and, (4) facilitation of participation of developing countries and recognition of special circumstances of LDCs.

Commitments in Financial Services ('the Understanding'),[8] a document setting a series of (additional) standards for market access and national treatment commitments but also additional obligations which Members might voluntarily undertake;[9] and countries' GATS schedules of financial services commitments. In short, thereafter all the commitments been accorded would be referred to as 'GATS financial services commitments'.

Thereafter capital account liberalization becomes considered as a goal for the GATS, particularly endorsed in Article XI.1[10] and the footnote to Article XVI.[11] Henceforth, under certain circumstances, capital controls may even constitute a breach of GATS commitments.[12] Nevertheless, WTO members do still maintain some room to introduce controls (Gallagher, 2013). In particular, the Annex on Financial Services, which permits the introduction of prudential defensive measures states, 'Notwithstanding any other provisions of the Agreement, a Member shall not be prevented form taking measures for prudential reasons.' In sum, at least three specific exceptions might be allowing member states to elude GATS limitations, as follows:

- ✓ **FIRST, member states are allowed to introduce capital controls satisfying an IMF request (GATS Article XI-2)**. According to Article XV.9 (a) of the GATT (1994), a measure restricting capital transactions that is consistent with IMF obligations should not lead to a finding of breach of GATT/WTO provisions.
- ✓ **SECOND, an exception is allowed in order to safeguard member states' balance of payments (GATS Article XII)**. It follows that members are not only permitted to impose temporary trade restrictions but they can also introduce (current account) restrictions on service-related payments.
- ✓ **THIRD, and finally, controls can also be introduced in order to ensure the integrity and stability of the financial service sector (Article 2-a of the Financial Services Annex – GATS)**. This prudential carve-out clause can be adopted regardless of the member state's specific commitments on market access and national treatment.[13]

8. Initially binding for a tiny group of EMEs, which committed to advance in financial market deregulation.
9. Forty countries were participating in this list, including all members of the EU plus Australia, Canada, Iceland, Japan, Liechtenstein, New Zealand, Nigeria, Norway, Sri Lanka, Switzerland, Turkey and the United States.
10. Article XI.1 (Payments and Transfers) states that, after undertaking market access and NT commitments for specific services sectors, a state has to liberalize the connected current and capital movements.
11. Footnote 8 to Art. XVI (Market Access), on the other hand, states that capital controls on both inflows and outflows are prohibited for financial services provided under Mode 1, and for all services provided under Mode 3.
12. In particular, CARs may be constrained by the market-access clauses (Article XVI plus Footnote 8), when the introduced measure amounts to a ban or to a quantitative limitation. But CARs use might also be prevented by the presence of the National Treatment (Art. XVII) Clause, when the measure accords less favourable treatment to foreign services suppliers.
13. See for more details in the next section.

The relatively stable and functional multilateral trade system created by the WTO did, nevertheless, experience certain significant challenges. One of the most serious problems concerned the latest negotiations of the WTO – the Doha Round – ostensibly named the 'Development Round', as developing countries insisted on increased concrete benefits. Nevertheless, more restrictive clauses were appearing in BITs and FTAs, limiting participating countries to imposing controls on a wide basis on capital inflows. Binding clauses are generally included in the treaties' investment chapters, certainly proving harmful for economic development and financial stability.

What is even worse is the lack of any sort of balance-of-payments safeguard in FTAs/ BITs or a prudential carve-out clause – particularly those initiated by US negotiators.[14] Whereas older agreements allow for some form of safeguard until a balance-of-payments crisis, the new ones have none.[15] This change came into light in the nineties when developed countries embraced financial liberalization and rushed to ban any type of measure affecting the international movement of capital flows – and including the issuance of special dispute settlement procedures related to capital controls.[16] If present, safeguard clauses should just express a micro-prudential concern. These types of agreements also introduce a too-broad definition of investments, restricting the government's policy options. The wording in free transfer clauses, in contrast, expresses excessive guarantees that could prevent the use of controls by the sovereign state – in particular, investments must be allowed to be transferred 'freely and without delay' among parties to an agreement. As observed by M. Waibel (2009), 'free transfer clauses limit the host country's monetary sovereignty'.

The IMF staff has recently adopted a critical stance on the restrictive approach adopted by BITs and FTAs, for the reduced flexibility introduced by these schemes.[17] Furthermore, they (the IMF) declared, 'the proposed institutional view could help foster a more consistent approach to the design of policy space for CFMs under bilateral and regional agreements. Recognizing the macroeconomics, IMS, and global stability goals that underpin the institutional view, members drafting such agreement in the future, as well as the various international bodies that promote these agreements, could take into account this view in designing the circumstances under which both inflows and outflows CFMs may be imposed within the scope of their agreements' (IMF, 2012c, p. 32).

14. By contrast, the G-20 FSB forum has pledged to maintain this clause in FTAs (Helleiner, 2012, p. 144).
15. Surprisingly, all exceptions were negotiated during the presidency of Reagan. Exceptionality could also be observed in several FTAs (Singapore–Australia; Malaysia–New Zealand; Canada–Chile; EU–Korea; Japan–Malaysia) or BITs (Peru–Japan) (Anderson, 2011).
16. For example, at the negotiation table US representatives forced their Chilean counterparts to discontinue that country's *encaje* ("strongbox") policy, which was used to force foreign investors to freeze their portfolio investments for one year. A similar requirement was made of Singapore, one of the Asian nations profoundly affected by the 1997 crisis.
17. See K. Gallagher. 2013. *Capital Account Regulations and the Trading System: A Compatibility Review*. Pardee Center Task Force Report. Boston University. The Frederick S. Pardee Center for the Study of the Longer Range Future.

Surprisingly, and despite the great economic turmoil generated by the latest financial crisis, developed countries continue to push for capital account openness and financial liberalization. The US stance during the negotiations of the Trans-Pacific Partnership (TPP) trade agreement is a leading example of such an extreme position.[18]

Banking Internationalization and Financial Service Deregulation under WTO–GATS

The Bretton Woods framework basically centred on dealing with macro imbalances, monetary issues and how to coordinate them. Financial issues, by contrast, were left behind as financial markets (and banks, in particular) were 'international in life and national in death' (Bank of England Governor Mervyn King and economist Charles Goodhart), and financial services were under a nation state's scrutiny. When a new financial pattern emerged, it lacked any sort of institutional backing. In order to fill this gap, advanced economies began to press towards a new setting, crowning financial services liberalization (FSL) in the centre. The push originated in the United States, whose authorities envisioned to generalize the institutional transformation beginning to be adopted by the Reagan administration. US bankers were also driving for relaxation, however, particularly after the North American Free Trade Agreement (NAFTA) bypassed a series of rules surrounding mergers between commercial and investment banks – and, henceforth, permitted the emergence of 'universal banking'.[19] Nevertheless, and despite not being universally adopted, either being convinced (for example, in exchange for trade benefits) or being under threat (for example, of being sanctioned by the IMF), numerous developing countries finally accepted to open their financial services markets to foreign competition

The multilateral agreement reached after the Uruguay Round would become the first to deal with trade in services (including financial services), but also one which provided the principles and rules for government policies and regulation affecting this trade. Rules on cross-border transactions and the commercial presence of foreign banks would be settled under the WTO–GATS framework, in particular, the financial services commitments approved in the late nineties (1997).

The GATS agreement defines four ways of trading services. The first mode, which comprises cross-border supply, entails the provision of a service of one country (a Brazilian client using a Brazilian bank) to another country (to pay a supplier in China). The next is labelled consumption abroad, as a client from another country (Indian expatriate) consumes locally (in Korea). The GATS third mode is establishment, and it is associated with a global bank (from China) opening a subsidiary or a branch in another country (Argentina). The last GATS mode is associated with the presence of natural

18. The list of countries includes Australia, Brunei Darussalam, Canada, Chile, Japan, Malaysia, Mexico, New Zealand, Peru, Singapore, the United States and Vietnam.
19. NAFTA was signed in 1994, years before the passage of the Gramm-Leach-Bliley Act in 1999.

persons, as for example, the temporary travel of a (Argentinean insurer) professional to supply their services to a client resident in another country (Brazil).

GATS provisions are divided between general obligations and specific commitments. The former applies to all measures subject to the GATS agreement, and the main obligation is the most-favoured-nation (MFN) requirement. Commitments apply to those services the country has agreed to liberalize – a negative approach, which grants more room to local regulators in dealing with market-access demands.[20] Each WTO member (or potential member) was required to submit a schedule of commitments, although some exceptions (to liberalize trade in services) were granted to those requiring it. Thereafter, specific commitments made by members were to be backed by national treatment and market-access clauses, both determining the liberalizing impact of the agreement (Hoeckman and Kostecki, 2009). Commitments made under GATS also advanced on behalf of foreign suppliers of financial services, particularly by improving market-access conditions and providing them non-discriminatory treatment. Finally, by virtue of GATS Article XVI (Footnote 8 – Market Access), a member country could be pushed to maintain a capital account liberalization and deregulation policy against its will if it previously committed to opening the economy to cross-border flows (Stichele, 2004).[21]

The regulation of financial services was also a matter of interest at the time of negotiation. A series of general obligations were then introduced, including the mutual recognition of standards between contracting parties and a list of measures that should be prohibited, a priori, when dealing with market-access provisions.[22] Another regulatory issue relates to the provision of new services, for instance, a new financial service to be offered by an already established foreign bank. According to a provision included in the *GATS Understandings*, a foreign entity would be free to supply them, and this would not require preapproval from the local regulator.[23] In the same direction, the attempt by a member to dismantle the universal banking model could be challenged by the standstill rule (although the GATS does not specifically dictate any proposal regarding a bank's corporate form).[24] Finally, in relation to market entrance, and although not properly

20. Article XVI(1) GATS 'with respect to market access through the modes of supply, each Member shall accord services and services suppliers of any other Member treatment not less favourable than that provided for under the terms, limitations and conditions agreed and specified in its Schedule'.
21. 'GATS rules do not only influence what cross-border capital flows are permitted, they also influence how restrictions on those flows are managed' (Stichele, 2004).
22. The list of prohibited measures includes limitations on the number of services suppliers; limitations on the total value of service operations; limitations on the number of natural persons employed, requiring specific types of legal entity or joint venture in order to supply a service; and limitations on foreign capital participation. As a consequence of the positive commitment approach adopted under GATS, limitations apply on all those services which have been approved by the host country.
23. 'A Member shall permit financial services suppliers of any other Member established in its territory to offer in its territory any new financial service.'
24. By virtue of the GATS standstill rule, members may not roll back deregulation and liberalization once a sector is bound to GATS. Paradoxically, the first attempts to dismantle the

specified at the time of the agreement (as stated in GATS Article XVI.2), branches (and not subsidiaries) obtained developed countries' support as it was considered the most liberal of the alternatives. If a member wishes to roll back regulations in this realm it might be required to modify or be forced to withdraw from a prior commitments made under the GATS (Delimatisis and Sauvé, 2010).[25] Surprisingly, and despite the renewed enthusiasm towards subsidiarization observed among developed countries after the GFC, developing countries continued to be pressed to recognize other forms of entry (i.e. branches) (UNCTAD, 2014, p. 9).

The deregulatory and liberalized measures were considered as a minimum playing field to be enhanced in future negotiations. Unfortunately, none of them made provisions for financial stability nor considered the need for more detailed supervision. In this sense, and despite all the constraints originally promised, the GATS provisions remained limited as countries were proposing their (liberalization) commitments until the WTO. Nobody was forcing them to show their own financial liberalization commitments to the rest of the world. A positive list approach prevailed at the bilateral level. BITs and FTAs, in contrast, were pushing (developing and EMEs') host countries to liberalize their financial systems and reducing regulators' degree of freedom. In order to obtain market access in developed countries (for their raw materials) (weaker) developing countries were forced to open their economy (including its financial sector), which left them with less freedom and less autonomy.

Market deregulation, as observed, easily muted into underregulation – particularly benefiting global banks. Financial regulators remained silent on the problems posed by cross-border funding and related systemic risks. The GFC would come to challenge this vision, with both global leaders and IFIs now advocating for financial sector re-regulation.

The Bilateral Push towards Financial Deregulation

In considering the extent of FSL commitments being drafted in FTAs, two different approaches soon emerged: a *soft approach* being (originally) followed by the EU, and a *hard approach* initially proposed by the United States (initially observed in NAFTA but later introduced in the KORUS FTA), and now being adopted by EU negotiators. Below, we introduce a brief analysis of the latest and most relevant treaties.

---

universal scheme came from the North and, up to now, no case has arrived at WTO–DSU (Dispute Settlements Understanding) tribunals yet.

25. In this sense, the refusal of China to subscribe to this advice was highly criticized in the past (Crosby, 2008). But, as part of the negotiations at the time of its accession at the WTO, China obtained a five-year grace period after which it was accepted that foreign financial institutions meeting the conditions would be permitted 'to establish a subsidiary of a foreign bank or a foreign finance company in China, permitted to establish a branch of a foreign bank in China, and permit to establish a Chinese – foreign joint bank or a Chinese – foreign joint finance in China'. Chinese authorities' policy option was, first, to induce foreigners to associate with local banks. Foreigners were also allowed to enter into the local market through a minority participation in a local (but private) financial institution or through direct entry – as a subsidiary.

The TPP, a mega-FTA deal recently concluded and involving 12 countries from the Pacific basin area has enormous implications for FSL (Kelsey, 2010). The TPP is a 'very different kind of pact' from NAFTA, however, as it definitively leaves aside tariffs to concentrate in services (Guillen, 2015). The agreement includes core obligations (National Treatment; NT, Most Favored Nation; MFN, Market Access) observed in older FTAs as in GATS–WTO. But it pushes financial liberalization even further, as it bans members from imposing any specific type of legal entity or joint venture, or quantitative restrictions on the supply of services. For example, the agreement prohibits local regulators from asking foreign banks to establish an office or affiliate, or to be resident, in its territory in order to supply a service. The agreement, however, limits financial innovation as the extent to which a supplier of a TPP party (a US bank) may be able to provide a new (financial) service in another TPP market (Korea), only if domestic companies (locally owned Korean banks) in that market are allowed to do so (US government, 2015).[26] As commonly observed, the TPP follows a 'negative-list' approach – although exceptions are agreed to and negotiated in advance.[27]

The EU 'hard approach' is certainly present in the recently proposed EU Trade in Financial Services agreement with ASEAN countries (Robles, 2014),[28] and is fairly extended. As stated at the European Parliament (2014) report, the financial services sector has emerged as a key priority for Europe, particularly since 2006.[29] EU is pushing (liberalization) commitments further in the mode of commercial presence or establishment (mode 3). The new standard model is following a somewhat particular positive list approach – called 'hybrid' – in both national treatment and market-access obligations. As related to regulation, all new agreements are framed in the WTO–GATS approach permitting signatories countries to use a carve-out clause for prudential reasons.[30] Another example of the effects of the GFC in expanding EU flexibility is the recognition of subsidies (among other forms), now considered the subject of a carve-out clause. In

26. See US Trade Representative (USTR) at: https://ustr.gov/about-us/policy-offices/press-office/press-releases/2015/october/summary-trans-pacific-partnership.
27. 'TPP Parties adopt a "negative-list" basis, meaning that their markets are fully open to foreign investors, except where they have taken an exception (non-conforming measure) in one of two country-specific annexes: (1) current measures on which a Party accepts an obligation not to make its measures more restrictive in the future and to bind any future liberalization, and (2) measures and policies on which a Party retains full discretion in the future' (https://ustr.gov/about-us/policy-offices/press-office/press-releases/2015/october/summary-trans-pacific-partnership).
28. EU negotiators are demanding a unilateral opening of financial markets, including the removal of restrictions on (European) financial institutions' cross-border lending to Southeast Asia (mode 1). Furthermore, the EU is pushing Asian regulators to grant (European) financial institutions the freedom to invest in Southeast Asia and to engage in operations once established there (mode 3) (Robles, 2014).
29. Although the interest in opening financial markets abroad is previous, at least since the nineties (see previous chapter), it was in 2006 when, for the first time, all EU PTAs (Preferential Trade Agreements) began to include detailed rules and commitments covering trade in services.
30. As the financial crisis affected Europe harshly, the new agreements have expanded the (somewhat limited and vague) original carve-out clause. Among the modifications being included, can be mentioned the *prohibition of particular financial services or activities for prudential reasons,*

sum, the presence of two elements in the EU approach to the carve-out clause might be considered as novel: a guide on the application and a filter mechanism (to be exceptional use, and for prudential reasons). All these new agreements now include protection for financial services under the investor-state dispute settlement (ISDS) framework, although filtering legal disputes originated in the carve-out clause. Another distinctive aspect of the new approach on financial services treatment is associated with the twofold partition of the market-access obligation concept, one related to cross-border supply and the other with its establishment (European Parliament, 2014).[31]

In sum, the bilateral agenda has become a renewed playing field where developed countries can push deregulation and liberalization a little bit further. A similar picture is emerging at the multilateral level if a new Trade in Service Agreement (TiSA) continues to mature. Proposed by the United States in early 2012, and as a consequence of the impasse observed at the Doha round, the (so-called 'Real Good Friends') group actually encompasses an important number of developed and developing countries.[32] The group is being led by the United States, the EU and, unsurprisingly, Panama (a Central American financial 'tax haven', country) (Denae Trasher, 2014). Although it actually presents some similarities with the GATS–WTO, it maintains important differences (WEED, 2014). Among the former can be mentioned the presence of the NT requirement, the positive list approach to market access, the maintenance of the standstill clause and the state-to-state arbitration scheme also observed at the WTO. Differences arise in the presence of a 'ratchet effect clause',[33] the adoption of the negative list approach

provided such provisions are applied on a non-discriminatory basis. For instance, a sovereign state could ban CDS instruments if it understands them to be extremely dangerous and harmful for financial stability.

31. As previously mentioned, the establishment phase is where most of the constraining requirements are observed, including measures restricting or requiring specific types of a legal entity or joint venture in which a service supplier may supply a service; limitations on the participation of foreign capital in terms of maximum percentage or limits on foreign shareholding or the total value of individual or aggregate foreign investment; limitations on the total value of services transactions or assets in the form of numerical quotas or the requirement of an economic need test and so on.
32. The TiSA group listed 16 members, rapidly expanding to 78, including 28 EU members plus 13 other developed or high-income countries (Australia, Canada, Hong Kong, Iceland, Israel, Japan, South Korea, Liechtenstein, New Zealand, Norway, Switzerland, Taiwan and the United States), 8 emerging economies or upper-middle-income countries (Chile, Colombia, Costa Rica, Mauritius, Mexico, Panama, Peru and Turkey), and 1 developing or lower-middle-income country (Pakistan).
33. Whereas through the standstill clause members are banned from creating a new regulation for those services, they formerly agreed to liberalize. For example, country A and country B sign an agreement. Country B agrees to liberalize options and futures. But a couple of years later, authorities realize that futures markets are highly volatile, which affects the country's macro sustainability. Unfortunately, due to the FTA agreements which were previously signed, they are legally blocked from doing that. The ratchet clause states that any liberalization steps that take place after the agreement are not reversible. This latest clause reflects the possibility authorities will have to introduce regulatory measures later and be forced to permit the operation of any sort of financial instrument. In other words, the first clause locks in existing

for national treatment, a series of cross-sectorial measures and the liberalization in individual sectors – including financial services. Surprisingly, the 'progressive liberalization' consideration that figures in the GATS preamble is omitted by the TiSA. In contrast to GATS, in order to limit host countries' policy space, the TiSA wants to transfer the discussion on mergers and acquisitions to international forums, which, in practice, would further open the financial sector to foreigners. In sum, under such a scenario foreign investors' political power would tremendously enhanced (Mashavekhi and Tuerk, 2006; Wouters and Coppens, 2008; Denae Trasher, 2014).

What seems contradictory, however, is the re-regulation trend observed within the United States and other developed nations such as the United Kingdom or the EU, and their ambitions of maintaining an unregulated financial system abroad. On the one hand, those in charge of regulation at home claim the importance of regaining national space in order to control global banks' risky behaviour. For instance, consider what Fed member, D. Tarullo, recently stated: 'proposals to include prudential regulation or, more precisely, to include limitations on prudential requirements in trade agreements would lead us farther away from the aforementioned goal of emphasizing shared financial stability interests, in favour of an approach to prudential matters informed principally by considerations of commercial advantages' (2014, p. 19). In this sense, as Brummer recently highlighted, 'nation-states are unlikely to cede power to a global financial regulator as long as they retain the responsibility for guaranteeing liquidity, serving as the capital providers of last resort, and protecting the public treasury' (2012, cited in Eric Helleiner, *The Status Quo Crisis: Global Financial Governance after the 2008 Meltdown*, Oxford University Press). A similar statement is observed in Sheng (2012), when he recognizes the specific character that regulatory practices should follow: 'we must accept that there can be no "one size fits all" approach to financial regulation, reform, crisis prevention or resolution' (Sheng, p. 361). In sum, the GFC reinstalled the regulatory issue in the policy debate, putting the regulation of global banks at the top of the agenda.

On the other hand, in flagrant opposition to a prudential mandate like this, those negotiating trade deal agreements stubbornly support financial liberalization abroad despite the risks posed by (unregulated) global financial entities. In order to access developed country's markets, developing countries and some emerging economies are prone to accept financial instability. Nevertheless, some sovereign governments seem savvier at the negotiation table than others or, supported by their size, some countries remain (institutionally) untouched.

If we recall the adverse effects of the cross-border supply of services and the wide-ranging liberalization of foreign direct investment (FDI), the question is whether countries like the United States or the EU are still demanding FSL. Certainly, and despite all the contradictory effects associated with it, the financial industry is highly relevant for both economies (Cooper et al., 2010; Barbee and Lester, 2013; Robles, 2014; European Parliament, 2014).

---

levels of liberalization, whereas the second locks in future in future liberalization (European Parliament, 2014).

The OTC Market and the US Push for ET Regulation

Whereas the preceding paragraphs demonstrated the pressure being exerted by a group of developed countries to maintain financial markets unregulated, in their search for tame OTC markets and dealers, the United States took the first steps in a series of initiatives in order to regulate this market (also at the EU). Deregulation came in hand with the Commodity Futures Modernization Act, passed in 2000 by the US Congress. Ten years later, when the Dodd–Frank Act was finally passed by the Congress, US legislators would turn the OTC market upside down (see previous chapter).

As noted, this market shows a high degree of cross-border interconnection. Thus, in order to avoid excessive risk taking, the new legislation came to establish that rules could be applied outside the national border: the extra-territoriality (ET) issue (Cervone, 2015).[34] As regulation become the cornerstone of the reforming agenda in Washington, US policymakers fiercely induced other participants at the G20 select club to follow in their re-regulating agenda[35] – yet except Europe, all other members showed little interest in the issue (Knaack, 2014).

The ET rule embedded in the Volcker ('Final') Rule presents stronger effects than those proclaimed by the EU: whereas both jurisdictions have extraterritoriality effects, the new norm entitles US authorities to act unilaterally. Consequently, although the extraterritoriality option was devoted to controlling systemic risks (affecting the US financial sector)[36] its inclusion has resulted in a vivid controversy – particularly in political circles in the EU.[37] The controversy, however, exceeded the politicians' debate to include academics – particularly lawyers established on both sides of the Atlantic. A significant number of politicians in Washington,[38] but well-known academics too, have

34. Until now, the United States has followed a national treatment model, especially in the securities market (Greene and Potiha, 2013).
35. Under supervision of the G20 FSB, the International Organization of Securities Commissions (IOSCO) was put in charge of coordinating the OTC market reform. In April 2010 the FSB created the OTC derivatives working group (ODWG), which comprised regulators from nine different jurisdictions, officials of several financial institutions and representatives from IOSCO, the Basel Committee and the Committee on Payment and Settlement Systems (CPSS). After one year, and given the lack of progress, Mark Carney (FSB chairman) decided to organize a new group (OTC Derivatives Coordination Group). Another year passed and nothing transpired but the formation of a new group (Derivatives Regulators Group).
36. Section 715 Title VII of the Dodd–Frank Act provides that, with certain exceptions, 'If the Commodity Futures Trading Commission or the Securities and Exchange Commission determines that the regulation of swaps or security-based swaps markets in a foreign country undermines the stability of the United States financial system, either Commission, in consultation with the Secretary of the Treasury, may prohibit an entity domiciled in the foreign country from participating in the United States in any swap or security-based swap activities.'
37. She also observes the challenge imposed by ET to the traditional Westphalian concept of sovereignty.
38. In this sense, and despite the opposition observed abroad, a group of US senators wrote a letter urging the US Commodities Futures Trading Commission (CFTC) authorities to implement cross-border derivatives rules under Dodd–Frank as originally proposed (joint letter from

supported the extraterritoriality of the US regulation. One of the most conspicuous defenders is John Coffee,[39] for whom the efforts to control the market proved insufficient, and for whom the regulator's frustration relates to its 'inability (or unwillingness) to reach extraterritoriality end runs around their rules'. Voices against this hard stance are certainly strong abroad. Europeans were among the most conspicuous critics of the US ET approach including, among others, Michel Barnier (EU commissioner for financial services), who declared that it was 'not acceptable that US rules have such a wide effect on other nations' (Knaack, 2014, p. 22). A series of financial articles were also hardly critical of the ET concept, as it ignored national sovereignty, representing instead 'an alleged return to a prior tradition of US imperialism under which the United States assumed that its preferred financial practices could be mandated for the rest of the world' (Braithwaite et al., *FT*, 26 September 2013) or 'The United States is coming to be seen as a global treat, acting unilaterally with aggressive new market rules [...] [with] the new buzzword [...] [being] extraterritoriality or ET' (Huw Jones, *Reuters*, 5 February 2012). As for academics, in a series of articles Edward F. Greene and Ilona Potiha supported the convenience of establishing a coordinated framework granting 'mutual recognition, with effective agreements coupled with exemptions' and, henceforth, challenging the unilateral vision embedded in the substituted compliance concept (2013, p. 6). Market participants also reject the US ET stance, highlighting the risks of a unilateral advance (ISDA et al., 2011). Somehow, in the middle ground, Dr Elisabetta Cervone, a distinguished academic in the field and a World Bank consultant, while recognizing the efforts made by US policymakers in bypassing the 'Final Rule', highlighted the negative effects that such a rule could have on US financial markets. In this sense, she shares the vision of other academics and market participants, both warning of the possibility of a 'fragmentation' in the derivatives market (Cervone, 2015.[40] Civil society organizations also favoured an intermediate position, but supported a mutual recognition perspective.

Another controversy could be detected in some of the actions being undertaken by the US government, as for example the exception granted by the US Treasury to FX swaps as authorities judged that those swaps contained high levels of transparency and management (Greene and Potiha, 2013, p. 13). In particular, what would be the reaction if a US or EU firm involved in Brazilian FX swaps were being forced to comply with a Brazilian OTC regulatory framework (ANBIMA, 2014)?[41] Although the Brazilian OTC

Senators Sherrod Brown, Tom Harkin, Jeff Merkley, Carl Levin, Elizabeth Warren and Diane Feinstein to Gary Gensler, Chairman, Commodities Futures Trading Commission, *Support for the CFT's Proposed Rules Implementing Cross-Border Swaps Provisions Mandated under Title VII of the Dodd-Frank Act.* 22 May 2013).

39. Professor of Law at Columbia Law School and director of the Columbia Center on Corporate Governance

40. In a letter sent to Treasury Secretary Jack Lew, the EU's commissioner for internal market and services (Barnier) plus senior financial regulators from Brazil, France, Germany, Japan, Russia and South Africa expressed their concern on 'fragmentation' in the OTC market if the United States insisted on applying extraterritoriality.

41. According to ANBIMA, Brazil's rules – in particularly those regarding registration, are several steps ahead of G20 proposals (ANBIMA, 2014, p. 10).

market is far from perfect, from a regulatory perspective Brazil is 'topping the league table' (Freeman, 2011).[42]

Tensions at the negotiation table after all did not prevent UE and US negotiators from bargaining over a new agreement. From this perspective, *minilateralism* seems to be one of the lessons inherited after the GFC.[43] Nevertheless, limiting participation in order to reach an agreement could mask important costs, for instance, an agreement between US regulators and the EU Commission on derivative OTC regulation, as together these players have sufficient 'leverage in encouraging other nations to play by their rules' (Coffee, 2014, 1288). But why would Brazil (whose futures FX market ranks among world leaders) be left aside? Independently of the present relevance, nobody doubts that China's market would become larger in the foreseeable future. How can its present exclusion from the negotiation table be explained?

According to Simmons (2001), 'the decisions of regulators in dominant centres can drastically change the choices available to other countries, they create a paradigm shift, and any negotiations that follow are merely splitting hairs' (Simmons, 2001, p. 591). Minilateralism could work if followers have the incentive to participate (adopting the rules brings them scarce capital) but also if they are afraid of the (negative) externalities from being excluded (investors would ask a higher yield in order to participate).

For some scholars, minilateralism is associated with leading financial centres having the right incentives to control systemic risk (Coffee, 2014, p. 1266). So developing countries and emerging economies have become constrained by BITs or FTAs. Financial regulation has always masked important distributional consequences. Developing nations and emerging economies were certainly aware of the challenges imposed by financial liberalization. Unfortunately only after the GFC did US representative noticed the costs imposed by a highly unregulated banking industry. After the GFC, perhaps, 'no longer would emerging economies accept the role of "rule takers" while allowing Washington and its wealthy allies to be "rule makers" ' (Blustein, 2013, p. 96). The incoming future will show us whether this prophecy becomes real.

Exchange Rate Policies under (Renewed) Scrutiny

The institutional transformation being described, though, goes beyond the management of the capital account. US representatives are now pushing for the inclusion of an ER manipulation clause in all new treaty agreements.

As observed in Chapter 2, currency manipulation has certainly become a very 'hot' issue in the international macro debate. In fact, several academics and policymakers around the world are endorsing China, Germany and a group of oil exporter countries

42. T. Freeman, 'Brazil a Possible Model for Derivatives Reform', *FT*, 19 August 2011.
43. Moises Naim, an influential policy adviser and international relations expert and long-time editor of *Foreign Policy*, coined the term. See 'Minilateralism: The Magic Number to Get Real International Action', *Foreign Policy*, 22 June 2009. Minilateralism, however, is hardly a new phenomenon in the international financial architecture.

as the main culprits in the US debacle (Bergsten, 2014; Scott, 2015).[44] Accordingly, the presence of global imbalances and undervalued currencies might be generating a new type of currency crisis, which calls for a different solution.[45] Furthermore, US legislators consider the purchase and accumulation of FX reserve by monetary authorities around the world as unfair. Even though sovereign fund holdings of US bonds are blamed as harmful – surprisingly, the Fed quantitative easing (QE) policy is by no means considered pernicious by those advocating ER manipulation.[46]

In the IMF Articles of Agreement, member states 'were required to declare a par value for their currencies in terms of US dollars or gold (the common denominator of the par-value system) and to intervene in the money markets to limit exchange rate fluctuations within a band of one per cent above or below parity' (Viterbo, 2012, p. 291). A sort of 'fundamental disequilibrium' in the balance of payments was considered a cause of change in the par value, a theoretical clause binding for both deficit and surplus countries.[47] When the Bretton Woods system collapsed, IMF members were then permitted to freely adopt the scheme of their choice – although limitations on ER movements were inserted and currency manipulation directly banned.[48] In particular, fund' norms and rules considered that members' FX and monetary policies were aimed at pursuing orderly economic growth and financial stability and that they should avoid manipulation of ER. When the guidelines were first revised in 1977, the floating ER system was just being adopted but cross-border capital flows remained trivial (Blustein, 2015). This new clause (IMF Article IV, Section iii) also contemplated international monetary system manipulation, but the concept has never been clarified (Viterbo, 2012).[49]

After the IMF 2007 Surveillance Decision (SD), ER manipulation was defined as 'a member will only be considered to be manipulating exchange rates in order to gain an unfair competitive advantage over other members if the Fund determines both that: (A) the member is engaged in these policies for the purposes of securing fundamental exchange rate misalignment in the form of an undervalued exchange rate and (B) the

44. US automakers and steel producers are among the main advocates for the inclusion.
45. Ben Bernanke, former chairman of the US Federal Reserve, affirmed, 'the maintenance of undervalued currencies by some countries has contributed to a pattern of global spending that is unbalanced and unsustainable. Such imbalances include those not only between emerging markets and advanced economies, but also among the emerging market economies themselves, as those countries that have allowed their exchange rates to be determined primarily by market forces have seen their competitiveness erode relative to countries that have intervened more aggressively in foreign exchange markets' (Speech at the G20 Meeting in Paris, 18–19 February 2011).
46. For those favouring the manipulation clause the same policy instrumented by a foreign country, like Japan, has important effects on the value of the US dollar (Scott, 2015).
47. It was theoretical rather than practical, as the clause was left undefined by the IMF articles.
48. In particular, 'to promote exchange stability, to maintain orderly exchange arrangements among members, and to avoid competitive exchange depreciation' (IMF, Article I-iii)
49. According to the ER clause, members are committed to 'avoid[ing] manipulating the exchange rate or the international monetary system in order to prevent effective balance of payments adjustments or to gain unfair competitive advantage over other members'.

purpose of securing such misalignment is to increase net exports'. This decision came to replace a previous one (dated from 1977), designed for a period (widely expanded use) of fixed ER regimes and pervasive capital controls.[50]

Maintaining the country's external stability (i.e. to avoid the country's current and capital account balances being in excessive disequilibrium) surges was one of the key objectives pursued by the new framework.[51] Henceforth, as the economy remains balanced, the probability is reduced of generating disruptive real exchange rate movement. The problem with this definition lies in the explicit link to the RER and that it leaves untouched other core policies (monetary or fiscal and those affecting the financial sector) that could also have a direct effect on the country's external stability. The SD decision also introduced the term 'currency manipulator', specifying that it is carried out through intervention policies directed at keeping the national currency undervalued and, thus, at obtaining an (artificial) increase in net exports.[52] It has also came to clarify the different ways manipulation can occur, ranging from market intervention to the imposition of capital controls.[53] Control is left to IMF staffs, which is required to evaluate whether members' are 'fundamentally misaligned'.

In any event, and although ER manipulation might be demonstrated, the Fund's enforcement power is restricted by its lack of either the necessary tools or the political leadership to deal with it.[54] Furthermore, as the issue remains highly controversial, IMF staff have avoided making an announcement on ER policy (Lavigne and Schembri,

50. According to Zhou Xiaochuan, PBoC governor, 'The Chinese government expresses her deep concern over the Fund's intentions to call the Board of Directors to vote' (letter addressed to the IMF managing director, Rodrigo de Rato (quoted in Blustein, 2015, p. 52).
51. The new directive states that 'a Member should avoid exchange rate policies that result in external stability'.
52. An important group of EMEs expressed their concerns on how the Decision would be implemented. Four of the five countries being analysed in the present book (Argentina, Brazil, China and India) were among those that questioned the IMF 2007 Decision – see the International Monetary and Financial Committee statements on behalf of these and associated countries (Miceli, Mantega, Zhou and Chidambaram).
53. In a seminar in Nanjing, China, Timothy Geithner (at the time US secretary of the treasury) said, 'The most compelling gaps in the present system are the weaknesses and inconsistencies in the approaches that govern exchange rate policy and the use of capital controls, and in the incentives for cooperative policy action to limit economic imbalances. The major currencies are all flexible, with essentially full capital mobility. Most major emerging economies now operate largely flexible exchange rate regimes, with very open capital accounts. Some emerging markets run tightly managed exchange rate regimes with very extensive capital controls, though this is starting to change. This asymmetry in exchange rate policies creates a lot of tension. It magnifies upward pressure on those emerging market exchange rates that are allowed to move and where capital accounts are much more open. It intensifies inflation risk in those emerging economies with undervalued exchange rates. And, finally, it generates protectionist pressures (Statement by Secretary of the Treasury Tim Geithner at the 'High-level Seminar on the International Monetary System', Nanjing, China, 31 March 2011).
54. Following the 2007 Decision, the Fund staff decided to accuse China of fundamental misalignment, but the report was never publicly realized. After the Lehman Brothers collapse, nobody was interested in wrestling with Beijing (Blustein, 2015, p. 56).

2009; Sanford, 2011).[55] Consequently, and trying to act against China's ER policy, US authorities were seeking after WTO legal norms. The rules remain unclear, however, as exceptions mitigate a sovereign state's obligation not to misalign the ER: in particular, there will not be a breach of the GATT if a country's ER policy is consistent with the IMF articles.[56] Even if a currency dispute is settled until the WTO Dispute Settlement scheme, its jurisdiction remains debatable, as ER policy does not fit within the WTO definition of export subsidy. Jurisdiction is also being challenged by those countries that believe that the issue should remain under IMF scrutiny – or be part of inter-agency cooperation and, thereby, profit from the Fund's expertise.[57] There is an important debate on whether the GATT rules underlying the legal architecture in the field remain valid, despite the vast transformation being experienced in recent years by the international system of the ER (Sanford, 2011).

The fact that both entities have the credentials to deal with currency manipulation (but the Fund lacks an enforcement mechanism, whereas WTO instruments remain somewhat vague (Sanford, 2011; Viterbo, 2012)), G20 leaders, led by the United States, began working on the issue and focusing on a satisfactory arrangement for dealing with the problem.[58] The first attempts were observed at the meeting of 21–23 October 2010 in Gyoungju, Korea, where leaders committed to 'move towards more market determined exchange rate systems that reflect the underlying economic fundamentals and refrain from competitive devaluation of currencies' (*FT*, 'G20 Agrees to Avoid Currency Wars, 17 February 2013). Finance ministers and central bank governors who gathered in Paris in February 2011 agreed on the need to 'ensure systematic stability, promote orderly adjustment, and avoid disruptive fluctuations in capital flows, disorderly movements in exchange rates – including advanced economies with reserve currencies being vigilant against excess volatility – and persistent misalignment of exchange rates' (Reuters Staff,

55. It might be remembered that every single year, the Fund evaluates the exchange rate policies of each member during its annual economic review of the country.
56. GATT Article XV:4 states that members of both the IMF and the GATT are requested not to frustrate the intent of the GATT provisions by means of 'exchange action', nor the intent of the IMF Articles through 'trade action'. This provision, however, is mitigated by the exception established by GATT Article XV:9(a), prescribing that exchange controls or exchange restrictions adopted in conformity with the IMF Articles of Agreement cannot be considered as amounting to a breach of the WTO obligations.
57. Both organizations (formerly the IMF and the GATT, later the WTO) were envisioned as cooperating each other from the very start. A new agreement was made in 1996, establishing cooperation on 'matters of mutual interest'.
58. As an example, consider Geithner addressed the Nanjing Conference, saying, 'This is the most important problem to solve in the international monetary system today. But it is not a complicated problem to solve. It does not require a new treaty, or a new institution. It can be achieved by national actions to follow through on the work we have already begun in the G-20 to promote more balanced growth and address excessive imbalances. It can be achieved by building a stronger set of international norms and standards that will hold for the future (Statement by Secretary of the Treasury Tim Geithner at the 'High-level Seminar on the International Monetary System', Nanjing, China, 31 March 2011).

'G20 Finance Ministers, Paris February 19 Communiqué'. Markets News, 19 February 2011). Two years later, G20 finance ministers were claiming, 'We will refrain from competitive devaluation. We will not target our exchange rates for competitive purposes', but the currency war idea was in the air – particularly after an aggressive easing of monetary policy from Japan was discovered (*FT*, 'G20 Agrees to Avoid Currency Wars', 17 February 2013). Similar statements were made at the regional level (for instance at the Asia-Pacific Economic Cooperation, APEC, forum), or directly introducing the issue on the bilateral agenda (as observed at US–China high-level talks) (Sanford, 2011). In a recent communiqué, G7 leaders condemned those intervening in the market: 'We, the G7 Ministers and Governors, reaffirm our longstanding commitment to market determined exchange rates', although they avoided being accused of being manipulators by declaring, 'We reaffirm that our fiscal and monetary policies have been and will remain oriented towards meeting our respective domestic objectives using domestic instruments, and that we will not target exchange rates.'[59]

As pressure in political circles and among lobby groups in Washington mounted,[60] US politicians began to ask for the inclusion of a specific clause in their bilateral agreements, whereas others directly advocated including a currency chapter – with an effective dispute resolution mechanism to deal with it (Bergsten, 2014).[61] An earlier question naturally might arise at this point, as to how to determine 'misalignment'. Concerning this matter, Bergsten proposed to examine three variables: current account surpluses, level of reserves and amount of interventions. Nonetheless, a problem arose at this particular moment: how disruptive might a (bilateral) current account surplus be (for the affected country) and the time span for the surplus? What amount of reserves should be taken into account? What level of intervention could be acceptable? Consensus is lacking on what responses should be, and also on the convenience of such a clause. For instance, Brookings Institution researcher Mireya Solís asks whether a tiny group of nations could become the vehicle to change a major point of doctrine (the jurisdiction over the exchange rate), from multilateralism to bilateralism (2014). For her, if such a transition were finally made, the multilateral regime would become seriously eroded. Harvard University professor Jeffrey Frankel has also joined the opposition camp, presenting 10 reasons to explain why qualifying China as a manipulator remains theoretically incorrect and empirically unviable (2015). Among others, the sovereign right to intervene becomes one of the most controversial reasons not to introduce the (currency manipulator) label, as the practice remains in use in several countries – even among developed nations, as observed during the mid-eighties when the United States joined with Japan, Germany

59. 'Statement by G7 Finance Ministers and Central Bank Governors', 12 February 2013, www.g8.utoronto.ca/finance/fm130212.htm.
60. The US the undervaluation of the Chinese RMB has been at the centre of the debate, and a bipartisan issue in the Congress regarding several legislative initiatives.
61. For those countries violating the clause, the author proposes a set of sanctions, including the withdrawal of concessions made in the trade agreement, the imposition of countervailing duties, import surcharges, monetary fines or countervailing currency intervention (CCI) (Bergsten, 2014, p. 7).

and other G7 countries in concerted intervention at the Plaza Accord in order to push the dollar down. He also defends the purchase of US assets by sovereign states (including the PBoC and China's Sovereign Wealth Funds), even if this policy artificially keeps the value of the national currency lower (vis-à-vis the US dollar). Finally, in recognizing the external effects of the Fed's QE policy, he suggests that this 'had the effect of depreciating the dollar from 2009 to 2011, prompting the same charges of beggar thy neighbour policies that US congressmen now level against others' ('The Top Ten Reasons Why Trade Agreements Should Not Cover Currency Manipulation', Jeffrey Frankel Website, 13 June 2015).

Thus, being seduced or pressed by US negotiators, countries participating in the TPP have committed to refrain from competitive currency devaluations and to be transparent with their ER policies. In their declaration, almost all TPP members are committed to increasing the transparency of their actions in the FX market, including monthly reports of FX reserves and quarterly reports of intervention – inviting the IMF to provide independent input and to enhance transparency.[62] But what about the weight of the United States in the burden of adjustment for imbalances on other countries, which the effects of the Fed's QE policies in other countries?[63] US negotiators might be trying to introduce a 'new gold standard for the twenty-first century' (Ji Xianbai, '"Free" Trade and the Sovereignty Squeeze', 28 October 2014), a standard centred on the US dollar.

The Globalization Paradox and the Political Economy Perspective

The GFC has came to demonstrate the vast challenges unrestricted globalization has imposed, an inconvenient truth for those advocating for free capital movements and unlimited financial deregulation. Development economist Dani Rodrik remains one the main critics of this trend, describing the challenge being posed by hyperglobalization forces on democratic governments around the world. For him, as the globalization process advances (towards the 'hyper', or unregulated stage), it pushes developing countries towards a new dilemma: moving away from democracy or abandoning any attempt at maintaining national sovereignty. This political trilemma could lead to three different scenarios, as follows:

The first scenario (a *golden straightjacket*) is one where undeterred capital flows match national sovereignty, as observed during the nineteenth-century Victorian era. This policy space, however, remains narrowly defined: the sovereign has little freedom to manage the free flow of capital and goods. National economies were compelled to adjust, and quickly (including prices and wages), if international conditions were

62. Brunei, Malaysia, Singapore and Vietnam have been temporarily exempted.

63. In this sense, 'Wasn't America's overconsumption, low saving rate and government budget deficit just as important as China's currency in causing the imbalances, if not more so?' (Blustein, 2015, p. 59). As a consequence, there are chances to find a highly misaligned greenback: according to the IMF, in 2006 the US dollar was certainly overvalued – somewhere between 10 and 30 per cent overvalued (IMF, 2007 'United States: Article IV Consultation – Staff Report' (quoted in Blustein, 2015, p. 79)).

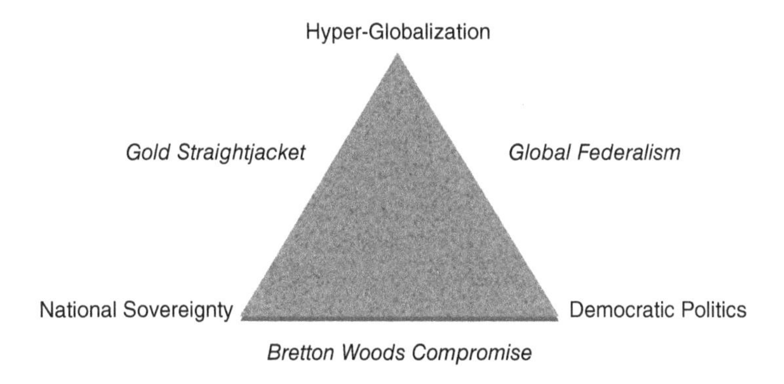

Figure 4.2 Dani Rodrik's hyper-globalization trilemma
Source: Rodrik (2011)

required to do so. In short, this configuration required national leaders to 'agree on requiring the domestic economy to pay the price necessary to realize the benefits of integration into the world economy' (Frieden, 2006, p. 12). Twenty-first-century globalization resembles a weakly regulated financial system, where banks and other financial actors exercise micro regulation (as observed under the Basel II framework). Local authorities are also incapable of protecting social contracts, a setting incompatible with democracy as the system leaves social problems unsolved (Rodrik, 2011). In sum, as Martin Wolf highlights in the preface of his latest book, this alternative, if viable, is not convenient as it not only increases financial instability but also increases inequality, which leaves liberal democracy at risk (Wolf, 2015, p. xxi). This matches K. Polanyi's assertion on the long-term instability of this scenario, as it 'is destined to fail because society would not tolerate the instabilities and upheavals that accompanied an economic order based on the self-regulating market' (Helleiner, 1995, p. 150, on Polanyi's argument).

The second (*Bretton Woods compromise*) scenario is associated with a less open economy (although not necessarily closed to trade and investment flows), where local authorities maintain ample degrees of freedom, and democracy remains relatively less constrained by external forces. This scenario resembles a 'cooperative decentralization' solution observed in the aftermath of the Second World War (Helleiner and Pagliari, 2011), when local authorities maintained regulatory control over cross-border flows. If conflict between leading economic powers increases and regulatory fragmentation continues, this could help this scenario be realized (Helleiner, 2014). It also resembles Rodrik's (2013) limited globalization notion: a particular institutionalization design, which differentiates nations by geography and cultural heterogeneity. Furthermore, by avoiding a 'hyper-globalization' scenario liberal democracy is likely to endure, as the sovereign is capable of offering both freedom and citizenship.

Finally, a third (*global federalism*) scenario is one where free-moving capital would benefit global citizenship, whereas an ideal 'global planner' would discipline global financial entities. The dismantling of the nation state was advocated as welfare improved (as reduced transaction costs), whereas globalization was achievable through regulatory harmonization (Rodrik, 2013). As expressed by Barry Eichengreen (2010), a 'more comprehensive, binding, and coordinated international regulation will be crucial to financial stability worldwide, now and in the future' (p. 114). But, in order to work, the central planner (global regulator) should be flexible enough to consider participants' specific aspects (stage of development, degree of financial market's liberalization and so on). Such a case could be labelled as a 'soft-regulated global federalism' scenario. Legal academics do not agree on its benefits, as they remain afraid of the renegotiation costs imposed by this type of regime. In any case, countries would be more comfortable in stripping down their policy space if they participated in the process of setting up international standards. Nevertheless, if parties to the agreement behave cooperatively, then a soft approach might be feasible. But whereas the relevance of cooperation has been extensively shown, the aftermath of the latest financial crisis might have demonstrated how difficult it (a cooperative agreement) is.[64]

A different sort of global scenario arises when harmonization is viewed as a way to force the weakest countries to introduce a homogeneous norm. In such a case flexibility is certainly necessary, yet power remains king. For Brummer (2012), existing theories 'ultimately assume a considerable consonance of interests between regulatory players', but in reality there are significant distributive considerations in international finance when positive and negative benefits can arise in different countries from the same rule (Baker, 2014). Harmonization, in addition, has 'weakened the very national institutions of governance that previously has ensured that the spread or the growth of domestic or national markets could provide for the prosperity for all' (Rodrik, 2012 p. 396). In sum, this 'one size fits all' framework is what defines a 'hard-regulated global federalism' scenario, which could prove inconvenient for EMEs. As long as harmonization prevails and uniform implementation is required, this leaves no manoeuvring space for local regulators to deal with issues. Institutional harmonization could, at the extreme, be maintained by the local government at the cost of significant political turmoil – 'hard law' to be later rejected, as the Latin American experience exemplifies. Henceforth, and above all, the match between globalization and democracy remains unsolved. To some extent, this latter scenario (hard-regulated global federalism) might reflect the rules and norms being imposed at bilateral negotiations by advanced economies – thus, we could label it as 'hyper-globalization', though for beginners.

Policy space, nonetheless, remains legally unrestricted for just a few. In the case of larger developed countries, holding power has allowed them to create rules and design institutions (Mortimore and Stanley, 2010; Gallagher, 2015). For 'emerging giants', size and power has permitted them to bypass tough rules and, more recently, to be increasingly listened to by IFIs. Brazil, for example, has remained an exception as authorities

64. Eichengreen advocates for the creation of a world financial organization (WFO), an international body empowered to impose hard sanctions on those who violate the agreement] – as observed with the WTO. A proposal made by Garicano and Lastra is to empower the IMF to become a 'global sheriff' and, henceforth, avoid the costs associated with the creation of a new international body.

never ratified their BITs nor signed (until now) any FTAs. India represents another exception, whose government has recently introduced a new investment model for development. Finally, there is China. This rising global power has been aware of the perils and restrictions imposed by international rules and norms. In sum, it is a savvy emerging giant that has played the globalization game by Bretton Woods rules rather than by hyper-globalization rules (Rodrik, 2013, p. 9). Even for those who have signed trade and investment agreements, there may still maintain an escape valve that allows them not to give foreign investors excessive prerogatives. The largest EMEs obtained notable exceptions to BIT standard clauses, as size permitted them to gain more policy room. Agreements undertaken by Asian countries, in particular, recognized the importance of CARs and other barriers to the free flow of external finance flows (Montes, 2013).

Every sovereign nation should be free to choose how to couple with other nations in international financial markets, a process which entails important macroeconomic, sectorial and institutional challenges. Developed countries led by the United States have maintained their one-size-fits-all discourse on the institutional front, leading emerging economies and developing nations into a race for the installation of global standard institutions (GSI) (Chang, 2007), which is not necessarily beneficial for them. But, as Nobel Laureate Douglass North once noted, 'crisis is an event but development is a process' (Sheng, 2012, p. 10). As such, and considering it is desirable to participate in global financial markets, what national governments should carefully scrutinize is which institutions would fit with their membership and how they can confront the challenges imposed by unfettered finance. From this perspective, no institutional design fits all, and no regulatory scheme might work all the time or for every country (Rodrik, 2007;[65] Reinert, 2007)

The preceding discussion has tried to demonstrate how difficult a homogeneous global governance scenario could be, particularly when global power is unequally distributed and the leading countries have no interest in behaving as a benevolent planner. The GFC and the costs associated with it, alongside the rise of China and India, might, however, hopefully help challenge the present 'hyper-globalization' scenario. On the one side, pushed by the high fiscal costs facing them in the aftermath of the crisis, even developed countries' governments are now challenging the deregulatory trend observed in the past. Emerging giants, on the other side, remained unenthusiastic with the set of hyper-globalization rules imposed by developed countries and, directly or indirectly and either in-group or individually, they have worked to transform them. China, but also India and the rest of the BRICS (Brazil, Russia, India, China, and South Africa)

65. As expressed by Rodrik, 'The key lesson of the past half-century is that policymakers must be strategic, rather than comprehensive. They have to do the best with what they have instead of wishing they could transform their society wholesale. They need to identify priorities and opportunities, and work on them. They must seek sequential, cumulative change rather than a single, all-inclusive breakthrough' ('World Too Complex for One-Size-Fits-All Models', *Post-Autistic Economics Review*, 44 (9 December 2007): 73–74, http://www.paecon.net/PAEReview/issue44/Rodrik44.pdf.

members, continue to place greater emphasis on national sovereignty.[66] In the middle, a vast group of emerging economies and developing countries remains, anticipating whether the world will finally move towards re-regulation or whether deregulation of financial markets may persist. Nevertheless, in view of the recent experiences, a group of emerging economies and developing countries are beginning to renegotiate their original commitments (BITs/FTAs), in order to modify restrictive clauses affecting them.

I would like to finish this chapter by quoting a passage from Columbia Law School professor Katherine Pistor's (2012) presentation at the INET Conference, which reveals the challenge actually observed on the institutional front: 'what is needed are instrumental arrangements that will help mitigate risks for countries not only at the top, but on the periphery of the system. Absent such answers these peripheral countries will resort to self-help, even if this adversely affects the global system – and they hardly be blamed for it' (Pistor, 2012, pp. 23–24). In other words, those who have no voice can, eventually, choose to exit.[67]

66. This trend is being observed in the appearance of a set of new developmental banks and international institutions, basically centred on China and a vast list of participants.
67. As recognized by K. Pistor, this latest paragraph is inspired by Hirschman (1970), which helps her explain the political economy of financial governance (Pistor, 2012).

Part 2

A Comparative Analysis

Chapter Five

ARGENTINA

Introduction to Stop-Go Macroeconomics

Until the mid-1970s Argentina followed an ISI strategy, which permitted the country to have an average of 4.4 per cent of GDP growth during the 1964–74 period. Under this model the state became an important economic actor, with a leading role in the financial front through the fixing of interest rates and by rationing resources to (selected) investors or projects. Capital inflows and outflows were strictly limited, including important restrictions on remittances and limitations in FX transactions. Despite growth record growth the substitutive model began to periodically exhibit cycles of boom and burst responding to either the absence or the presence of an external gap. Inflation was certainly a key factor in explaining this pattern because it eroded industrial competitiveness by virtue of real exchange rate appreciation. Devaluating the national currency ideally permitted the government to boost (traditional) exports but simultaneously diminish (superfluous) imports. Manufacturing imports, however, were strongly affected by ER devaluation. So it happened with industrial activity, and additionally ER ups and downs prevented local firms from engaging in long-term planning. But devaluation also affected workers' real wages. Eventually, inflationary pressures were erupting sooner rather than later, preventing a competitive ER for long-term equilibrium from being reinstalled. In other words, the national economy was cyclically confronting up and down movements, *stop and go variations*.

Notwithstanding, in 1975 the country suffered an important macroeconomic crisis – and, certainly, vast political turmoil, which ended in the coup d'état of 24 March 1976. In order to curb the crisis, the dictatorship took the initiative of implementing an ambitious liberalization package, shock therapy to remove or reduce regulations over the economy, including the reduction of trade barriers, the gradual removal of capital controls and the freeing of interest rates. The stabilization programme introduced a new exchange rate regime: a pre-announced rate of crawl (the *tablita*), captivated financial investors the most as it promised important and (apparently) safe returns. Additionally, the economy began to experience a series of current account deficits as well as a permanent increase in the country's foreign debt.[1] Obviously, this lead to real exchange rate appreciation. The programme's credibility came under stress, however, after the Central Bank of Argentina (CBA) was forced to rescue several banks from systemic failure in March 1980. Problems

1. However, this position was considered to be irrelevant for the theoretical framework of the programme: the monetary approach to balance of payments.

were further aggravated thereafter as monetary authorities were required to finance the public sector deficit. Henceforth, and in order to seduce investors, the government raised interest rates on peso deposits.[2] An opportunity for arbitrage was evident. In early 1981, a balance-of-payment crisis marked the end for the dictatorship duo Videla–Martinez de Hoz, although the military would remain in power for another two years.

Thereafter liberalization measures were reversed, reintroducing most of the previously dismantled controls including those affecting the capital account. Democratically elected authorities introduced a (heterodox) macroeconomic programme (the Austral Plan), which reduced but also muted economic agents' inflationary expectations (now, they were expecting lower inflation levels), but harshly constrained by the external debt and low commodity prices the national economy failed to recover.[3] In the spring of 1989, inflation spiralled out of control, and President R. Alfonsín was forced to resign six months ahead of schedule and, sooner than expected, C. Menem became the new resident at 'La Rosada'. After the failure of Argentina's initial anti-inflationary plan, the elected president entrusted the Finance Ministry to D. Cavallo – and a new era began. The convertibility plan introduced a fixed one-to-one dollar–peso exchange rate, which rapidly enabled the new government to stabilize the economy.[4] Dollarization of the local economy became highly encouraged by the national government, by making it legally feasible to write contracts in foreign currencies and by allowing foreign currencies to be used as an alternative means of payments. More or less simultaneously, Argentina embarked on a vast process of deregulation and liberalization, and tariffs and other barriers to trade in goods were (practically) eliminated. Likewise, authorities lifted almost all previous restrictions on international investments, including those banning or limiting foreign participation in key economic sectors.[5] In considering the trilemma, the Menem–Cavallo option implied a hard choice: by introducing a fixed parity and by opening the capital account, authorities at the central bank were left at the mercy of US monetary policy – as we show, hard choices were also made on both the financial and the institutional front. This configuration pushed Argentina towards fiscal discipline, a stable financial sector to support investment and savings, and (overall) a positive balance of international reserves. Henceforth, authorities were permanently forced to attract foreign investors to maintain this inflow of capital entering the

2. Under the new legislation passed in 1977, banks were allowed to accept deposits in foreign currencies by non-residents. Initially, investors were obliged to keep deposits for a year, but the requirement was soon relaxed until it was abandoned in 1979. A year later, the interest rate differential adjusted by pre-announced depreciation was approximately 3% per month.
3. During the period 1981–89, average real GDP decreased by −0.7% annually.
4. The plan required the monetary base to be backed with international reserves (2/3) and dollar-denominated Argentina central bank securities at market prices (1/3). Argentina's central bank was effectively converted into a currency board which could only issue domestic currency in exchange for foreign currency at a fixed rate.
5. In 1994, the country granted foreign investors national treatment status, including those participating in the financial sector.

country. Promises were increased every time investors' expectations turned negative, so were the constraints being imposed.

Privatization soon became one of the pillars of the new economic programme, enabling the government to reduce its external debt, remove the financial liabilities generated by public utilities from the public sphere, and last but not least, attract fresh FDI.[6] Argentina's macroeconomic performance improved notably, and the country entered a solid upward spiral of growth, with the economy expanding by around 9 per cent per year in 1994 and also experiencing an important increase in productivity. However, the exposure of the economy to international capital flow volatility remained strong.[7] Moreover, suddenly, the Tequila crisis was knocking at the central bank's door. As a consequence the economy slumped, with GDP falling by 2.8 per cent in 1995. Authorities played tough enough, allowing interest rates to increase up to 40 per cent and raising (unpopular) taxes (basically, the VAT rate from 18 to 21 per cent), demonstrating their commitment to the model and to the economic orthodoxy. Challenges to the plan were quickly overcome, however, and the economy recovered a year later. Thereafter, Argentina would transform into a showcase of successful reform in Latin America and the Caribbean (LAC), whereas President Menem was hailed as an example to follow in the 1998 annual meeting of the IMF and the World Bank in Washington.[8] Things were not equal once a new series of financial crises broke out, starting in East Asia, and the economy slipped into a downward spiral towards depression and crisis.

The Argentinean GDP experienced a 3.4 per cent plunge in 1999, mostly driven by an impressive fall in investment (13.6 per cent). Decreasing consumption, however, came to overturn trade balance deficits as imports almost collapsed. As public debt keep increasing (surpassing the $100 billion barrier), foreign investors began to carefully observe the Argentinean fiscal deficit: they were starting to show detachment towards perpetual lending.[9] Nonetheless, as the government offered higher yields, they kept on buying Argentinean bonds.[10] Once the newly elected government of Fernando de la Rúa took office in December 1999, recession was definitively installed. Nevertheless, investing

6. Privatization revenues, however, postponed the resolution of the historical low savings rate of the Argentina.
7. The scope for sterilization was certainly minimal under the hard peg.
8. As exemplified by the enthusiastic words pronounced by the former IMF director Michael Camdenssus on the occasion, '[I]n many respects the experience of Argentina in recent years has been exemplary, including in particular the adoption of the proper strategy at the beginning of the 1990s and the very courageous adaptation of it when the tequila crisis put the overall subcontinent at risk of major turmoil [...] [S]o clearly, Argentina has a story to tell the world: a story which is about the importance of fiscal discipline, of structural change, and of monetary policy rigorously maintained' (quoted in Blustein, 2005, p. 58).
9. An important number of academics blamed the government fiscal policy as inconsistent with the currency board. As debt levels continued to climb, the government's lose fiscal policy began to undermine confidence in convertibility. By the end of 2001, provincial debt rose to over US$23 billion.
10. The influence of investment banks and rating agencies in attracting foreign investors was superb, although they certainly did not force local authorities to avoid a prudent fiscal policy.

banks and rating agencies maintained their interest in the country (or just showed their appetite for risks), continuing the selling of Argentinean bonds, particularly among less-informed investors in Europe and Japan.[11] In order to keep alive the convertibility plan, the government also agreed to a three-year standby arrangement for $7.2 billion in March 2000, augmented by $13.7 billion in January 2001. The bailout agreement (the *blindaje*) was an initiative commonly introduced by the Fund in order to assist emerging countries in financial distress.[12] In September 2001, the IMF loan was newly extended to up to US$ $22 billion, of which (US$)$3 billion was used in support of a possible debt-restructuring operation

Macroeconomic perceptions among local businessman were waning fast, however. Unemployment and social indicators were getting worse, but the new economic team preferred to reassure foreign investors' expectations by introducing a tightened fiscal policy. The new package did not help in reversing pessimistic perceptions, condemning the convertibility to fall instead. In the latest attempt to rescue the plan and impede massive capital outflows and a generalized run on banks, the government decided to introduce financial controls (termed the *Corralito*, or little fence'). Likewise, foreign currency transactions were prohibited, preventing both local and foreign investors from transferring funds abroad. A month later, in January 2002, the peso was officially devalued, and all the bank deposits and debts converted into pesos.[13] Argentina, once again, plunged into a devastating macroeconomic crisis.

Previous liberalization measures on the capital account were (once again) phased out, as the government was forced to introduce several controls to track the crisis.[14] In particular, and following the 2001–2 crisis, the Central Bank of Argentina (BCRA) introduced a 90-day residence requirement (to be further extended up to a one-year residence period) and a 30 per cent tax on incoming funds.[15] Restrictions also affected commercial operations: importers needed prior approval from monetary authorities for their

11. Syndicated investment banks tailored a number of their offerings to Europe, attracted by regulatory leaks and small investors' appetite for higher yields. Consequently, Italian retail investors were among those convinced they should sue Argentina at (international) tribunals to claim the full payment of their bonds. From January to September 2000, the Argentine government borrowed nearly US$6 billion by selling dollar-denominated bonds, at an interest rate from 11 3/8 per cent to 12 per cent. It borrowed another US$4 billion plus by selling euro-denominated bonds, mostly to European retail investors, paying an annual interest of 8 1/8 per cent to 10 1/4 per cent (Blustein, 2005).
12. By fixing the loan at US$ 14 billion, the bank surpassed Argentine's lending limits.
13. Dollar deposits were converted at 1.4 pesos to the dollar, while dollar loans were subject to one-to-one conversions.
14. As Argentina maintained its capital account open until the last days of the convertibility scheme, outflows of capital increased during 2000–1 ([US$]$23 billion left the country in that period). Controls were reintroduced in December 2001, but funds poured out through the stock market channel.
15. BCRA A/3712 September 2002. It would be extended to 180 days one year later (BCRA A/3972), and up to one year (BCRA A/4359).

Table 5.1 Argentina, basic macroeconomic indicators

Argentina Macro Performance									
Year	GDP growth (annual per cent)	GDP (current millions of international dollars)	GDP per capita (current US$)	Inflation, consumer prices for Argentina, per cent, annual, not seasonally adjusted	Current account balance (balance of payments, current millions of US$)	External debt stocks, total (debt outstanding and disbursed, current billions of US$)	External debt stocks, long-term (debt outstanding and disbursed, current billions of US$)	Exchange rate (ARG $ per US$)	Domestic public debt (per cent GDP, end of period)
1990	–2.40	141,352.37	4,318.77	2313.96	4,552.00	62.50	48.90	0.49	6.74
1994	5.84	257,440.00	7,449.48	4.18	–10,979.45	75.00	63.70	1.00	7.79
1998	3.85	298,948.25	8,248.76	0.92	–14,482.00	140.10	103.70	1.00	8.10
2002	–10.89	97,724.51	2,579.20	25.87	8,766.61	145.60	116.10	3.06	13.16
2006	8.40	262,666.52	6,639.91	10.90	7,767.04	118.40	89.60	3.05	26.73
2010	9.45	461,640.24	11,198.64	10.780	–1,516.50	111.70	94.70	3.90	12.78
2014	0.45	548,054.87	12,751.39		–8,074.73			8.08	

Source: Own elaboration based on World Bank and INDEC

requirements of hard currency, and exporters became obliged to convert their currency earnings at the central bank's coffers.

*Macro*economics or *Makro*: From Twin Surplus to Populism

Predictably, economic turmoil and sharp devaluation followed the collapse, but authorities managed to stabilize the exchange rate around mid-2002. Around the same time, President E. Duhalde obtained extraordinary emergency powers to tackle the crisis, putting the country into a new political era – although his presidency would remain politically weak and under permanent political scrutiny by a hardly active and mobilized citizenship. The crisis also came to impose a social agenda on the government, as poverty was now at record levels, with a quarter of the population remaining unemployment – mostly without social protection. Consequently, the severity of the crisis would, although certainly unexpectedly, bring back the state into the national economy.[16] A year later, democratic elections would bring N. Kirchner into office, whose government would maintain policies and several ministers from the outgoing administration – including R. Lavagna at the Ministry of Economy.

The local economy started to recuperate thereafter, to a great extent, thanks to the introduction of a competitive real exchange rate policy. External factors were also favouring Argentina now (like most countries in the Southern Cone of Latin America), as the ascent of China (and India) boosted demand for raw materials and energy goods, raising commodity prices to a new plateau. Additionally, Argentina would benefited from the technological revolution and the consequent expansion of its agrarian frontier.[17] The commodity boom came to transform the former deficits into surplus, at both the trade and fiscal accounts.[18] The new macro model combined a managed exchange rate scheme, an active policy of FX reserves accumulation and a monetary aggregate targeting programme (Argentinean Government, 2005).[19] Restrictions on cross-border flows were initially maintained, however, to be later lifted and resumed in 2008. In short, Argentinean political authorities were seeking to gain policy space by moving to the middle ground this macro configuration which permitted them to avoid the constraints posed by the trilemma.

---

16. From the expenditure side, the situation forced economic authorities to subsidize transport, energy and other public services. From the revenue side, it induced a new set of measures, taxing primary goods and raw materials exports.
17. The technological revolution involved a huge process of transformation (seed varieties and so on), and an important organizational change (pool of harvest and so on).
18. As previously observed, the new administration reinstalled the burden tax on both agricultural and energy exports. The boom in soybean prices would become the engine of growth in Argentina's exports during the next decade and, additionally, it would become key in backing the ambitious social spending programme started by the Kirchner administration.
19. According to the official communication to Congress, the intention of the exchange rate programme was to protect the national economy 'against sudden reversals in capital inflows, but also to be used as an insurance against an eventual financial crisis'.

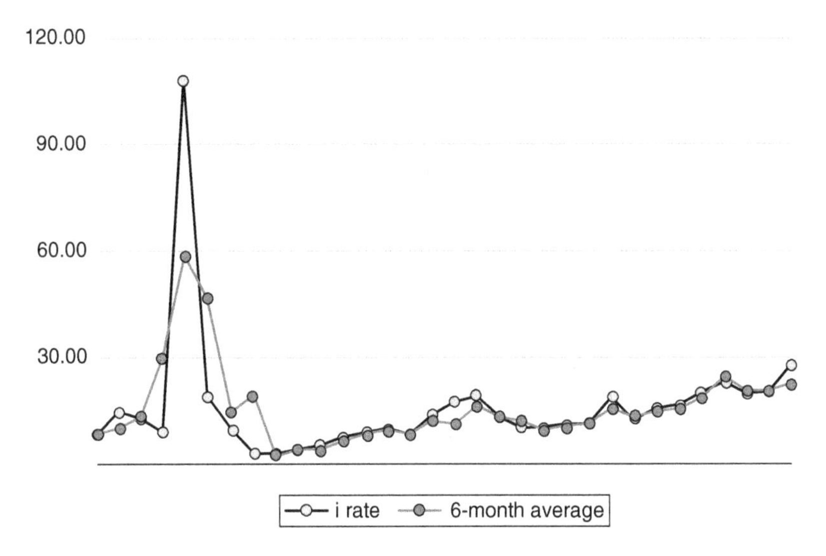

Figure 5.1 BADLAR interest rates, private banks
Source: BCRA

Argentina would become one of the few countries in the region not to follow an interest-targeting policy. The adoption of a quantitative instrument (monetary aggregate) instead of price (interest rate) relates to particular circumstances: at the time uncertainty and the shortening of horizons hindered the existence of a benchmark interest curve (Redrado, 2008).[20] In order to accomplish their objectives, monetary authorities were relying on OMOs and swaps, basically traded through the inter-banking market system.[21] In particular, and with the immediate objective of finding an instrument to absorb market liquidity, authorities started to introduce short-to-medium-term debt instruments: the so-called Lebacs and Nobacs.[22] The Buenos Aires Deposit Large Amount Rate (BADLAR),[23] in turn, became the market's leading rate after the 2001–2 crisis.

20. Initially the programme was based on quarterly targets of monetary base, later replaced by quarterly M2 in pesos.
21. The inter-banking system is divided into two different segments: a secured and an unsecured, or call, market. In this latest market, financial entities trade short-term liquidity positions.
22. With Argentinean bonds in default, and incapable of issuing new debt, the BCRA introduced two new instruments (BCRA B/7155 (March 2002) and BCRA B/8064 (December 2003)). Lebacs are financial actives with zero coupons – capital redeemed at the expiration date, and with zero interest. Nobacs are notes in pesos and indexed by Reference Stabilization Coefficient, or Coeficiente de Estabilización de Referencia (CER), with a four-year redemption date – the note's yield is a spread over the BADLAR.
23. The BADLAR (Buenos Aires Deposit Large Amount Rate) is the weighted average interest rate of time deposits between 30 and 35 days, although it reflects the rate obtained for those depositing more than $1 million.

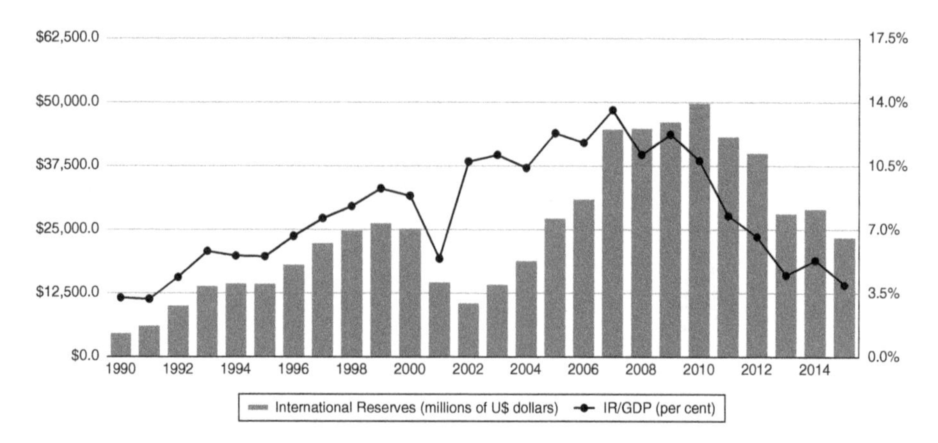

Figure 5.2 Argentina's international reserves (not seasonally adjusted)
Source: Federal Reserve Bank of St. Louis

The central bank used these bills and notes, financial repos and some additional transactions[24] to sterilize the FX surplus – and reduce FX appreciation pressures associated with capital inflows. In parallel, the BCRA introduced a series of norms directed at minimizing the currency mismatch problem. Additionally, but also in order to manage market liquidity, the BCRA made extensive use of reserve requirement ratios (*encajes*), fixing a 15 per cent for peso deposits (up to 25 per cent for deposits in foreign currencies). Both instruments permitted authorities to avoid sharp fluctuations in the monetary base and to impede short-term nominal volatility in the peso/dollar parity. More importantly, the scheme permitted authorities to maintain a competitive real exchange rate (or SCRER) during the 2003–8 period. A managed rate, in turn, revealed the key to avoiding instability problems (short-term) and appreciation (long-term) bias (Rapetti, 2013; Damill et al., 2015). In sum, during the 2003–9 period, the Argentinean GDP grew at a rate of 8.5 per cent.

FX reserves were also mounting, increasing from US$ 9 billion in the aftermath of the crisis to almost US$ 50 billion in early 2008. As previously observed, a series of financial tools permitted the government to neutralize pesos obtained by currency purchase, although it simultaneously increased the amount of contingent liquidity to be managed by the BCRA. Although the scheme brought important benefits (in keeping the monetary base at shore), it also brought with it (quasi-fiscal) costs, challenging its effectiveness. But given the country uniqueness at the time (being away from international capital markets and, henceforth, facing larger financial costs than most sovereigns), sterilization costs were largely offset by the benefits (Frenkel, 2007; Redrado, 2008).

Despite all these promising numbers, some issues remained unsolved, including the interest rate resistance to reducing it below a 10 per cent plateau. To some extent the

24. Cancellation of rediscounts received by banks during the 2001–2 crisis became an important way to tighten the market.

figure reflected the eruption of inflationary pressures after 2004,[25] a problem the government refused to acknowledge and would later try to mask.[26] In any case, and feeling strong about the macro trend, the government decided to (partially) relax capital controls.

Back in Populism

Too much of a good thing can turn dangerous or create addiction. After recovering from the crisis and having regained some national policy space, authorities thought something other than macro constraints would be politically affordable. Thus, they began to relax former rules (such as those implemented by Nestor Kirchner) aimed at obtaining a fiscal surplus. As fiscal policies were relaxed, inflation inevitably resumed. In order to solve the problem (or rather, to mask the situation), the government (now led by Cristina Fernández de Kirchner; CFK) decided to intervene in the national agency for statistics (INDEC), and allegations of underreporting or outright manipulation of inflation data followed.[27] INDEC's intervention signalled a new institutional path, certainly one (now openly) exhibiting a strong populist bias. This confrontational attitude would become entrenched in CFK's administration, and would be once again observed in the conflict with the farming sector in March 2008. Instead of looking for cooperation with farmers, she decidedly sought to confront them and their policy constituencies.

When the Lehman crisis erupted, Argentina was certainly in better (economic) shape than in previous years (and, certainly stronger than in the previous crisis), although somewhat altered from a political standpoint after the clash with farmers' organizations. The twin surpluses evidenced in the past were now granting local authorities – and particularly the BCRA – great 'fire power' to act. (Financial sector) vulnerability to risk was by this time minimal, as neither the public nor the private sector were showing signs of exposure in terms of accumulated debt. Nevertheless, and despite the resiliency, the GFC would severely impact on the local economy. On the one trade front, Argentina was affected by a simultaneous fall in quantities and commodity prices. In addition, the crisis had an impact on the financial front by virtue of a large capital flow reversal (flight-to-quality phenomenon). From a monetary perspective, the crisis triggered a sharp reduction in bank deposits,[28] alongside a significant increase in all

25. The 2001–2 crisis settled down prices, with inflation stabilizing at below 4% in 2003. A year later, as the recovery continued, inflation accelerated to 6.1% to surpass the 10% level in 2004 and 2005 – inducing the finance minister to act in order to curb agents' expectations. In the end, the government did not act, as Minister R. Lavagna resigned in late 2005.
26. The national government implemented a different strategy: price controls. The agreements negotiated by Guillermo Moreno, then undersecretary of commerce, were highly ineffective at curbing inflationary pressures.
27. The failure of the price agreements and controls mechanism was regarded as one of the reasons for the INDEC intervention. For several academics and market analysts, this decision became a turning point, initiating a period of confrontation with the media and markets.
28. A resurgence in dollar-denominated deposits was signalling, once again, local agents' permanent search for hard currency during the turmoil.

market rates (inter-bank, wholesale and retail) in order to contain the former trend. Nevertheless, the fundamentals proved sound, and the economy resisted and did so pretty well (Damill et al., 2015). The effects on trade were also less permanent than expected, as the resilience observed in China kept global demand afloat and commodity prices somewhat stable. As for the FX market, in order to adjust to the external shock, authorities allowed the exchange rate to depreciate against the US dollar, although by a rate (19 per cent) far below those observed among other floaters in the region. Despite all this, the national economy contracted by 8.1 per cent between the third quarter of 2008 and the second quarter of 2009.[29]

Henceforth, and in order to reduce the impact, the government enacted a fiscal stimulus package plus a complimentary series of monetary policy measures. In order to ensure the availability of credit and revert expectations, authorities injected liquidity into markets: renewing maturities, establishing a series of repo actions and implementing a new channel for daily automatic repurchase in real time form notes and bills in the secondary market (Redrado, 2008).[30] By the same token, and in order to increase disposable funds for foreign trade, monetary authorities reduced minimum cash requirements on foreign currency deposits. Furthermore, and in order to curb currency depreciation expectations, the BCRA decidedly acted over both spot and future FX markets – in coordinated action with the main state-owned banks.[31] Additionally, the government obtained international help after the signature of a swap agreement with the PRCs (which agreed to extend this conditional line for RMB 70 billion and a three-year period).[32] Finally, the national government reinstated regulatory controls on the capital account, including now some macro-prudential measures directed at preventing distortions in the FX market and deterring volatility.[33]

On the fiscal front, authorities implementing a vast stimulus programme aimed to boost private demand and increase public investment. Decisions could be supported by the presence of a relaxed position on both the external and the fiscal front (Econometrica newsletter, 2012). Tax exemptions were mainly directed at stimulating consumption and

29. To the negative financial shock generated by the GFC, Argentina added some real effects: soybean prices plummet by 37% (during 2009) plus a severe drought affecting the 2009 harvest. Both factors explain a reduction in exports for U$ 15 billion and a 2.5% to 3% fall in the national GDP.
30. During the 2007–9 period, the monetary base expanded by approximately AR$ 35 billion, despite the US dollar purchase by private agents. Expansion, in turn, was explained by transactions on Lebacs and Nobacs at the OMOs.
31. Authorities decidedly acted in futures markets by expanding their limits but also by compromising by allowing the Emerging Market Trade Association (EMTA) to fix the benchmark FX rate (applicable to futures and forward transactions). Additionally, the government created a mechanism of repos in USD.
32. Although authorities were able to sign another swap agreement with Brazil (the Banco Central do Brazil; BCB), they were not able to obtain a similar agreement with the US Fed – as the country remained in financial distress.
33. For example, since 2007 the BCRA banned foreigners from trading in Lebacs (BCRA Communication A 4715).

labour demand (as for example by introducing a temporary moratorium on fiscal and social obligations), whose fiscal costs were still affordable. In addition, on 20 October the government decided to nationalize the country private pension funds system (a sort of grab on pensioners' assets).[34] If we add the official manipulation of public statistics, the attempt to modify export taxes, and pension funds nationalization, what emerges is a generalized clash with private investors.

Despite the signals the economy proved resilient to the crisis and started to recover by the second half of 2009, basically fuelled by Chinese demand and a new commodity boom. Consequently, the national economy regained *Chinese growth rates* in 2010. Unfortunately, the government misunderstood the lessons from the past and stubbornly refused to reduce the expansionary bias once the first overheating signals of profligacy appeared on the radar. Moreover, and once again, Argentinean authorities would replace the fiscal surplus objective with a loose fiscal policy.[35] As commodity prices began to descend and export-related taxes to vanish, the inflationary tax would become the main instrument to fund the expansionary fiscal policy.

Monetary authorities were definitively playing the expansionary game, particularly after the forced resignation of central bank president M. Redrado in January 2010.[36] Two years later, the government transformed the BCRA Charter, introducing a vast monetary policy mandate to those in charge of monetary policy: 'to promote monetary stability, financial stability, employment, and economic development with social equity'. By eliminating the formerly required ratio of the international reserves to the monetary base, the CFK government diminished the BCRA's power (reserving for itself a greater role in managing FX reserves). Lastly, and as a result of the intervention in the INDEC, bondholders began to get rid of bonds, prices began to fall and the sovereign risk premium climbed. Further controls on FX transactions were imposed starting in November 2011,[37] leading to a parallel exchange rate market (the so-called *dólar blue*). As the external front continued deteriorating, and hard currency availability to evaporate, authorities

34. The measure permitted to raise $23 billion in assets, ensuring there would be funds for the ambitious public-works programme started by the national government ('Harvesting Pensions', *The Economist*, 28 November 2008).
35. For example, in 2008 the consolidated primary fiscal position (nation + provinces) over GDP evidenced a 2.5% surplus, whereas the same figure for 2011 turned into a 1.1% deficit – a figure that increased to 2.3% if debt interest is considered (Econometrica newsletter, December 2011).
36. His resignation came as a consequence of his refusal to comply with an emergency decree to transfer $6.5 billion of reserves to a planned new government fund to repay debt ('Argentina's Central Bank Chief Resigns', *FT*, 30 January 2010).
37. As capital flights continued accumulating during the whole year, totalling U$ 25MM by the end of 2011, the government decided to impose controls on the exchange market (the so-called *cepo cambiario*, or clamp) to deter locals from buying US dollars. As macro tensions persisted, the parallel market maintained its relevance, despite government repressive measures to diminish it. In order to reduce tensions, yet incapable of bringing the dollars to the market, authorities decided to fractionalize the market, installing an official dollar but also a tourism-linked-dollar, or an differentiated exchange rate, for credit-card transactions.

rushed to set several trade barriers.[38] By 2012, the machine was somewhat exhausted and the economy was deteriorating fast, the collusion against the external restriction became inevitable: although the currency exchange blockade (*cepo cambiario*) initially functioned sooner than later, economic agents discovered how to bypass it.[39] Therefore, and despite the resilience observed in the aftermath of the crisis, the government's actions were now signalling the return to populist macroeconomics – or MacroPopulism.[40]

MacroPopulism basically neglects the role of internal and/or external factors in unravelling the crisis, but unsustainable policies are never questioned. Challenged by globalization, populist regimes of this sort were sooner than later reverting to old autarkical macro policies – a solution that permitted them to overcome constraints imposed by the monetary trilemma but at a higher cost.[41] Once again, this new era of populism implied an increase in government expenditures not matched by genuine tax revenues or by foreign sources (as the capital account became practically closed), henceforth leading to a process of public debt monetization and the return of the inflationary tax. Any attempt to link monetary emission to inflationary pressures was decidedly abandoned after the arrival of A. Kicilof at the Ministry of Economy – which occurred in November 2013. Consequently, lacking a comprehensive anti-inflationary plan, the effects of devaluation were condemned to fall short, even for a substantial depreciation such as the one observed in January 2014.[42] The experiment in curbing inflation by controlling prices also failed. In sum, a process of exchange rate appreciation was initiated, basically pushed by inflationary pressures. Furthermore, the decision to maintain a freeze on public services tariffs undermined both the fiscal (subsidies) and the external account (energy-related

38. A differential ER market or devaluation would be an alternative, although the government opted to maintain the currency and to introduce (exchange) controls. One of the effects generated by this policy was the (re)introduction of an illegal market for dollars (popularized as the *blue dollar* market in Argentina). Controls were also affecting Argentina´s commerce, and deeply, as importers were now forced to declare their operations in advance.
39. Once again, a 'cheap' (undervalued) US dollar generated enthusiasm among Argentineans to travel abroad (from a US$ 200 MM surplus in 2010 it transformed into a US$ 6,000 MM deficit in 2013).
40. Independently of the positive attributes associated to the first model (for example, fiscal discipline), decisions always respond to short-term priorities and to increased economic power (the 'cash is king' motto). In short, macro populism was in the roots of the Kirchner administration.
41. Following the Bresser–Pereira analogy, we categorize macro populism in two different types: developmental and liberal. Whereas the first type neglects internal (or fiscal balance) constraints and has a bias towards autarky, the second type recognizes the importance of fiscal discipline but disregards the external (or balance-of-payment) constraint. In other words, whereas the first type can be associated to the dupla Kiciloff–Fernández de Kirchner, the second type is easily recognized under the Cavalllo–Menem convertibility programme.
42. In 2010, authorities left the peso devalued by 4%, whereas inflation reached 22%. The next year the national currency lost 5%, again well below the observed inflation rate (25%). A sharp devaluation occurred in January 2014, when the peso plummeted by more than 12% in two days – yet the real effects of devaluation (to put the local currency on a competitive path) were shortening fast, in a question of months, as authorities refused to act on the inflationary front.

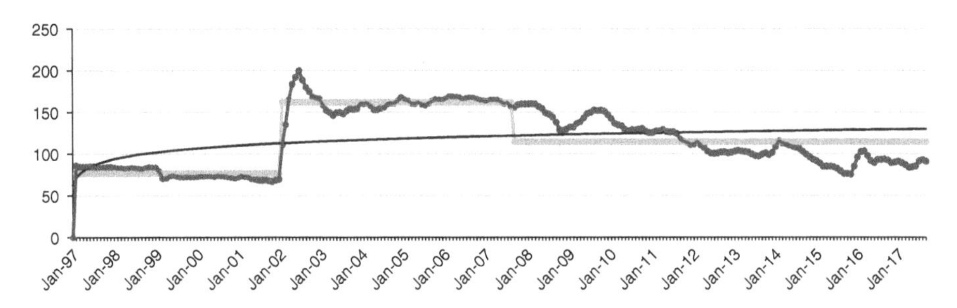

Figure 5.3 Argentina: Real exchange rate, monthly average
(Index 17-12-2015: 100)
Source: BCRA–ITCRM Series

imports).[43] When the commodity boom reverted and with it the former exogenous bonus that blessed South American countries in the past, the former current account surplus suddenly began to vanish.[44] The twin surpluses that signalled the first government were both rapidly muting into deficits. In sum, CFK's last (and desperate) step was to stimulate aggregate demand disregarding all macro fundamentals. Unfortunately, the situation would limit the next government's actions – even restricting the possibility of implementing a gradual approach.

The above graph shows how the multilateral RER evolved in Argentina during the latest 20 years. As a BCRA technical paper observes, there were clearly three different stages. The first stage, with a highly appreciated multilateral real exchange rate (MRER) (an average value of 76.5 for January 1997–January 2002), covered the Convertibility years.[45] As previously stated, following the collapse of the plan, a new economic plan was implemented, basically oriented towards maintaining an SCRER. During the whole period (February 2002–August 2007), the average value reached 161.9. After the arrival of CFK, a new macro model was implemented, basically oriented towards boost consumption. Thereafter, inflationary pressures resumed, and the SCRER was one of the first casualties of this policy orientation. Thus, a huge appreciation bias characterizes the last period under analysis (from September 2007 to present): with an average MRER of 114.2.

43. The attitude of maintaining an artificially low price at the upstream, eliminated firms' incentive for exploration. As the policy was maintained, Argentina was forced to import oil, reverting to the self-sufficiency condition it followed in the past.
44. For example, whereas the current account over GDP ratio observed a surplus of 2.1%, it turned into a 1.1% deficit in 2011. The increase in the oil import bill would become key, transforming the sectorial trade balance as Argentina passed from a US$ 3.5 billion surplus in 2008 to a 3.2 billion deficit in 2011 (Econometrica newsletter, December 2011). As public utilities rates remained basically unaltered, 2013 exports associated with a record harvest were insufficient to match the energy-driven import bill (Econometrica–Quantum newsletter, 2013).
45. The convertibility started in 1991, and the BCRA historical series was initiated in January 1997.

In sum, Argentina, which transformed into a textbook examples of macro populism, was forced to reintroduce controls to deter massive capital flights. By the end of the presidential mandate, a highly predicable outcome emerged: currency appreciation, a negative interest rate and high inflation. Meanwhile external reserves continued to disappear and fast. One of the first economic measures introduced by Mauricio Macri's government was to unclamp the exchange rate, a tight monetary policy came along to avoid an ER overshooting – the country still suffers from strong inflationary pressures. It is still in two-digit figures (above 20 per cent for 2017, after two years of the new administration).

Financial Markets and the Financial Trilemma

Under the ISI model, the Argentinean financial sector became characterized by financial repression (affecting both prices and quantities), alongside the strong participation of state-owned banks. Financial liberalization transformed the former, whereas the passing of a new financial entities law converted the banking industry structure – permitting financial institutions to organize themselves as universal banks. Financial deregulation continued its pace under Menem, whose government advanced further on the liberalization front. The Mexican crisis severely affected the sector. With deposits plunging by 18 per cent, the government rushed to assist financial entities facing problems. Several actions were undertaken, including the passing of new legislation encouraging the arrival of foreign entities.[46]

Accordingly, whereas in 1994 only 15 per cent of total Argentine banking system assets was held in foreign banks, their market share increased faster (to 55 per cent in 1998 to reach an astonishing 73 per cent in 2000) (De la Torre, Levy Yeyati and Schmukler, 2003). Denationalization would coincide with a huge concentration process (Burdisso and D'Amato, 1999; Damill et al., 2010): the number of entities in operation decreased from 205 to 168; 67 per cent of all deposits was concentrated in nine banks; and with two public institutions leading the list, six out of the seven following ones were foreign-owned banks (*The Economist*, 4 March 2000). Additionally, the government started a vast banking privatization process, getting rid of practically everything with the sole exception of the two leading state-owned bank (SOB) entities (the National Bank and the Buenos Aires Provincial Bank).

When evaluating the role of foreign banks, the picture is more nuanced than (initially) expected. Interest rate spreads did not diminish despite the system's gain in efficiency, but arbitrage was further encouraged (Damill et al., 2010).[47] Furthermore, as financial risk increased, they began to reduce their exposure in the country (Dominguez and Tesar, 2005), unmasking their proclaimed fortress – in particular, when looking at the limited assistance from headquarters to subsidiaries in distress (Moguillansky et al.,

46. Menem's administration had previously modified the Law of Financial Entities granting national treatment to foreign banks and removing a former ban on market entrance.
47. Foreign banks were benefited (and henceforth, ready to arbitrate) as they could rely on lower hedging costs (funds were obtained at their headquarters, where they centrally managed liquidity).

2004; Damill et al., 2010).[48] Nor did foreign banks perform better in terms of credit allocation, though they certainly failed in allocating credit to small and medium-size enterprises (Stiglitz, 2002). Independent of their origin, private banks operations during the nineties were mainly oriented towards redirecting funds towards private consumption, real estate mortgages and commercial lending. Lending to private agents, however, began to be curtailed following the Asian crisis. Private entities (both local and foreign) did not reduce after all their lending to public sector entities – despite the presence of weaker repayment guarantees. When the crisis arrived, asymmetric *pessification* would exacerbate local banks' balance-sheet problems.[49] Foreign banks' balance sheets were also hardly disturbed, as most entities were being forced (by their headquarters) to (pre) cancel foreign currency credits. This also contrasts with their theoretical financial resilience, often associated to their preferential access to finance but certainly absent when the crisis appeared (Stichele, 2004).

To be sure, under the currency board the Argentine banking system was heavily exposed to a devaluation of the peso against the US dollar. For this reason, and as a consequence of the limited deposit insurance scheme designed under the convertibility plan, regulatory authorities considered liquidity provisions in detail. Likewise, and in order to preserve the solvency of the financial system, they introduced strong capital requirements – going beyond the 8 per cent ratio recommended by the Basel Committee at the time. Argentinean authorities had also accepted strong (liberalizing) commitments at the WTO GATS, generous in terms of both coverage and depth. In sum, Argentina's (de)regulatory behaviour was characterized as 'exemplary' in policy circles in Washington (Bouzas and Soltz, 2003). De-regulatory offers at the WTO-GATS were aiming to lock-in regulatory reform. In this sense, the offer was not just constraining the policy space for current but also for future administrations. Reputation is not a free lunch: it might be highly costly for future incumbents to alter multilateral rules previously accepted.

48. In the case of the United States, 'legislation establish[ed] that a bank is not obliged to pay deposits made in a subsidiary abroad if it is unable to do so because: a) a state of war, insurrection or civil revolt exists; or b) because it is prevented by an action or instrument of the government of the host country, undertaken without explicit agreement with the bank. This law was added to the existing legislation in 1994, after Citibank was taken to court by depositors in the Philippines and Vietnam and lost the respective cases' [Section 25C of the Federal Reserve Act, section 326 of the Riegle-Neal Interstate Banking and Branching Efficiency Act, codified in 12 US Code Section 633] (Moguillansky et al., 2004).

49. As explained by Blustein (2005, pp. 192–93), 'To head off mass bankruptcy, the government decreed that most people who had borrowed in dollars could repay their loans in depreciated pesos, at the rate of one peso per dollar. At the same time, to appease savers, the authorities announced deposits would be converted at a different rate – 1.4 pesos per dollar. As a result, the banking system, which was already on its knees, was rendered prostrate. The disparity between what banks could collect from their borrowers, and what they owed their deposits, added up to billions of dollars in new losses [...] As for depositors, they felt cheated, notwithstanding the concession the government had given them [...] Their angry reaction lead to a deepening of the banking system's woes, as thousands of them obtained court orders requiring the return of their deposits in full, and money began draining anew from the banking system.'

Despite all these measures and the promises being made, however, the regulatory front presented a few inconsistencies. To begin with, in the case of a sudden FX movement, alternatives were absent for non-tradable producers dealing with repayment problems (aggravating their exchange rate risk). Likewise, high regulatory standards (introduced via Basel Accord) failed to prevent the excessive risk introduced by public sector lending (Damill et al., 2010). Therefore, deterioration in the fiscal burden that widened the exchange risk, automatically forced an increase in interest rates in order to avoid a sudden reversal in capital flows.[50] In sum, the local banking system became overexposed to a sovereign state's default (increasing banks' solvency problem) and, additionally and by the end, systematically crowding out funds from private agents.

Following the 2001 crisis, the government regained policy space. Important changes in prudential regulation were introduced, including a reduction in the minimum risk-weighted regulatory capital coefficient.[51] The central bank also banned foreign currency lending to private agents (except for those having incomes in US$), whereas it introduced a ceiling to commercial banks' liquidity holdings of foreign currencies – which related to banks' deposits in foreign currencies. External source irrelevance is explained not only by this new regulatory scheme but also by the new funding strategy adopted by foreign banks operating in the country.[52] Meanwhile, deposits were transformed into the main source of funding for banks, whose credits would now benefit both firms and households (BIS, 2008).

A couple of years later, and following the recovery of the national economy, banks were finally moving away from the crisis – honouring their obligations with the BCRA. Furthermore, and despite the short period that had elapsed since the collapse, the local financial system was showing renewed signs of solvency. The system remained not just underdeveloped but also profoundly disconnected from the world (cross-border flows were minimal). Unexpectedly, this would be beneficial for the local banking industry, as it permitted to minimize the impact of the GFC. As external funds were highly limited during the Kirchner government, local banks were able to avoid currency mis-match risks – although risks were further reduced after the *cepo* was introduced. In sum, whereas in the past Argentina had become trapped by the dynamics of the financial trilemma the (almost) absence of cross-border flows during the CFK government left the local banking system unaffected by its constraints. But the fortress was illusory, however, as the country exhibited a banking system incapable of bridging economic agents' financial necessities.

---

50. After the arrival of the crisis in 1998, the fiscal burden deteriorated progressively, both at the national and the provincial level. As the recession advanced, some provinces were forced to introduce quasi money.
51. By June 2007 it became fixed at 16.8%, almost duplicating the Basel recommended value (Redrado, 2008).
52. As previously observed, once the GFC erupted, the BCRA established a perfect match (deposits in dollars could only be used to make loans in dollars), with the aggregate that loans (in dollars) should only be granted to companies and households recording dollar-linked income (BIS, 2008).

'**Living *La Vida Loca*': Argentina's Institutional Path**

Foreign investment played a very important but volatile role in the Argentine economy in the past, strong during the 1970s and the 1990s, when inflows reached highs of 8 per cent of GDP, and was virtually absent during the 1980s debt crisis and in the last decade. These highs were associated with three different types of investor: first, in the 1970s, transnational banks that extended large syndicated loans; then, in the 1990s, financial intermediaries which lent voluminous sums in bonds, and TNCs that made very significant direct investments. In other words, Argentina was attractive to a multitude of different foreign investors although in an on-again-off-again manner.

Argentina's new ability to attract foreign capital was based in good part on improved market prospects in the context of the neo-liberal reform programme introduced by the Menem government in the early 1990s. The Convertibility Law enacted in March 1991 was fundamental to stabilizing the economy, based on the introduction of a fixed one-to-one dollar–peso exchange rate, after the inflationary chaos that followed the debt crisis of the 1980s. This extreme measure was costly in economic policy terms as it effectively tied the hands of national policymakers in fiscal and monetary matters; however, it greatly enhanced Argentina's credibility with the international investor community and the Washington-based international financial institutions (IMF, World Bank and InterAmerican Development Bank (IDB)).

Argentina signed over 50 BITs in the 1990s to provide increased protection to foreign investors in the hope of attracting much greater quantities of foreign investment. More or less simultaneously, Argentina moved ahead with an ambitious programme of privatizations along a wide deregulation and liberalization process. The privatizations soon became one of the pillars of the new economic programme. From an aggregate point of view, the sale of public assets and the use of the debt-capitalization scheme enabled Argentina to attract fresh foreign investment, reduce its external debt and remove the financial liabilities generated by public utilities from the public sphere. Privatization was also seen as focusing on a quest for credibility, tying the fate of the privatized firms inextricably to the success of the convertibility plan.

On 23 December 2001, Argentina shook the international financial community by announcing a default on its external public debt of over US$ 100 billion – at the time, a quarter of all debt traded in the emerging bonds market. In January 2002, the Argentine peso declined to one-third of its value and the government *pesified* public utility rates (converting dollar-denominated contract provisions to pesos), provoking a large number of ISDS cases.[53]

A little over three years later and with no help whatsoever from the IMF, Argentina shed its default status when its unilateral offer was widely accepted (by over 75 per cent) by external public debt bondholders.[54] Argentina achieved what no country had achieved

53. US president Franklin Roosevelt introduced a similar policy in 1933, when he passed a resolution nullifying the gold clauses in both private and public debt contracts. The validity of the resolution was challenged in court, but the Supreme Court upheld it.
54. In June 2010, Argentina reopened its debt exchange, bringing the total amount of restructured debt to 92.6%. The high level of acceptance could mainly be attributed to the share of

before, that is, the bondholders not only accepted a large cut in principal but also agreed to a lengthening of maturity and a reduction in the interest rates to be paid. The outcome of the swap far exceeded Argentina's expectations, especially given that it had worked out its default unilaterally without the intervention of the IFIs or the assistance of G7 governments. A group of unsatisfied bondholders went to court (US tribunals), yet few among them opted for International Centre for Settlement of Investment Disputes (ICSID) facilities.[55] Unfortunately, ICSID tribunals lack the institutional competence to determine the debtor country's ability to pay following default (Weibel, 2011).

With regards to the FDI crisis, the abrupt end of exchange rate parity opened a new front in the dispute with foreign investors, in this case with those who had invested in the real sector, especially public utilities.[56] Under the agreements signed in the 1990s, foreign investors felt that they were entitled to full compensation from the government. Although most foreign investors in Argentina were affected by the change in the exchange rate model, the bulk of the complaints came from those with some kind of interest in public utilities, mainly those associated with the energy industry (gas and electric power). The predominance of this type of foreign investment was due not only to the guarantees offered under BITs but also the advantages related to national regulations (for example, rates set in dollars and indexed to the US wholesale price index). As a result, national legislative provisions, regulatory terms and the BIT network bound the contractual framework.[57]

This mechanism helped the Menem government demonstrate its commitment to the new international standards promoted by investor countries and the Washington financial institutions, yet, unfortunately, it also became the main base for foreign investors' legal proceedings. The spirit of the restrictions Argentina had imposed upon itself (the

---

distressed bonds held by banks (U$ 10 billion over a total of U$ 20 billion). Investment funds hold another U$ 4 billion, whereas the rest was in the hands of individuals and other creditors (iMarketNews.com, 23 March 2010). This second restructuring did not include defaulted Brady bonds, debt which Argentina was seeking to solve (DowJones.com, 6 December 2010).

55. The Argentinean default lead to the presentation of series of claims until ICSID tribunals, lead by different groups of Italian bondholders: Abaclat v. Argentine Republic (ICSID case N ARB/07/5), Ambiente Ufficio v Argentine Republic (ICSID case N ARB/08/9), and Alemanni v Argentine Republic (ICSID case N AR/07/8). At different time, ICSID tribunals granted all of them jurisdiction.
56. It should be mentioned that five of these were filed while the convertibility regime was still in place. At ICSID were registered 43 cases, whereas 3 cases were filled under the UN Commission on International Trade Law (UNCITRAL) rules. Awards have been issued in 12 cases (three of them denying the jurisdictions of the Claimants, and one later suspended); an annulment decision has been issued in only one case and requests for annulment are pending in other six cases; one award is being challenged before the Washington, DC, courts. Seventeen cases are still pending (plus one recently started but is unrelated to the 2001 crisis), and proceedings have been suspended or discontinued in 18 cases.
57. Thus, seeking to attract foreign investors and guarantee the success of the reforms, the neoliberal Menem government ended up accepting a system of 'complete' contracts, and thereby accepting risks that normally would be shouldered by the foreign investor. Argentinean sovereign bonds were also affected by the problem of 'complete' contracts (Stanley, 2009).

convertibility scheme combined with BITs) was to minimize the possibility of contract renegotiation with privatized firms, since the magnitude of the commitments made any alteration, however necessary, too costly. Ultimately, the crisis demonstrated the intrinsic 'incompleteness' of the contract scheme implicit in the regulatory framework.

When the Argentine crisis broke out, the international system failed to provide a solution to either the losses of foreign investors caused by the country's inability to apply the rates stipulated in the original contracts or the sovereign default. Foreign direct investors were shocked to find that the World Bank was incapable of obliging the Argentine authorities to abide by the original terms of utility contracts. The bondholders discovered that the IMF was unable to force the Argentine government to renegotiate its debt under any kind of pre-existing scheme or provide assistance to bondholders who opted *not* to accept the swap offer – 'holdouts' – in the hope of a better deal from the government of Argentina. For its part, the Argentine government, in its dual capacity as host country and debtor, was appalled by the functioning of the international system, because of the way it explicitly favoured foreign investors, the lack of objectivity of the international financial institutions (basically the IMF) and attempts to condition the country's economic policy on fulfilment of (by then impossible) international commitments. As a result, and in view of the social dimension of the crisis, the government found itself forced to choose between using scarce resources to alleviate the economic and social suffering of the Argentine population caused by the crises, and allocating them to meet their international obligations to foreign investors. Action taken by the Argentina government spawned, in turn, 'the greatest wave of claims by foreign investors against a single host country in recent history' (Alvarez and Khamsi, 2009).

Ultimately, the international finance and investment community, which had celebrated Argentina's adoption of a risky neo-liberal policy framework, failed to provide the country with specific solutions to resolve the multiple crises it was facing. It proved to be another example of one government limiting the policy options of succeeding governments to deal with the crises provoked in large part by the policies of the former.

Yet, what is striking is the fact that Argentinean authorities did not manage to terminate (or replace) this contract scheme during the past decade, failing to profit from the fact that several treaties were expiring.[58] Neither the government become interested in introducing a new template (for example, as offered recently by India), to alter the strong pro-investor bias that characterized older BITs.[59] A similar passive attitude was observed on the dispute settlement front, as Argentina did not alter its pertinence to ICSID (or

58. As for example, and related to the sovereign debt restructuring (SDR) issue, some countries manage to include special provisions in their new treaties (or a particular annex on public debt) ('*Sovereign Debt Restructuring and International Investment Agreements*', UN, Issues Note. July 2011). According to the report, among other agreements including this particular clause are Peru–Singapore (2008), US–Uruguay BIT (2005), Chile–US FTA (2003) and China–Peru FTA (2009).

59. Most of Argentina´s BITs are drawn on an old template, where environmental or social issues are not recognized.

similar international arbitral tribunals) nor tried to modify its status.[60] In sum, and despite the high costs observed after the crisis, the CFK government remained attached to both the old BITs template and to the IA-ISDS scheme.

Argentina and Dani Rodrik's Political Trilemma

When the Convertibility Plan imploded, vast political turmoil emerged and people took to the historical Plaza de Mayo calling out, 'que se vayan todos!' (all of them must go!). As observed by Rodrik, during the nineties the (Argentinean) nation state responded to the needs of the international economy.[61] The Menem–Cavallo hyperglobalization strategy permanently forced Argentina to attract foreign investors as to grant them guarantees in excess (to keep them coming). During this decade, the government undertook a series of bold reforms, transforming the financial system as well as the country's economic structure. In sum, the fate of the Convertibility plan became associated to the persistence of capital inflows. All institutional measures being adopted by the government (laws, regulations, BITs network) were aimed at demonstrating the irreversibility of the plan.

Once the viability of the plan was put into question, the De la Rúa–Cavallo dupla decided to push for the internal adjustment but '*not to skip a cent of their obligations with foreign creditors*' (Rodrik, 2003, p. 18). In other words, and despite the meagre results generated by each of the several (and failed) attempts to revive the economy, authorities continued privileging the maintenance of the Convertibility plan. In the end, this modern *golden straightjacket* proved incompatible with a modern democratic society, and (new and provisory) authorities were suddenly forced to choose between two hard options: either to maintain democracy (defaulting on external debt) or to avoid default (although imposing a huge social cost). To some extent, a somewhat similar option was confronting European countries during the interwar period: either to sustain democracy or to maintain the gold standard economic orthodoxy (Rodrik, 2007, p. 202).

When the crisis erupted Argentineans were not blaming only local politicians. They also mobilized against bankers, international financial institutions and market fundamentalism. The IMF became highly criticized not just for its fundamental role during the Convertibility but also for leaving authorities alone during the crisis. In sum, after a decade of market fundamentalism (hyperglobalization) people were ready for new alternatives. Henceforth, confronted with two (hard and totalizing) options (hyperglobalization versus democracy), and confronting a popular mobilization and political turmoil, politicians finally opted for their constituency.

---

60. The pro-investor bias of the actual IA-ISDS scheme is widely recognized, and several voices have called for a change. In this direction, it could be mentioned that the European Commission proposed a 'new and transparent system for resolving disputes between investors and states – the Investment Court System', which is supposed to replace the existing ISDS mechanisms in all ongoing and future EU investment negotiations (European Commission, 2015a,b).
61. In particular, see http://rodrik.typepad.com/dani_rodriks_weblog/2007/06/the-inescapable.html.

For those who assumed a high-rank provision during the 2001–2 crisis following the fall of de La Rúa government, their actions were now closely observed by a highly active and mobilized population. Those members of government proved (economically) rational and (socially) sensible, installing a developmental model with social inclusion, which avoided inflationary bias, basically maintained a competitive real exchange rate and rapidly led to a twin (fiscal and external) surplus. Unfortunately, sometime around 2007 the developmental experiment ran out of steam and the government began to play the populist game – avoiding the trilemma by (re)implanting a now (populist) dilemma. When the GFC arrived, MacroPopulism was deepened, and the anti-market discourse endured. Argentina's exceptional status, in the sense of belonging to a particular group of middle-income countries which recurrently go from booms to burst, is a widely studied phenomenon, a subject of analysis for academics working in different scientific areas and of passion for policymakers trying to understand the country's exceptionality. How national authorities misused the opportunity observed in the past decade would add another chapter in this perennial search.

The failure of populism, however, should not serve to favour a new hyperglobalization experiment. Argentina, certainly, should advance towards a new strategy for the world market of reinserting itself into global markets and attracting investors. There is no doubt about this. This means it must undertake a proactive and strategic stance at the negotiation table, avoiding to remain attached to rules which could affect the country in the future – as observed in the past. Since the arrival of M. Macri to office, international capital is back. But most of the funds are short term in essence, attracted by the business opportunities originating from agents' ER expectations and the interest rate differential (carry trade). Nor does the arrival of FDI flows guarantee a sustainable development path, per se. Take, for example, those funds directed to finance the development of an enclave mining project, whose social and environmental costs are not internalized. In other words, nobody is talking about the risks posed by the arrival of short-term capital flows or the benefits associated with FDI flows.[62] Argentina needs funds and investments, for sure. But it also needs a long-term perspective: a strategic approach.

Unfortunately, in its relationship with foreign investors, Argentina has followed a rather schizophrenic approach: simply rejecting them or promising everything to them. This reflects the Argentinean passive institutional approach: either reject or take it. This binary behaviour should be replaced by a more equilibrated, sequential and consensual approach. This proactive approach might certainly be more tedious, but the emerging institutions would be perdurable.

62. Additionally, both types of investments show an exchange rate appreciation bias (representing different sorts of the so-called Dutch disease phenomenon).

Chapter Six

BRAZIL

Macro at the Corners: Economic Policy in Stormy Waters

For several years Brazil was considered an outstanding outsider in the Latin American region due to its excellent economic record from the mid-sixties to the early eighties.[1] Those were the 'Brazilian miracle' years, with GDP per capita continually increasing by a yearly rate of over 6 per cent from 1968 to 1980. Until the early nineties, the country followed the ISI model,[2] with the strong involvement of multinational (market-seeking) companies (MNCs),[3] which permitted Brazil to definitively leave behind a backward economy. In sum, foreign investors in tandem with local companies and the national government recreated a so-called *triade* (Evans, 1995), which was highly successful in converting Brazil into Latin America's industrial powerhouse and rapidly transforming the local society and the state.

As widely observed in other Latin American countries at the time, the Brazilian state adopted a more proactive role, and the society (or some portions of it) began to enjoy the emergence of the 'welfare state'. From the start, the substitutive model profited from instruments and policies tools available in the developmental large class, including a multiple exchange rate policy and a crawling peg scheme, which periodically adjusted the local currency to the US dollar (Canuto and Holland, 2001).

The large degrees of freedom in policymaking were, certainly, highly correlated to the capital account foreclosure alternative being adopted. Isolation, in turn, granted

1. Brazil exceptional status basically relates to its colonial legacy and the different historical path it has adopted since its independence from the Portuguese rule.
2. The first attempt to industrialize the country was observed during the First World War, but this was reversed once the war finished and coffee remained the mainstay of the economy. The decade of the 1930s saw a plethora of political changes, beginning with the revolution that ended with the 'Old Republic' (1889–1930), politically controlled by the agrarian oligarchy (fazendas owners). The 1930s were also represented by a series of economic transformations which introduced Brazil to an industrialization path. The Estado Novo finally installed the ISI model, and economic policy was reinforced in the aftermath of the Second World War.
3. MNCs became attracted by the promise of the internal market rather than any legal protection available (i.e. Law 4131/62), and in spite of the existence of some sectorial restrictions consistent with the ISI model, foreign investors were obliged to register with the central bank in keeping with existing foreign exchange and tax controls. However, the government passed legislation (Law 4131) guaranteeing MNCs the 'right of return' and of profit remittances (Carvalho and Souza, 2010).

monetary authorities important degrees of freedom in their design of monetary policy.[4] Nonetheless, this highly autonomous environment presented some negative side effects, particularly for those at the central bank: monetary policy became highly dependent on the *fisc*. Furthermore, as industrialization advanced, the country became more nor less dependent on foreign inputs, pushing the economy to a recurrent balance-of-payments crisis – a pattern also observed in Argentina. Last but not least, and in order to bypass the increasing saving gap imposed by the model, the government began to rely on foreign credits.[5]

The rise in global interest rise coupled with a sharp rise in oil prices (at the time, Brazil was an oil importer country) exposed Brazil's large structural weakness. In the mid-1980s the external debt crisis aggravated the fiscal and financial gaps of the balance of payments, whereas the collapse of the demand of the internal market put a damper on foreign investors' expectations (Bacha, 1990). All the country' macroeconomic *gaps* were suddenly appearing by the time democracy returned, which hardly affected the economy and Brazilian society. A perfect storm of mounting social demands and diminishing degrees of freedom magically emerged to challenge those administering the economy and trying to overcome poverty and record inequality.[6] Tensions like this became apparent in the Brazilian treatment of FDI. Decree-Law No. 1986/82 introduced important restrictions for foreign companies in order to operate in the local capital market. Two years later, a constitutional amendment would introduce further restrictions, including a ban on foreign investors participating in the local banking industry. The new scenario would put the economy into an inflationary vicious circle lasting until the mid-1990s, despite several deregulatory initiatives and liberalization measures undertaken under both the Fernando Collor de Melo and the Itamar Franco government.[7]

Unsolved tensions forced the government to monetize the mounting fiscal deficit, thus pushing the society to an annual rate of inflation exceeding 100 per cent every year from 1981 to 1994. Henceforth, for those aiming to obtain public support at the ballot box, combating inflation came to the centre of the political agenda, and politicians affirmatively responded. Thereafter a series of heterodox programmes were introduced (1985 Plan, 1987 Bresser Plan and 1989 Summer Plan), which initially helped reduce inflation

4. Monetary authorities introduced OMOs as early as in the 1970s – alongside the creation of the central bank reserves market. Two decades later, OMOs would be replaced as the government preferred to rely on intermediate targets in order to control monetary policy. The mid-1996 movement also discontinued OMO operations in the secondary market (BCB, 1999, p. 81).
5. Commercial lending was mainly attached to oil imports, although loans were also directed to finance public investment.
6. Brazil has always been described as a highly unequal country, even by Latin American standards. At the time of the miracle, some observers were describing this contrast as 'Bel-India' – that is, as affluence favouring a tiny sector of the society but with the rest falling below poverty levels.
7. Among other measures, the Brazilian government opened the domestic securities market to foreign investors and granted companies permission to transfer financial resources abroad without proof of previous internment through the so-called CC5 results.

rates, but pressure caused it to resume sooner rather than later.[8] Consequently, at the beginning of the 1990s inflation was again out of control – surpassing an annual rate of 5,000 per cent in June 1994 (CBB, 1999). The situation motivated policymakers to act, and bravely.

Playing at the Corners: How Sustainable Can a Fixed ER Scheme Be?

On July 1994, the government introduced the Real Plan aimed at curbing the inflationary problem by committing itself to maintaining an exchange rate ceiling of one-to-one parity with the dollar.[9] A few months earlier, Brazil had achieved an agreement with the international banking sector on the external debt issue (i.e. Brady Plan), normalizing its international financial relations. Authorities now decided to install a more liberal and market-friendly approach towards national development and foreign investors' involvement.[10] The Real Plan was fully successful in settling the inflation down, putting an end to indexation and the chronic high inflation observed in the past. The architect of the plan, Fernando Henrique Cardoso (or FHC, for short, as he has famously been known in Brazil), was at the time Minister of Finance and later twice elected president of the Federal Republic of Brazil from 1994 to 2002.[11] During his term in office, Brazil would attract numerous foreign investors (Mortimore and Stanley, 2010).[12]

The success of the Plan generated some complications, however, including an important bias towards exchange rate appreciation,[13] demand expansion (pulling for

8. As observed in other countries in the region, notably Argentina, the central elements associated with a freeze in the main macro prices (including wages), prohibiting financial indexation and fixing the exchange rate regime.
9. In contrast to the Convertibility Plan in Argentina, the monetary authorities in Brazil did not explicitly state the relationship between changes in the monetary base and foreign reserves movements, thus allowing for some discretionary leeway – a crawling peg scheme.
10. Brazil, as other countries in the region, embarked on an ambitious privatization programme, which attracted several firms – particularly from Europe and also the United States.
11. FHC is also a leading intellectual figure in Latin America. A sociologist, he would in the 1960s become one of the founding fathers of the dependence theory. On his return to Brazil, he began his political career, being twice elected to the Senate (1982 and 1986). He took part in the 1987–88 National Constituent Assembly that drafted and later approved the (new) Brazilian Constitution. Before becoming head of the Ministry of Finance, he served as Minister of Foreign Affairs (from October 1992 to May 1993) – both charges under President Franco.
12. Capital inflows increased spectacularly in the nineties, in both FDI and financial flows: whereas in 1990 capital flows represented 0.9% of Brazilian GDP, ten years later they totalled 3.8%. Regarding the 1990–2000 period, mid- and long-term inflows totalled US$ 95.8 billion – mostly commercial notes (71.0%), followed by inter-firm credits (17.1%), bonds (5.9%) and commercial papers (4.3%). Short-term flows, in turn, were important until 1995, and thereafter monetary authorities began to bet hard against speculative capital, reintroducing controls (Terra and Sohiet, 2006, pp. 728–31).
13. As observed by E. Cardoso, 'despite minor devaluations between 1995 and 1998, the REER at the end of 1998 was still as high as it was at the beginning of 1996. There was no structural changes or anticipated growth to justify such a significant real appreciation.' The slow growth of exports is another sign of the plan bias towards appreciation' ('Brazil Currency Crisis: The

increasing imports)[14] and, unfortunately, the persistence of a lower savings trend. Trade liberalization plus currency appreciation turned the current account into deficit from 1995 to 1999. The Plan was also incapable of untangling old fiscal problems, inducing instead an external debt rise – which proved necessary to maintain the economy at work. Despite the evident fiscal problems, the Banco Central do Brazil (BCB) (the Brazilian central bank) decided to play it tight – yet increase the interest rate differential. Unable to alter the exchange rate in the event of external shocks, the government left aside the bulk of the adjustment on the interest rate policy (Canuto and Holland, 2001), a decision whose consequences are still challenging Brazil.

As external imbalances intensified, the economy remained at the mercy of financial speculators.[15] Therefore, in order to reduce volatility, and despite the liberalization path being initiated, economic authorities decided to introduce a series of controls on capital inflows.[16] On the one hand, authorities decided to introduce price-based schemes including explicit taxes on capital flows on stock market investments, foreign loans and certain exchange transactions.[17]

On the other hand, the government also maintained different administrative controls as outright prohibitions against (or minimum maturity requirement for) certain type of inflows (*sand in the wheel* provisions). An institutional view would observe that the legal framework regarding the issue still contained some old norms and rules, all of them dated from the Vargas administration and originally focused on preventing capital outflows (Carvalho and Garcia, 2006).[18] Independently of legal enforcement, the regime became

---

Shift from an Exchange Rate Anchor to a Flexible Regime', chapter 4 in *Exchange Rate Politics in Latin America*, ed. Carol Wise and Riordan Roett (Washington, DC: Brookings Institution Press, 2000), p. 80.

14. The enthusiasm generated by the boom, led economic authorities to raise minimum wages and government wages and salaries.
15. In might be important to emphasize the low interest rate level observed among industrialized countries in the nineties. Henceforth, lower interest rates in DCs (developed countries) induced investors towards some EMEs like Brazil, whose economy was then characterized by open capital accounts, a fixed exchange rate and an important interest rate differential (carry trade). During the Asian crisis, Brazil lost US$ 11 billion in reserves in three months, forcing the central bank to raise interest rates from a 19% annual average to 46% in November 1997. A few months later, high interest rates pulled foreign investors back, although 'temporarily': the Russian crisis pulled them out again (Carvalho and Souza, 2010).
16. As an example, Terra and Sohiet (2006) mentioned the approval of two resolutions (No. 1832/91 and No. 1482/92) reducing the short-term capital stance, along with the CBB Resolution No. 2388 constituting the foreign capital fixed-rent fund. Since 1997, the FHC government had introduced a series of rules and measures, resuming the opening of the capital account. The Asian crisis and the increase in capital outflows that resulted thereafter, however, caused authorities to discontinue this trend.
17. The so-called tax on financial operations (or Imposto sobre Operações Financeiras – IOF) was introduced in June 1994 through Law No. 8.894. Inflows were mostly charged at 2% – although some operations were exempted, such as those involving the state (local, regional or national) and their related companies and payments accruing to import and exports operations.
18. The Brazilian legal framework included (in 2006) the following requirements: foreign exchange must be converted into the national currency; export revenues and resources secured offshore

highly contested by mainstream pundits/experts], which tilted capital controls to be ineffective in keeping speculators at bay.[19] In sum, although controls increased policymakers' space, the country remained exposed to global capital flows as some legal leaks permitted investors to arbitrage. As in the Argentinean case, the strategy of using the exchange rate as an anti-inflationary anchor remained highly vulnerable – and investors became well aware of this.

The End of an Affair: Inflation Targeting as a New Anchor

In order to maintain the exchange rate, the government profited from an IMF syndicate loan in late September 1998, which, unfortunately, proved incapable of restoring market confidence.[20] International reserves were almost exhausted, and financial flows remained negative. As the macroeconomic environment worsened, economic agents began to transform their holdings from BRL (Brazilian reals) to US$ dollars. Incapable of maintaining the peg, the re-elected president (FHC) decided in January 1999 to allow the real to float, convincing both politicians and public opinion that the currency would be less vulnerable to future speculative attacks if it were flexible. To settle down economic agents' expectations, economic authorities introduced an inflation-targeting regime along with adding more pressure to achieve a primary fiscal surplus (Fiscal Responsibility Law, approved by the National Congress in May 2000).

Thereafter, the economy grew at very low rates, a phenomenon that could be explained by several factors, among them, a contractive fiscal policy, very high real interest rates impeding new investment financing and, last but not least, the maintenance of high external volatility. All these factors were adding stress on the macro front. A series of external shocks (Russia, Argentina, the dot.com bubble in the United States) would come to aggravate the external front, whereas the perspective of Luiz Inácio Lula de Silva's victory in the presidential election affected the internal one.[21] Confronted with a fresh crisis, new economic authorities acted similarly to the previous ones: raising interest rates and causing the economy to contract (Carvalho and Souza, 2010).

must be brought back into the country; and private exchange rate transactions were prohibited (Carvalho and Garcia, 2006).

19. A series of papers analyse this period, including the effectiveness of capital controls: Cardoso and Goldfajn (1997); Sohiet (2002); Paula, Oreiro and Silva (2003); Carvalho and Garcia (2006). Costa da Silva and Cunha Resende give a more optimistic opinion – promoting the necessity to reinforce these types of controls with more restrictive measures (2010). Cardoso and Golpin (1997) introduce an index of capital controls describing all legal transformations affecting capital inflows, including all the norms and rules introduced by the central bank of Brazil. Scholars classified the rules affecting the capital flows as being pro-market (liberalize) or anti-market (restrictive).
20. The package was orchestrated among the IMF, the World Bank, the Inter-American Development Bank (IDB) and a group of industrialized nations, with the BIS articulating it. As compensation for aid, the agreement stipulated an adjustment programme.
21. Lula finally won the Brazilian presidency in the 2002 elections, after three unsuccessful runs (1989, 1994 and 1998).

Table 6.1 Brazil IT, evolution since 1999

BRAZIL inflation- targeting evolution (1999 to 2015)						
Year	Target	Tolerance interval (p.p.)	Upper limit (%)	Lower limit (%)	Actual inflation (IPCA,% p.a)	Difference
1999	8	2	10	6	8.94	–0.94
2000	6	2	8	4	5.97	0.03
2001	4	2	6	2	7.67	–3.67
2002	3.5	2	5.5	1.5	12.53	–9.03
2003	4	2.5	6.5	1.5	9.3	–5.3
2004	3.25	2.5	5.75	0.75	7.6	–4.35
2005	4	2.5	6.5	1.5	5.69	–1.69
2006	3.75	2.5	6.25	1.25	3.14	0.61
2007	5.5	2	7.5	3.5	4.46	1.04
2008	4.5	2	6.5	2.5	5.9	–1.4
2009	4.5	2	6.5	2.5	4.31	0.19
2010	4.5	2	6.5	2.5	5.91	–1.41
2011	4.5	2	6.5	2.5	6.5	–2
2012	4.5	2	6.5	2.5	5.84	–1.34
2013	4.5	2	6.5	2.5	5.91	–1.41
2014	4.5	2	6.5	2.5	6.41	–1.91
2015	4.5	2	6.5	2.5	10.67	–6.17

Source: BCB

Once again authorities were pushing monetary policies too far: stabilization become a strong mandate for the BCB (and a weak one for those covering the fiscal front). Certainly, an important number of academics posed the problem on the monetary front. But, unfortunately, Brazil real interest rates are among the EMEs highest – particularly when compared with Asian EMEs. The Special Clearance and Escrow System (SELIC) is the basic rate dictated by the government in order to alienate demand and supply of money. Being settled by the central bank's Monetary Policy Committee (hereinafter referred as COPOM), this overnight rate indexes the Brazilian Treasury notes, or Letras Financieras do Tesouro (LFTs).[22] As the notes are automatically indexed by SELIC, its guarantees investors zero *Maculay* duration.[23] As a consequence, by guaranteeing high liquidity and

22. Treasury Indexed Bonds were originally introduced in 1964, and particularly directed at enhancing OMO' liquidity (Branco and Paula, 2015, p. 111). LFTs were introduced by the 1988 Constitution, as it prohibited the federal government from obtaining (direct or indirect) financing throughout the BCB. The new law granted the federal government a unique account at the central bank, permitting the BCB to introduce the notes in the monetary toolkit (Oreiro et al., 2012, p. 568),
23. Macaulay duration is used to measure how sensitive a bond price is to change in interest rates. Thus, bonds have zero interest rate risk, reducing the wealth effect of monetary policy.

limited risks, LFTs remain the most preferred financial instrument among federal government domestic debt (Oreiro et al., 2012), at the cost of perpetually postponing the fiscal problem solution. An increase in SELIC automatically raises the public debt; however, it generates a contagion effect of public debt that 'changes the term structure of interest rates' (Holanda Barbosa, 2006) and prevents the creation of a long-term market for government bonds.

Whereas prior experience showed how vulnerable a monetary – *fisc* –liaison might be in a closed economy context, the situation is aggravated further when the economy is open to the world as foreign investors are now entitled to mediate monetary instruments. This explains why LFTs are in Brazil highly correlated with foreign reserves, as the BCB uses them (reserves) to sterilize operations with indexed Treasury notes.[24] This correlation, in turn, generates an extreme interest rate dependence on exchange rate movements (Oreiro, 2014, p. 214). In short, the LFTs exhibit high negative effects on the Brazilian economy, particularly affecting the effectiveness of BCB monetary policy under an inflation-targeting scheme (Oreiro et al., 2012). Nevertheless, and despite all commented limitations imposed by high real interest rates, the scheme proved successful in preventing the Brazilian economy from dollarizing during the hyperinflationary years (Holland Barbosa, 2006), certainly 'an object of desire for many EMEs' (Bacha et al., 2007, p. 16).

Along with the flexible exchange-rate-cum-inflation-targeting regime, and in order to limit volatility shocks, Brazilian authorities began to use derivatives instruments (FX options). In particular, the BCB decided to intervene in the domestic market via the use of derivative swaps to maintain the ER parity within a certain range of value – and without necessarily being forced to alter the country's FX reserves![25] This policy tool, be that as it may, proved problematic to manage as economic agents converted it into a highly speculative weapon.[26] In addition, the increasing importance of the derivative market altered the normal exchange rate determination process: instead of being formed at the spot market, it was the futures market which determined the ER value determined not by the spot but rather (or strongly affected) by future market operations (Franco, 2000; Dodd and Griffith-Jones, 2007; Ventura and Garcia, 2009).[27] Besides this undesirable bias, FX derivatives (coupled with the

24. Treasury notes are used to regulate market liquidity. If the market exhibits excess demand of LFTs, then the central bank is forced to grant liquidity in order to maintain the monetary base in equilibrium. However, if the market is exhibiting an excess supply of LFTs, authorities are forced to use their reserves in order to liquidate them (Oreiro, 2015, p. 112).
25. Monetary authorities first commercialized the dollar/real future contracts in November 1996, with the BCB trying to defend the crawling peg. As, due to legislation, FX futures are non-deliverable, the central bank is not forced to use its international reserves.
26. Speculation might not be bad if it is bidirectional, but economic agents' bets turned unidirectional (Rossi, 2015).
27. As, for example, in August 2013, the daily turnover of the futures market was four times greater than the spot market: US$ 27.0 billion against US$ 6.4 billion (Rossi, 2015)\, p. 718.

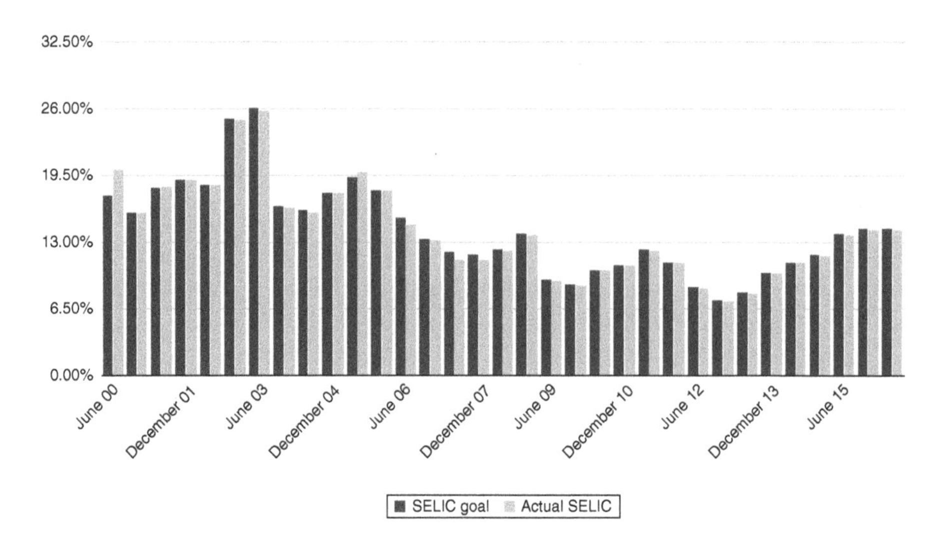

Figure 6.1 Brazil, SELIC rate
Source: Central Bank of Brazil

presence of assets indexed to foreign exchange) permitted to install 'a barrier that strongly attenuated the transmission of financial instability to the economy' (Prates and Farhi, 2015, p. 16).[28]

The arrival of Lula to the presidency did not lead to alteration of FHC's macroeconomic programme, but orthodox measures further expanded – which received important criticism from the heterodox Keynesian camp. The BCB maintained the inflation-targeting scheme almost intact, reinforcing the tightening approach on monetary policy.[29] The exchange rate regime continued untouched, although the real was not left at the mercy of market forces as monetary authorities began to periodically intervene. Fiscal policy became more ambitious, as authorities were now pushing for a primary surplus of 4.25 per cent of GDP (Williamson, 2010). It might be remembered that Lula's first term began in January 2003. At that time the effects of the EME crisis were still latent, but external conditions would become favourable soon and some heterodox policies begin to gain space.

After 2003, the external front would become more generous to Brazil, as commodity prices improved and exports continued to rise (the China factor). This boom transformed Brazil's pattern of commerce, introducing a new normal as the balance quickly moved from deficit to surplus.[30] The always-problematic fiscal front became less traumatic as

28. Liquidity, in turn, is explained by the BCB's attitude of continuing with the selling of US$ dollars.
29. In his first year in office, the SELIC averaged 15.4% per year.
30. Brazil's main exports to China were concentrated in a small batch of commodities, particularly soybeans and other seeds, iron ore and concentrates, oil and derivatives, pulp and waste paper and meat.

Table 6.2 Brazil international reserves and basic indicators (1990–2015)

Year	Total Reserves (includes gold, current millions of US$)	Total Reserves to GDP ratio (%)	Total Reserves in months of imports	Total Reserves to Short-Term Debt	Total Reserves to M2	GDP PPP (current millions of US$)
1990	9,199.60	1.99	2.6959	257.7820	15.2623	461,951.78
1991	8,748.60	1.45	2.7053	300.7501	24.1386	602,860.00
1992	23,264.50	5.81	7.5251	103.5314	10.4921	400,599.25
1993	31,746.90	7.25	8.1952	98.6635	12.9158	437,798.58
1994	38,491.70	6.90	8.4307	83.5785	6.4513	558,112.00
1995	51,477.30	6.55	7.9343	60.6502	4.8493	785,643.46
1996	59,685.40	7.02	8.5729	59.5602	5.0038	850,425.83
1997	51,705.50	5.85	6.4080	66.5250	6.3141	883,199.44
1998	43,902.10	5.08	5.3244	68.0615	7.7381	863,723.40
1999	36,342.30	6.06	5.0955	80.4308	7.0608	599,388.88
2000	33,015.20	5.04	4.2562	93.8145	9.2285	655,421.15
2001	35,866.40	6.41	4.5473	78.8293	9.1098	559,372.50
2002	37,832.10	7.45	5.5186	61.8389	7.3911	507,962.74
2003	49,297.20	8.83	6.9927	49.8897	6.3526	558,320.12
2004	52,934.80	7.91	6.1843	47.7323	7.1347	669,316.24
2005	53,799.20	6.03	5.1330	44.5972	10.0129	891,629.97
2006	85,842.80	7.75	6.7141	23.6747	8.3321	1,107,640.33
2007	180,333.60	12.91	10.8977	21.7630	5.4084	1,397,084.38
2008	193,783.30	11.43	8.5080	18.9098	6.3479	1,695,824.52
2009	238,539.40	14.31	13.1785	16.6790	5.5221	1,667,020.11
2010	288,574.60	13.06	10.5444	22.6951	6.0660	2,208,872.21
2011	352,010.20	13.46	10.6835	11.9713	6.0930	2,614,573.17
2012	369,565.90	15.02	12.2090	8.7316	5.6810	2,460,658.44
2013	358,808.00	14.55	11.6298	9.3381	5.7561	2,465,773.85
2014	363,551.00	15.04	11.3669	16.0016	5.9269	2,417,046.32
2015	356,464.00	20.09	14.3830		4.7374	1,774,724.82

Total Reserves: Total reserves comprise holdings of monetary gold, special drawing rights, reserves of IMF members held by the IMF and holdings of foreign exchange under the control of monetary authorities.

Total Reserves to Imports: This item shows reserves expressed in terms of the number of months of imports of goods and services they could pay for (Reserves/(Imports/12)).

Total Reserves to ST Debt: Short-term debt includes all debt having an original maturity of one year or less and interest in arrears on long-term debt.

Total Reserves to M2: Broad money is the sum of currency outside banks; demand deposits other than those of the central government; the time, savings, and foreign currency deposits of resident sectors other than the central government; bank and traveller's cheques; and other securities such as certificates of deposit and commercial paper.

Source: World Bank

the economy recovered and the government's revenues increased. Favoured by the new external scenario, Brazil also began to increase its gross international reserves up to US$ 200 billion in 2008. Last but not least, local interest rates began to diminish, albeit at very slow rates. All this set the Brazilian economy on a more relaxed path. Additionally, the discovery of the pre-salt oil fields in the seabed off the southern coast increased the government's confidence in the foreseeable future.[31] The new international environment backed the Lula administration in adding a social content to his previous market-oriented economic model. The China effect led those in the government think that Brazil's grand destiny was now firmly installed.[32] Unfortunately, some confused the success of these short-term policies and the apparent resilience of the Brazilian economy as a guarantee of a sustainable development path.[33] In sum, this 'social-developmental' (but populist) programme would, unfortunately, prove unsustainable (Bresser Pereira, 2015).[34]

Brazil, the GFC and Beyond: A New *Caiphirina* Moment?

The GFC seriously affected the Brazilian economy, both on the real and the financial side. External markets were suddenly depressed; GDP contracted by 0.6 per cent on a yearly basis; and the ER experienced a harsh depreciation, as investors were leaving the country en mass. This flight-to-quality phenomenon involved portfolio investors but also MNCs' subsidiaries, which unexpectedly began to increase their remittances and payments abroad. What proved more destabilizing, however, was the unrestricted access obtained by investors in both the spot and derivative segments of the Brazilian financial market (Prates, 2014, p. 155). Attitudes like this just added pressure to the real exchange rate, forcing economic authorities to lead the market initiative in order to avoid a sudden devaluation of the real. The prudent macro policies being followed until the financial crack did not help immunize the national economy nor did the vast FX reserves that had been previously accumulated.

Despite the storm and in order to gain initiative, the Lula government introduced an ambitious stimulus package while altering government's policies on the monetary, fiscal and industrial fronts. Among the measures undertaken were an important motivation for credit expansion, including both (direct) monetary instruments[35] and the enactment

---

31. Petrobras, Brazil's leading oil company, made a series of important discoveries in 2007 and 2009. Although the reserves are important, so are the associated costs of extraction.
32. Brazil was now included in a selected group of emerging giants, the so-called BRICs group (Brazil, Russia, India, and, China). Originally given this name by Jim O'Neill in 2001 (by then, chairman of Goldman Sachs), they finally assembled as a group and had their first formal summit in 2009 in Yekaterinburg. South Africa would join the group in 2010, henceforth becoming known by the BRICS acronym.
33. An important increase in the minimum wage was among the principal measures benefiting the lower class, but they were also gained from two additional policies introduced by the Lula administration: the *bolsa familia* and an increase in the share of GDP devoted to social spending.
34. 'We will have more oil to face up to this financial crisis', Lula da Silva said after Petrobras discovered the pre-salt reserves in 2008 ('Pre-Salt Oilfield Creates Biggest Challenge Yet for Petrobras', *FT*, 22 October 2013).
35. In order to push financial institutions towards credit, the government introduced penalties in the reserve requirement of time deposits. Another important set of measures was related to the development of the discount windows procedures and of the Credit Guarantee Fund (CGF). The creation of a special type of time deposit (six months, backed by the Fundo Garantidor

of new credit lines at the Brazilian Development Bank (BNDES) (Sobreira and Paula, 2010).[36] The government was assigning a countercyclical role to most federal public banks (Banco do Brasil; BB, Caixa Economica Federal; CEF and Banco Nacional de Desenvolvimento Econômico y Social; BNDES) (Moreira Cunha, et al., 2011, p. 705). On the monetary front, the BCB started with an easing policy in order to lower the policy target rate and simultaneously increase market liquidity (Moreira Cunha et al., 2011). Liquidity qualms were avoided by the BCB through a series of measures, including the reduction in the SELIC rate and reserve requirements on cash deposits and time deposits, and auctions of loan reserves. Monetary authorities also rushed to shield the financial system from a systemic crisis, including new rediscount lines and the enactment of renewed regulatory rules and prudential measures. Finally, a swap agreement was negotiated with the US Fed, which was highly valuable in relaxing pressures on the exchange rate (EX) market.

On the fiscal front, actions were oriented towards incentivizing both consumption and investment expenses, introducing a more adaptable position over the previous more orthodox approach.[37] Finally, Dilma Rousseff, the first female president of Brazil and the resident at the Palácio da Alvorada since 1 January 2011, reintroduced capital controls by issuing a 2 per cent annual tax on foreign loans.[38]

According to Mesquita and Torós (2010), the main lesson to be extracted from the GFC experience is that a country characterized by inflation targeting, prudential monetary policy and conservative banking rules and practices enters into a crisis later and exits sooner, all along with lower price volatility. Certainly, Brazil entered into the crisis exhibiting strong fundamentals (international reserves, fiscal accounts, external front and so on). As noted by Wise and Tedesco Lins (2015, p. 177), many observers were happy to proclaim a triumphal narrative, but resilience towards the GFC was ultimately confounded by an indefinite future of prosperity.

Nevertheless, induced by the Fed's policies, capital continued to arrive in Brazil, and in a massive way. These new massive inflows of capital plus the funds available after the stimulus package would generate important effects over the macro (exchange rate appreciation, increasing deficit in the current account, mounting inflation and so on). The local stock market was now the main destiny of inflows, fuelling a credit boom that particularly

de Credito (FGC), or CGF by its English acronym) became another valuable instrument introduced by monetary authorities (Mesquita Toro, 2010).

36. According to Silva (2009), the BCB avoided to install a tight monetary policy thanks to the availability of FX reserves and by the use of FX derivative swaps.
37. In order to stimulate demand, the fiscal package introduced several measures, including (1) an expansion of the PAC; (2) a construction programme (Minha Casa, Minha Vida); (3) budget transfer to municipalities; and (4) an expansion of unemployment benefits (Moreira Cunha, 2011).
38. In her inaugural speech Dilma Rousseff stated that Brazil would protect 'the country from unfair competition and from the indiscriminate flow of speculative capital' ('Dilma Rousseff Inauguration Speech: Brazil's First Female President Addresses Congress in Brasilia', *Huffington Post*, https://www.huffingtonpost.com/2011/01/03/dilma-rousseff-inaugurati_1_n_803450.html, 3 January 2011).

Table 6.3 Brazil fiscal indicators (2002–15)

Key macro indicators after the 2008 crisis (2008-2015)														
	2002	2003	2004	2005	2006	2007	2008	2009	2010	2011	2012	2013	2014	2015
Real GDP change (%)	2.7%	1.1%	5.7%	3.2%	4.0%	6.1%	5.0%	-0.2%	7.6%	3.9%	1.8%	2.7%	1.0%	–3.5%
Primary result (% of GDP)	3.2%	3.2%	3.7%	3.7%	3.2%	3.2%	3.3%	1.9%	2.6%	2.9%	2.2%	1.8%	–0.6%	–2.1%
Nominal result (% of GDP)	–4.4%	–5.2%	–2.9%	–3.5%	–3.6%	–2.7%	–0.2%	–3.2%	–2.4%	–2.6%	–2.3%	–3.1%	–6.2%	–11.1%
Gross General Government Debt (% of GDP)	66.7%	60.9%	56.2%	56.1%	55.5%	56.8%	56.0%	59.3%	51.8%	51.3%	54.8%	53.3%	58.9%	69.0%
Net Public Debt (% of GDP)	59.8%	54.2%	50.2%	47.9%	46.5%	44.6%	37.6%	40.9%	38.0%	34.5%	32.9%	31.5%	34.1%	33.0%
Net Tax Revenue (% of GDP)	17.7%	17.2%	18.0%	18.6%	18.7%	18.9%	18.8%	18.3%	20.0%	18.7%	18.7%	19.2%	18.4%	18.7%
Primary expenditure (% of GDP)	15.5%	14.9%	15.4%	16.1%	16.6%	16.7%	16.0%	17.2%	18.0%	16.5%	17.1%	17.7%	18.7%	19.0%
Foreign Public Net Debt (% of GDP)	15.6%	11.0%	7.8%	3.1%	–1.2%	–7.3%	–10.7%	–8.8%	–9.3%	-12.3%	–12.9%	–13.4%	–13.8%	–19.5%

Source: Own elaboration, based on Holland (2015), World Bank and Brazilian Central Bank

benefited Brazilian households and kept stimulating sales in both the retail and the auto market. In sum, quantitative easing policies have strong spillover effects on the Brazilian economy (Barroso et al., 2013, p. 30), certainly benefiting households' consumption but disruptive to manufacturing and real investment.

One would say that when dancers perceive the music will stop soon, they begin to exit. This pattern was observed among savvy investors after they perceived the end of the Fed QE programme – the so-called taper-tantrum moment which began in May 2013.[39] They smelled Brazil's (macroeconomic) weakness and, thus, helped transform a (once qualified) rising global star into an inconsistent example of macro populism. The Brazilian macro was, once again, confronting a series of disruptions on the fiscal, monetary and exchange rate fronts.

Both political and economics forces were, one more time, pushing the country towards recession and a tremendous devaluation. The local currency plunged from a high of about $1.5 to the dollar in July 2011 to $3.83 in September 2015 ('Dilma in the Vortex: Brazil's Economic and Political Crises Are Reinforcing Each Other', *The Economist*, 1 October 2015). The real economy contracted fast, as confidence began to reduce households' consumption plans alongside destimulating firms' investment plans. Furthermore, inflationary pressures were back, with rising prices in food, electricity and transport adding pressure on the BCB target range. Inflation forced monetary authorities to tight interest rates,[40] but, unfortunately, the movement also led to a new debt spiral.[41] In any event, the situation put the fiscal front back into the scene, and the government now became forced to rebalance its budget after the overspending bias generated by the prolonged fiscal stimulus. As authorities evidenced weak enthusiasm for disentangling the fiscal burden, leading rating agencies ended up downgrading Brazilian external bonds to the junk category in September 2015. To sum up, depreciation and recession induced a huge contraction in the national economy, which contracted by nearly a quarter that year in dollar terms.[42] Despite the storm, foreign investors remained interested in National

39. Tapering is a system of slowly reducing the amount of money the Fed puts into the economy, which, in theory, gradually reduces the economy's reliance on that money. However, if the public hears that the Fed is planning to engage in tapering, panic can still ensue; that panic is called a taper tantrum (investopia: http://www.investopedia.com/terms/t/taper-tantrum.asp#ixzz4vo3wQSKW). See also Gerald D. Cohen, 'Emerging Markets' Taper Tantrum', at Brookings.edu, 29 January 2014.
40. Considering the period from October 2014 to early June 2015, the SELIC rate increased by 275 basis points ('Brazil Raises Rates for Sixth Straight Time', *FT*, 4 June 2015), to finally reach 14.25% at the end of July – its highest level since August 2006 ('Brazil Raises Rates to 14.25% to Combat Inflation', *FT*, 30 July 2015).
41. With a 64.5% debt-to-GDP ratio, it reached a new plateau in September 2015, but forecasts predicted the ratio would surpass 70% soon ('Brazil Struggles to Fix Fiscal Crisis', *FT*, 2 September 2015). Private sector debt also jumped to 55% of GDP in recent years, from a mere 25% level observed in 2005 ('The Crash of a Titan', *The Economist*, 28 February 2015).
42. From a figure of US$ 2.353 billion in 2014, Brazilian GDP was expected to reach US$ 1.812 in 2015 ('Brazil Economy to Contract Nearly One-Quarter This Year in Dollar Terms', *FT*, 25 May 2015).

Treasury Finance (NTF) notes, as Brazilian bonds continued to offer one of the most attractive yields in the world.[43] Some other actors, however, were rather pessimistic regarding the monetary tightness, arguing that the government was pushing further this contractive phase of the cycle.

For some academics and policymakers, the latest news came to confirm the challenges posed by incomplete modernization (Wise and Tedesco Lins, 2015), or the changes introduced under the Rousseff government that reversed prior market-friendly measures.[44] However, other academics would assert that these 'end-of-the-party' sorts of problems showed their historical roots in Latin America, as those countries cyclically observe a highly volatile macro scenario. Still others highlighted the challenges posed by the massive arrival of capital, the appreciation bias and the strong deindustrialization path followed in last decades (Bresser Pereira, 2015).[45] To make the scene worse, wages kept increasing despite the weak performance in labour productivity recently observed (Oreiro, 2015a).

The Financial System and the Trilemma: New Actors, Renewed Constraints

Until the mid-eighties, Brazil's financial system was characterized as a repressed model. As observed in Argentina, the state was fixing prices (interest rates) and rationing quantities (credit). Likewise, the presence of foreign banks was severely limited, whereas public sector/state-owned banks were warmly embraced. In particular, this reflected highly restrictive legislation covering banking, with foreign banks entry being considered only on a reciprocal basis and subject to special capital requirements (Freitas, 2009).[46]

Thereafter, the Brazilian financial system underwent profound changes, including the end of the 'floating' scheme after the introduction of the Real Plan.[47] Once Brazil left behind

43. In June 2015 non-residents owned R$ 480 billion, or 20.5% of Brazil's local currency government debt ('Foreign Ownership of Brazil's Local Debt Hits Highest Ever Level, EM Squared', *FT* 5 June 2015, https://www.ft.com/content/7981d1bc-0aa8-11e5-a8e8-00144feabdc0).
44. As, for example, by augmenting state involvement in the economy by reducing BCB independence, by increasing trade protectionism or, finally, by lowering the tax basis (Oreiro, 2015).
45. He also blames Rousseff's irresponsibility on the fiscal front. Additionally, Bresser Pereira considers unacceptable the narrow inflationary target maintained by her government, which misunderstands 'two other goals of good macroeconomic policy: growth and financial stability' (Bresser-Pereira, 2015, 'The Macroeconomic Tripod and the Workers' Party Administrations'. Paper prepared for book edited by Lauro Mattei, March 2015).
46. Article 192 of the Brazil Federal Constitution and supplementary laws – approved at the National Congress under by a qualified quorum – are rules for foreign participation in domestic financial institutions. Authorization, originally granted in reciprocity or in the interest of the government, was subject to BCB analysis and approval.
47. Under the inflationary regime, an agent's lending capacity was basically directed towards buying governmental bonds. Indexation of contracts permitted Brazilian authorities to recreate a domestic reserve asset competing with massive dollarization of private agents portfolios (Carvalho and Souza, 2010).

the old macro scenario, the banking industry was pushed towards a tough dilemma: either sell their share in the market to other players (either new entrants or competitors) or maintain their stance and become competitive in this new environment. The new financial scenario turned more unpredictable, certainly, and particularly affected small and medium-size banks and public entities (Hermann, 2010).[48]

Henceforth, and in order to solve the dilemma, the Brazilian government introduced a series of measures aimed at attracting foreign investors (Carvalho and Souza, 2009).[49] Bankers from Europe or the United States were seen as more solid (both in terms of capital and liquidity provisions), along more efficient and, certainly, technologically on the front line. Consequently, since the mid-nineties foreign banks had begun to arrive, launching an important trend towards concentration and (partial) denationalization in the Brazilian banking industry.[50] Institutionally, the government removed former legal restrictions placed on foreign participation – including those introduced by the Brazilian Constitution.[51] In the same direction, the government decided to open the fixed-rent market to foreign capital (Annex VI, Resolution 1289/1993).[52] Thereafter, equity markets gained in relevance, although now with the important participation of foreigners.[53] Additionally, with the retreat of inflation Brazil recreated the debt market.

---

48. Only three big national banks were affected by the crisis (Banco Nacional, Banco Econômico and Bamerindas). BANERJE and BANESPA were the two biggest public-regional banks distressed by the mid-nineties crisis.
49. Two measures were particularly important. One is the creation of the PROER (Program of Incentives to the Restructuring and Strengthening of the National Financial System), whose objective was to assure the liquidity and solvency of the national financial system. In order to achieve this, the programme introduced a merger and acquisition policy, including important tax incentives and credit facilities for those interested in participating. The second one relates to the implementation of the PROES (Program of Incentives for the Reduction of the State´s Participation in Banking Activities), whose primary goal was to reduce the number of public sector participants in the financial system.
50. Foreign banks' entrance was mainly made throughout the acquisition of both public entities and (local) private banks. The purchases of Banco Meridional, Banco Bozano-Simonsen and Banco do Estado de São Paulo by Spanish Banco Santander transformed it into one of the most relevant entrants. Other European banks were also entering the Brazilian market in the late nineties, such as the Dutch ABN AMRO or the French Société Générale. The participation of foreign-controlled banks among the 15 largest banks increased from 6.5% to 34.0% between 1994 and 1998 (Fernando J. Cardim de Carvalho, 2002, 'The Recent Expansion of Foreign Banks in Brazil: First Results'. University of Oxford Centre for Brazilian Studies Working Paper Series. Working Paper Series CBS-18-01, pp. 22–23).
51. The issue was certainly unclear under the 1998 Federal Constitution. Foreigners with an interest in operating in the Brazilian market were obliged to ask for a special authorization from Congressional authorities.
52. The first steps towards attracting foreign investors were undertaken in the late eighties by introducing a special vehicle to participate in the market. In 1991, foreigners were allowed to operate without intermediaries.
53. Primary and secondary purchases made by this group of investors reached 71.2% of total primary and secondary markets in 2005 (Carvhalo and Souza, 2010, p. 27).

Monetary authorities were also introducing important changes on the regulatory front, and regulatory measures affected all financial markets.[54] In 1994, the National Monetary Council (NMC; Conselho Monetario Nacional)[55] adopted the 1988 Basel Accord (NMC Resolution 2099), permitting financial institutions to adopt the new rules including the new capital requirement ratio of 8 per cent, although opinions on the adjustment phase remain debatable (Arienti, 2007; Carvalho and Souza, 2010).[56] Prudential regulations were further expanded under the FHC government, introducing a new deposit assurance scheme (Fundo Garantidor de Créditos) along with an increase in the capital requirement ratio up to 11 per cent. Despite new rules aimed at shielding Brazilian banks from liquidity shortages, the system's fragility increased as profits began to diminish, and holding extra capital became a 'luxury that struggling institutions could not afford' (Sobreira and Paula, 2010), and, henceforth, system strength was confronted with market competition (Arienti, 2007). As a result, the 'rules of the game' introduced via the privatization programmes (PROER and PROES) and the new regulatory scheme (FGC) permitted foreign banks to increase their share in the local market.

The bank industry started on the route to a process of market concentration and denationalization, a path observed in several emerging countries at the time, particularly in Latin America and Eastern Europe. Foreign bank performance, however, did not match expectations, with their attitude towards credit lending and risk management being not dissimilar to what was observed among local private banks. Some facts are important to mention, which also differentiates this experience from others. First, and despite the arrival of new financial players from abroad, local players were also very active in the process of banking consolidation, since an important number of Brazilian private banks (including Bradesco, Itaú and Unibanco) decided to play an active role in the privatization process (Arienti, 2007). Secondly, foreign bank entry remaining bureaucratically restrained by different measures enacted by the government as well as by the BCB policy of permissions acting on a case-by-case basis (Paula and Sobreira, 2010).[57]

The banking internationalization process initiated in 1997 was suddenly discontinued after 2001, however, as foreigners become scared of the new political

54. With this stance the Brazilian government moved away from the Glass–Steagall- type organizational model introduced in the mid-1960s. Since 1988, have authorities recognized universal or multiple banks (Resolution 1524).
55. The CNM's resolution 2099 defined four risk 'buckets', with weights 0%, 20%, 50% and 100%. Brazil also adopted Basel II rules in 2004. It is important to note that, whereas financial regulation and supervision is conducted by the CMN, the BCB is in charge of monetary policy.
56. To be weighted by the risk of the bank's asset operations.
57. See previous footnote describing the role played by the BCB. In legal terms, Circular N 3317/2006 listed the information to be fulfilled by foreigners interested to enter. Six years later, Resolution N 4122/2012 and its further amendments implemented by Resolution N 4279/2012 and Resolution N 4308/2014, set down the requirements and procedures concerning the authorization for establishing and operating all types of banks (universal, commercial, investment, development and foreign exchange), and financial companies (credit, financing and investment, real estate credit, mortgage, development agencies, leasing, securities brokerage, securities distribution and foreign exchange brokerage).

and macroeconomic situation.[58] The new scenario induced public banks to reappear but, fundamentally, allowed local private banks a new opportunity to expand (an option from which Bradesco and Itaú profited). Among the SOBs, their revival involved a triad of giants: BNDES,[59] Caixa Economica Federal and Banco do Brasil.[60] Public banks, particularly the BNDES, were called in to help rescue big companies seriously affected by the FX derivative market (Farhi and Zanchetta Borghi, 2009).[61] In sum, nationally owned banks (private and public) gained in presence in the financial system, with some firms undertaking their initial steps towards internationalization, a process particularly relevant on a regional basis.

Brazilian Capital Markets: A Brief Guide

In the mid-nineties Brazilian authorities rediscovered capital markets and their role in economic development. Thereafter, the equity market started its meteoric rise in the *grand ligues*, and BOVESPA, the Brazilian main open market (actually BF&M-Bovespa), exploded (Russo and de Oliveira, 2015).[62] The transformation also has an institutional chapter, with the Security and Exchange Commission of Brazil (Comissao de Valores Mobiliários; CVM) introducing a series of new rules protecting minority stakeholders and others norms encouraging the adoption of higher standards for corporate governance.[63]

There are two main stock markets operating at the BF&M-Bovespa: the old one, where around 370 companies are listed, and the one at the Novo Mercado, where 134

58. Whereas in 2001 local financial institutions participated with 27% of total assets, five years later their share was at the level of 53.8% (Sobreira and de Paula, 2010, p. 86).
59. BNDES would become an artifice of the new development plan introduced by Lula's administration, although its relevance would increase after the GFC as the stimulus package gave federal public banks a leading role.
60. In June 2009, among the ten largest banking groups operating in the country, three were institutions owned by the federal government (occupying positions 1, 5 and 6), four corresponded to private domestic banks (positions 2, 3, 8 and 9) and the remaining three corresponded to foreign groups (positions 4, 7 and 10) (Fernando J. Cardim de Carvalho and Francisco Eduardo Pires de Souza, 2010, 'Financial Regulation and Macroeconomic Stability in Brazil in the Aftermath of the Russian Crisis'. Mimeo, p. 22, available at Research Gate https://www.researchgate.net/publication/264878765_Financial_regulation_and_macroeconomic_stability_in_Brazil_in_the_aftermath_of_the_Russian_crisis.
61. In the end, benefits were accruing to about 200 companies, not just those affected by the bet.
62. The boom occurred in 2004–6. In that period the number of primary emissions tripled to a total of U$ 28 billion, whereas the number of operations in the secondary market reached U$ 182 billion (Hermann, 2010, p. 269).
63. A complete list of prudential measures can be found at Hermann (2010). Independently of these measures, the Brazilian legislation still classifies shares into two different types: PN and ON. In particular, although those in possession of PN shares are entitled to have a minimum dividend to be paid before ON shares, they do not have voting rights. This makes the PN market more liquid but less protected from companies' owners (holding ON shares).

are quoted.[64] Local institutional investors (pension funds, insurance companies, mutual funds) are highly active.[65] Yet foreign investors explain between one-third (Hermann, 2010) to one-half of the operations (Larson, 2014), with most of the investors being domiciled in the United States and Europe (Park, 2012).[66]

Foreign investors are also very active in the bonds and derivatives markets. In terms of the former, there exist four different markets (local currency or US denominated) (sovereign or corporate bonds), with varying foreign relevance in each of them. Local residents, in turn, are the majority in the local currency sovereign bond market, where Brazilian leading companies are among the main issuers.

Finally, there is the market for futures and options, where trade is transacted at two main markets: the Bolsa Mercadeorías e Futuros (BMFBovespa), one of the world leaders in the field. There is also an OTC market, whose operations are required to be reported, either with BM&F or at CETIP, where the majority are registered, the latter being the most important in term of registered operations.[67]

Market contracts are basically associated to FX derivatives and local interest rate futures, offering a wide range of maturities. One of the leading products being commercialized by the BMFBovespa is the 'Cupom Cambial', a contract priced in basis points as an interest rate equal to the spread between the overnight interbank deposit rate and the exchange rate variation prior to maturity of the contract – an equivalent to the onshore US dollar interest rate (Dodd and Griffith-Jones, 2007). The presence of high interest rates raises local investors' minimum required returns, increasing volatility in equities and creating a bias towards fixed income. Certainly, a highly inflationary environment and the reliance on dollar funding has helped developed the derivative market (Stone, Walker and Yasui, 2009). Brazil's uniqueness also explains the importance of the non-deliverable forwards (NDFs) market, foreign exchange forwards that are 'cash settled' in one currency (reals if traded in Brazil or US dollars if traded offshore), but also the relevance of the future market in exchange rate determination (see below).

As observed in other regions, a few large dealers are dominating the OTC market – particularly, large multinational banks from the United States, the EU or Japan.[68]

64. Companies listed at the Novo Mercado are exposed to stricter standards of corporate governance than those determined by Brazilian corporate law.
65. However, investors' priorities are safe and liquid assets – as government bonds and repo transactions.
66. Notice that the Brazilian legislation does not discriminate between foreigners and local participants, as the former are entitled to acquire and invest in the same securities (equity, debt) as those that are available to local domestic investors (Russo and Oliveira, 2015).
67. This is a publicly held company located in Rio de Janeiro, which offers services related to registration, central securities depository (CSD), trading and settlement of assets and securities. The company is also Latin America's largest depositary of fixed income securities and Brazil's largest private asset clearinghouse (for more information, see https://www.cetip.com.br/?lang=en-us).
68. Foreigners' participation in the domestic derivative market, however, was originally restricted. When the government introduced Fixed Income Funds To Foreign Capital (FRFCE), these

Foreigners are active participants in the onshore market (explaining around one-third of the market's volume) and the majority in offshore ones. In terms of governance, Brazil's derivative market is differentiated from other ones as being more transparent and by the fact that most of their inter-dealing trading is conducted through exchange trading (Dodd and Griffith-Jones, 2007).

The GFC and the Financial Market

New measures were introduced in the aftermath of the GFC, which particularly affected banks' reserve requirements and liquidity provisions, including those oriented to reducing ER mismatching.[69] As a result of the crisis and investors' desire for liquidity, Brazil experienced an important shortage of US dollars – ultimately affecting local currency liquidity. Part of the problem, however, resided in the (relative) high exposure to derivatives products experienced by the corporative sector.

Economic policy was oriented towards a virtual separation between the monetary policy and liquidity administration (Mesquita e Torós, 2010). On the one hand, the National Monetary Council (CMN) introduced a series of measures aimed at protecting system liquidity, including the issuance of compulsory recognitions, the (re)introduction of a special fund and an aggressive policy of rediscounts.[70] Furthermore, according to BCB reports, capital coefficients were maintained well above the minimum required (Carvalho and Souza, 2010; Tabak et al., 2010),[71] along with reducing interest rates to historical levels (Tabak et al., 2010).[72] On the other hand, authorities had to keep an eye on the monetary aggregates, keeping (always present) inflationary expectations under control.

One of the main lessons arising from the latest crisis relates to the relevance of local actors in dealing with the crisis (Sobreira and Paula, 2010), along with the institutional maturity shown by the financial system (Mesquita and Torós, 2010) and the renaissance of public banks (Sobreira and Paula, 2010; Tabak et al., 2010). SOBs' participation in credit operations had been increasing since 2003, although what became decisive in

investors were prohibited from investing in mutual funds and private bonds as well as operations with options (Prates and Farhi, 2015).

69. Some measures were undertaken by the BCB in 2007, well before the outbreak of the international financial crisis. Thereafter, Brazilian authorities introduced a battery of measures, including active participation in the U$ dollar futures market, introduced to minimize supply shortages. The swap agreement reached with the US administration (29 August 2008) became another important measure in the previous direction (Moreira and Torós, 2010).
70. Although scarcely used by banks in order to avoid be signalled as under stress (Mesquita and Torós, 2010).
71. With 18.2% SOBs showing the highest margin requirement compared to other financial institutions, including private domestic banks (15.2%) and foreign owned banks (11.7%).
72. The Brazilian banking industry historically showed important levels of non-performing loans (NPLs), which might eroding system security. However, and despite the crisis, NPLs diminished in recent years, reflecting a level of 3.4% in June 2008. In comparative terms, SOBs present a lower number of NPLs, a performance that denotes a different lending profile (Tabak et al., 2010).

transforming private agents' mood was the role played by the public banks during the crisis ('Mutually Assured Existence', *The Economist*, 13 May 2010).[73] Regulatory changes were also important in the equity market, as the CMV passed a series of reforms directed at shielding firms from systemic risks posed on future operations. The Brazilian NMC introduced new legislation (Resolution N 4373/14) aimed at increasing foreign investors' legal status (Russo and Oliveira, 2015).

Authorities introduced a tax on financial transactions (IOF), which is levied on foreign exchange, securities or bonds, credit and insurance transactions. As foreign inflows resumed and became massive at the start of 2011, the government during the third quarter began to raise this tax to avoid BRL appreciation. To summarize, the crisis did not reverse prior [pro-liberalization] rules, and some financial risks would remain practically undealt with. The Brazilian financial sector is highly complex and most of it is profoundly integrated into world markets. This could be very beneficial, and indeed it might be, but it also leaves an ample room for regulatory arbitrage. The problem becomes more acute in the Brazilian context because coordination between regulatory agencies is far from good (Holanda Barbosa, 2014).

Financial Trilemma in Brazil

As introduced in Chapter 3 of this book, banking regulation remains key in Schoenmaker's financial trilemma: in the presence of cross-border funding, local authorities are incapable of guaranteeing financial stability. What is astonishing in the Brazilian case is that, although regulatory tools remained on the local regulators' side and regulations on banking flows were tough, local agents' international assets remained large. As previously observed, the Brazilian financial system presents a highly complex configuration, with participants in the FX market beyond local regulation.

Despite the relevance of foreign banks, local legislation in Brazil prevents cross-border arbitrage – at least, in the traditional sense. In particular, Brazilian laws prohibit deposits in foreign currency – and, thus, prevent non-residents from holding FX spot positions as observed in other countries (as in Argentina). A second and related explanation of why Brazilian banks were not severely affected by the GFC, lies in the conservative financial practices followed by the local regulator (i.e. by limiting cross-border flows) and reinforced by some foreign banks which opted for funding locally (see Chapter 3).

73. The expansion after the crisis benefited, in particular, three state-owned banks: Banco do Brasil (a listed commercial lender with a bias towards agriculture), Caixa Econômica Federal (a mortgage specialist) and the BNDES. The latest figures give these three banks a share of 42% of the assets in the Brazilian financial system. As observed in China, state-owned banks' expansion abroad remains incipient, basically 'near abroad' (Fernando Ferrari Filho, 'Brazil's response: How Did Financial regulation and Monetary Policy Influence Recovery?' *Brazilian Journal of Political Economy*, 31, no. 5 (Special edition 2011): 880–88; 'Mutually Assured Existence', *The Economist*, 13 May 2010; Rogerio Sobreira and Luiz Fernando de Paula, 'The 2008 Financial Crisis and Banking Behavior in Brazil: The Role of the Prudential Regulation', *Journal of Innovation Economics* 2, no. 6 (2010): 77–93.

The crisis, after all, hardly affected non-financial firms, particularly big-and-internationalized Brazilian ones – which were highly active in the FX derivative market, relying on highly complex financial instruments (Dodd, 2009).[74] But this practice came to alter the waters in the financial realm. Instead if relying on hedging to manage ER risk, they used (derivatives) for speculative purposes – betting against local currency appreciation (Dodd, 2009; Kregel, 2011). Once the crisis arrived and the real appreciation trend reversed, financial bets left local companies almost in bankruptcy, forcing them to enter into a vast restructuring process (Zeidan and Rodrigues, 2013).[75] Thus, and despite the practices being adopted in the realm of financial regulation, 'the operation of derivatives markets and in particular offshore derivatives market have created instability, in both the financing of firms, but also in the financial institutions themselves and in the exchange rate' (Kregel, 2011, p. 857).

As previously noted, arbitrage is intense in the derivative market as FX futures have become a leading reference to the Brazilian market. According to Rossi (2014), important loopholes in the regulatory front were key in explaining this: in contrast to *spot markets*, where only specialized institutions could participate and that are closely scrutinized by the regulatory agency, operations in the Brazilian *futures markets* remain less restrictive, whereas participant entities are weakly regulated. This regulatory bias, however, is ineffective in preventing markets from interconnecting or preventing FX's arbitrage. As previously noted, the presence of important restrictions on FX conversion forces arbitrage to be indirect (an NDF onshore market, and a derivable offshore market). By regulating the onshore market, the government is reducing arbitrage possibilities and market liquidity with it – but also transferring liquidity to the spot market (Rossi, 2014).

Foreign banks were central in the development of the futures market, and certainly they were key actors for their international connections (Prates and Farhi, 2015; Gallagher, 2015[76]). Banks are the only financial entities which benefited from the NMC to operate in the inter-banking market and, thus, to intermediate between Brazilian residents and non-residents.[77] Non-residents, in contrast, had had unrestricted access to the foreign exchange futures market since January 2000. Consequently, and from a legal perspective, they would enjoy similar rights to their Brazilian counterparts. Unfortunately, similar legal treatment would not be available for Brazilians abroad, as the Sadia/Aracruz case came to demonstrate (Gorga, 2015). In particular, both companies were confronting private

74. Among others the so-call Sell Target Forward (STF) contract.
75. Sadia S.A. and Aracruz Celulose were among the most-affected local companies, suffering billion dollar losses and leaving them almost bankrupt (as they were heavily participating in the futures market).
76. Ten banks controlled almost 80% of the FX derivatives market, but half of the market is controlled by just four: Deutsche Bank, Citigroup, Barclays and UBS (Gallagher, 2015, p. 77). Not only did banks intervene as dealers but also some of them were involved on their own account: Santander (with 60 firms as clients), Unibanco (33 firms), and Itaú (96 firms) (Kregel, 2011, p. 856).
77. As previously observed, local legislation prevents FX bank deposits. Therefore, in order to have access to short-term external credit lines in the international interbank market and to hold FX

litigation in the United States and Brazil, yet only American investors were able to obtain financial recoveries.[78] Moreover, as noted by Gorga (2015), the legal implications of the approach adopted after *Morrison v. National Australia Bank Ltd.* would have far-reaching consequences, eventually affecting the settlement of class actions in other jurisdictions or limiting foreign firms' benefits for participating in the American Deposit Receipt (ADR) market. The same author highlights, 'the fact that investors holding securities from the same companies suffered similar damages but were subject to such distinct legal remedies raises efficiency and fairness concerns for international securities markets' (Gorga 2015, p. 137).

Although prudential measures had been observed in the market since 1994 (Dodd and Griffith-Jones, 2007; Prates and Farhi, 2015), the crisis increased the demand for market transparency (Farhi and Zanchetta Borghi, 2009).[79] The government introduced a series of measures to tackle the transparency issue, including the issuance of new accounting rules.[80] Furthermore, and in order to gain in transparency, monetary authorities made mandatory the registration of financial derivatives linked to foreign loans. Private banks had also moved to increase market transparency, establishing the Centre for Exposure in Derivatives (CED) (Prates, 2014).[81] Whereas in the past, Brazilian OTC markets operated with no collateral requirement or standards (Dodd and Griffith-Jones, 2007), a transaction clearing and settlement scheme has been recently introduced which, under specific circumstances, acts as a central counterpart.[82]

In sum, the derivatives market risks opening the door to evading regulation, a challenge that neither CARs nor MPRs were originally designed to tackle. In the case of Brazil, and given the NDF characteristic of OTC contracts, non-financial agents and banks could circumvent the prudential objectives – which, for example, arise in the event

---

positions (in US$ dollars), banks need special authorization: an authorized dealer status. Only 17 banks are in this category, most of them MNC entities (Prates and Farhi, 2015).

78. Federal securities class actions were filed in New York (against Sadia S.A.) and Miami (against Aracruz Celulose S.A.). In brief, the US courts settled a large suit against Sadia ($ 27,000,000) and an even larger one against Aracruz ($ 37,500,000), sums accruing to US investors. Brazilian investors, in contrast, not only were not compensated but also (indirectly) bore the financial costs imposed by US courts. The US Supreme Court's decision in Morrison v. National Australia Bank Ltd. (2010) would alter the transnational securities litigation scenario by expanding the scope of the American legislation abroad (protecting local investors) yet limiting the issuance of claims in US territory (affecting foreign investors).
79. As, for example, CMN Resolution n 2042, enforcing actors to register their (swap) operations either at BM&F or at the CETIP.
80. In order to advance in data dissemination, the CVM promulgated Statement 475/08 and Resolution 566/08. The commission also intervened in the design of new accounting rules.
81. The CED lists the positions of companies that are registered with CETIP or BM&FBOvESPA, and that have voluntarily adhered to the system. It is worth noting that only the regulators have access to the data in the system, and that although participation is voluntary, the CED records cover 90% of the registered contracts in Brazil (http://www.bmfbovespa.com.br/en-us/bmfbovespa/download/BEST-BRAZIL.pdf).
82. Regardless of whether a settlement takes place in a guaranteed or in a non-guaranteed environment, the settlement model used in Brazil ensures the use of the strictest principles of

of an increase in the IOF tax. If contracts are disrupted, the highly interconnected character of this market calls for inter-jurisdictional cooperation to avoid unequal transfers between investors.[83] Inter-jurisdictional problems cannot be left to the market nor left in the hands of local authorities but rather call for cooperation. Those entering into a similar contract (securities–FX derivatives) should face the same (company-specific) risks 'instead of pure legal risk, diminishing the ability of companies to engage in legal arbitrage at the expense of a specific group of security holders' (Gorga, 2015, p. 179).

Brazil: No Longer an Institutional Outsider?

In spite of the magnitude of FDI inflows and a clearer definition of what Brazilian authorities expected from foreign investors in terms of its impact on national development, Brazil stands out for its active resistance to various aspects of post–Second World War foreign investment protection and liberalization initiatives. First, it never ratified the Washington Convention of 1965 (the ICSID Convention), which established the basis for an international framework for the resolution of investment disputes by way of international arbitration between individual foreign investors and host country governments. Secondly, Brazilian national FDI legislation maintained several important exceptions to national treatment of foreign investment and legal provisions for compensation in the event that expropriation did not wholly meet the commonly accepted international practice of 'prompt, adequate and effective' compensation. Thirdly, Brazil negotiated 14 BITs during the pro-FDI period following the fall of the Berlin Wall in the 1990s,[84] although it never ratified them, mainly because of the risks associated with the IA-ISDS clauses.[85] Fourthly, Brazil negotiated the two fundamental foreign investment agreements of the Southern Market (Mercosur) integration scheme, one covering investments by Mercosur members (Colonia Protocol) and the other those of non-members (Buenos Aires Protocol), but never ratified either of them. Finally, Brazil actively opposed several

---

delivery versus payment (DvP). This scheme is essential to eliminate the principal risk, thus avoiding the possibility that any of the parties involved in the transaction might be at risk of not having fulfilled their obligations, being deprived of the acquired right as a result of the counterparty having failed to meet its own obligations (http://www.bmfbovespa.com.br/en-us/bmfbovespa/download/BEST-BRAZIL.pdf).

83. This might be particularly acute when more than one type of investor (local and foreigners) participates in the market, and they are subject to different legal responses. In particular, this problem arises when two reasons are present: On the one hand, one of the jurisdictions may be biased in protecting buyers (investors), whereas the other tends to favour those issuing the contract (firms). On the other hand, whereas theoretically all investors independently of their type can present claims, only local investors can initiate class actions.
84. With industrialized countries, such as Belgium/Luxembourg, Denmark, France, Finland, Germany, Italy, the Netherlands, Portugal, Switzerland and the United Kingdom, and others, like Chile, Cuba, Republic of Korea and Venezuela.
85. For the members of Congress, it was inappropriate to grant foreign investors the right to settle investor–state disputes via international arbitration while this was not available to national investors.

aspects of the US RTA-like Free Trade Area of the Americas before its suspension in 2004 because it considered the initiative to be asymmetrical and to contain undesirable constraints on Latin American and Caribbean countries, including the proposed IA-ISDS procedures. In particular, its refusal to participate in the ALCA initiative can be explained by the stringent conditions introduced by the United States on the financial front, banning any sort of control on capital flows (Pudwell, 2003).[86] As a result of these actions, Brazil is not involved in any known ISDS investment disputes and carries virtually no IIA risks.

In sum, Brazil is a country that has demonstrated a welcoming approach to FDI and has accumulated a significant stock of inward FDI, thereby increasing its integration into the global economy. At the same time, Brazil has used its increasing negotiating strength, which derives in part from its attractiveness to TNCs (its large market and growing economy), to implement cautious policies that carefully limit or reduce to a minimum its IA-ISDS risks with respect to IIAs.

Rejection, however, could remain with the past autonomy (of being outside the BITs framework. Whereas the Argentinean traumatic experience with foreign investors (in the aftermath of the 2001 crisis) reaffirmed the Itamaraty's old stance, the expropriation of Petrobras/Bolivia in 2006 signalled a turning point for authorities at the Foreign Affairs Ministry to reconsider the investment treaty policy (Perrone and Cerqueira César, 2015). Interest rose as Brazil continued to gain relevance as a(n emerging) capital exporter, and as it increased its political credentials among developing countries and emerging economies.

In line with this new role, the Brazilian Foreign Office has recently begun to sign a series of investment agreements with Angola, Mozambique and Malawi – and maintained negotiations with others: Algeria, Morocco, South Africa and Tunisia. In contrast to traditional BITs, Brazil 'novo modelo de acordo de investimento' (new template/model of investment agreement) signed with African countries presents a peculiarity (IISD, 2015): a joint committee, where officials from the involved countries would be authorized to debate, monitor and expand the original contract.[87] An executive office would control directive/joint committee initiatives, including a leading role in dispute settlement. If disputes between parties cannot be resolved amicably, then an international judiciary instance is open: state-to-state schemes, which prevent private actors from directly suing sovereign states. The inclusion of a social responsibility chapter also differentiates these new agreements from traditional ones, as it tries to differentiate EMEs' TNC practices (mainly, those of older Chinese SOEs operating in Africa) from the common malpractices of MNCs – particularly Chinese involvement in Africa (Ana Garcia, 2015).[88] In sum, the

86. The signature of the FTA agreement with Chile could have worked as guidance, as Chile was forced to accept free movement of capital and rescind its former policy on the matter, which was included in all BITs signed by the country.
87. 'Side-by-side comparison of the Brazil-Mozambique and Brazil-Angola Cooperation and Investment Facilitation Agreements' (IISD, June 2015).
88. 'O Novo Acordo de Cooperação e Facilitacao do Investimento entre Brasil e Moçambique: algumas considerações' Departamento de Relação Internacionais da PUC Minas/grupo potencias medias'.

Brazilian approach remains quite different from the widely expanded neo-liberal template associated with property rights respect but focused instead on 'consolidating economic relations with its partners and establishing political mechanisms to promote FDI' (Perrone and Cerqueira César, 2015, p. 2.

The Itamaraty historical approach, however, might soon be abandoned if the new government maintains its bet on political redemption. Following a putsch, and in order to maintain himself in office, Michel Temer is dismissing Brazil's strategic attitude towards foreign investors. As those at power remain focused on buying time and avoiding impeachment, so they are willing to offer important concessions to investors interested in going ahead with agricultural projects in the Amazon[89] – including foreigners.[90] Similarly, authorities are now backing oil investments in the Amazon Reef, the environmental consequences of which remain highly contested.[91] Finally, the government is proposing to eliminate all former restrictions on land acquisition by foreigners – in fact, a very attractive notice for foreign investors, particularly the Chinese.[92] Although most of the measures will bring real capital to the depressed economy, all of this financial capital flows could put the country's short-term development in jeopardy. If finally all these changes are undertaken, the Brazilian economic structure will be shaken and the government's decisional power will be resented.

89. As, for example, ruralists. With a large number of representatives in the Congress Deputy Chamber (230 seats out of 513), this group advocates for less lenient laws for agricultural works in the Amazon (see 'Temer Pushes Amazon Deforestation Bill in Brazil', *FT*, 18 July 2017).
90. This new legislation might find opposition from another group of foreign investors: Norway (see 'Norway Issues $1bn Threat to Brazil over Rising Amazon Destruction', *The Guardian*, 22 June, 2017).
91. 'RPT-Total's Plans for Brazil's New Oil Frontier Snagged on Amazon Reef', *Market News*, 12 May 2017.
92. 'Brazil to Lift Limits on Foreigners' Owning of Land', *Business News*, 25 May 2017.

Chapter Seven

CHINA

From Mao to the GFC: The Comrades' Macro

When Comrade Mao Zedong and his communist forces arrived to power on 1 October 1949, a new country emerged – in a year which would certainly leave a hallmark in China's history (Naughton, 2007). Almost thirty years later, in December 1978, the Communist Party of China (CPC) decided to take the initial steps of a new long march, now towards a more balanced and successful economic model that entailed breaking with some traditional communist practices, including a closer association with the global economy in the form of international trade and foreign investment.[1] Economic transformation, however, would not erode the central role played by the public sector in the economy nor CPC influence. Nevertheless, sooner rather than later the country adopted an open policy towards foreign investors, although under a gradualist approach, transforming the country into one of the principal recipients of FDI (UNCTAD, 2008b).[2] Foreign investment, in turn, became massively involved in transforming the (mostly backward and agrarian) country into the world's leading export platform.[3] Both FDI attraction and export promotion become the drivers of China's exceptional growth, a path characterized by the simultaneous presence of commercial and capital account surplus.

Whereas FDI inflows were highly incentivized, other flows became certainly much less. Portfolio and foreign debt flows would definitely remain unimportant during the

---

1. The meeting of all China Communist Party (CChP) members (the so-called third plenum) at the 11th Central Committee on December 1978 initiated a new era for the country, including the return of Deng Xiaoping as a leader.
2. By 2005, the PRC was receiving annual FDI inflows of US$ 70 billion. It is important to notice that the bulk of the FDI originated in Asia, particularly from Hong Kong, Japan, Korea, Taiwan and Singapore.
3. China's cautious FDI policy originally focused on restricting FDI to the cheap labour export assembly activities in the special economic zones, for the most part reserving the domestic market for domestic companies or limiting it to joint ventures of foreign companies with local partners. For foreign investors, activities in the PRC were defined as prohibited, restricted, permitted and encouraged. MNCs were originally prevented from commercializing production in the countryside. In terms of country of origin, most funds were coming from the region, particularly from Hong Kong. However, FDI was subject to approval, and was later registered with both the planning and the foreign trade department of the government. After entry into the WTO in 2001, China's FDI rules became more liberal in the sense that they encouraged more activities and fewer restricted activities were maintained, and eventually 75% of all foreign companies were wholly owned foreign companies.

whole transformation process.[4] During the initial years authorities always prevented convertibility in the local currency, including important limitations on the purchase of FX by domestic importers.[5] The central government somewhat liberalized the FX regime in 1994, giving room to RMB convertibility, although on a partial basis and fiercely maintaining foreclosed capital account movements. When some timid proposals (from within the government) advanced towards the opening of the capital account, the Asian crisis persuaded authorities on the menaces posed by financial liberalization. Consequently, Chinese authorities followed a 'selective opening' strategy for the capital account (Prasad and Wei, 2004; Yu, 2010), keeping China away from market volatility.

On the monetary front, certainly a repressive model accompanied gradualism, with the government ever fixing interest rates and having an outstanding role in credit allocation. During the first years monetary authorities relied on quantitative-based instruments such as RRs in order to control monetary aggregates – certainly this tool remains highly relevant for those in charge of monetary policy. State participation in bank credit and low interest rates faced by productive firms remain key in explaining China ascension. Thereafter authorities began to introduce some flexibility in interest rates, but credit policies remain differentiated (PBC, 2010).

The persistence of a repressed financial model, in turn, validated a boom (loosen) and burst (tightening) monetary cyclical pattern, reflecting an inflationary bias in the economy. Certainly pressures were initially relevant, but after several failed attempts monetary authorities tamed inflation spurs in 1996 (Naughton, 2007).[6] Relaxation in credit policy as observed during booms would make banks expand, whereas a burst recurrently would force the central government to rescue them.[7] During the decade spanning from 1998 to 2007, average interest rate was fixed at 3.0 per cent per year, or 2.1 per cent in real terms.

Financial repression began to be dismantled, albeit timidly and sequentially. Some financial institutions were new but others were (re)created during the Republic period, making markets increasing relevant. Interbank money and bond markets were created in the late 1980s, whereas in the early 1990s the government decided to constitute the stock exchange market: first Shanghai (1990), and later Shenzhen (1991). Thus, stocks markets were tightly controlled at the beginning and both remained poorly connected to the real economy. However, in order to expand the interbank money market, People's Bank of

4. The policy might be expressed as 'welcome to FDI, but no thank-you to foreign debt and portfolio flows' (Prasad and Wei, 2004, p. 453).
5. To qualify for FX, domestic buyers first had to be eligible to import. For licensed imports, enterprises had to first obtain a license, whereas for non-licensed imports, SAFE approval was based on a 'priority list'.
6. Reformism did not preclude this cyclical pattern of high inflation and sectorial bottlenecks followed by retrenchment and slower growth, as peaks were observed in 1978, 1984–85, 1992–94 and 2003–5.
7. State ownership proved rather inefficient in allocating credits (Prasad and Wei, 2004), particularly contributing to the highly level of NPLs observed in the 1990s but slightly curtailed in the 2000s. In 2005, the NPL ratio was close to 5%, and even higher in 2010.

China (PBoC) authorities started to liberalize both the offered and the repo rate, granting markets greater leeway in bond pricing.[8] Also during the nineties monetary authorities decided to introduce OMOs, basically to control market liquidity (Yi, 2008). In sum, in 1996 the PBoC embarked on an interest rate liberalization reform although prioritizing deregulation of (a ceiling on) lending rates over that of (floors for) deposit rates.

In terms of ER policy, China maintained a differentiated regime until 1994, basically aimed at protecting local production from foreign competition. Until this date, the local currency remained inconvertible, in a strong sense. Afterwards, China decided to leave behind the differentiated scheme and set the RMB with the US dollar at a rate of about 6.8 yuan per dollar, a de facto fixed ER policy that lasted for more than a decade – a policy highly criticized by the American government for being 'mercantilist'.[9] Pegging, however, permitted Chinese monetary authorities to stabilize the national economy, acting as a nominal anchor in reducing economic agents' expectations (it might be remembered that, during this entire period the capital account remained closed). A stable environment, in turn, laid the foundations for an investment-cum-export-led growth model. The monumental increase in industrial production and the rapid rise of exports reflected the success of the model, generating a tremendous current account surplus. In July 2005, authorities introduced a new scheme by which the RMB would be determined by a basket of currencies (but the US dollar maintained its relevance).

Thereafter, monetary sterilization operations transformed into a crucial instrument to prevent financial volatility – although exhibiting some negative signs. Certainly, strong controls might be considered vital to explain the prolonged success of the ER pegging (at least, in theory). Yet in practice the picture was more nuanced, as the country became increasingly exposed to capital inflows – including speculative ones. This led Chinese authorities to act: by raising reserve requirements (Kawai and Lamberte, 2010)[10] or by beginning to sell central bank bills (CBBs) to commercial banks (Yongzhong, 2009; Yu, 2010).[11] Thus, by allowing for more (exchange rate) flexibility, the PBoC automatically expanded its policy space. Flexibility was also considered as helping monetary authorities in dealing with carry trade operations, to the extent that one-sided FX movements might be prevented. Further arguments for a more flexible FX arrangement were related to the costs and limits posed by sterilization policies. Exogenous forces were also observed, as they envisioned Chinese pegging as a modern mercantilism regime.

8. In 1998, the China Development Bank (CDB) issued the first market-priced policy bond, and, a year later, government bonds began to be issued through open bids (Asia Focus, 2014).
9. As, for example, supported by Dooley, Flokerts-Landau and Garber (2004) but also in articles by P. Krugman (2010a), 'Chinese New Year', *New York Times*, 1 January; and (2010b), 'China's Swan Song', *New York Times*, 11 March.
10. Reserve requirement were mainly introduced after 2005 in order to contain sterilization costs, as interest rate began to rise.
11. For Yu (2010), sterilization operations were truly successful as the broad monetary base (M2) has been in line with the needs of economic growth. Sustainability is in doubt, however, as the scheme has increased the share of low-yield assets in commercial banks' portfolios.

In relation to the capital account, the third axis in the triangle, authorities have always managed on a prudential basis. This posture does not imply an ideological vision: Chinese authorities have always envisioned an international role for the RMB. And, in order to achieve that, an open capital account becomes a necessary condition – at least from a theoretical perspective. Political ambitions, however, were always calibrated. The Asian financial crisis in 1997–98 brought to the attention of Chinese authorities all the vulnerabilities accompanying CAL policies. As China acceded to the WTO in 2002, however, authorities reintroduced the process with enthusiasm but did not set aside their suspicion (as referred to in the institutional section). Thereinafter, and after carefully taking into account all the hazards involved in this journey, Chinese authorities decided to advance. But they did so on a sequential basis. Constraints (affecting the capital account) continued to (slowly) ease, as when the government adopted a policy of *difficult in and easy out* aimed at loosening controls on capital outflows, indirectly benefiting the newly adopted *going global* strategy. After the passing of the qualified foreign institutional investors (QFII) scheme in December 2002, foreigners were authorized to invest in the local market. Some years later, the government introduced the qualified domestic institutional investors (QDII) scheme, granting local investors the possibility of maintaining portfolios in foreign currency-denominated assets. In both cases, conditions to participate were highly restrictive, at least at the beginning.[12] At the same time, control over cross-border capital inflows had become more tenuous since 2003, as domestic agents obtained access to new external sources of credit, including the surge in equity inflows (Yu, 2010).[13]

What did this (timid) liberalization movement reflect? On the one hand, and to a certain extent, the movement indicates the increasing inflationary pressures being confronted by authorities, particularly since 2004 when important overheating signs appeared.[14] With more options abroad, economic agents' decisions were now reducing pressure on the RMB (avoiding an appreciation bias). Greater de facto openness also reflected the losing power of capital controls as the government could not effectively isolate trade-related flows from the mounting flows of capital that continuously arrived at China's shores. But, on the other hand, this partial opening of the capital account would become instrumental in the increasing international role to be played by the RMB (see below).

A combination of stable ER, increasing trade surplus and large FDI inflows permitted international reserves to grow, and exponentially: from US$ 186.3 billion in 2000

12. Foreigners were allowed to invest in A shares, although funds were locked for one year, which was later shortened to three months. In order to qualify, investors were forced to exhibit prior experience and assets under management of at least $10 billion – to be reduced to $5 billion in September 2006. Local investors could invest abroad only through permitted brokers (qualified investment banks, security firms and insurance companies).
13. This relates to the issuance of IPOs by local enterprises in overseas stock markets, particularly on the Hong Kong Stock Exchange (HKSE)
14. The authority in charge of fixing the exchange rate policy is the State Administration of Foreign Exchange (SAFE), in cooperation with the PBoC. SAFE is the successor of the State General Administration of Foreign Exchange (SGAFE), an agency created in 1979 within the Bank of China to supervise all inflows and outflows of foreign exchange.

to US$ 1.53 trillion in 2007. Thus, and at aggregate level, the rise of China (export-led growth) coupled with its strategy of accumulating US bonds in order to prevent the RMB from appreciating (exchange rate policy) has contributed to generating the present global imbalance, a vision shared by an important group of policymakers, certainly with great support in US political circles.[15] However, increasing FX reserves began to raise concerns about monetary and inflation stability. Confronted with this vision, and conscious of the important costs imposed by the potential growth in money aggregates and prices, the government decided to continue with the sterilization game. Sterilization could certainly be managed by central authorities because the state-controlled financial system helps in reducing inflationary pressures at home, immunizing China against the US 'dollar weapon' (Helleiner and Kirshner, 2013). In any case, reserve accumulation also adds inflationary pressure that explains why the PBoC has historically criticized hoarding.[16] Yu Yongding is certainly one of the leading advocates of this latest position, supporting the idea that reserve accumulation represents a greater misallocation of resources.

China, the Global Financial Crisis and RMB Internationalization

In order to minimize the effects of the GFC, China started an ambitious stimulus package (around RMB 4 trillion), almost half of it financed by the central government and with the banking system channelizing nearly all of the funds to public investments (Lardy, 2012; García-Herrero and Santabárbara, 2013).[17] Additionally, the PBoC reversed previous tightening measures, including a reduction in benchmark interest rates as well on the reserve requirement ratio – basically introduced to favour the real demand for loans (Lardy, 2012).[18] The GFC also forced authorities to temporarily suspend the flex exchange rate regime introduced in 2004: the *peg* was back. And with it came all the pros and cons of the export-led growth model. The GFC also reinstated the debate over the issue of capital controls, although authorities now preferred to install 'new gates' instead of reinstating the 'old walls' policy. For example, the SAFE begun to think about tightening the management of banks' foreign-debt quotas and introducing new rules on their currency provisions,[19] although shortly before, the same regulatory agency had

15. This explains the interest in declaring the RMB as a misaligned currency (an issue analysed in Chapters 2 and 4).
16. Besides the instability problems, reserve hoarding is criticized because of the low returns associated with US Treasury notes – the main assets in China's foreign reserves.
17. This vast package was directed at improving infrastructure (highways, railroads and airports), and funds for affordable housing, public health and education. Additionally, China introduced an industrial restructuring programme directed at reducing obsolete capacity and at enhancing the use of energy-saving technologies.
18. In order to prevent the economy from forming a bubble in the household market, authorities initiated a series of tightening measures – particularly in the second half of 2007.
19. *Bloomberg Businessweek*, 10 November 2010.

advanced in easing some controls obstructing the debt market.[20] In sum, after the GFC the Chinese economy would prove resilient in renewing growth at home but also in transforming itself into a locomotive for the rest of the emerging world – and, to some extent, for the global economy. Chinese growing power would also emerge in the financial realm, with the PBC signing several swap agreements with both emerging economies and developed countries. The crisis affecting the EU would come to definitively establish China as a challenging new superpower: the G2 was born.

The GFC would also affect the pace of the RMB internationalization process (Stanley, 2013), as Chinese policymakers observed the alarming costs imposed by placing most of their savings in US Treasury bonds. If the idea of an international currency was envisioned from the very start, the previous financial crisis came to convince authorities of the convenience of postponing both (capital account) openness as well as financial market liberalization. Nevertheless, and despite the negative effects introduced by the Asian crisis in the late nineties, authorities resolved to (sequentially) move forward with the internationalization process almost immediately – with Hong Kong playing a leading role in this experiment (Minikin and Lau, 2013).[21] Nor did the GFC cause leaders' enthusiasm with the process to dwindle, as observed by the issuance of the 2009 PBC proposal to accelerate CAL and fully opening the capital account in a decade (PBC, 2012).[22] Finally, in November 2012 government CPC members gathered at the 18th Central Committee meeting decided to accelerate interest rate liberalization as to advance further with the internationalization process – supplementary authorities decided at the 2013 Party Congress to install a financial free trade zone (FFTZ) in Shanghai aimed to promote capital account openness further.[23]

Monetary authorities were extremely cautious in their first movements, certainly, but also decided to maintain the pace. In particular, China opted for a gradual dual-track strategy for RMB internationalization, maintaining a closed capital account at home yet

20. In August 2010, the SAFE allowed offshore banks and foreign central banks to invest in the RMB interbank bond market ('Easing China´s Capital Control', Milken Institute, 29 September 2010).
21. The emergence of Hong Kong as an offshore centre might have to do with political reasons – not just economic causes associated with the pro-market environment observed in this former British protectorate. The island´s economy was not just recovering from the Asian crisis but also from the SARs (severe acute respiratory syndrome) flu epidemic. In order to overcome this situation, Chinese authorities signed a special agreement (closer iconic partnership) and decided to grant more leeway to the HK financial district.
22. The PBoC programme divided the sequencing into three stages (short, middle and long term). In one to three years, in order to encourage the *go global* strategy, authorities would loosen direct controls on investments. In the middle term, loosening would now be on commercial lending and borrowing. Finally, the government compromised to ease regulatory measures on real estates, stocks and bonds. By the end, quantitative should be replaced by price controls.
23. Shanghai FFTZ allows companies and financial institutions settled in the area to invest in Shanghai securities and futures markets, while qualified overseas individuals in the zone may open accounts to trade local securities (Dai Haibo, Director of the Shanghai FFTZ, 'China Inaugurates Shanghai Zone, *Bloomberg News*, 30 September 2013).

Table 7.1 China's response to the GFC

	China's fiscal stimulus package	
Date	Announced at Nov. 2008	
Amount	RMB 4 trillion or US$ 586 billion over two years or 13.4% of GDP	Third world's largest package behind Russia and Saudi Arabia (in comparison to GDP)
	US$173 billion was to be central government spending, with the rest coming from local governments (US$180 billion) and Bank lending (US$233 billion)	Key role played by local government financial vehicles (LGFVs)
Indirect–Financial front	Total net new bank lending also rose, increasing by US$1.4 trillion in 2009, or almost 30% of GDP	Expansion of credit was vital to the success of the plan
Funding	Central government (30%), rest by local governments	
Directed to: Investment-based stimulus package	Infrastructure (70%)	More than two-thirds of the stimulus was allocated to infrastructure sectors, including railways, roads and grids, but also mega-projects as well as for the reconstruction effort for post-earthquake Sichuan (up to 25% of total funds)
	Technology and Environment (20%)	Low-carbon infrastructure was prioritized, with 8000 km of high-speed railway lines and grid modernization projects receiving significant allocations China intends to spend $46.9 billion in stimulus funding on energy efficiency, clean vehicles, grid infrastructure and other clean energy technology
	Social Measures (10%)	Including construction and renovation of cheap houses, and to improve social security and health services
Employment	Infrastructure-related employment has helped mitigate the impact of job losses in export-oriented processing industries	
Industrial Policy	10 sectorial industrial policies set by NDRC	favouring, among others, the steel, auto, textile, light industry, electronics, IT industries

Source: Based on Lardy (2012) and other sources

beginning to relax some operations in some locations abroad – initially in Hong Kong and later in other offshore centres in the region and then expanded worldwide (offshore RMB, thereafter). Few operations were authorized at the beginning, as for example, permitting traders to open special accounts in RMB at HK banks. The offshore market has

Table 7.2 China's onshore and offshore interest rates

	10-3-16	10-3-15	10-3-14	11-3-13
HIBOR – O/N	0.04929	0.06103	0.05959	0.09214
HIBOR 1 week	0.08	0.10929	0.12857	0.09714
HIBOR 1 month	0.23375	0.23857	0.21	0.21714
HIBOR 6 months	0.89529	0.54071	0.55	0.535
HIBOR 1 year	1.26634	0.84214	0.86846	0.845
SHIBOR O/N	1.945	3.35	2.358	2.2315
SHIBOR 1 week	2.282	4.763	2.625	2.998
SHIBOR 1 month	2.666	5.055	5.502	3.422
SHIBOR 6 months	3.016	4.7789	5	4.1001
SHIBOR 1 year	3.0955	4.7483	5	4.4

Source: Own elaboration, based on data from People's Bank of China and Hong Kong Monetary Authority

grown exponentially since then. Several specialized markets in (offshore) RMB are now under operation from stocks to bonds or futures, whereas new financial centres around the world are now operating with red back notes. In short, the RMB is increasingly mastering all the functions an international currency is called on to perform (medium of exchange, unit of account and reserve of value).[24]

As the capital account remained regulated, the RMB internationalization process led to the emergence of two differentiate interest rates: one repaying savers in the local market, and the other being paid to those saving in RMB-denominated financial vehicles in the Hong Kong offshore market – or any other offshore centre currently. The appearance of an offshore market also implied the coexistence of two different ER markets for currency forwards (onshore and offshore). As China continued to leave behind former regulations on the capital account, it became exposed to the real interest rate parity (RIRP) and the possibility for market arbitrage: raising it if macro inconsistency persisted.[25] Consequently, as the process of CAL deepens, economic authorities are being forced to strongly reduce all the gaps observed in these different markets. From this perspective, liberalization has pushed China to lower both the interest and the exchange rate existing market gaps, and thus, to advance towards a more market-based (macro) economy.

To the restrictions imposed by RMB internationalization, one should add the expanding relevance of China's macro policies for other countries' macro decisions. In fact, as trade and financial linkages are permanently widened, a growing number of policymakers in Asia (and increasingly around the world) are beginning to consider interest rate movements in China (Liu et al., 2013; Su et al., 2014). More and more trade and financial linkages are explaining why exchange rate movements in the Asia

24. The RMB is beginning to play the role of anchor currency for an important number of East Asian trading partners, moving away from the US dollar to the Chinese sphere (Stanley, 2015).
25. In particular, exchange rate expectations and interest rates both enter into determining RIRP.

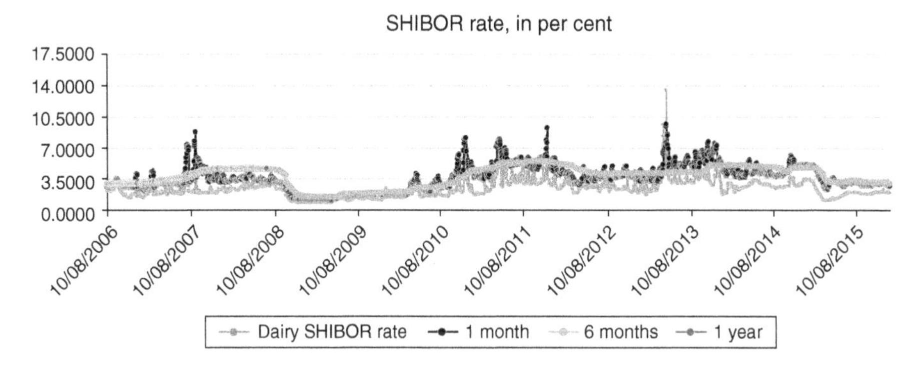

Figure 7.1 Interest rate in Hong Kong and continental China
Source: People's Bank of China and Hong Kong Monetary Authority

region move in tandem with the Chinese RMB rather than the US dollar (Stanley, 2015). The number of nations pegging their currencies to the Chinese RMB is expanding fast. Chinese RMB is also being increasingly used as a medium of exchange and a reserve currency, by both private entities and sovereign states around the world. In sum, by means of internationalizing, the government is widening RMB exposition to market forces it seen forced to advance in liberalizing both interest and exchange rate settings.

RMB internationalization is also pushing China to eliminate, one after another, all former restrictions on the capital account. Until recently, the country observed a myriad of restrictions, affecting both private investors and firms alike. Interested in introducing the RMB into global markets, though, the government has begun to eradicate former controls, benefiting both households and enterprises (Yu, 2010). In order to accomplish this, authorities further advanced with liberalizing funds through the enlargement of both the QDII and the QFII programme. By permitting foreigners to participate in the local market, authorities have tried to boost the (underdeveloped) bond market – although until recently it continued to be dominated by government issuers (Glick and Hutchinson, 2013).[26] China also reversed its former policy (difficult in, easy out) as it proved ineffective in preventing an increase in macroeconomic volatility. Furthermore, in order to maintain hard currency abroad and to control inflationary expectations at home, authorities also lifted former controls on exporters' foreign currency earnings[27] – a movement signalling Chinese firms' global expansion. To sum up, although important

26. Treasury and a reduced group of (policy) state-owned banks were the issuers of almost three-quarters of the bonds quoted at the market. Furthermore, trading remains limited, as banks hold most of the bonds (Glick and Hutchinson, 2013, p. 4).
27. The SAFE started the trial programme on 1 October, allowing 60 exporters in four cities and provinces (Beijing Municipality, Guangdong, Shandong and Jiangsu provinces) to keep their hard currencies abroad ('China Expands Its Easing of Capital Controls on Exporters'. The program was later expanded to the entire nation ('People's Daily on Line 'China to Allow More Exporters to Keep Revenues Overseas', 1 January 2011, http://en.people.cn/90001/90778/90862/7248466.html).

restrictions are still binding, most of the transactions included in the capital account are liberalized.

The GFC somewhat helped Chinese leaders recognize the increasing limitations of the once successful development path implemented after 1978, leaving the investment and external demand model for a new one based on domestic consumption (El-Erian, 2016). Independently of the sources, excess demand (easy mortgage loans inducing a real state market bubble) and overinvestment (mainly associated with bureaucrats at the provincial and the regional level) initiated a career for fixed assets, added new tensions on the monetary front – a soft inflationary bias. Furthermore, as financial repression persisted, non-traditional (and highly unregulated) financial entities (shadow banking) advanced in financial intermediation (see Chapter 3). Tensions were placing the PBoC back into the picture, tightening its monetary policy and also favouring the decision to reintroduce the floating scheme.

In sum, short-term capital inflows are gaining in importance, a trend further reinforced by the government's attitude of easing former controls on capital flows. As the process of RMB internationalization advances, monetary authorities have decided to push the liberalization process even further but also grant markets more room in determining both interest and FX rates.[28] China has also advanced on the FX front, not just by reintroducing some flexibility to the scheme but also by granting markets more room in the exchange rate setting. Among the policies being recently adopted, the PBoC introduced a 'two-way floating process' in order to end the prevalent unidirectional movement of the RMB rate (Sen, 2014) – basically directed at avoiding carry trade operations.[29] More important is the fact that China has left the GFC untouched, as compared with other bigger economies, maintaining 'its creditor status and its provision of balance of payment finance' (Helleiner and Kirshner, 2014).

RMB internationalization would certainly add new macro challenges, risks which some economists consider highly problematic (Gallagher et al., 2014).[30] One of the most uncertain issues facing China since it has opened up, relates to the likelihood of massive capital outflows and the increasing volatility the initiative might introduce on all macro variables (Bayoumi and Ohnsorge, 2013; Zhang, 2014; Arora and Ohnsorge, 2014). Authorities, instead, should maintain the sequencing: advance first with liberalizing both the interest and the exchange rate; continue after that with the reform of

28. Authorities removed all limits on bank lending rates on July 2013. In October 2013, the PBoC began to publish a prime-lending rate – based on the lending rate quotes submitted by nine lending commercial banks (Asia Focus, 2014).
29. In April 2012, monetary authorities decided to widen the (exchange rate) band – from 0.5% to 1%. Two years later it was further amplified to the 2% range.
30. A recent book by Gallagher et al. (2014) introduces a series of articles from leading economists around the world, which presents all the challenges posed by RMB internationalization. Although not necessarily critical of the objective, some of the papers appearing in the book are critical of the PBoC attitude towards the issue. In brief, RMB internationalization is being pushed as an instrument to alienate the national economy under a new growth model based on consumption.

the domestic financial market (including, first, an increasing involvement of the private sector and, thereafter, the adoption of comprehensive macro-prudential policies); and, finally, liberalize the capital account (Zhang, 2014; Arora and Ohnsorge, 2014). China has advanced on the monetary and exchange rate fronts, liberalizing and deepening markets – in the sense that monetary liberalization suggests the search of interest rate convergence.

The process, however, has confronted challenges and tensions, recurrent ups and downs. As recently as mid-2014, and disrupted by a modest fall against the US dollar, the Chinese RMB began to experience a period of financial turbulence – which particularly affected the equity market.[31] As anxiety mounted, citizens took their wealth out of the country, a capital flight process that forced Chinese authorities to direct funds from its FX reserves in order to revert it.[32] If turbulence continues, and the RMB continues to depreciate, Chinese officials might have few options: continuing to use their FX reserves, reversing the opening process, reinstalling more tight controls on capital flows movements, and letting the market settle the ER.[33] Reserves are certainly not finite, and it remains a strategic asset – one that is not solely explained by economic factors (Steinberg, 2014).[34] In other words, although monetary authorities can deplete some funds in order to stop a (non-fundamental) fall in the market's prices, nobody in the central government would accept a huge lose of reserves in order to return to a massive speculative attack in the FX market.[35] A devaluated RMB, However, it would certainly shock the global economy and, henceforth, raise worldwide tensions (El-Erian, 2016). This left the Chinese government with just one policy option: to reinstall capital controls or to postpone the opening process. In this sense, it should be remembered that Chinese leaders have always prioritized economic stability, a condition that guarantees them the possibility of maintaining power (Cohen, 2012). In other words, as authorities continued with the RMB internationalization process and advanced with the opening of its capital

31. As problems increased and the stock plunged, the Chinese government intervened the market – for the first time in August 2015. As tensions on economic fundamental persisted the market continued to experiment strong swings, which led authorities to introduce a new mechanism (known as a circuit breaker) directed at halting trade when losses reach a threshold (Keith Bradsher and Amie Tsang, 'Stock Markets Shudder after Chinese Stock Plunge Forces a Trading Halt', *New York Times*, 6 January 2016).
32. From June 2014 to the end of 2015, China's FX reserves diminished by at least US$ 700 billion – with $ 108 billion in just one month (December) ('China's Forex Reserves Drop by Record $108bn in December', *FT*, 7 January 2016).
33. 'Capital Flight Is at the Core of China's Dilemma', *FT*, 13 January 2016.
34. According to Steinberg (2014), reserve accumulation is characterized by a conflict between different political factions. Among supporters are those favouring the export-led growth model, whereas those at the PBoC criticize this policy as one in which FX accumulation is favoured by exporters (permitted to maintain a depreciated ER) because it adds to inflationary pressures. Support is also seen among those at the lower levels of government, as reserves could be used to solve economic mismanagement in several areas – for instance, recapitalizing insolvent banks.
35. Chinese officials are well aware of the deterrent effect of reserves, which are key in the effort to stabilize the FX rate.

account, this has left China's monetary and exchange rate policy options increasingly constrained, as Nobel laureate R. Mundell predicted 50 years ago.

Chinese Financial Markets: A Brief History of the Chinese Banking Industry

Under Mao's regime the PBoC performed monetary policy functions, although it also acted as a commercial bank.[36] China's financial system began to be transformed after the 11th National People's Congress in 1978. The creation of four state-owned banks became one of the initial measures undertaken by the new government: the Agricultural Bank of China (ABC), the Bank of China (BOC), the Construction Bank of China (CBOC) and the Industrial and Commercial Bank of China (ICBC).[37] PBoC functions were decoupled two years later, with commercial activities being funding by the ICBC, and the PBoC transforming itself into the official central bank with responsibility for monetary policy and financial system supervision. Financial regulation lay with the PBoC until the early nineties when the government decided to separate the regulations: securities (China Securities Regulatory Commission, 1993); insurance (China Insurance Regulatory Commission, 1999); and banking (China Banking Regulatory Commission, 2003), whereas the State Council was in charge of coordinating the four entities (three regulatory commissions plus the central bank). When observing the vast transformation undertaken by the Chinese financial system, we can see that the results of institutional progress are amazing (Garcia Herrero and Santabárbara, 2013).[38] The relatively lengthy process of interest rate liberalization has, however, provided leeway for China's banking sector to improve (Asia Focus, 2014).

Overall, the banking system was, and remains, the main source of financing in China. The banking model comprises a multiplicity of competing large, medium-sized and small local banks, most of them state owned. Legally, this collective was transformed in 1995 following the enactment of 'The PRC Commercial Bank Law'.[39] The law also implemented a market-based scheme for credit allocation, pushing SOBs to operate as

36. In those days the PBoC controlled almost four-fifths of all bank deposits and provided 93% of all loans. Following the founding of the PRC, communist authorities dismantled both the stock and the insurance market.
37. China's 'big four' composition in 2009 was as follows: (1) ICBC: government of China 70.7%, H-shares 13.4%, foreign strategic investors 7.2%, A-shares 4.5%, other domestic investors 4.2%; (2) CCB: government of China 57.02%. H-shares 25.22%, foreign strategic investors 10.95%, A-shares 3.85%, H-shares held by domestic firms 2.96%; (3) BOC: government of China 70.79%, H-shares 26.65% and A-shares 2.56%; (4) ABC: Ministry of Finance 50% and Huijin (state-owned company) 50% (although this composition altered after the 2010 IPO; see previous footnote).
38. In the banking sector, regulatory changes involve changes in asset quality (a five-tier credit classification system introduced in 2002, which was further transformed later, in 2005 and 2009), bankruptcy procedures, regulatory capital (2003 Basel I, 2008 Basel II) and supervision.
39. Prior to this, in 1986 the government enacted the 'Provisional Regulation on the Control of Banks', the first sectorial regulation in post-Mao China (Luehr, 2011, quoted at Rana, 2012).

commercial entities with accountability for profits and losses. Market competition was further strengthened in the late 1990s, when the government implemented a four-tier system: the first covering new commercial banks,[40] the second comprising state-owned policy banks, the third including pro-development banking[41] and the fourth related to SOEs, local enterprises and local governments.[42] The Asian crisis and the resulting economic meltdown increased the number of Chinese banks' NPLs, (affecting up 30 per cent to 50 per cent of the loans), and the possibility of a domestic crisis was one of the main concerns among Chinese officials (Yu, 2010).[43] This led to a governmental bailout and,[44] after a series of frustrated recapitalization attempts, the decision to restructure the banking industry. The crisis also alerted authorities to the necessity for further reforms – including the above-mentioned institutional movements (Rana, 2012, p. 221).

A new process of corporate reform and financial restructuring was initiated a decade later, including the transformation of SOBs into state-controlled joint-stock commercial banks (JSCBs).[45] In parallel, they advanced with privatization, a process beginning with the public listing of the Bank of Communications (BOCOM).[46] From then on, the

40. Shanghai Bank, Shenzhen Development Bank, Guangdong Development Bank and Everbright Bank were among the new entities. A new wave of commercial banks started in the late eighties, when they began to expand like mushrooms.
41. CDB, Agricultural Development Bank of China (ADBC), the Export-Import Bank of China (EIBC), and the Bank of China (BCI foreign currency bank) (CBRC, 2011).
42. Additionally, the Postal Savings Bank of China (PSBC). With more than 37,000 branches on its own, the PSBC has played an important role in expanding the banking system in every corner of the country.
43. Authorities scale down the problem by injecting capital and writing-off NPLs from banks' balance sheets – transferring them to newly created asset management companies (AMCs). The process lasted for more than a decade: in 2009 authorities finally decided to roll over 10-year AMC bonds for a similar period – now with an explicit guarantee from the Ministry of Finance.
44. Despite those measures, banks continued to suffer further loan losses (i.e. NPLs), forcing Chinese authorities to increase the bailout. A major injection of money occurred in 2004, benefiting two big state-owned banks (Construction Bank of China (CBC) and the Bank of China (BOC)), and two years later aid went to the ICBC.
45. The first initial public offerings (IPOs) were introduced in 2005. By the end of 2008, there were 14 Chinese banks publicly listed (3 City Commercial Banks (CCBs) created by restructuring and merging urban credit cooperatives] and 11 State-Owned Commercial Banks (SOCBs) and Joint-Stock Commercial Banks (JSCBs)). Banking equity involves different types of shares: (1) class A, which are only allowed to be held by Chinese residents, (2) class H, for those traded at Hong Kong and (3) class B for foreigners (Stanley, 2011; Alicia García-Herrero, Sergio Gaviláy and Daniel Santabarbara, 'China's Banking Reform: An Assessment of its Evolution and Possible Impact', *CESifo Economic Studies* 52, no. 2 (2006): 304–63, doi:10.1093/cesifo/ifl006.
46. 'Domestic Duties', *The Economist*, 13 May 2010. BOCOM raised US$ 2 billion at the IPO. Shortly thereafter, in October 2005, CCB obtained US$ 8 billion. In June 2006, BOC raised US$ 10 billion in capital, followed soon by ICBC with US$ 22 billion. The last 'big' of the Chinese commercial banks to be listed was ABC, which raised US$ 22.1 billion in July 2010. Listings also involved small and medium-sized rural financial institutions, a path initiated by the Chongquing Rural Commercial Bank in December 2010 (CBRC, 2011).

Table 7.3 Chinese banking system, ratios and performance

	RMB 100 million					
Institution / Year	2008	Returns	2012	Returns	2014	Returns
Banking Institutions						
Total Assets	CNY 631515.00	0.9%	CNY 1336224.00	1.1%	CNY 1723355.00	1.1%
Total Liabilities	CNY 593614.00		CNY 1249515.00		CNY 1600222.00	
Total Owner Equity	CNY 37900.00	15.4%	CNY 86708.00	17.4%	CNY 123132.00	15.7%
Profit after taxes	CNY 5833.60		CNY 15115.50		CNY 19277.40	
Policy Banks and the CDB						
Total Assets	CNY 56454.00	0.4%	CNY 112174.00	0.7%	CNY 156140.00	0.7%
Total Liabilities	CNY 52648.00		CNY 106647.00		CNY 148704.00	
Total Owner Equity	CNY 3806.00	6.0%	CNY 5527.00	13.3%	CNY 7436.00	14.5%
Profit after taxes	CNY 229.80		CNY 736.30		CNY 1079.60	
Large Commercial Banks						
Total Assets	CNY 325751.00	1.1%	CNY 600401.00	1.3%	CNY 710141.00	1.3%
Total Liabilities	CNY 306142.00		CNY 560879.00		CNY 657135.00	
Total Owner Equity	CNY 19608.00	18.1%	CNY 39522.00	19.1%	CNY 53006.00	16.8%
Profit after taxes	CNY 3542.20		CNY 7545.80		CNY 8897.50	
Joint-Stock Commercial Banks						
Total Assets	CNY 88337.00	1.0%	CNY 235271.00	1.1%	CNY 313801.00	1.0%
Total Liabilities	CNY 83924.00		CNY 222130.00		CNY 294641.00	
Total Owner Equity	CNY 4414.00	19.1%	CNY 13142.00	19.2%	CNY 19161.00	16.8%

Table 7.3 (*cont.*)

	RMB 100 million					
Institution / Year	2008	Returns	2012	Returns	2014	Returns
Profit after taxes	CNY 841.40		CNY 2526.30		CNY 3211.10	
City Commercial Banks						
Total Assets	CNY 41320.00	1.0%	CNY 123469.00	1.1%	CNY 180842.00	1.0%
Total Liabilities	CNY 38651.00		CNY 115395.00		CNY 168372.00	
Total Owner Equity	CNY 2669.00	15.3%	CNY 8075.00	16.9%	CNY 12470.00	14.9%
Profit after taxes	CNY 407.90		CNY 1367.60		CNY 1859.50	
Rural Commercial Banks						
Total Assets	CNY 9291.00	0.8%	CNY 62751.00	1.2%	CNY 115273.00	1.2%
Total Liabilities	CNY 8756.00		CNY 57841.00		CNY 105954.00	
Total Owner Equity	CNY 534.00	13.7%	CNY 4910.00	15.9%	CNY 9318.00	14.8%
Profit after taxes	CNY 73.20		CNY 782.80		CNY 1383.00	
Rural Cooperative Banks						
Total Assets	CNY 10033.00	1.0%	CNY 12835.00	1.3%	CNY 9570.00	1.3%
Total Liabilities	CNY 9381.00		CNY 11796.00		CNY 8732.00	
Total Owner Equity	CNY 653.00	15.9%	CNY 1039.00	16.6%	CNY 838.00	15.0%
Profit after taxes	CNY 103.60		CNY 172.20		CNY 125.50	
Urban Credit Cooperatives						
Total Assets	CNY 804.00	0.8%				
Total Liabilities	CNY 757.00					

(*continued*)

Table 7.3 *(cont.)*

	RMB 100 million					
Institution / Year	2008	Returns	2012	Returns	2014	Returns
Total Owner Equity	CNY 47.00	13.2%				
Profit after taxes	CNY 6.20					
Rural Credit Cooperatives						
Total Assets	CNY 52113.00	0.4%	CNY 79535.00	0.8%	CNY 88312.00	0.9%
Total Liabilities	CNY 49893.00		CNY 75521.00		CNY 83270.00	
Total Owner Equity	CNY 2220.00	9.9%	CNY 4014.00	16.3%	CNY 5042.00	16.5%
Profit after taxes	CNY 219.10		CNY 654.00		CNY 829.80	
Non-Banks Financial Institutions						
Total Assets	CNY 11802.00	2.4%	CNY 32299.00	2.6%	CNY 50123.00	2.5%
Total Liabilities	CNY 9492.00		CNY 26194.00		CNY 40384.00	
Total Owner Equity	CNY 2310.00	12.3%	CNY 6105.00	13.5%	CNY 9738.00	13.0%
Profit after taxes	CNY 284.50		CNY 825.50		CNY 1265.20	
Foreign Banks						
Total Assets	CNY 13448.00	0.9%	CNY 23804.00	0.7%	CNY 27921.00	0.6%
Total Liabilities	CNY 12028.00		CNY 21249.00		CNY 24832.00	
Total Owner Equity	CNY 1420.00	8.4%	CNY 2555.00	6.4%	CNY 3089.00	5.8%
Profit after taxes	CNY 119.20		CNY 163.40		CNY 179.20	
New type rural financial institutions & Postal Saving Banks						
Total Assets	CNY 22163.00	0.0%	CNY 53511.00	0.6%	CNY 70981.00	0.6%

Table 7.3 *(cont.)*

	RMB 100 million					
Institution / Year	2008	Returns	2012	Returns	2014	Returns
Total Liabilities	CNY 21942.00		CNY 51712.00		CNY 67972.00	
Total Owner Equity	CNY 221.00	2.9%	CNY 1799.00	18.9%	CNY 3009.00	14.2%
Profit after taxes	CNY 6.50		CNY 340.70		CNY 427.30	

Source: Own elaboration after CRCB data

assets of the Chinese banking system kept on growing, eclipsing Americans' competitors and transforming banking global league tables.[47] SOBs are certainly protected from international competition at home.[48] The banking system also greatly benefited from the latest stimulus package introduced by the government to deal with the GFC.[49] Meanwhile, some Chinese entities decided to go abroad – although the process remains barely extended.[50] Foreign banks' presence, in contrast, became active starting in 2002, after the entrance of banks from Taiwan, Province of China; South Korea; and Hong Kong SAR.

47. 'China's Banks: Great Wall Street', *The Economist*, 8 July 2010; 'Domestic Duties', *The Economist*, 13 May 2010. The Chinese banking industry involves more than 5,600 financial institutions, holding assets for 78.8 trillion yuan ($ 11.54 trillion) in 2009 (*Chinese Banks Have Become World Class Institutions*, Thomas White Global Investing, BRIC Spotlight Report, February 2010). Among the top 10 biggest banks by market capitalization in December 2012, four were Chinese: the Industrial and Commercial Bank of China (ICBC) (first) displaced Bank of America to become the world's biggest bank by Tier-1 capital (which is mostly common stock and retained earnings), followed by CCB (second), BOC (seventh) and ABC (eighth) ('World's Biggest Banks', *The Economist*, 13 July 2013).
48. The big two banks of China have over 15,000 branches each, against a few hundred owned by foreign firms. Henceforth, this latest group has a small market share of 2% of total assets ('World's Biggest Banks', *The Economist*, 13 July 2013,
49. The government package totalled 4 trillion yuan, about 601 billion US$ dollars ('China's Banking Regulator Urges Structural Reforms', *Global Times*, 24 October 2010). In sectorial terms, the PBOC directed banks to provide additional credit to 10 key sectors, including infrastructure projects, public facility management, communication and transportation, real estate, postal service, warehousing, and environmental protection (PBC, 2010).
50. As of the end of 2010, China's fabulous five had set up 89 branches and subsidiaries abroad, but they also acquired or invested in 10 foreign banks (Garcia Herrero and Santabárbara, 2013, p. 161).

Securities markets were reintroduced in the early 1980s, experiencing a definitive transformation when the government decided to install the Shanghai Stock Exchange – SSE (1990) and Zhengzhou Stock Exchange – ZSE (1991).[51] Additionally, the market has followed a classical boom-burst pattern – whose latest crash had worldwide consequences.[52] Market segmentation is a distinctive characteristic of the stock market, however, as regulations maintain different listing segments. After the 2015–16 turbulent events, and in attempt to advance towards more transparency, the market regulator (China Securities Regulatory Commission; CSRC) introduced new rules.

The boom pattern observed in the stock market was induced by the government, as authorities considered it as the 'best place to make the "China Dream" come true' (G. Li and H. Zhou, 'The Systematic Politicization of China's Stock Markets', *Journal of Contemporary China* 25, no. 99 (2016): 422–37). Toward this end, the CSRC loosened its regulation, inducing individuals to bet on the market and trading stock with debt. But, and despite the crisis, the relative small size of the market impeded the transformation of the large share-price fall into a threat ('The Stockmarket's Collapse Kicks Up Political Fallout for Xi Jinping', *The Economist*, 26 August 2015.

In view of the scale, the interconnectedness and the complexity of Chinese banks, the sectorial regulator decided to further advance with the implementation of 'higher standards for banks whose degree of systematic importance is relative large' (CRBC, 2014). An enlargement of the shadow-banking system could result in a side effect of this disclosure. In relation to the activities, since the enactment of the first Commercial Bank Law in 1995, commercial and investment banks have been separated.[53] Yet, 10 years later Chinese authorities began to introduce a series of pilot schemes integrating both activities (Loechel, Packham and Li, 2010).

---

51. Besides the two mentioned, four other futures markets are important: the Zhengzhou Commodity exchange, the Dalian Commodity Exchange; the Shanghai Futures exchange and, the China Financial Futures Exchange.
52. The turbulence began on mid-June 2015 and ended in early February 2016. During this period, the A-shares on the Shanghai Stock Exchange lost a third of their value. Major events, however, occurred in one single day: the so-called Black Monday, in July 2015 ('The Causes and Consequences of China's Market Crash', *The Economist*, 24 August 2015; Jennifer Duggan, 'Chinese Stock Markets Continue to Nosedive As Regulator Warns of Panic', *The Guardian*, 8 July 2015). The turbulence shocked financial markets worldwide, becoming a trending topic at 2015 IMF annual meetings of finance ministers and central bankers (Anatole Kaletsky, 'China is Not Collapsing', Project Syndicate, 12 October 2015, https://www.project-syndicate.org/commentary/why-china-is-not-collapsing-by-anatole-kaletsky-2015-10).
53. Separation followed the bankruptcy of two Trust and Investment Companies in Hainan and Shenzhen, which massively redirected deposits into stock markets and real estate speculation.

Managing the Financial Trilemma

Institutions are key in managing the financial trilemma, either to prevent or to induce its appearance. From a policy perspective, Chinese authorities have always kept regulatory measures on pace with the government's macroeconomic and developmental objectives (Bell and Chao, 2010). In particular, officials shielded the domestic financial system from capital inflows by both limiting the entry of foreign banks[54] and maintaining important convertibility restrictions on the foreign currency transactions by domestic financial institutions.[55] Likewise, the government banned local settled banks from raising funds abroad for lending onshore. Prudence was also observed by those in charge of stock market regulation, preventing foreigners from entering until very recently.[56] This led to market segmentation, with shares being differentiated into shares for domestic investors (A shares) or foreign investors (B shares), for local firms listed in Hong Kong (H shares) or on the New York Stock Exchange (N shares). In addition, A shares could be further differentiated into three subsets: state shares, legal persons shares or public individual shares. In contrast to deregulatory trends which were in vogue, banking authorities decided to dismantle the universal banking model during 1994 reforms, prioritizing a traditional banking industry oriented towards creating '*liquidity for customers through the acceptance function*' (Liang, 2012). The regulatory framework helped, certainly. The limited exposure (to international financial markets), and the companying resilience during the GFC, would be difficult to explain if capital controls are left in the discussion.

In sum, Chinese authorities followed a conservative approach on the regulatory front, which contributed to shielding commercial banks from contagion from the past as well the latest financial crisis. The government also made important advances on the prudential front, which helped ameliorate the governance of the financial system, including harsh control on banks' lending practices to real estate markets (BCRC, 2011). Authorities also raised the capital adequacy ratio for JSCBs from a previous effective 5 per cent level to an actual 11.4 per cent.[57] Along with a set of new dynamic provisioning requirements,

54. The Rules Governing the Equity Investment in Chinese Financial Institutions by Overseas Financial Institutions states that 'the equity investment provision of a single overseas financial institution in a Chinese financial institution shall not exceed 20 per cent, and the activities shall be granted the approval of the CBRC, and operates under its regulation and supervision' (China Banking Regulatory Commission; CBRC, Order of China Banking Regulatory Commission (No. 6, 2003)).
55. The inconvertibility prevents offshore banks from making foreign currency loans to Chinese companies.
56. It was on 7 January 2011 that the government granted approval to JP Morgan and Morgan Stanley to enter the country's domestic securities market ('Hope over Experience: Foreign Investment Banks Are Allowed a Toehold in the Chinese Market', *The Economist*, 13 January 2011).
57. Although China accepted international standards, only a small part of state-owned banks and some shareholding commercial banks met the 8% capital ratio requirement in 2003 (He and Fan, 2004). Actually, all 239 commercial banks met the capital adequacy requirement (Liang, 2012). The percentage above (11.4%) corresponds to the weighted average capital adequacy ratio of commercial banks by the end of 2009 (PBC, 2010).

the regulator implemented new leverage and liquidity requirements (CBRC, 2011). An important improvement is also noticeable in banks' staff, which are becoming more prepared to face competition and more receptive to introducing new financial products.

Thirty years ago, the financial system in China was, without doubt, an example of a repressed and underdeveloped system. At the end of 2010, it ranked among the 'big four' in the top world league, and eighty-fourth in the world's top 1,000, and yet most of its main earnings are coming from a local basis.[58] Also, at the end of 2010, the total assets of China's banking institutions increased by RMB 15.8 trillion, with total assets of almost RMB 100 trillion (CBRC, 2011). Despite the local bias, however, some Chinese leading banks are gaining global relevance and, henceforth, becoming listed as SIFIs.[59] What is more shocking is to observe Chinese banks' after-tax figures for 2008/09, and compare them with those of leading TNC banks (Liang, 2012).

Although China advanced in deregulating its local financial system, monetary authorities were extremely prudent in opening its market to foreigners. In particular, and despite China's market-access commitments at the GATS, global banks penetration remains minimal. Furthermore, and as previously noted, important restrictions on capital flow movements have kept cross-border flow at bay (Liang, 2012). Foreign bank assets are minimal compared with total bank' assets observed in the country. The maintenance of a relatively autarkic banking system permitted authorities to avoid being entangled in the financial trilemma. However, the financial sector is going global, and fast. How Chinese authorities will confront with the challenges posed by the (financial) trilemma remains an open question.

Institutional Development: Third World Leader Transformed into a Globalizer Champion

In the time of Deng Xiaoping, China remained an autarky – an option which had as much to do with China's reaction to colonial practices as with Marxist ideology.[60] For

58. Despite the relevance acquired by the Chinese banks, their attitude towards internalization became extremely cautious. For instance, although local banks generated 22% of their 2009 pre-tax profits outside mainland China, most of this was from Hong Kong and Macau. ICBC, which has shown the most expansionist instincts, derived only 4% of profits from abroad ('Domestic Duties: CCB, China's Second-Biggest Bank, Exemplifies The Size of the Task at Home', *The Economist*, 13 May 2010).
59. The following Chinese banks are on the latest FSB G-SIB list: Agricultural Bank of China, Bank of China, China Construction Bank, Industrial and Commercial Bank of China Limited (http://www.financialstabilityboard.org/wp-content/uploads/2015-update-of-list-of-global-systemically-important-banks-G-SIBs.pdf).
60. By way of the Nanjing Treaty in 1842, a weak China was forced to sign a series of unequal treaties that resulted in a complete loss of control over vital aspects of its relationship with the international economy, particularly import tariff policy. China was forced to open five port cities (Xiamen, Guangzhou, Fuzhou, Ningbo and Shanghai) to foreign investments and international trade, and it was even forced to maintain a British citizen as the head of customs from 1863 until 1908. A year later (1843), it was the turn of the United States and France, which condemned China to sign similar humiliating treaties, whereas 1858 would become the time of

this reason, the PRC's opening to foreign investment in 1978 can be considered so dramatic but it also suggests why the adopted FDI policy was so cautious, evolving slowly based on China's own experience of linking foreign investments directly to national goals defined in the national development strategy. In the past 30 years, the PRC has progressively opened up investment to foreigners and, consequently, received voluminous FDI inflows. From an institutional perspective, China opted for a proactive insertion, prioritizing gradualism over shock.

International investment treaties progressively gained in importance, in tandem with PRC's proactive FDI policy. Enthusiasm, however, did not mean a non-critical adoption of external rules. Chinese authorities were aware of their bargaining power in dealing with other governments and foreign investors. In 1982, China became a signatory of the International Centre for Settlement in Investment Disputes (ICSID) Convention, although it formally joined it (entered into force) on February 1993. In 1988, authorities also decided to accept membership in the World Bank's Multilateral Investment Guarantee Agency (MIGA). The first BIT was signed in 1982 with (the Kingdom of) Sweden, which allowed China to later become an active player in this scheme. In fact, the Chinese government transformed into one of the most enthusiastic adherents to the scheme, which encompassed 130 bilateral agreements (UNCTAD, 2015). The FTA signed with Pakistan in 2009 initiated a new institutional era, which nowadays is flourishing, where investment-related aspects are increasingly gaining in relevance (Stanley and Fernandez Alonso, 2015).

The treaties signed by the PRC are quite special and vary considerably according to their date of signature (Rooney, 2007). First-generation BITs extended from the early 1980s to the end of the 1990s were extremely cautious regarding FDI protection and guarantees. Older treaties generally excluded any sort of IA-ISDS provisions, preventing foreign investors from presenting a lawsuit against China until international courts, although some among them included arbitration clauses that permitted investors to discuss the amount of compensation payable following an expropriation (Stanley, 2007; Heyman, 2008; Rooney, 2008).[61] Earliest agreements do not contained national treatment clause or, diffuse when included.[62] The defensive approach began to relax at mid-1990s,

---

Russia. Ironically, the origin of all the conflict was the English addiction to tea, which resulted in the opium wars: in order to avoid an increasing current account deficit, British officials decided to triangle Bengali opium. The British East India Company established a monopoly on opium cultivation in the Indian province of Bengal, where they developed a method of growing opium poppies cheaply and abundantly ('Opium Trade: British and Chinese History'. *Britannica*, https://www.britannica.com/topic/opium-trade) to pay for Chinese luxuries ('The Opium War and Foreign Encroachment', Asia for Educators, http://afe.easia.columbia.edu/special/china_1750_opium.htm).

61. As stated in the notification note, *'the Chinese government would only consider submitting to the jurisdiction of ICSID disputes over compensation resulting from expropriation or nationalization'. Authorities* also delayed the implementation of New York and Washington treaties, which affected the enforcement of any awards (Rooney, 2007, p. 707).
62. Observe, for example, the language used in the China–UK BIT, when parties accept to grant (NT) 'to the extent possible'.

signalling the start of a new generation of treaties (Schill, 2007). New agreements were introducing restricted DS provisions, to finally advance towards unrestricted access after the 1997 BIT signed with South Africa (Hadley, 2013, p. 304). Earlier agreements included a brief definition of investment, generally excluding indirect investments[63] – a concept to be firstly introduced in the 1988 agreement with Australia (Schill, 2007; Hadley, 2013). China's most – favoured – nation (MFN) clause has barely changed, although some minor changes are introduced at FTAs with New Zealand and Canada (Hadley, 2013). The national treatment (NT) clause, by contrast, has notoriously changed over time, reflecting the increasing capital-exporting role played by China (Schill, 2007; Hadley, 2013).[64] The so-called *capital transfer clause* has also experienced a monumental transformation in recent years: whereas originally transfers were subject to 'a party's law and regulations', China now accepts freer capital movements – not just to avoid conflicts with foreign investors but also increasingly to prevent third (host) countries from blocking Chinese firms' repatriation transfers (to their home country). The capital exporter role assumed by China is also transforming the expropriation clause, prohibiting (after the BIT signed with Mauritius in 1998) both direct and indirect expropriation (Hadley, 2013). Similarly, whereas earliest agreements referred to 'compensation', new investment treaties are clearer in addressing the standard of compensation (Schill, 2007). Finally, the 1988 BIT signed with Australia became the first to include a transparency clause.

A third wave emerged in recent years, when Chinese authorities finally responded to the impasse observed at the Doha Development Round (DDR) (Yunling and Shen, 2011). This new pattern can be observed in the trilateral deal under negotiation with Korea, Japan and other economies from the East Asia and the Pacific region still with countries in the Middle East or in Latin America. This Regional Comprehensive Economic Partnership (RCEP)[65] has been considered as rivalling the US-led TPP.[66] Obviously, the picture has dramatically changed since the election of Donald Trump as the forty-fifth president of the United States, which has allowed China to take a leading role in the Asia region.[67] All these agreements are under the FTA

63. Investors could own or control a specific asset. An investor could have a 'substantial interest' by means of 'the exercise of control or decisive influence' over an investment.
64. The 1998 Sino–Japanese BIT or the 2000 BIT signed with Botswana were among the first to include the NT clause.
65. The RCEP is a proposed FTA between the 10 member states of ASEAN (Brunei, Burma (Myanmar), Cambodia, Indonesia, Laos, Malaysia, the Philippines, Singapore, Thailand, Vietnam) and the 6 states with which ASEAN has existing FTAs (Australia, China, India, Japan, South Korea and New Zealand). RCEP negotiations formally started in November 2012 at the ASEAN Summit in Cambodia (en.wilkipedia.org).
66. From the perspective of the US government, which scheme will finally prevail will definitively answer the question about whether East Asian integration will be based on US initiatives or led by China (McBride, 2015). According to E. Alden, senior fellow at the Council on Foreign Relations (CFR), the TPP versus RCEP dispute 'has acquired a geopolitical dimension' (quoted at McBride, 2015, blog hosted at the Council on Foreign Relations, cfr.org).
67. According to Edward Alden (Council on Foreign Relations senior fellow), by killing the TPP, 'Trump has just unilaterally given away the biggest piece of leverage he had to deal with the

logic, activism that can be explained by economic or strategic reasons.[68] In particular, China's engagement is directed at gaining leverage in setting the rules of global trade (Zeng, 2010) – and why not? – for those related to investment.

Yet despite the tensions, all the new institutional arrangements (BITs, TPPs) are surprisingly close to the US wording, as observed in the recently adopted definition of investment or by modifying its dispute settlement (DS) clause – narrowing its consent to arbitration (Sauvant and Nolan, 2015).[69] Additionally, Chinese negotiators included a new clause allowing 'states to derogate from the duties they would otherwise be compelled to abide, provided certain circumstances occur', to be applicable in different circumstances (as, for example, when the economy is under financial stress). Also worth mentioning is the restricted meaning granted to the indirect expropriation clause in new agreements signed by China (Sauvant and Nolan, 2015).[70] In sum, the institutional evolution might be reflecting the increasing relevance of China as a global exporter rather than a receiver of capital (Schill, 2007; Hadley, 2013).

China's global expansion strategy has also led authorities to sign new investment agreements (basically FTAs) with developed nations.[71] From a legal perspective, investment chapters have been skipped in most signed agreements, nor is the ISDS scheme considered by the totality of them; instead, some are fixing a WTO DS-type scheme.[72] As a capital-exporting country, but as a huge internal market for multinationals' appetite, negotiators push partners to open their economies (benefiting Chinese firms' entry), although maintaining tough conditions at home (preventing foreign firms' entrance). This asymmetrical treatment can be observed in the recently signed Sino–Canadian Foreign Investment Promotion and Protection Agreement (FIPPA), and has been denounced by legal specialist Gus Van Harten – as a new type of 'North–South' relationship, with Canada performing the role of supplier of raw materials (Van Harten, 2014).

Another deal involving a developed partner is the proposed EU–China bilateral investment agreement (EU–China BIA), certainly, a challenging task for those in charge

---

biggest challenge in the world of trade, which is the increasingly troubling behavior by the world's second largest economy, China'.

68. In particular, at the negotiation table Chinese leaders obtained the inclusion of special provisions granting China market economy status – like Australia – at bilateral negotiations, China has often use its leverage to obtain the market economy status (MES).
69. The new agreement specifically excludes certain business transactions (particularly some financial related transactions) from the definition of qualified investment.
70. Similarly, more recent treaties consider that 'deprivation of property (through) measures taken in the exercise of a state's regulatory powers as may be reasonable justified in the protection of the public welfare [...] shall not constitute an indirect expropriation' – as observed in the China–New Zealand FTA – Annex 13; the China–Peru FTA – Annex 9; or the China–India BIT.
71. The list of actual partners includes Hong Kong, Macau, Taiwan, ASEAN 10, Chile, Costa Rica, Pakistan, Peru, South Africa Customs Union, Switzerland, Iceland, New Zealand, Australia and the Gulf Cooperative Council (GCC). Authorities are actually negotiating agreements with India, Colombia, Maldives, Georgia and Moldova.
72. As observed in the FTAs signed with Pakistan, Singapore or the GCC.

of negotiations.[73] Launched in 2012, the deal becomes a priority for both sides.[74] Seen as an opportunity to increase FDI flows (which actually are minimal) on both sides. For European negotiators, the agreement is basically directed at improving market-access guarantees – as China's access investment rules continue to highly discriminate against foreigners (Godement and Stanzel, 2015; Ewert, 2016). Market access is not an issue for Chinese negotiators, as the EU is already open to foreigners – including those coming from the Middle Kingdom. Whether negotiators are able to expand the ISDS scheme remains doubtful, particularly as scepticism is shared – certainly, few foreigners would be interested in pushing the issue further (Godement and Stanzel, 2015). Pushing Chinese authorities to assume further liberalization commitments (at both the pre- and the post-investment phases) remains difficult (Bickenbach, Liu and Li, 2015). The importance of the agreement is more political, instead, for two different reasons, one internal and the other external. As observed in the case of RMB internationalization, the agreement gives more leeway to those favouring a new accumulation model with markets having greater space in economic decision (Zhang, 2015). From an external perspective benefits accrue for those Chinese firms investing abroad, particularly in developed countries. By obtaining an agreement with the EU, however, Chinese negotiators gain leverage at another negotiation table: the one dealing with recognizing market economy status (MES) for China (Bickenbach et al., 2015; Ewert, 2016).[75]

Institutions and China's Commitments

A savvy attitude at the negotiation table permitted China to attract foreign investors while avoiding been caught in exorbitant claims. The maintenance of tough regulations preventing capital from freely flowing shielded China's financial markets from an international crisis. A highly restrictive norm still prevents foreign banks from expanding their local market share. The following paragraphs explain this performance.

China's banking commitments made under the GATS established a gradual opening scheme from 2002 to December 2006. When the five-year transitional period was culminating, market expectations mounted as the schedule prevented that any 'non prudential

73. Chinese negotiators would prefer a different kind of agreement: an FTA (Godement and Stanzel, 2015).
74. The proposed agreement replaces all previous ones (mostly signed in the 1980s and 1990s). From a political economy perspective, multiplicity grants China a greater bargaining advantage vis-à-vis individual European countries.
75. China joined the WTO in 2001 through its Protocol of Accession, in which the country committed to a series of obligations that should theoretically lead it into a market economy. After joining the Protocol, other country members were allowed to consider China as a Non-Market Economy until the end of 2016. In a nutshell, those countries which recognize China as a market economy would have a fewer antidumping investigations than those that are still treating Beijing as a Non Market Economy: this is the key reason of why the Chinese Government has been campaigning vigorously since 2001 to gain a MES status by a larger number of its economic partners. Whether prices are determined by market forces or the government has some influence on it?

measures restricting ownership operation and juridical form of foreign financial institutions, including on internal branching and licenses, shall be *eliminated*' (Crosby, 2008; Rana, 2012).[76] Theoretically, commitments were important and far-reaching (Whalley, 2003; Crosby, 2008; Yu, 2010).[77] Expectations somewhat vanished once regulation emerged. For instance, the new norm adopted once the five-year transitional period expired, forced foreign banks to enter through subsidiaries instead of branches – a path also adopted by India (see next chapter). Foreign financial entities are also subject to the Chinese Regulatory Banking Commission (CRBC) rule necessitating higher capital requirements for them – a trend being recently followed by the United States and other developed countries (as explained in Chapter 3).[78] In all the cases, limitations and requirements were justified on prudential grounds. Nevertheless, and independent of the fairness of the measures, their effectiveness is not discussed: with a mere 1.73 per cent of China's total banking assets in 2013, foreign banks' participation remains poorly significant.[79]

The foreign strategic investment rules issued by China's Banking Regulatory Commission continue to limit foreign bank participation in the local bank industry to a minority stake: 20 per cent per investor, and an aggregate of 25 per cent.[80] Furthermore, and despite their seat on the board, foreign investors have little or no ability to influence the company's management (Bell and Chao, 2010). China also asserted that some of the actions were undertaken to nurture the country's financial regulatory and prudential measures. Additionally, those interested were banned from entering by the acquiring of existing banks. For instance, as foreigners are prevented from having more than a 20 per cent stake in local banks' capital,[81] they are condemned to build their presence

76. A 'commercial presence' commitment in banking services requires the relevant member to allow banks of other WTO members to be established in their market by constituting a new bank or acquiring state-owned, state-invested or privately owned banks that wish to sell all or part of their business subject only to the limitations that the member has scheduled on market access and national treatment.
77. According to Crosby, China accorded to permit foreign institutions 'to establish a commercial presence in China to supply banking services for deposits, all types of lending, and financial leasing, as well as payment and money transmission services, including credit, charge, and debit cards (including import and export settlement), guarantees and commitments, and foreign exchange/Renminbi trading' (2008, p. 84).
78. Foreign banks are obliged to maintain a minimal capital requirement for every branch or subsidiary they seek to open in the country – the initial amount rose to RMB 1 billion (each subsidiary) or to RMB 100 million (each branch).
79. Local banks are also outperforming foreigners in terms of returns, both on equity (19.2% versus 5.6%) and on assets (1.3% versus 0.5%) (all the numbers correspond to 2013) ('Lenders of Little Resort', *The Economist*, 28 June 2014).
80. As indicated in the notes included at the WTO Committee on Trade and Financial Services, limits on foreign equity participation were expansive, particularly since 2006 (as the five-year gradualism period culminated). As restrictions on foreign ownership remained, the United States and other developed countries complained that Chinese authorities still maintained their stance.
81. Up to 25% for joint foreign investment. In sum, before the GFC, almost 30% of local commercial banks maintained a partnership relation with a foreign bank.

from scratch – implying higher capital requirements for those interested in entering.[82] Foreign banks' operations in local currency are also extremely limited, although the government has recently adopted a series of measures easing the RMB license enforcement (FT, 2014).[83] Leaders' interest in moving forward with RMB internationalization and the greater global role of Chinese banks, without doubt, help explain this latest movement. The approach to the entry of foreign banks undertaken by Chinese financial authorities was not only cautious but also strategic, and certainly did not give foreign banks room for any dream of 'obtain[ing] controlling positions in existing banks, accessing infrastructure and customers through branches or subsidiaries on a level playing field, and in operation independent electronic payment networks' (Crosby, 2008).

Henceforth, and considering China's (apparent) misconduct, a number of WTO members initiated a series of complaints (Raja, 2007; Crosby, 2008). In particular, a dispute arises concerning whether Chinese authorities were rejecting the entry of foreign rivals or whether foreign banks were expecting a unilateral opening from local ones.[84] Developed countries' negotiators have also rejected China's behaviour in limiting foreign banks' domestic operations, which they found contrary to the GATS and beyond the prudential carve-out scope (Crosby, 2008).[85] Restrictions, however, were not challenged until the WTO tribunals.

In conclusion, during China's 'long journey towards development', Chinese authorities managed not to be caught by the hyperglobalization trap.

82. For instance, in order to compete with the BOC (more than 2,690 subsidiaries), HSBC had to expand the number of its branches more than 10 times – by mid-2014 it owned 190 branches ('Lenders of Little Resort', *The Economist*, 28 June 2014).
83. Whereas in the past, foreign banks interested in conducting RMB operations were forced to wait for a period of three years, authorities have recently reduced the waiting period to one year (*FT*, 'China Ease Rules for Foreign Banks', 21 December 2014).
84. The GATS only limits certain restrictive or discriminatory government measures, and does not create rights for foreign firms to invest in particular Chinese banks. The GATS neither compels privately owned banks to sell interest to foreign investors, nor requires full or partial privatization of government-owned services suppliers (Crosby, 2008).
85. For instance, Crosby considers the tension arising from the wrong interpretation of domestic regulation by the Chinese as stated by GATS Article VI. As detailed in Chapter 3, prudential carve-outs are permitted in order to protect 'investors, depositors, policy holders, or persons to whom a fiduciary duty is owed by a financial services supplier, or to ensure the integrity and stability of the financial system' (Crosby 2008).

Chapter Eight

INDIA

Macroeconomics in an Open and Integrated World: Avoiding the Extremes

A number of important things distinguish India from other emerging economies. In terms of population, with 1252 MM (2013) people, it ranks second behind China, but India has demography on its side as youth make up a majority. India, however, still ranks as a relatively poor country, although an active middle class has flourished in recent years. But if something differentiates this country from the rest of the countries being analysed in this book, it is the country's democratic performance, which has never been interrupted since it achieved independence from British rule on 15 August 1947. In this sense, as the world's largest elected democracy, public authorities receive constant scrutiny from its citizens, in contrast to China's autocratic government.

From an economic perspective, and after a brief period of FDI promotion on receiving independence, India established a relatively closed economy with considerable state intervention in industrial policy and multiple controls over private investment. Authorities were implementing a national development strategy characterized as a highly interventionist industrialization model, popularly known as the 'licence raj', which affects both local and foreign investors. The legal scheme introduced by the Foreign Exchange and Regulation Act (FERA) in 1947 (and reformed in 1957) imposed a 40 per cent ceiling on foreign investors' participation in industrial projects, sometimes even preventing TNCs from using their own brands in India (Kumar, 1995). Development, in turn, is internally financed from resources mobilized domestically as the national economy remains inaccessible to capital from abroad (FERA legislation prohibits most FOREX transactions).

On the monetary side, authorities' emphasis has been on generating resources for public investment, whereas a highly repressed model characterized the local financial sector. A close capital account granted enormous policy autonomy for those working at the Reserve Bank of India (RBI), which immunized them against the monetary trilemma. Finally, this highly centralized and substitutive setting installed a pegged exchange rate system that (initially) fixed the rupee value in tandem with the sterling pound.[1] Overall, the model introduced after independence proved satisfactory as the economy exhibited

1. In particular, there was a par value system of exchange rate that fixed the rupee at 4–15 grains of fine gold with the pound sterling working as the intervention currency (Dua and Ranjan, 2012, p. 28).

positive growth rates from 1950 to 1980 – an average of 3.5 per cent growth per year. This is a poor record if net population growth is considered, but outperform the near-stagnant growth performance observed during colonial Rule (Reddy, 2010, p. 97). The inward-looking-cum-centralized model made the monetary policy a servant to *fisc* (Morah, 2009, p. 11), although inflation records were below those observed at Latin American. Nevertheless, by the late eighties the licence raj model began to exhibit signs of deterioration and the country to experience severe (and recurrent) foreign exchange constraints.[2] But the Gulf crisis of 1991 would become a turning point, forcing policymakers to rethink policies. Authorities were now realizing the recurrence of current account deficits, the impossibility of sustaining a fixed exchange rate, and the danger introduced by relying on short-term debt financing to maintain the model alive. India was now short of funds: capital inflows were needed.

The Gulf crisis changed politicians' minds; they finally agree to open the economy. As Reddy (2010, p. 45) comments, 'Policy actions were initiated as part of the overall macroeconomic management, well-coordinated to simultaneously achieve stabilization with structural change.' Consequently, and as a result of the liberalization movement, Indian authorities were now beginning to realize the constraints imposed by Mundell's monetary trilemma.

Avoiding the Corners: India's Cautious Insertion into Global Financial Markets

On the real side, the government introduced a new industrial policy, which included the launching of a price liberalization scheme coupled with an important reduction in external tariffs, which, progressively, began to dismantle the old system. Thus, a gradualist approach would characterize the whole (CAL) process (Bhattacharya, 2006). Indian authorities were also beginning to eliminate controls on the trade channel and to ease former prohibitions on investment flows (Panagariya, 2004; Ahluwalia, 2002) – a timid liberalization in the capital account was initiated, but important restrictions on debt flows were maintained (Shah and Patna, 2004).

Institutionally, the process of current account convertibility ended in June 2000, when the government finally replaced the 1973 FERA by a new scheme: the Foreign Exchange Management Act (FEMA). Thereafter, all transactions were permitted unless expressly prohibited or regulated by the government. Transactions involving the capital account remained highly regulated.[3] Similarly, restrictions on capital outflows were maintained,

2. Another similarity with Latin America's ISI experience is the expansive use of regulations and FX rationing to address foreign constraints.
3. In contrast to trade, investment flows remained highly regulated. Furthermore, authorities opted for liberalized portfolio investments before FDI. Under the FEMA, foreign international investors (FIIs) are entitled to invest in listed shares and convertible debentures, but not to sink investments in some specific sectors. Obviously, foreign investors' participation is subject to a cap, whose ceiling remains attached to a specific sectorial policy.

affecting both householders and local firms massively – at least until the Indian government began to encourage local enterprises to go global.[4]

The cautious approach which was adopted, not only dismantled the repressive model but also simultaneously helped eliminate the automatic monetization of the public deficit that was observed in the past. Consequently, by reducing monetary dependence on fiscal policy, the RBI gained in independence. Furthermore, in order to enhance monetary policy power, authorities decided to move from direct to indirect instruments of monetary control, introducing a set of different market mechanisms for interest rate discovering interest rates (Mohan, 2009, p. 253).[5] For example, they induced financial intermediaries[6] to elucidate rates through their participation in OMOs for government securities.[7] By the same token authorities introduced the so-called Liquidity Assistant Facility (LAF) channel in June 2000, which further aided economic agents in discovering rates on the overnight market.[8] The RBI, however, sequentially implemented liberalization. All those measures permitted the primary market to grow alongside expanding liquidity in the secondary market.

By the same token, monetary authorities gradually reduced the public sector relevance in interest rate determination. From a policy perspective, measures were aimed at installing a new (and different) macro environment, linking money, government securities and FOREX markets (Reddy, 2005; Mohan, 2009). Interest rate liberalization, however, was only accomplished after the government stabilized its balance of payments, not before (Bhatacharya, 2006). The importance given to the process of discovering interest rate was by no means synonymous with inflation targeting nor with the unique policy pursued by the RBI. Indian monetary authorities were interested in ensuring an adequate flow of credit to the economy but were decidedly convinced to combat financial instability. This idea lay behind this 'multiple indicator approach'[9] undertaken by

---

4. Outflow liberalization was basically aimed at encouraging the globalization of national companies, maintaining important restrictions on capital movements for local residents.
5. As expressed by the Chakravarty Committee, 'There does appear to be a strong case for greater reliance on the interest rate instrument with a view to promoting the effective use of credit, and in short term monetary management. Over the years quantitative controls on credit have increasingly borne the major burden of adjustment required under anti-inflationary policies and have in the process given rise to distortions in credit allocations at the micro level' (pp. 161–62).
6. Originally, the RBI was able to participate in the primary auction of government securities, but no longer after 1 April 2006. Independently of their participation, from the start the new regimen implied the end of cheap borrowing for the government: market rates were determining fiscal costs!
7. There are no restrictions on the use of OMOs, yet private agents' willingness to participate in the market has been (historically) minor. Its expansionary use permitted authorities to diminish the role of the cash reserve ratio (CRR) in monetary policy decisions.
8. The LAF is designed to nudge overnight interest rates within a specific corridor, the difference between the fixed repo (injection) and reverse repo (absorption) rates (Mohan, 2009, p. 20).
9. The multiple indicator approach followed since 1998 has a multiple target (money, capital, currency and so on). Monetary authorities were previously attached to so-called 'monetary targeting with feedback' (a slightly different version of the traditional MT approach) with M3 as a nominal anchor, reserve money as the operating target and bank reserves as the operating instrument (Bhattacharya, 2006).

the RBI, in order to balance price stability with economic growth and to prevent the economy from receiving instability shocks caused by large and volatile capital flows that integration into global financial markets would made feasible.[10] Extensive management practices in the monetary realm, in contrast, were possible thanks to the presence of voluminous capital controls and the limited integration into international financial markets reported by India at the time (Khurana, 2007). Henceforth, and overall, RBI authorities exhibited important degrees of autonomy during the CAL process.

As (a relatively small) open economy (although relatively closed in terms of capital), monetary policy transmission is highly dependent on the exchange rate channel. Henceforth, ER regime selection became a hot issue for policymakers. With the liberalization process initiated in the nineties India embarked on a more flexible exchange rate regime, first, by introducing a basket of currencies and, later, by setting a (theoretical) market-determined floating exchange rate scheme.

As the RBI actively participated in the market to prevent extreme volatility and influence the market price, it was rapidly classified by academic circles as a 'de facto' peg.[11] Nevertheless, and despite some punctual interventions by the RBI, since 1993, market forces which were responding to demand and supply conditions have determined the Indian rupee.[12] Exchange rate determination, however, was not blind to external disturbances in capital markets, and isolated episodes of volatility also had an impact. Anxiety affecting the (FX) markets, for example, was observable when the Asian financial crisis occurred, or following the September 11 terrorist attack in the United States, or after the attack on the Indian Parliament on 13 December 2001. Under such circumstances the RBI intervention was crucial to calm the market's operators and restrict FX volatility. Beyond punctual interventions to curb market volatility, movements in the Indian rupee are basically determined by trade rather than capital flows (Dua and Rajan, 2012, p. 58). Remember that India exhibits a structural deficit in its current account.

Intervention in the FOREX market, however, was radically transformed in April 2004 following the introduction of the MSS, a mechanism thought to absorb liquidity and reduce sterilization costs.[13] Authorities further intervened through the use of OMOs plus LAFs. Additionally, to curb pressures on the exchange rate further, the RBI makes use of CRRs. Other market-deepening measures involved the introduction of forward

10. By this time, India's political environment was highly volatile, preventing the RBI to install an inflation-targeting regime (Bhattacharya, 2006, p. 83.
11. Those who tested the *dirty-floating* scheme indicated that the rupee continued to be pegged to the US$ dollar. For Patnaik (2010), the peg remained in force all throughout the 1993–2008 period.
12. Banks, corporations and FIIs are the main players in the FX market – direct intervention has been reduced. In recent years, futures and options have performed as the relevant markets.
13. The excess of FX assets obviously forces the RBI to expand the system liquidity, at least on a partial basis, with the remaining maintained as government securities to be sold on the market. If the government uses this to finance its fiscal expenditures, the amount the central bank could sterilize under this mechanism would be finite. Henceforth, and since April 2004, India has initiated the MSS, which prevents the government from financing its expenditures through the sale of these securities (Chandrasekhar, 2008).

and hedging contracts, basically aimed at managing the market's risks (Dua and Rajan, 2012, p. 49).[14]

In terms of CAL, India's attitude can be described as consensual and cautious in character. Politicians were clever enough to discuss the issue at a highly technical level, a committee of experts, and grant them autonomy and enough time to elaborate the response. After a decade and a half of deliberations, experts' recommendations tilted towards a gradualist (CAL) approach.[15] To sum up, India's gradual path involved the opening of long-term (FDI)[16] over short-term (portfolio) flows, the strict regulation of short-term external commercial borrowing[17] and a gradual liberalization of outflows (Dua and Rajan, p. 135).

On the whole, capital inflows were mainly directed at financing India's current account deficits, as export recipes proved insufficient to finance the mounting increase in imports. Among several sources of external funding, the increasing importance of Indian expatriates' remittances in the capital account proved distinctive.[18] The trend continued thereafter, with liberalization measures facilitating India's stock market renaissance – including benefits favouring FIIs' arrival.[19]

After the Asian crisis, a sequential approach to rupee convertibility was finally established,[20] which was a step-by-step project subject to (moving) ceilings (Chandrasekhar, 2008).[21] Whereas in April 1998 FIIs were permitted to invest in government bonds, the government decided in January 2003 to remove all remaining limitations for participation in the local currency market. Likewise, FIIs' participation in local firms increased to 40 per cent in March 2000 from a previous ceiling of 30 per cent (to 49 per cent a

14. In recent years market turnover augmented considerably, totalizing a daily average of US$ 18 billion in 2007–8 – from a mere US$ 5 billion ten years before (Dua and Rajan, p. 66). Half of the trade is made on the spot market, whereas market shares are split between merchant and inter-bank operators.
15. Experts focusing on the CAL issue released three different reports. The one led by C. Rangarajan, the *Report of the High Level Committee on Balance of Payments*, appeared in 1993 and particularly aimed at correcting the deficiencies observed following the 1991 BoP crisis. Three years later, the first of two reports on capital account convertibility was published, under the direction of S. S. Tarapore, while the last one was finally published in 2006.
16. However, FDI flows continued to be subject to sectorial ceilings, whose values are periodically changed by economic authorities depending on the country's technological needs.
17. Private investors obtained a similar privilege under the Indian Depositary Receipts (IDRs) programme. Under this programme, foreign companies were allowed to list their depositary receipts on Indian stock exchanges and mobilize capital from India (Dua and Rajan, p. 137).
18. To highlight the absence of any sort of sovereign debt programme, multilateral lending (as for example, IMF lending in arrears) is practically null, as it has been the case with foreign aid.
19. Consequently, pension funds as well as other big players began to arrive, receiving permission (to enter) at both the primary and secondary markets. Ceilings were initially settled at 5% for a particular entity and 24% for all FIIs participating in the market (later expanded to 30%).
20. The committee chaired by S. S. Tarapore had drawn up a road map to full convertibility, although the crisis prevented the government from opting immediately for such a policy.
21. Chandrasekhar (2008) offers a complete list of liberalization measures benefiting capital account convertibility.

Table 8.1 Composition of capital inflows to India

Item		1990–91	2000–2001	2010–11	2014–15	
Net Capital Inflows	US$ million	$7,056.00	$8,840.00	$59,738.00	$92,398.00	
1. Non-Debt-Creating Inflows	%	1.5%	76.8%	91.8%	79.6%	$73,561.00
a) Foreign Direct Investment		1.4%	45.6%	39.1%	35.3%	$32,627.00
b) Portfolio Investment		0.1%	31.2%	52.7%	44.3%	$40,934.00
2. Debt-Creating Inflows		83.1%	78.9%	51.4%	18.8%	$17,411.00
a) External assistance		31.1%	4.8%	8.3%	1.8%	$1,630.00
b) External Commercial Borrowing		31.9%	48.7%	19.4%	3.0%	$2,729.00
c) Short-Term Credits		15.2%	6.2%	18.4%	–1.0%	–$924.00
d) NRI Deposits		21.8%	26.2%	5.4%	15.2%	$14,057.00
e) Rupee Debt Service		–16.9%	–7.0%	–0.1%	–0.1%	–$81.00
3. Other Capital		15.0%	–55.0%	–43.2%	1.5%	$1,426.00
		100%	101%	100%	100.0%	$92,398.00

Source: RBI (2016) and Das and Rajan (2012). Based on data from Das and Rajan (2013) and Reserve Bank of India (2016)

year later).[22] As for domestic companies, they were entitled to issue ADRs and Global Depository Receipts (GDRs).[23] By the same token, the government permitted local investors to go abroad, authorizing domestic mutual funds to invest in foreign securities – up to U$ 1 billion in overseas exchange-traded funds for some qualified funds (Reddy, 2009). Consistent with a sequential approach, however, Indian authorities restricted foreigners from participating the market for government securities (Shah and Patnaik, 2004), a decision basically adopted to maintain autonomy over its monetary decision–making process (Chandrasekhar, 2008; 'India and Capital Flows: A World Apart', *The Economist*, 29 October 2009). Analogously, the RBI retained several constraints on foreign currency borrowing by local firms, by fixing both the maturity and the interest rate of the loan, and banning short-term borrowing ('India and Capital Flows: A World Apart', *The Economist*, 29 October 2009). In sum, and despite the above-discussed liberalization trend initiated in the early 1990s, capital accounts remained under control during the whole process – although cross-border flows increased (and significantly) during this period.

22. A legal movement that obviously increases the feasibility of Indian firms being taken over by foreign entities (Chandrasekhar, 2008).
23. Contrary to other EMEs, India's experience with ADRs and GDRs become short-lived as Indian local enterprises maintained the domestic stock market for funding (Shah and Patnaik, 2010) (further details below).

Economic performance in the post-reform period began to show many positive features. Average growth rate put India among ascending EMEs. As the economy kept on growing, domestic demand flourished, whereas a constant increase in the savings rate permitted India to (autonomously) sustain high rates of gross capital formation. Simultaneously, economic authorities advanced on the fiscal front, reducing their financing needs and with concomitant inflationary pressures being recurrently observed in the past. Unfortunately, high commodity prices at international markets kept inflationary expectations alive – as the country is a net importer of oil. On the positive side, expatriate remittances helped reduce the external gap, further reducing the continued expansion of the services sector.[24] This buoyant economic scenario rapidly attracted FDI flows (mainly attached to the information technology (IT industry) but also portfolio investments, funds primarily directed towards bank loans and external commercial borrowing. External debt has not presented a problematic pattern as most of the debt flow showed a long-term horizon. Furthermore, and since 2001–2, India began to build up an important amount of foreign reserves, totalling US$ 309.7 billion on 31 March 2008.[25] Consequently, as previously observed in the aftermath of the Asian crisis, the Indian economy proved resilient to the financial turmoil affecting most developed countries following the Lehman collapse.

Sailing against the Wind: India's Performance after the GFC

As the liberalization trend continued, India's economy became further entrenched in the constraints imposed by Mundell's monetary trilemma. Authorities maintained the path towards CAL while simultaneously granting more relevance to markets in money and exchange rate determination. And the more interconnected, the more exposed to external shocks the Indian economy became. The crisis hit the Indian economy through three channels: real, financial and confidence.

Following Lehman's bankruptcy, the rupee experienced a sharp depreciation against the US dollar, forcing RBI authorities to provide dollar liquidity in order to curb excessive volatility on FX markets (Das and Ranjan, 2013, p. 96). Furthermore, and despite fundamentals, the crisis hit the local stock market as foreign investors suddenly lost confidence in the Indian economy (Chandrasekhar, 2008), with the BSE index falling from a peak of 20.783 points on 8 January 2008 to 8.160 points in March 2009. As inflationary pressures continued mounting, monetary authorities raised the interest rate (RBI, 2010). Trade imbalances grew significantly, as exports recipes plummeted and demand for imports increased. All these factors help explain how the GFC affected the

24. Services were further increasing its relevance, now accounting for more than half of the country's output and becoming an important source of FX. Services expansion has also transformed India into a top FDI destination, transforming its ranking to third, just after China and the United States (UNCTAD, 2005).
25. Compared with other EMEs, India's foreign reserves are not associated with current account surpluses but with excess in capital flows far in excess of the absorptive capacity of the country. In other words, reserves might be better classified as being 'borrowed' not 'earned' (RBI, 2013).

Table 8.2 India's FX reserves

Date	Foreign Currency Assets	Gold	Reserve Tranche Position	SDRs	Total
01-Apr-2016	$ 335,686.6	$ 20,115.0	$ 2,456.3	$ 1,501.9	$ 359,759.8
03-Apr-2015	$ 318,642.7	$ 19,038.0	$ 1,303.4	$ 4,021.5	$ 343,005.6
04-Apr-2014	$ 278,805.8	$ 21,566.8	$ 1,827.0	$ 4,447.9	$ 306,647.5
05-Apr-2013	$ 261,513.4	$ 25,692.0	$ 2,303.9	$ 4,333.7	$ 293,843.0
06-Apr-2012	$ 258,650.1	$ 27,023.1	$ 2,816.4	$ 4,437.8	$ 292,927.4
01-Apr-2011	$ 275,019.0	$ 22,972.0	$ 2,939.0	$ 4,556.0	$ 305,486.0
02-Apr-2010	$ 254,730.0	$ 17,986.0	$ 1,379.0	$ 5,001.0	$ 279,096.0
03-Apr-2009	$ 244,597.0	$ 9,577.0	$ 985.0	$ 1.0	$ 255,160.0
04-Apr-2008	$ 301,394.0	$ 10,039.0	$ 434.0	$ 18.0	$ 311,885.0
06-Apr-2007	$ 193,075.0	$ 6,784.0	$ 459.0	$ 2.0	$ 200,320.0
07-Apr-2006	$ 147,692.0	$ 5,755.0	$ 759.0	$ 3.0	$ 154,209.0
01-Apr-2005	$ 135,262.0	$ 4,500.0	$ 1,437.0	$ 5.0	$ 141,204.0
02-Apr-2004	$ 107,175.0	$ 4,198.0	$ 1,315.0	$ 2.0	$ 112,690.0
04-Apr-2003	$ 71,502.0	$ 3,534.0	$ 666.0	$ 4.0	$ 75,706.0
05-Apr-2002	$ 51,498.0	$ 3,047.0	$ 612.0	$ 10.0	$ 55,167.0
06-Apr-2001	$ 39,962.0	$ 2,725.0	.	$ 2.0	$ 42,689.0

Notes: 1) Foreign Currency Assets excludes US $ 250.00 million (as also its equivalent value in the Indian rupee) invested in foreign currency-denominated bonds issued by the IIFC (UK) since 20 March 2009, excludes US $ 380.00 million since 16 September 2011, excludes US $ 550.00 million since 27 February 2012, excludes US $ 673 million since 30 March 2012 and excludes US $ 790 million since 5 July 2012 (as also its equivalent value in the Indian rupee).
Source: Reserve Bank of India

capital account: the economy saw a sharp decline in portfolio inflows, external commercial borrowings, trade credit and the overseas borrowing of banks (Dua and Rajan, p. 98).

Thus, and in order to stimulate aggregate demand, the government introduced a series of monetary policy initiatives along with advancing with important fiscal stimulus measures (RBI, 2010).[26] From a monetary perspective, authorities were targeting objectives on three different fronts: exchange rate, monetary liquidity and credit supply. In order to curb excess volatility, authorities decided to be actively involved in FX markets (mostly through purchases/sales of the US dollar) (Dua and Rajan, p. 162). Authorities also worked hard to avoid a credit crunch, injecting liquidity into the system (Dua and Rajan, 2013, p. 99). To this end, they cut the policy rate from 9.00 per cent to 4.75 per cent, and the cash reserve ratio from 9.00 per cent to 5.00 per cent. They also started with a series of unconventional measures such as opening refinancing facilities to SIDBI and EXIM banks, and reversing former prudential norms on provisioning and risk weight.[27] The RBI also launched a series of FOREX liquidity measures, such as an increase in the interest rate ceiling on non-resident deposits and the easing of restrictions on external commercial borrowing and on short-term trade credits.

But RBI intervention also aimed at curbing volatility and also maintaining the rupee at a competitive level (the so-called real effective exchange rate; REER) (RBI, 2013). Monetary authorities also decided to negotiate a series of swap agreements in order to avoid stress in the exchange rate markets. However, the country persisted in its cautious approach with regard to capital flows and financial integration (Dua and Rajan, 2013)

The active monetary policy pursued by the US Fed added to EMEs' resilience sooner than later reversed agent's expectations, and portfolio flows were back. In the case of India, between April and December 2009, inflows nearly equalled the accumulated 2000 to 2005 total.[28] This massive inflow affected local ER competitiveness, which led the government to seriously discuss the reintroduction of more stringent capital controls (Chandrasekhar, 2009). Increasing commodity prices were also affecting the economy, as oil imports were becoming more expensive and, henceforth, increasing the country's current account deficit.[29] What made things worse was the sudden increase in gold imports, as private consumers historically demand this precious metal as a store of value. Finally, as a consequence of the stimulus package, the fiscal front was back under stress, and inflationary pressures soon followed. All these factors – an appreciated exchange rate, a mounting current account deficit and the fiscal deficit – placed India among the most vulnerable EMEs to Fed's reversing crisis-era monetary policy. Furthermore, interest rates were high enough prior to the movement, leaving less room for more tightening – although it would increase further the following year. A final remark: external reserves, although important (around U$ 300 billion) were now declining when compared with pre-crisis GDP coverage levels, and, thus, making the economy more vulnerable to

26. The active fiscal policy implemented in the aftermath of the crisis came to challenge prior responsibility norms introduced by the Fiscal Responsibility and Budget Management (FRBM) Act, sanctioned by the Parliament in 2003.
27. Certainly, all these measures were tackling the ER problem, too, trying to minimize the side effects of the crisis on the Indian rupee.
28. 'India Considers Capital Controls', gulfnews.com, 3 May 2010.
29. Since 2006, the deficit has continued to increase, reaching five points of the GDP in 2013.

Table 8.3 Annualized volatility of Indian rupee vis-à-vis major currencies

Year	US dollar	Pound Sterling	Euro	Yen
2016	0.30%	0.86%	0.54%	0.91%
2015	0.31%	0.57%	0.80%	0.57%
2014	0.38%	0.51%	0.51%	0.67%
2013	0.78%	0.79%	0.75%	1.08%
2012	0.62%	0.56%	0.60%	0.79%
2011	0.52%	0.55%	0.68%	0.81%
2010	0.52%	0.65%	0.65%	0.91%
2009	0.60%	0.92%	0.68%	1.11%
2008	0.68%	1.04%	0.97%	1.38%
2007	0.37%	0.49%	0.48%	0.81%
2006	0.26%	0.48%	0.47%	0.49%
2005	0.22%	0.47%	0.52%	0.65%
2004	0.32%	0.64%	0.71%	0.62%
2003	0.14%	0.55%	0.68%	0.53%
2002	0.10%	0.42%	0.57%	0.63%
2001	0.13%	0.54%	0.77%	0.67%
2000	0.15%	0.57%	0.84%	0.65%

Note: Volatility is the standard deviation of per cent changes in exchange rates of Indian rupee 2016, from January 1 to August 12
Source: Das and Rajan (2012) and Reserve Bank of India (2016)

external shocks (Basu et al., 2014, p. 28). As is recognized, a signal can be enough to make investors nervous – particularly for those with positions in the 'fragile five' group which, at that time, included India.[30]

As with the tapering talks that took place from April to August 2013, the rupee experienced a 15.70 per cent depreciation against the US dollar, external reserves diminished by 5.89 per cent and the stock market index declined by almost 10 per cent (Basu et al., 2014, p. 6). In order to avoid further casualties, RBI authorities implemented a series of precautionary measures on the monetary front (such as increasing interest rates[31] or raising the duty on gold imports) in the exchange rate market (intervening to limit ER volatility and prevent overshooting,[32] opening a separate window for oil-importing companies), or affecting the capital account (restricting residents' capital outflows, inducing capital inflows from non-residents). The government also signed a swap-line agreement with Japan (U$ 15 billion), the first and only one for the time being signed by India.[33] Once again, the savvy attitude

30. The other four were Brazil, Indonesia, Turkey and South Africa.
31. The highest level was observed on 15 July 2013 when the RBI increased by 200 basic points the overnight lending rate, leaving it at 10.25.
32. Authorities spent some US$ 13 billion between the end of May and the end of September 2013.
33. Authorities also signed a contingent reserve agreement (CRA), an agreement among BRICs members, with US$ 100 billion of reserves. India could withdraw as much as US$ 36 billion, twice its share in the agreement (Basu et al., 2014, p. 33).

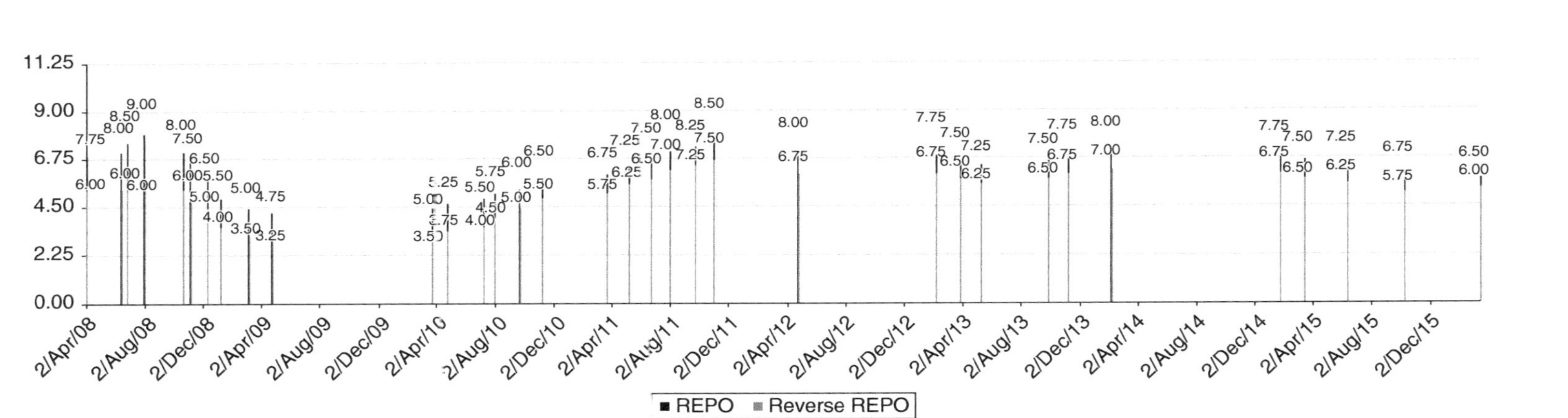

Figure 8.1 India policy rates (repo and reverse repo)
Source: Reserve Bank of India

of Indian policymakers, in particular those at the RBI, paved the way for a soft-landing scenario.[34]

After Raghuram Rajan took office as the twenty-third governor on September 2013, the RBI introduced a series of complementary measures in order to halt investors' pessimism, including an extension of the existing swap agreement with Japan (up to U$ 50 billion) and further incentives in deposits to induce capital inflows by non-residents – whereas it partially relaxed previous restrictions on capital outflows.

The cautious path is again under stress among EMEs, now from pressures originating from the presence of a strong US dollar alongside the supposed end of the commodity super-cycle and the consequent flight to quality observed in among international investors. Monetary conditions in advanced economies, particularly in the United States, remain accommodating, but the situation is different in EMEs whose post-crisis investment and credit boom is now part of the past. By comparison, the fall in commodity prices benefited India twice, by lowering inflationary expectations as well by mitigating current account deficits as oil prices plummeted. This positive trade shock is fuelling an increase in domestic demand (IMF, 2015), however, and it mighty renew inflationary pressures in the near future. This would prove the resilience of the recently introduced inflation targeting policy.[35] This new landscape has led to considering India as a rising start – separate from the 'fragile five' group, at least for the moment.

In sum, authorities' vigilant attitude towards financial globalization prevented India from experiencing the effects of the GFC, to which it was just partially exposed through trade and financial channels. A similar attitude was observed years later, when exogenous circumstances pushed the country towards a fragile position. Once again, capital controls and prudential controls permitted the economy to sail against the wind. As the next paragraphs show, a similar cautionary attitude was observed on the financial front. The high professionalism and pragmatism of RBI officials has certainly helped India avoid outrageous policies.

Financial Markets: Avoiding Financial Instability

The establishment of the Bank of Hindustan in 1770 signalled the emergence of the Indian banking sector (Sharda, Swamy and Singh, 2014). Years later, financial markets expanded after a group of public sector banks appeared and, after 1850, with the

34. To add suspense, the storm came at the time Rajan was assuming office as the twenty-third governor of the RBI. A Chicago professor, he was famous for his exuberant critical approach to financial markets at IMF meetings in Jackson Hole, Wyoming, in 2005.
35. In February 2015, the RBI governor (Rajan) signed an agreement with the government (Narendra Modi) to establish a formal inflation-targeting framework. The objective: to reduce inflation to below 6% by January 2016 and 4% thereafter. The RBI's powers might be restrained, however, if the government finally introduced the Monetary Policy Committee, an academic group of experts in charge of making interest rate decisions stipulated in the draft Indian Financial Code ('Rajan Stresses RBI Policy Independence', *FT*, 4 August 2015).

entrance of a group of foreign banks (Reddy, 2009; Singh, 2011).[36] Once the country obtained its independence, market dynamism somewhat waned and the state's voice gained room. Henceforth, and until the nineties, the Indian financial system developed into a highly repressed model, with the state fixing prices (interest rates) and rationing quantities (credit). Additionally, and in order to expand banking to rural areas and benefit vast groups of the population, the government established a mandatory priority sector lending (PSL) scheme. Leading banks were nationalized by the government in the late 1960s, as a means to accomplish their development objectives which were established in five-year plans. Six more banks went public in the early eighties, a policy which would be discontinued thereafter.[37]

Despite its apparent drawbacks, the financial system deepened and branches expanded nationwide, helping the government increase the local savings rate (Goyal, 2011). A series of crises revealed banks' poor performance records, and the RBI's unviability persisted with fiscal deficit monetization. A partial deregulation of interest rates transformed into one of the main policy challenges to be faced by the government. In view of that, monetary authorities decided to initiate a series of reports in order to transform the financial industry, beginning with the Narasimham Committee in 1991.[38]

Financial Markets and Actors

Since the late eighties, several entry barriers were fully or partially dismantled in different service sectors, including banking and insurance. Although the new policy allowed 100 per cent foreign ownership in a large number of industries and majority ownership in most service sectors, the banking sector remained exempted, permitting up to 49 per cent foreign participation.[39] A different picture emerged on the stock market, with the government authorizing foreign institutional investors to purchase shares of Indian companies, opening a window for portfolio investment at existing companies. In parallel, the federal government inaugurated a more receptive FDI attraction policy, including a series of

36. Three of today's most important foreign banks were already established in the mid-nineteenth century.
37. In the early nineties, almost 90% of the banking system came to be owned by the central government. During the first wave, the 14 largest banks were nationalized, increasing the public sector banks' share of deposits from 31% to 86%. Following the second wave, the percentage increased to 92%.
38. One of their first recommendations was to deregulate the interest rate determination process. The Narasimham Committee also recommended a reduction from 40% to 10% in priority sector lending, although this latest recommendation never became implemented. The committee also advanced on the institutional front, particularly by strengthening prudential norms and the supervisory framework, leading monetary authorities to adopt the Basel Accord in 1992.
39. Foreign investors' participation also became constrained in the following industries: insurance (26%); financial companies (51%); telecommunications (49%); Internet (74%); air transport (40%); foreign and exchange trade companies (51%); radio (49%); publicity (74%); and up to 51% in health or educational companies.

incentives packages (Government of India, 2006), the end of discrimination between local and foreign investors and the (already mentioned) transformation of FERA into FEMA.[40] Reforms also expanded the ownership base among India's domestic banks, particularly by allowing private equity into public sector banks (Reddy, 2009). In 2004, the Ministry of Commerce and Industry revised the existing guidelines on FDI in the banking sector (RBI, 2005). But foreign investors continued to require government approval in order to enter in the market (IBEF, 2008). Thus, by 2010 the prospect of entrance continued to be minimal, with foreigners allowed to enter only those operations identified by the RBI for restructuring and respecting an upper limit of 74 per cent (RBI, 2011). Likewise, portfolio inflows continued to be conditional on the fulfilment of important restrictions as, for example, those constraining corporate bond ownership or equity investments by foreigners (Khurana, 2007).

India's financial sector is primarily bank based, and mainly associated with public sector entities with a nationwide presence – and under RBI regulation. Created under colonial rule and later nationalized by Indian authorities, the RBI is organized on a federal basis (like the US Fed), although with a unique character granted by its foundational act. As recognized by the funding act, the central bank has a development commitment, which has been maintained throughout different governments and political periods. The RBI is not a fully independent entity but an arm of the executive since the country's independence, although since the reform it has gained in autonomy.

Reforms of the banking sector were implemented from the start, particularly those related to improving the financial health of commercial banks in terms of capital adequacy, profitability and asset quality (Khurana, 2007; Reddy, 2009). Remarkably, and in contrast to what happened in other EMEs (as in Latin America), institutional reforms did not follow a financial crisis nor were they the outcome of any structural support package (Reddy, 2009). This, in turn, gave policymakers more freedom to introduce a proper sequencing, an approach certainly respected in the *Raghuram Rajam Report* (Rajan, 2008), and also helped avoid endless ideological debates about whether state banks should be privatized ('India and the Credit Crisis: How India Could Benefit in the Long Term', *The Economist*, 14 October 2008). Some restrictions remain binding, however, particularly those related to overseas operations by the banking industry (Shah and Patnaik, 2004). Similarly, the RBI imposed controls on currency borrowing by firms in order to keep currency mismatching under control. The new financial opportunities given by the liberalization package, however, permitted them to diversify their basket of products by including insurance, asset management and similar products, leading to the emergence of financial conglomerates.

From a structural perspective, the Indian banking industry is divided between a commercial and a cooperative sector, with public entities leading the former group.[41] The

40. Although the new legislation permitted full foreign ownership in the manufacture sector, FDI continued to be excluded from some sectors and limited in others.
41. Public Sector Banks (PSBs) account for more of 75% of the industry's total assets, followed by private (but national) banks with a participation of 18%, and foreign banks with a mere 6.5%.

exposure to government securities is particularly important, although not necessarily inaccurate.[42] The asset quality of Indian banks, however, saw constant improvement in recent years, although non-performing assets increased during 2009 (RBI, 2010).[43] The relevance of SOBs was not eclipsed by the reforms; instead, the government opted for injecting them with more money (Reddy, 2009). Following the emergence of the GFC, foreign branches decided to limit their credit market exposure – an option undermining their market share (RIB, 2011; BBA, 2011; Singh, 2011).[44] As a consequence, people's attitude towards SOBs changed for the better after the crisis as these entities continued to supply credit to the economy during the downturn ('Rambo in Cuffs: Balance-Sheets Are Less Powerful Than They Look', *The Economist*, 13 May 2010) and converting the State Bank of India into the main lending agent. Financial reforms, in contrast, are certainly far from being completed, as India has not yet solved the accessibility to credit, particularly for those living in rural areas.[45] To sum up, and as a consequence of past nationalization policies and banks' attitude towards the GFC, most of the Indian financial system remains in public hands. This could change in the near future, if Prime Minister Modi's plans are enacted. Although authorities plan to sell down stakes, the state will remain the majority shareholder in state-backed banks.[46]

Foreign banks operating in India are basically oriented towards niche segments or new products and basically focus on activities in urban areas.[47] From an institutional perspective, after the 1991 *Narasimham Report* foreigners were allowed to enter into joint ventures with private banks or to operate on their own as a branches or wholly owned subsidiaries (WOSs). A new report by the RBI (*Roadmap for Presence of Foreign Banks in India*), which appeared in 2005, reaffirmed the interest in boosting sector efficiency, and it also traced a two-phase plan (Sharda et al., 2014). Whereas the initial focus was directed towards consolidating the (banking) industry, after 2009 authorities' interest was in ring-fencing

PSBs include three types of banks: the nationalized banks, the Bank of India and the regional rural banks ('Mutually Assured Existence', *The Economist*, 13 May 2010).

42. Banks are obliged to use about a quarter of their deposits to buy government debt ('Rambo in Cuffs: Balance-Sheets Are Less Powerful Than They Look', *The Economist*, 13 May 13 2010).
43. Public sector banks performed better, whereas more doubtful and loss-making assets were presented by foreign and new private sector banks (RBI, 2010).
44. Foreign banks not only reduced their lending but some also decided to exit or shrink their operations, such as the United Kingdom's Royal Bank of Scotland (Singh, 2011).
45. For Chandrasekhar (2008), it worsened. He evaluates the 1990–2004 evolution of the credit-deposit ratio along the ratio of investments in government securities over total earning assets. Commercial banks restructured their assets, reducing their exposure to the private sector at the same time as they were increasing their exposure to risk-free government securities. The new policy also harmed credit delivery to rural India and small-scale industry.
46. The government planned to sell down stakes in 27 state-backed banks by 2009, cutting its holdings to 52% in all cases – down from between 56% and 84% (Rashmi Kumar, 'India Paves Way for $26bn Bank Equity Issuance', *Global Capital Asia* 12 December 2014).
47. There are actually 41 foreign banks operating in India, with the Standard Chartered Bank the most important among them.

foreign banks' operations in the country. The Nair Committee released a new report in 2011, reaffirming the recommendations previously set by the RBI but also including new provisions fixing important duties to foreigners: they were now forced to increase their lending to the priority sector.[48]

The latest reforms were basically directed at boosting a WOS legal scheme, as the GFC sided with RBI authorities with this legal form.[49] Subsidiarization became the leading scheme for those entering, as in the recommended legal figure for those (foreign entities) already established in the country.[50] According to the RBI, 'conversion is also desirable from the financial perspective [...] (as) it ensures that there is clear delineation between assets and liabilities of the domestic bank and those of its foreign parent and clearly provides for ring-fenced capital and assets within the host country'.[51]

FDI is permitted through four different channels: in public sector banks (a 20 per cent cap), in private sector banks (a 74 per cent cap), branches, or WOSs. Thus, WOS is mandatory for some categories of foreign banks[52] or in the event that they become systematically important by virtue of their balance sheet size.[53] Foreign banks' growth plans remained under the scrutiny of local authorities: according the Indian commitments at the WTO, the expansion of the branch network of foreign banks (both existing and new entrants) is restricted to 12 per year (Department of Financial Services, Ministry of Finance). In terms of treatment, RBI president Rajan made sure that foreign entities enjoy (near) national treatment status, although with a couple of conditions – particularly, reciprocity.[54]

Capital markets have historically few participants and highly inactive ones, which induces more volatility. During recent years, however, the importance of the stock market began to rise, as seen in the rocketing increase experienced by SENSEX,[55] the daily stock

---

48. The priority sector target (PST) was increased to 40% of the adjusted net bank credit (ANBC) or CEOBE (credit equivalent of off-balance sheet exposure). The new regulation also included an additional sub-target of 15% for exports and 15% for the MSE sector.
49. *Foreign Investment Policy for Banking Sector in India – Present Status*: A presentation by Department of Financial Services, Ministry of Finance /PPT presentation, undated.
50. According to (former) RBI Governor Raghuram Rajan, 'By setting up wholly owned subsidiaries, foreign banks will get more opportunities to expand in India [...] That is going to be a big-big opening because one could even contemplate taking over Indian banks, small Indian banks and so on' (Speech at an event of the Institute of International Finance (IIF), Washington, DC, October 2013.
51. 'RBI Opens Doors to M&As for Foreign Banks in India', *Economic Times*, 7 November 2013.
52. In particular: (1) banks incorporated into a jurisdiction that has legislation which gives deposit made/credit conferred, in that jurisdiction a preferential claim in a winding up; (2) banks which do not provide adequate disclosure in the home jurisdiction, (3) banks with complex structures; (4) banks which are not widely held and (5) if the RBI is not satisfied that supervisory arrangements and market discipline in the country of their incorporation is adequate.
53. In case their assets become 0.25% of the total assets of all scheduled commercial banks in India.
54. 'Policy of Entry of Foreign Banks Soon: RBI' (*Business Today*, 14 October 2013).
55. On 25 July 1990, the SENSEX Index was fixed at 1,000 points, reaching 6,000 points ten years later and 17,000 points by September 2007.

price index of the Bombay Stock Exchange (BSE).[56] Certainly, FIIs have an important role in this surge, but it is also true that their arrival became highly induced by a set of fiscal initiatives emanating from the government[57] and, more recently, by the events set in motion by several IPOs of state-owned firms.[58] The surge in equity financing, however, has had more consequences in the pattern of ownership of the corporate sector than in the structure of financing (Chandrasekhar, 2008), scattering the perception among policymakers of the threat imposed by this financial instrument of widespread foreign takeover. The boom reinforced policymakers' and politicians' fears of a rise in foreign takeovers]

Offshore financing has also been an important channel of financing, and many Indian firms are issuing equity abroad (American Depository Receipts / Global Depositary Receipts (ADR/GDR)). Despite becoming an important vehicle for financial globalization in the early nineties as local firms circumvented local regulation, once reforms were bypassed and the local stock market modernized, Indian firms returned to the local equity market for funding (Shah and Patnaik, 2010). What is more, their success increased the attractiveness of the domestic equity market, inducing the arrival of global investors, which, in the end, led the government to restrain them from entering, but this failed. Interested in encouraging the arrival of capital, the government in 2012 decided to further advance with pro liberalization measures, increasing foreign private investors' benefits.[59] In the same direction, the SEBI announced new deregulatory measures in June 2013.[60] As a consequence of all those changes, led by institutional investors, foreigners now dominate the Indian equity market – although local investors[61] are intending to return (*FT*, 2015).[62]

India and the Financial Trilemma

The banking system remained strong and well capitalized, a position that directly relates to the fact that Indian banks are 'hav[e] greater exposure to domestic conventional assets' (Dua and Rajan, 2013).[63] As for the credits, RBI's historical compromise with financial

56. In addition to the BSE (founded in 1875), the National Stock Exchange (NSE) was established in 1992. Although most important firms are listed in both markets, the BSE remains dominant in spot trading and the majority player in derivative trading.
57. As for example, addressing the Congress, the authorities compromised to 'abolish the tax on long-term capital gains from securities transactions altogether', a fiscal concession that (might) trigger the speculative surge in stock markets.
58. In mid-October 2010, the state-owned Coal India announced an IPO expected to rise to $ 3 billion. Previously, Power Grid Corporation and Steel Authority of India adopted a similar path ('Rupee Off Highs as Capital Controls Talks Weigh', *Economic Times*, 11 October 2010).
59. 'India Opens Stock Market to Foreign Investors', *The Telegraph*, 4 January 2012.
60. 'India's Stock Market Regulator, SEBI, Announces Significant Amendments to Foreign Investment Norms', *International Business Times*, 27 June 2013.
61. Local investors have historically relied on gold and property, although they turned to the local equity market in search of new (and more lucrative) investment alternatives.
62. 'Domestic Investors Board India Equity Run', *FT*, 3 June 2015.
63. It might be remembered that private firms were practically banned from issuing debt in foreign currency, nor did the issuance of ADRs by local firms become important.

stability and the effective use of macro-prudential regulations should be highlighted. In other words, and in terms of the financial trilemma, the RBI avoided extremes by carefully regulating financial intermediaries' exposure to FX liabilities (RBI, 2010). Furthermore, RBI authorities always pushed foreign banks to ring-fence their activities.

The question which remains unanswered in this chapter is whether this (semi-) autonomous financial pattern will predominate for the coming future or whether India will be pushed towards the constraints imposed by the financial trilemma. If global banking assumes a more important role, the local regulator authority would certainly diminish, demonstrating the 'inevitable tension between the benefits that such global conglomerates bring and some regulatory and market structure and competition that might arise' (R. Mohan, 2009, p. 164). Similar tensions would arise if Indian stock markets become financially interconnected with global ones, and local regulations are suddenly bypassed. Both Prime Minister Modi and RBI Governor Rajan are persuaded of the need to modernize the country, but they have also decided to recognize a more important role for international capital. They have adopted a prudent attitude and, as the next paragraphs demonstrate, new rules have been introduced in the same direction.

Institutions

India has always been characterized by a hot and cold relationship with foreign investors. In spite of its colonial past and the traumatizing experience with the Bhopal disaster at the US Union Carbide plant in the mid-eighties, India avidly emerged from its licence raj model to embrace market liberalization in the 1990s (Mortimore and Stanley, 2010).

The new fervour towards market liberalization was reflected in the IIA network signed by India, which included close to 50 BITs, on top of a special agreement with the United States in 1987.[64] More recently, the country began to be more active on this front, adhering to several new RTAs and FTAs, several of which contain special chapters dealing with investment issues, reflecting the new focus of Indian policy on consolidating regional trade agreements in South Asia, ASEAN and, in the future, in Northeast Asia. India also initiated talks with main developed countries, such as Japan, in July 2005, whereas negotiations with the EU were originally announced in 2007 – and are still in progress[65] as numerous controversies have continued plaguing the talks.[66] As in the case of China, this trend towards bilateralism and regionalism accelerated following

64. The *Investment Incentive Agreement* aimed to protect and promote American investment in India, particularly in energy and power, telecommunications, manufacturing and services. The agreement contained a state-to-state dispute resolution mechanism.
65. Further details are available at: http://ec.europa.eu/trade/policy/countries-and-regions/countries/india/.
66. India pushed to relax EU stringent food safety criteria, which penalized their farm and fishery exports. Additionally, Delhi negotiators are interested in making it easier for Indian professionals to work in Europe. (EU–India, http://www.bilaterals.org/?-EU-India-&lang=en). EU negotiators, on their side, are interested in India's service sector (for more information, see the discussion below).

the breakdown in WTO negotiations (Aggarwal and Mukherji, 2008). Even so, India's policy with regards to IIAs has remained quite cautious – although it confronted nine cases of international arbitration stemming from earlier IIAs. Its 48 BITs in force with 14 industrialized countries and 34 others do not provide foreign investors any rights to establish investment in its territory, and India's more recent RTAs and FTAs with countries like Canada and Singapore carry important qualifications that limit future IA-ISDS risks (Mortimore and Stanley, 2010).[67] Furthermore, India still remains out of the ICSID Convention. In sum, this large-market developing country has attempted to use its increasing negotiating strength to reduce or limit risks associated with IA-ISDS clauses in IIAs. The recent RTA with Singapore demonstrates a much more coherent and clearer policy with regards to the management of such risks.

In 2012, the government began an important initiative to modify the 1993 India BIT model.[68] The new model will reduce foreign investors' protection in several ways. It adopts a definition of investment centre in enterprise, thereby narrowing the scope to FDI – and particularly excluding portfolio investments. Likewise, the new model eliminates the MFN clause provision and reduces the scope of the national treatment (NT) clause by inserting an 'in like circumstances' sentence.[69] Furthermore, pre-treatment guarantees already considered in previous treaties are now left aside, as it also remains silent on the so-called umbrella clause. In relation to investors' claims, the new investment model requires investors to exhaust all local remedies (judicial and administrative) before initiating international arbitration. In sum, the 2015 BIT model adopts a development-centric approach 'intended to preserve the policy space of host states' (Singh, 2015a, p. 1). To this end the new BIT model presents carve-out and reservations clauses, or provides a list of funds which are eligible for unrestricted transfer although subject to 'the imposition of temporary restrictions in the event of serious balance of payments difficulties or in cases where capital movements pose serious difficulties in the management of monetary and exchange rate policies' (Singh, 2015c, p. 1).[70]

As stated in the previous discussion, foreign-owned banks were almost non-existent under the Raj model. Liberalization measures started in the nineties, and benefiting foreign investors was certainly not expanded to the banking sector. As India applied for WTO membership, pressure mounted to liberalize its financial sector. The first attempt, although interrupted by the Asian crisis, permitted an important expansion of foreign banks (Gopalan and Pajan, 2010). The government established a new 'roadmap for presence of foreign banks in India' in 2005 (Reserve Bank of India; RBI,

67. The appearance of the new BIT model would certainly force India to renegotiate all existing BITs
68. Kavaljit Singh 'India and Bilateral Investment Treaties – Are They Worth It? Beyond BRICS blog, *FT*, 21 January 2015.
69. Although present in previous BITs signed by India, the MNF was excluded from the investment chapters of FTAs signed with Singapore (2006) and South Korea (2009) (Singh, 2015b).
70. Such as including contributions to capital, profits, dividends, capital gains, interest, royalty payments, technical assistance fees and payments related to contracts and loans.

https://m.rbi.org.in/upload/content/pdfs/RoadMap.pdf). Market entry road map stipulated a two-phase approach, which started by consolidating the local banks, both private and SOBs. WOSs become the legal figure for those interested in entering and the most appropriate for those already established as branches (RBI, 2010).[71] Nevertheless, monetary authorities should also look at the commitments made up until the WTO when considering the legal figure to be adopted by foreign banks (RBI, 2011; BBA, 2011). At this point the debate started (when India was applying for membership in the WTO) (BBA, 2011). If considering the commitments made by India at the WTO, authorities could even block licensing a particular foreign bank when the share of foreigners in the total domestic banking system exceeds 15 per cent (Madhyam, Briefing Paper, 2015). Likewise, and despite the fact that authorities recognized different (and better) treatment for WOSs than branches, foreigners will not receive full (but near) national treatment (Department of Financial Services, Ministry of Finance, undated; Rajan, 2013). Obviously, not recognizing full NT and having a different approach to branch licensing, it is being considered as discriminatory by foreign actors (BBA, 2011).

The RBI road map has also advanced on corporate governance issues, asking for a predominant role for Indian directors.[72] Monetary authorities are also debating whether foreign banks should be allowed to raise funds in the local market in order to augment their non-equity capital in India. Foreign banks, in contrast, are required to extend lending to the priority sector up to 32 per cent, which is below the percentage fixed for local banks. Finally, and despite the liberalization measures undertaken, authorities maintained very restricted measures by limiting the issuance of new licenses when foreigners' branches exceed 15 per cent of total banking assets.

Pressures to foster financial services liberalization are observed at the FTA negotiation table, however. As in the case of India – EU FTA talks, as European negotiators are asking for the removal of all barriers affecting market access but also they request for national treatment commitments (Singh, 2011). The EU banking industry, in particular, is demanding the removal of all restrictions pertaining to branch licenses, foreign ownership, numerical quotas, equity ceilings, differential taxation and voting rights. In addition, they are seeking to remove all restrictions on priority lending. Although some

71. Whether an international bank should legally constitute a legal branch or a subsidiary became acute after the crisis. The former are not separate legal entities (i.e. legally attached to the headquarters), whereas subsidiaries are locally separated legal entities and, henceforth, able to participate in (host country) deposit insurance schemes. In other words, it ensures a clear delineation between the assets and liabilities of the domestic bank and those of its foreign partner and clearly provides for ring-fenced capital within the host country. Another advantage relates to the increasing effectiveness of control under this legal type.
72. In particular, monetary authorities were suggesting that: (1) not less than 50% of the directors should be Indian national residents in India, (2) not less than 50% of the directors should be non-executive directors, (3) a minimum of one-third of the directors should be totally independent of the management of the subsidiary in India, its parent or associates and (4) the directors shall conform to the 'Fit and Proper' criteria established in the former RBI circular of 25 June 2004 (RBI, 2011).

restrictions might be lifted by the government, problems could remain if partners are not predisposed to grant similar treatment.[73] Banking-related discussions are being (aggressively) conducted by negotiators in the United Kingdom, one of the leading centres for global banking.[74]

This condition forces economic authorities to be cautious - when considering the degree of capital account openness (RBI, 2013). In this sense, monetary authorities are permanently well aware of the problems posed by (and are under continued pressure to avoid) excess volatility and exchange rate appreciation. Henceforth, India's successful macro records could certainly been associated with the correct policy choices adopted by its policymakers in assessing all different macro scenarios. Authorities were savvy enough to protect the country against all-powerful storms generated in global financial markets – both originated in East Asia by the end of the nineties, like the one initiated in the United States a decade later. But macro success could not, in any case, be associated with a return to a closed framework, as a simple observation of returning capital controls might suggest. In the whole period, all policy changes were granting markets further relevance. Interest rate settlement is now a market-based phenomenon, as also is the mechanism for exchange rate determination. All this does not mean, however, authorities are disinterested in the rupee market's value nor are they disregarding the challenges imposed by exchange rate extreme volatility. Proper policy decisions could also explain why authorities refused to introduce inflation targeting in the past, although to understand why becomes perhaps relevant for the future. Meanwhile, the RBI has begun to notice of the problems the eruption of asset bubbles might generate, a situation that can lead to the introduction of prudential regulatory measures. Consequently, the ability of local banks to raise funds abroad remains strictly regulated – insulating the Indian financial sector from overseas capital markets. Similarly, the RBI has introduced a series of guidelines affecting the operation of foreign banks and particularly directed towards ring-fencing the local financial system from an exogenous crisis. All of these measures seem to be consistently matched in the institutional arena, a front in which Indian negotiators have maintained a careful approach.

In short, if the Indian experience with financial globalization and institutions can be summarized, it is found in the following statement from Y. V. Reddy, former RBI central bank chief: 'The basic features of the Indian approach are gradualism; coordination with other economic policies; pragmatism rather than ideology; relevance of the context; consultative processes; dynamism and good sequencing' (Reddy, 2005, p. 61). For Indian policymakers framing options, efficiency objectives are considered in tandem with stability considerations. Another distinctive feature of the Indian approach is the recognition of the uniqueness of the context when designing the policy. Authorities stress the importance of an appropriate mix between elements of continuity and change in the process of reform (Reddy, 2009). The new BIT model introduced by the government

73. For example, by virtue of the India–Singapore Comprehensive Economic Cooperation Agreement (2005), the RBI permitted the access of three Singaporean banks, but Singapore monetary authorities continued to refuse Indian banks' entry (Madhyam, 2013).

74. German banks are also active.

is certainly a worthy and interesting example. By prioritizing a developmental model, authorities are recognizing the problems posed by external sector vulnerabilities and the convenience of maintaining its policy space.

A cautious integration with global financial markets also characterizes the Indian approach, as observed by R. Mohan, deputy governor at the RBI: 'One distinguish feature of our trajectory is that financial stability has been successfully maintained despite repeated shocks, both international and domestic. Even in the ongoing global financial crisis, our banks continued to exhibit significant financial stability' [R. Mohan, 2009. *Monetary Policy in a Globalized Economy*]. The RBI's specific two-track approach to ensuring both price and financial stability differentiates it from most EMEs' central banks. Financial stability, in sum, was obtained by the maintenance of prudential policies by the RBI, regulation that prevented Indian banks from engaging in excessive risk-taking.

In sum, Indian authorities managed not to be caught by the hyperglobalization trap.

Chapter Nine
SOUTH KOREA

Macroeconomics from Korea Inc to Market Liberalization

From General Park's establishment of wide-ranging economic reform in 1963 until 1997, real per capita income growth averaged above 6 per cent annually in Korea. Undoubtedly, the Korean miracle rested on a particular mix of market incentives and state direction, together with a highly repressed financial market where domestic savings (plus international aid) financed capital accumulation. Industrial policy guided financial system behaviour, with (national) banks directing funds to the productive sector.

As occurred in many Asian countries, after a brief experiment with flexible exchange rates, the Korean won was formally pegged to the dollar, and it would remain that way until 1980, when a currency basket replaced the peg (although it remained centred on the US dollar). Likewise, international capital flows were highly controlled and financial repression widely extended. Controls were present in several sectors, and strict restrictions were imposed on FDI if not directly banning it. Similarly, outward FDI required prior official approval to go ahead. Trade policy was also under government scrutiny, which was particularly vigilant on the import side of the balance. The local currency was nonconvertible and, as experienced by other developing countries at the time, the Korean government also discouraged any offshore market in won or won-denominated instruments. The current account was also firmly controlled and strict exchange restrictions were applied to all capital outflows until the 1980s.

When General Chun came to power, in 1979, liberalization began to gain momentum (Nolan, 2005), although liberal policies were timid and not extensively implemented (Cho, 2010). Thereafter, interest rates began to be determined on the market, marking the beginning of the end of the financial repression era – although the government maintained de facto control over the same rates. A similar erratic liberalization was observed with the new ER determination scheme, as authorities did not leave the currency to freely move. At the same time, the government also promoted the emergence of a powerful shadow-banking sector. Finally, and despite all these (timid) liberalization efforts, Korea's financial markets remained closed to foreigners.

Further liberalization measures were adopted in the mid-1990s, and were particularly aimed at opening the local financial sector to the outside world. The Kim Young-Sam government resumed the reform process, further liberalizing both ER and money markets.[1] Likewise, the new authorities were phasing out old legislation which prevented

1. The interest rate approach implied a two-step process, first liberalizing lending rates and then

foreign investors from participating in the local stock market (although a 10 per cent ceiling on foreign holdings over private firms' equity was maintained). Similarly, and despite the fact that authorities permitted local firms to contract short-term commercial loans abroad, important restrictions were maintained, preventing them from having direct access to foreign capital markets. Unfortunately, the incapability to finance investments with long-term funds, push local firms to rely in short-term loans which, in the end, led to important inconsistencies, including the appearance of exchange rate and maturity mismatch problems – problems that easily transformed into the seeds of future crisis. In parallel, the government was now authorizing the arrival of FDI flows, although permissions were only benefiting some specific manufacturing sectors. Thus, all these measures plus a conjunction of a stable foreign exchange and an attractive interest rate differential pulled foreign investors into the country.[2] The housing finance system was also deregulated in 1996, and commercial banks entered the mortgage business.[3] As a result, capital inflows were rapidly surpassing foreign reserves and, simultaneously, inducing an increase in short-term debt, which by the time of the crisis was seven times larger than the former.[4]

A good performance prevented authorities from perceiving the growing inconsistencies, at least initially: the growth rate surpassed the 5 per cent benchmark during the whole 1990–97 period, and inflationary pressures remained low. In terms of ER policy, authorities were following a tightly managed float with the won/dollar rate moving in a narrow range. But whereas bank lending remained stable, other funding sources soared (in particular, lending by non-banking financial institutions –NBFIs) particularly after 1994. Consequently, strong macro fundamentals coupled with a relatively stable exchange rate led borrowers and lenders to underestimate both currency and maturity mismatch problems. After that point internal financial imbalances would began to characterize the Korean economy.

In addition, a series of external factors began to affect the local economy in the mid-1990s, including a term of trade reversal and an important currency devaluation by Korea's main competitor: Japan (Chopra et al., 2001). But, attached to maintain the *won*/dollar parity, monetary authorities made no allowance for a broader basket – and, henceforth, this tended to affect the country's multilateral exchange rate. On the monetary front, inflationary concerns led monetary authorities to tighten interest rate since mid-1996 – indirectly benefiting non-banking institutions. The devaluation of the Thai bath in July 1997, followed by the abandonment of the pegging by Taiwan three months

---

deposit rates. Furthermore, and despite the announcements, monetary authorities maintained important controls on both corporate rates and banks' lending rates (Cho, 2010).

2. OECD membership benefited the country's risk assessment but converted into another factor generating stress on the capital account.
3. Liberalization measures were followed by the privatization of the Korean Housing Bank (KHB), the monopolistic provider of low-interest, long-term housing loans, in 1997 (Igan and Kam, 2011).
4. Short-term debt rose from $ 40 billion in 1993 to $ 98 billion at the end of September 1997 (Chopra et al., 2001).

later, eroded foreign investors' confidence in the Korean national currency, initiating a capital flow reversal. As FX reserves were vanishing and constrained from rolling over chaebols' short-term debt, authorities permitted the won to depreciate. A twin banking and exchange rate crisis erupted, and the economy collapsed.

The 1997 Crisis and the Neo-liberal Response

There were several views over the origins of the crisis. One school of thought found financial market reforms responsible, and the negative effects associated with financial market liberalization (Sachs and Radelet, 1998 and 1999; Forman and Stiglitz, 1999). In order to avoid this situation occurring again, this group asked to undertake a more prudential approach – in terms of CAL. Another group of academics emphasized the negative role being played by Korea's chaebols, as the crony capitalism model behind this (Krueger and Yoo, 2002). For them, the crisis was easy to overcome: to continue with the opening of the economy and to advance further with market liberalization, in order to transform Korea's corporate sector and to eliminate chaebols' discretionary power. The government blamed both the financial sector and industrial conglomerates' corporate governance limitations as the culprits in the crisis.[5]

Thus, in the aftermath of the financial crisis of 1997 authorities decided to switch to the second option, placing the economy on a new neo-liberal path. The government signed a stand-by arrangement with the IMF, and consequently the government led by Kim Dae-Jung implemented the restructuring programme being suggested (Turner, 2010; Lee, 2010).[6] Recession was acute in 1998. That year is considered the worst in Korean post-war economic history, with GDP plunging 6.9 per cent whereas consumption fell by 10.6 per cent. The corporate sector suffered the most from the IMF's recessive policies, as the credit crunch left local firms with less funds (Lee, 2010). Corporate investment finally collapsed in 1998, and fixed investment shrank by more than 20 per cent.[7]

Accepting the IMF's advice, Korean authorities continued with both liberalization and deregulation measures (Noland, 2005; Lee, 2010). In this sense, the enactment of the Foreign Investment Promotion Act (FIPA) and the passing of the Foreign Exchange Transaction Act (FETA) were signalling the beginning of a new era: allowing all capital account transactions except those expressly forbidden (Kim and Yang, 2010).[8]

---

5. Importantly enough, the crisis would definitely bring sequencing into the picture. The IMF began to analyse the challenges posed by shocks: capital account and financial deregulation should be properly analysed.
6. The US$ 21 billion rescue package which was granted, was the largest in IMF history – and represented 19 times Korea's IMF quota. IMF's lending, however, became highly contested due to the breadth and depth of structural conditionality being introduced – particularly aimed at transforming Korea's corporate governance and at restructuring the country's financial system.
7. Although firms' cash flows were recovering fast, Korean bosses paid their debts and maintained liquidity. Henceforth, the low investment ratio would persist even after the 2004 recovery.
8. The former removed many of the former restrictions on, among others, cross-border M&A operations.

Restrictions on remittances were completely lifted, guaranteeing foreign investors unconditional transfer of funds, even under circumstances of exogenous shocks. Financial institutions' foreign currency transactions were now being accepted (Lee, 2010; Kim and Yang, 2010). Furthermore, and despite prior experience, the government maintained weak supervision over derivative markets. Liberalization measures on the mergers and acquisitions (M&A) front, along with lower asset prices and depreciation of the won, encouraged foreign companies to enter the local market (Lee, 2010). The government allowed long-term deposits by non-residents in domestic financial institutions, domestic firms' short-term borrowing was deregulated and partial deregulation of real estate investment abroad was put in place. In sum, all previous regulations on corporate bonds, equity and money markets were phased out, and a new neo-liberal package was put in place.

Despite this trend, the Korean government decided to undertake important regulatory reforms, basically directed at strengthening markets' resilience and financial stability (Lee, 2013). Among the vast set of prudential measures and new instruments, authorities introduced a FX liquidity ratio – basically directed at avoiding futures maturity mismatch problems.[9] A so-called domestic currency (DC) liquidity ratio was also proposed, directed at evaluating local banks' risks.[10] In order to maintain stability in the housing market,[11] two new instruments were announced: the loan-to-value (LTV)[12] and the debt-to-income (DTI)[13]. In sum, following the 1997 crisis, monetary authorities installed a series of macro-prudential policies (MAPPs), basically oriented to curbing investors' speculative behaviour in all targeted areas (the real estate market, the financial sector and the derivative markets).

From a macro perspective, and in order to tackle the crisis, the government now introduced a floating ER regime. For the day forward, short-term interest rates were raised alongside installing a more restrictive fiscal policy (both in the IMF toolkit). Additionally, authorities decided to set an inflation-targeting approach towards monetary

9. This ratio compares (foreign currency) liquid assets and liabilities, both with maturity of three months or less. When a particular measure was introduced in July 1997, days before the Asian Financial Crisis (AFC). A year later authorities decided to extend its coverage and to further adjust the ratio (from 70% to 80%). By introducing different liquidity ratios and several maturity ranges, authorities further advanced in tackling currency mismatch risks.
10. This ratio compares (domestic currency) liquid assets and liabilities, both with maturity of three months or less. Originally introduced in January 1999, this ratio guideline was strengthened two years later. In 2006, authorities decided to ease the ratio.
11. Housing price stability was defined as the annual house price appreciation moving between the range zero to nominal GDP growth rate. LTV and DTI were part of the battery of tools to accomplish such an objective. But the price stability goal was further complemented by strict regulation of land use and redevelopment (Igan and Kang, 2011).
12. This ratio considers the amount of mortgage loans, senior lending on houses and rent security received against house prices. In order to maintain prices stability, authorities set a 60% threshold level, beyond which tight measures applied – and further strengthened it to 40% in some regions.
13. This ratio compares annual mortgage and other loan payments against annual income.

Table 9.1 Classification of core and non-core liabilities

Degree of liquidity	Core liabilities	Intermediate	Non-core liabilities
Highly Liquid	Cash Demand deposits (H)	Demand deposits (NFC)	Repos Call loans Short-term bank debt
Intermediate	Time deposits and CDs (H)	Time deposits and CDs (NFC)	Time deposits and CDs (B&SF)
Illiquid	Trust accounts (H) Covered bonds (H)	Trust accounts (NFCs)	Long-term debt securities (B&SF) ABS & MBS

Notes: H, Households; NFCs, non-financial corporations
Source: Shin (2013)

policy – a trend now vividly supported by the academy and backed by the IMF. Finally, and in order to lessen capital inflow pressures over the exchange rate and to increase its monetary policy space, authorities initiated a policy of FX reserve accumulation which in the end helped reduce FX volatility and preserve monetary policy space.

Macroeconomic performance was ameliorated with the arrival of the new millennium. Recovery put Korea back into a new macro trend. Important capital inflows and large incentives introduced to favour private consumption were facilitating the recovery. The banking industry was directing loans from corporations to households, initially benefiting consumption and later the real estate sector. Tight regulatory measures prompted a decline in housing prices and an increase in mortgage lending as compared to the past.[14]

After years of ostracism, Korean financial institutions were now competing for new clients: households' loans (mortgages). With a focus on price stability, however, monetary authorities disregarded financial stability risks. They were incapable of seeing the risks posed by new financial instruments and off-shoring operations. Consequently, conditions were suddenly mature to inflate a bubble, which exploded in spite of the introduction of a series of macro-prudential regulations – including the previously mentioned LTV and DTI limits (Kim, 2013, Lee, 2013).[15]

As observed by Shin (2011), the post-Asian crisis Korean banking industry became less attached to traditional core liabilities in order to increase its exposure to new funding sources (non-core liabilities), particularly FX borrowing, REPOs and other non-deposit-related items. Consequently, commercial banks' balance

14. In particular, LTV tightening induced a 1.7% fall in the rate of increase in housing prices, whereas new DTI regulations generated a further 0.8% reduction. The effects of both measures were also important for mortgage lending: the volume of increase in mortgage lending fell on average by 43.9% (6.2 trillion won) after a tightening of LTV regulations and by 44.4% (4.9 trillion won) after a tightening of DTI regulations (Kim, 2013).
15. In August 2008, the LTV ratio peaked at 142%, versus 80% during the 1997 Asian crisis.

sheets began to reflect an increasing gap between deposits and loans as non-core liabilities complemented households' and firms' financing. Among other sectors, non-core liabilities financed the real estate boom, as denoted by the remarkable values attached to LTVs. Furthermore, the appearance of a regulatory bias induced an enlargement in foreign bank branches (FBBs) non-core liabilities as monetary authorities freed them from the constraints imposed by the FX liquidity ratio (Lee, 2013, p. 256).[16]

Derivative operations were also transforming the Korean financial landscape, but, to a large extent, they have also accounted for the exchange rate dynamics of the period. In particular, the so-called KIKO (knock-in-knock-out) foreign exchange options would become (particularly foreign) banks' favourite money-making product. Korean shipbuilders used this option to hedge against won appreciation – particularly after 2006.[17] By expecting the local currency to further appreciate, they increased their hedging ratio, thereby inducing an increase in capital inflows and bypassing their risk towards a local bank – by opening a forward contract (note the similarity with the Brazilian case previously analysed). Local banks were, in turn, borrowing hard currency (mostly USD) from foreign banks, proceeding to exchange these dollars for won on the spot market and, henceforth, hedging the risk embedded in their forward position. With the proceeds from the operation (won in exchange for USD), foreign banks bought certificates of deposit or other domestic bonds and sold the won forward for US dollars (Lee, Kim and Song, 2010; Prates and Fritz, 2013). From then on, (particularly foreign) banks engaged in interest rate arbitrage operations actively led to foreign capital inflow, though they also stimulated massive capital outflow as the boom turned to bust. Bond investments were motivated by arbitrage opportunities or deviations from covered interest parity conditions (CIP).[18] In other words, carry trade was rampant. As previously mentioned, foreign banks were buying short-maturity bonds from the proceedings of their FX swap transactions. As the FX forward market was too small, it became too dependent on these operations and, as a result, they tended to push the exchange rate up. This, in turn, drove the forward discount rate above the interest rate differential between the US and Korea (Baba and Shim, 2011), and, therefore, it led to higher expected returns on bonds (Lee, Kim and Song, 2010).

Nevertheless, and again, during the period 2000–8, macro problems were practically unimportant. Growth rates were positive, although lower than those observed during

16. The hidden agenda behind this norm was to favour foreign banks, as authorities thought of them as having greater access to international capital: injecting liquidity. As the crisis showed, funds proved short for Korea when banks were hit in the home market.
17. The typical contract involves a long time interval since the shipbuilder receives the order and the product is then eventually delivered. As the exchange rate is always subject to high risk, shipbuilders in Korea (the leading worldwide shipbuilder) have a great incentive to hedge them.
18. CIP is defined as the difference between the forward discount rate in an FX swap minus the interest rate differential. The former is defined as ln (USD/Korean won forward rate) minus ln (USD/Korean won spot rate, whereas the latter is defined as three-month USD LIBOR minus 91-day Korean won certificate of deposit rate).

the 1990–97 period. Inflationary pressures, however, were almost absent, reflecting the government's more serious stance on monetary stability. The bank lending rate dropped below 15 per cent per year. Furthermore, and in contrast to the previous pre-crisis period, the current account had now remained positive during all pre-GFC years, reflecting the government's relaunching of a new export-led growth era. Consequent with their neoliberal credentials, authorities dismantled most capital flow restrictions by 2007 (Baba and Kokenyne, 2011), leaving capital flow dynamics at the market's mercy (Kim and Yang, 2010).

As capital account liberalization led to won appreciation, however, the government forced domestic financial institutions to purchase MSBs in order to sterilize capital inflows.[19] Unfortunately, OMOs increased the Bank of Korea's vulnerability to the interest rate differential as to exchange rate fluctuations. Henceforth, and in order to limit appreciation, authorities subsequently introduced a set of measures encouraging capital outflow, including the relaxation of restrictions affecting overseas real estate investments.

Real estate-related measures were associated with LTV and DTI regulations, aimed at influencing housing prices and mortgage lending. After 2006, capital net flows turned negative, including the balance of portfolio investments, as foreigners decided to go short on their investments (BOK, 2009; Lee, 2010; Kim and Yang, 2010).[20] As the current account remained positive, however, the foreign exchange deficit was not further enlarged.[21] Nevertheless, the fact that the BOK maintained its differential interest rate (in order to suppress real estate price increases), induced Korean banks to attract capital from abroad and, consequently, to increase the country's capital account surplus. Two years later, however, the subprime crisis would produce an abrupt change in investors' expectations and a sudden change in this capital account position. Once again short-term borrowing basically explained the reversal in capital flow, although sizeable portfolio investments were also leaving the country.[22] Rising expectations for ER appreciation, however, led foreign investors to flee derivative contracts and remain liquid (Kim and Yang, 2010; BOK, 2010). The deficit in the capital account, resulting from the massive capital outflow, coupled with a current account, also turned negative.

19. MSB returns were highly costly for the government (Kim, et al., 2008). A variable deposit requirement (VDR) on capital inflows was an alternative. Despite being a controversial instrument, and potentially challenged by foreign investors, it become explicitly authorized under the Foreign Exchange Act of 1999 (Noland, 2005).
20. Residents' investments abroad in real estate increased from US$ 22 million in 2005, to US$ 2.7 billion in 2007! Overseas equity investment also grew during these years, but less spectacularly: from US$ 11 billion to US$ 50 billion.
21. The foreign exchange shortage is defined as the sum of current account deficit and capital account deficit, representing the amount needed to finance a decrease in reserve assets.
22. According to BOK figures, US$ 48.4 billion were associated with short-term borrowing and equity investments amounted to US$ 4.3 billion, whereas bond-related outflows reached US$ 10.0 billion.

Table 9.2 Korea, main macroeconomic indicators

		1990	1994	1998	2000	2004	2008	2014
GDP	current, millions of U$ dollars	$ 284,757.12	$ 458,704.21	$ 376,481.98	$ 561,633.04	$ 764,880.64	$ 1,002,219.05	$ 1,411,333.93
GDP growth	%	9.30	8.77	–5.71	8.83	4.90	2.83	3.34
Inflation – CPI, yearly basis	%	8.57	6.27	7.53	2.26	3.59	4.67	1.28
Current Account	% of GDP	–0.84	–0.97	10.64	1.86	3.89	0.32	5.98
M2	% (y-o-y)	25.3	21.1	23.65	5.23	6.31	11.96	8.14
Domestic Lending	% of GDP	50.5262238655709	49.8658647403214	62.9042397997487	73.6033231289491	109.775838150408	148.34046985574	138.358170522932
Interest rate	%	16.5	12.9	15.1	9.4	4.7	7	4.2
Stock Traded, total value	% of GDP	26.2033973804665	62.5303609211227	42.5970618405893	88.2009954891532	68.7458133025339	118.459360404761	90.9564736004906
Gross Savings	% of GDP	33.90	33.36	34.14	34.25	35.34	32.87	34.47
Gross Capital Formation	% of GDP	34.75	34.11	22.94	32.94	32.12	33.02	29.28
Exports of Goods and Services	% of GDP	25.89	24.59	42.36	35.01	38.30	49.96	50.28
Net Financial Account (BOP)	current, millions of U$ dollars	–$ 3,529.20	–$ 6,297.50	$ 33,969.40	$ 9,619.70	$ 34,332.30	-$ 6,591.60	$ 89,334.00

Source: World Bank

The GFC and Korea: Economic Turmoil and Macro-Prudential Policies

Korea became the economy in Asia most affected by the GFC, initiating a new era of exchange rate volatility and sudden reversal in capital flows. The crisis did not just have an impact on the financial side but also presented important contractive effects on the real side, as demand in the United States and Europe halted and depressed Korean exports. When Lee Ayung-Bak assumed the presidency, Korea had a conservative leader to sort out the crisis.

The contraction of financial markets seriously hit the local banking industry, which was now highly interconnected to global markets and, thus, introduced further stress to the real economy as credit lines were almost instantly curtailed. All of the above led to the collapse of stock prices and created notorious instability on both the domestic financial and the foreign exchange market (Lee, et al., 2010). In sum, and certainly resembling the picture of the 1997 crisis, the economy was suffering from another currency-mismatch problem: most banks' balance sheets confronted long-term dollar claims against short-term dollar liabilities. This deleveraging trend left the Korean financial system particularly vulnerable to the GFC (Bruno and Shin, 2012, p. 2), confirming the 'pro-cyclicality' of the banking sector. In contrast to the previous crisis, however, non-core funding (comprising FX borrowing, debt securities, REPOs, Promissory Notes type 1 and 2, and Certificates of Deposit) were highly relevant now. The relevance of this new source became evident when compared to the monetary base: non-core liabilities as a proportion of M2 ranged from around 15 per cent to a peak of 50 per cent in the Lehman crisis (Shin and Shin, 2011; Lee, 2013). The crisis also came to show the weakness of the regulatory scheme introduced after 1997, as banking regulations reflected a micro perspective but did not recognized macro conditions and their challenges (Lee, 2013).

Local currency depreciated 50 per cent against the US dollar during 2008 (see graph below), despite the huge amounts of foreign reserves held by the Korean government. In order to regain the market's confidence, authorities signed a series of swap arrangements with foreign institutions, including the US Fed (U$ 30billion), the Bank of Japan (U$ 20billion) and the PBoC (26.5billion). Likewise, but in sharp contrast to what previously happened, Korean authorities during the 2008–9 crisis decided to implement an expansionary fiscal and monetary policy (Cho, 2010; OECD, 2010) – and a strong fiscal position certainly helped at the time in introducing a countercyclical policy (Stalling, 2015).

Sooner rather than later the Korean economy was again on a growth path: by 2010 a 6.3 per cent rate eclipsed the previous year's 0.9 per cent. The recovery, however, brought with it a new wave of capital flows and, certainly, new instability concerns. The excess in global liquidity and an accommodating monetary policy in developed countries were now benefiting Korea, as was happening in other EMEs. In this sense, though internal factors also contributed, the economic recovery was mainly led by global portfolio flows into debt and equity markets (Fritz and Prates, 2013). Nonetheless, and despite their former advocacy of financial liberalization and capital account openness, economic authorities, starting in June 2010, began to announce a sequence of prudential measures particularly aimed at moderating 'the pro cyclicality of the banking sector by dampening

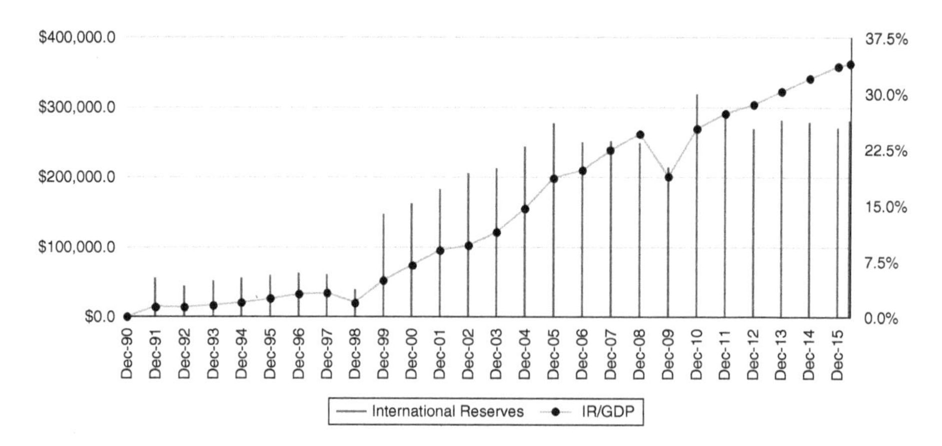

Figure 9.1 Korean WON dynamics, annual exchange rate variations against main competitors (2000–15)

the fluctuations in the growth of so-called non-core bank liabilities, especially cross-border banking sector liabilities' (Bruno and Shin, 2012).

Consequently, following growing military tension in the Korean Peninsula and frightened by the prospect of a sudden reversal of flows, authorities announced their intention to apply a levy on banks' FX-denominated liabilities (those conforming to the non-core liabilities of the bank) (Bruno and Shin, 2012).[23] In October 2010, the government also imposed a leverage cap, a limit of 250 per cent of equity capital on foreign banks and 50 per cent on domestic banks to reduce volatility in capital flows (Bloomberg, 2010).[24] Further controls were introduced in order to curb capital inflows, including a withholding tax on foreign investors' bond holdings and further limits on currency forward trading (*FT*, 19 October 2010).[25] Similarly, a series of FX-related measures were

23. Although this levy began to operate in August 2011, it was originally discussed at the beginning of 2010, but formally announced in December of that year and passed in the National Congress in April 2011. The finance vice minister announced the government's intention 'to regulate systemic risk from excessive capital inflows and outflows', deciding to introduce a bank levy to curb this problem (Bloomberg.com), 'South Korea Imposes Levy on Foreign Exchange Borrowings to Stop Outflows', 20 December 2010).
24. The government is preparing new measures in order to stop the won from appreciating. For example, it might be tightening the cap on banks' holdings of foreign-exchange derivatives. Furthermore, in order to deal with speculators, South Korean regulators began to audit how banks should handle foreign-currency derivatives. Likewise, on 8 December 2010 the National Assembly passed a bill that would, starting on 1 January 2011, tax interest income from treasury and central bank bonds by as much as 14% and put a 20% levy on capital gains from their sale.
25. Yoon Jeung-hyun, South Korea's finance minister at the time, declared to Parliament, 'We are preparing to counter the potential problems that liquidity flows into emerging countries sparked by low interest rates worldwide can cause (quoted at Cardiff Garcia, 'S Korea Plans Capital Controls', FT – Alphaville, 19 October 2010).

inserted to reduce derivative market risky performance – measures that were particularly aimed at exchange derivatives, as investors continued to be highly leveraged (Prates and Fritz, 2013). Monetary authorities later placed a tax on capital gains from foreign investment in bonds (*FT*, 18 September 2013). In sum, an array of new regulations was now in place in order to limit foreign currency mismatch, such as by constraining effective foreign borrowing by the corporate sector and wholesale funding by banks. All measures were introduced followed the government initiative titled *Plan to Mitigate the Volatility of Capital Flows*, which started in June 2010.[26] The Plan's main points were '*a reduction of banks' excessive short-term borrowing, the reining in of unnecessary and non-urgent demand for foreign currency and strengthening the management of the soundness of banks' foreign exchange business*' (BOK, 2010). The Bank of Korea (BOK) has also restated its commitment to financial stability, periodically analysing the potential risks threatening the Korean financial sector.[27]

According to Bruno and Shin (2012), the set of macro-prudential measures has helped reduce capital inflows' sensitiveness to global factors. Measures also proved useful for extending the maturity structure of the external debt.[28] Macro-prudential measures and leverage caps eased (in the two-year time span initiated by mid-2010) the maturity mismatch (mostly attached to foreign banks branches), observing an important decrease in short-term borrowing (U$ 35 billion) along with an increase in long-term borrowing (U$ 20 billion) (Kim, 2013).

Financial Market Evolution and the Financial Trilemma

Korea has largely been seen as a financially repressed economy, particularly since the renationalization of commercial banks, which started in 1961. Korean firms relied basically on bank financing, with banks acting as chaebols' financial partners, leaving no room for capital markets to develop.

Financial deregulation started in the early 1980s, including the reprivatization of commercial banks, the removing of interest rate ceilings as well a reduction in government-direct lending – although the state continued to exert influence on their functioning.[29] Authorities advanced further in reducing restrictions on FX transactions, whereas greater autonomy was given to bank management. Financial deregulation permitted

26. Authorities obtained greater support (for the capital control measures) at the G20 summit in Seoul, in November 2010 (Cho, 2010; Bruno and Shin, 2012).
27. Financial stability is regarded as one of the policy goals that must be achieved by the BOK, together with price stability and economic growth. Twice a year the Bank of Korea publishes the Financial Stability Report (FSR), which it submits to the Korean National Assembly (BOK, 2013).
28. Leverage caps could be assimilated to quantitative restrictions, directly affecting banks' foreign borrowing. Macro-prudential stability levies (MSLs), in contrast, can be thought of as price restrictions, affecting banks' borrowing through costs or net returns (Kim, 2013).
29. Particularly, because it continued with the appointment of senior management in the new privatized banks. But also as the state remained the owner of the largest two banks: the Korea Development Bank (KDB) and the Korea Import and Export Bank (KEXIM).

Table 9.3 A brief description of Korea's macro-prudential tools

	Type of regulation	Objective		Time	Ratio
Macro-prudential policy tools	Foreign Exchange liquidity	Designed for curing the potential weakness in domestic banking and FX transactions	AACs	FX liquidity ratio introduced in 1997	FX liquidity ratio: (Liquid assets with maturity of 3 months or less / Liquid liabilities with 3 months or less) x 100
	Maturity mismatch	To ensure FX liquidity		Maturity mismatch ratio in 1999	MM ratio: ((FX Assets – FX liabilities) / Total FX Assets) * 100
	Long-term borrowing	To curb loan-term FX loans		It was originally applied in 1991	LTB ratio: (FX borrowing of 3 years or + / FX loans of 3 years or +) * 100
	FX position management	Introduced to reduce FX risks		Oldest MaPP: 1964	
	Domestic currency	To regulate banks' risk management	AACs	DC liquidity ratio introduced in 1999, reinforced after 2002	DC liquidity ratio: (liquid assets with maturity of 3 months or less / liquid liabilities with maturity of 3 months or less) * 100
	Loan to Deposit	Regulate the amount of credit supply or bank's individual balance sheet items	AACs	Initially introduced in 2002, later abolished and replaced by the DC liquidity ratio	
	Loan to Value		AACs	LTV introduced in 2002	LTV ratio: (mortgage loans + senior lending on houses + rent security received) / house price

Table 9.3 *(cont.)*

	Type of regulation	Objective		Time	Ratio
	Debt to Income		AACs	DTI first appeared in 2005	DTI ratio: annual mortgage and other loan payments / annual income
	Macro-prudential Stability Level	Affects the operating margins and funding costs of financial institutions. Levy on the outstanding amounts of non-deposit FX liabilities, with rates varying from 2 to 20 basic points depending on the maturity of the liabilities	AGFCs	MSL introduced in 2011	
	Loan-to-deposit	To improve domestic banks' liquidity conditions and suppress their competition to expand their asset sizes through reliance on wholesale funding. To reduce banks' wholesale funding	AGFCs	LtD ratio introduce in 2009	

Source: Own elaboration based on Lee and Shin (2013)

first the expansion of a group of NBFIs, and later of those acting as merchant banking corporations (MBCs).[30]

During the early 1990s, authorities bypassed a series of normative changes, helping eliminate former differences among MBC (long-term lending) and IFI institutions (short-term lending), which particularly benefited former IFIs as they were previously

30. Until the early 1990s, the Korean financial system included both MBCs and investment finance companies (IFCs), with the former oriented to long-term business and the latter to short-term operations

prevented from entering the FX business. Chaebols also highly benefited from this new institutional scheme, as MBCs were now granting credits to them at very competitive rates. Conglomerates were also profiting from the rules governing the banking system, as lending decisions now relied on clients' collateral and inter-company guarantees (Chopra et al., 2001). On the whole, most operations consisted of borrowing short term from financial institutions abroad to lend long term to local industrial conglomerates at home. Henceforth, banks' short-term foreign liabilities increased significantly, particularly those working in close association with MBCs. A highly favourable interest rate differential was the key attraction for those intending to enter business, and also helps explain the strong connection observed between foreign liabilities attributed to the financial sector and Korean foreign liabilities.

When international lenders finally started to refuse to roll over short-term loans to MBCs, Korean firms began to experience an important maturity-mismatch problem involving foreign currency assets and liabilities. Undoubtedly, a weak regulatory environment and a rather complex supervisory system came to explain the collapse of commercial banks at that time (Choi and Lee, 2006).[31] Financial regulation and supervision of MBCs resulted in either weak or non-existent entities, and fragmentation between the office of banking supervision (at the Bank of Korea) and the Ministry of Finance and Economy (MOFE) (Chopra et al., 2001). Institutional weakness is also related to poorer capital requirement conditions for entry and to maintaining relatively modest supervision over the FX business.

The crisis compelled the Korean government to intervene in financial markets,[32] even forcing monetary authorities to acquire two distressed commercial banks[33] and to suspend an important number of merchant banks and close 10 among them as insolvency maintained. Afterwards, banking regulation was reinforced, bypassing a strict set of prudential measures (Lee, 2010), including a BIS capital adequacy ratio for MBCs (Choi and Lee, 2006), and new rules to avoid maturity and exchange rate mismatches (Lee, 2010). New regulation was now limiting lending to chaebol entities and their affiliates, introducing tough disclosure requirements. Korean authorities also decided to consolidate supervision into a single independent agency (FSC) and its executive branch (FSS), which

31. Among various supervisory institutions participating in banking supervision: the Ministry of Finance and Economics (MOFE), the Office of Bank Supervision (OBS) and the Bank of Korea (BOK). In 1999, Korean authorities integrated four supervisory bodies (the OBS, the Securities Supervisory Body (SSB), the Insurance Supervisory Board (ISB) and the Non-bank Supervisory Authority (NBSA) into a single new entity (the Financial Supervisory Service).
32. Two agencies were installed after the crisis. The Korea Deposit Insurance Corporation (KDIC) was in charge of financial entities' recapitalization, loss coverage and depositor protection, whereas Korean Asset Management Corporation (KAMCO) became responsible for the purchase of impaired assets and liabilities from all financial institutions covered by the deposit guarantee, to minimize the public burden of financial restructuring (Chopra et al., 2001, p. 45).
33. The Korea First Bank (KFB) and the Seoul Bank. As the initial policies showed limited success, the government made known a new wave of nationalization in 2000, increasing the number of commercial banks under governmental control to eight.

began to scrutinize the real estate market in late 2002 (Igan and Kang, 2011). To sum up, the new regulations introduced after the collapse were expected to increase banking supervision and to improve system transparency, but unfortunately prudential regulation would adopt a micro, not macro, perspective.

After the collapse, Korean authorities firmly encouraged the entry of foreign banks (Yi, et al., 2009; Lee, 2010), and the Foreign Investment Promotion Act of 1998 the legal instrument opened up financial institutions to foreign investors – which were now entitled to buy a hundred per cent of local banks. Consequently, and after a second round of bank restructuring,[34] foreign banks' market share further advanced, totalling now more than 70 per cent of total market share.[35] In sum, the crisis transformed the local banking industry: a more concentrated and denationalized financial system emerged. Another seaside transformation was implemented after the passing of the Financial Company Act (2000), which permitted the breakthrough of so-called supermarket banks (Cho, 2010). The government decided to ease prior restrictions affecting foreign banks' activities in Korea. For example, FBBs net borrowing from their parent bank came to be considered as conforming to FBBs' capital. In doing so, authorities indirectly induced cross-border funding and the altering of FBBs' balance sheets.[36] FX market regulation was also significantly altered, fully liberalizing all current account transactions, whereas authorities adopted a negative list approach towards capital account transactions (Cho, 2010). The legal metamorphosis also touched Korea's capital markets, as authorities were now promoting a new financial mix for local firms: equity replacing debt. Nevertheless, and despite (or because of) the observed transformation, financial markets would end up adding more volatility to the system.

Korean banks were now borrowing US dollars almost exclusively from foreign bank branches (Kim, 2009). Dependence on foreign banks, however, increased even further as domestic banks relied heavily on FX swap transactions (Lee, 2010; Baba and Shim, 2011). This near-monopoly status in supplying US dollars to the Korean market certainly reflected their power after liberalization. Foreign banks were also privileged by financial regulations as it included an asymmetrical treatment; they were free to have any liquidity ratio and a different regulation than that applicable to local banks (Cho, 2010; Baba and Kokenyne, 2011). They were just subject to risk management standards.

When the Lehman Brothers collapse occurred, banks began to suffer from deleverage. As a result, and resembling the 1997 crisis, the economy exhibited another

34. In October 2000, new legislation was passed (Financial Holding Company Act), permitting authorities to advance with banking mergers. Consequently, in April 2001 the Woori Finance Holding Company was created.
35. Three out of the top ten foreigners operating in the country were from the United States, and they controlled 25% of the commercial banking market – with Citibank ranking first among them (USITC, 2010)
36. This regulation has also induced foreign banks to enter into arbitrage: FBBs were borrowing money (US) from headquarters offices and selling them hard-currency/US$] at the local ER market to purchase higher-yielding Korean sovereign bonds. Thereafter, increased liquidity permitted FBBs to inflate the asset bubble.

currency-mismatching problem, but now banks were among the most affected players.[37] Things got worse as most banks relied on short-debt for funding, introducing a maturity mismatch problem [to the commented, currency mismatch one] (Kim, 2013).[38] As FBBs decided to aggressively compete in the funding of the real estate sector, they expanded both mortgage loans (households) and credits (construction companies), and they became hardly exposed to the GFC. Furthermore, the previously mentioned (incomplete) interest rate liberalization process ended up affecting both households (as the rate on deposits remained under regulation) and also banks (as they were absorbing fewer deposits). Consequently, banks were now forced to look for new sources of funds in order to fill the gap, a position that apparently benefited FBBs: they could easily obtain funds from their headquarters. Alternatively, households tried to diversify their risk by investing in the local stock market. The banking industry (and particularly FBBs) was also interested in the search for new alternatives, as the new legislation was forcing banks to look for new business opportunities. This led to an increase in the use of cross-border funding, which induced banks to lend beyond what prudence might dictate. The burst worsened even more, however, as local agents' appetite for liquidity drained funds away from the stock market, and local branches of foreign banks were suddenly asked to revert to previous capital inflows. Henceforth, and overall, the crisis confirmed the 'pro-cyclicality' of the banking sector, besides the excessive exposure showed by the Korean financial system following the GFC. Korea's experience additionally indicates the need to evaluate the stabilizing or the destabilizing role of foreign banks (Jeon, Li and Wu, 2014). State banks, in contrast, showed outstanding behaviour during the crisis, guaranteeing loans to small to medium firms and channelling government funds (Stallings, 2015, p. 59).

In contrast to the post-Asian crisis, policymakers were now trying to somewhat disentangle the prior banking industry denationalization path. Public-owned banks (POBs) or local investors were now heading the list of financial institutions, and the government has little interest in selling them to foreign investors (*FT*, 11 May 2011). Korean authorities were also raising regulatory standards, now discriminating against foreign bankers.[39] Henceforth, and because revenues and profits continue to squeeze,[40] some

37. From the first quarter of 2006 to the third quarter of 2008, US$ 168 billion flowed into Korea. From this total, US$ 137.4 billion was funded by the banking sector. After the fourth quarter of 2008, despite the Korean government's declaring a loan guarantee, lenders withdrew US$ 59 billion from banks. (Data from Kim, n.d.).
38. For the banking sector as a whole, and prior to the GFC, currency and maturity mismatches peaked at US$ 68 billion and US$ 85 billion, respectively (Kim, 2013).
39. Banks' CEOs complained about new government regulatory measures, including restrictions on dividend payments, requests for the reduction of fees and interest rates and a requirement that subsidiaries of foreign financial groups process data in South Korea instead of at regional headquarters (*FT*, 'Foreign Banks Struggle in South Korea', 18 September 2013).
40. Since the latest crisis, the banking sector has experienced an important shrinking in the loan-to-deposit interest rate spread, which explains the above-mentioned contraction. Profitability is further limited by an increase in banks' credit risks (FSR–BOK, 2014).

international banks began to reduce their exposure,[41] either leaving or drastically reducing their operations in the country.[42] Enthusiasm for foreigners was reduced among Korean policymakers, however. In December 2010, the Korean government announced it was abandoning the announced plan to sell its majority stake in Chohung Bank and Hanvit Bank, and its minority stake in KFB and Korea Exchange Bank (Yi et al., 2009). Korea has also maintained its majority stake in Woori Bank, Korea's largest financial group by assets. After the latest crisis, SOBs regained importance, particularly the KDB, the Expo-Import Bank of Korea and Korea Finance Corporation.

To sum up, Korean economic authorities seem to have renewed their faith in local banks alongside dwindling enthusiasm on foreign banks. Government now sees the financial system as 'a semi-public utility that should help the growth of the manufacturing sector rather than a industry that stands alone'.[43] However, the latest crisis has once again revealed the unstable role of non-banking financial institutions as, for example, in generating the real state bubble.

Korean Financial Sector, Foreign Banks and the Financial Trilemma

As observed in the first part of the book, in Chapter 3, when a country's financial system becomes highly interconnected to global markets, the government's ability to regulate it is severely diminished. As a matter of fact, when cross-border funding remains uncontrolled, national authorities become prevented from pursuing the goal of financial stabilization by themselves. As observed in other latitudes, financial liberalization has radically altered the traditional banking sector's balance sheet. In particular, cross-border non-core liabilities transformed into a leading source of funds for Korean banks – demonstrating the challenges posed by the financial trilemma.

The expansion in non-core liabilities permitted an increase in the rate of growth of credit, but it also induced a boost in financial system vulnerability. Risks are reduced by the effect of the rapid increase in credit availability, but risk perception by agents is often misplaced as they observe prices continuing to increase (a trend associated with a low probability of default) (Bruno and Shin, 2013). In sum, as observed by Borio and Disyatat (2011), when optimism in markets prevails, financial constraints are relaxed

41. The fall in profits could also be attributed to exogenous factors. According to Kim Woo-jin, a researcher at the Korea Institute of Finance, 'The profitability of the Korean retail banking market continues to fall because of falling growth and rising bad loans amid the slowing economy' (*FT*, 'HSBC to Exit Korean Retail Banking', 5 July 2013).
42. Citigroup recently announced its intention to close nearly 30% of its retail branches in the country. HSBC closed its retail banking and wealth management units in 2013, whereas Standard Chartered took a $ 1 billion write-down at its South Korean subsidiary – and expected to cut branches 25% further (*FT*, 'Citigroup to Close Swath of South Korean Retail Branches', 8 April 2014).
43. The statement comes from Hwang Young-key, a former chairman at Woory and Kb, one of the leading financial groups in Korea (*FT*, 'Foreign Banks Struggle in South Korea', 18 September 2013).

beyond what prudence might dictate: an *excess financial elasticity* trend appears. As the cycle is reversed, this extraordinary source of funds vanishes and the local financial system is hardly affected, as observed in the aftermath of the GFC. As previously observed, during the years preceding the GFC, Korean authorities decided to ease prior restrictions applying to FBBs. They graciously welcomed cross-border funding practices and certainly disregarded the challenges imposed by off-balance sheet operations.

As the crisis began, Korea experienced a substantial reversal in capital flows, which were mainly associated with banking deleveraging operations (Bruno and Shin, 2012) – mainly involving FBBs, particularly those coming from the United States (Jeon et al., 2013). As previously observed, regulation was biased towards them, as local regulators regarded foreigners as a guarantee of efficiency and stability. When the crisis arose, however, FBBs' leaders and foreigners examined the situation in detail, and authorities rushed to re-regulate the market (Bruno and Shin, 2012).

The Korean experience has also came to demonstrate how banks respond to host country monetary policy measures with FBBs playing 'a buffering or even hampering role by adjusting loan growth in a way opposite', particularly during a crisis (to domestic banks) (Jean et al., 2013). The presence of this buffering effect relates to FBBs' non-core funding. Banks' leverage now responds to global factors, not to local policies: VIX index measures. In order to curb this procyclicality bias, the government introduced an specific levy (on non-core liabilities), which proved successful in two ways, as it reduced the channelling of global funds and also made the country less sensitive to fluctuations in global funding (Bruno and Shin, 2012).

In the absence of a global regulatory body, Korea's re-regulation can be thought of as a second-best response in line with the prescriptions set by the Committee on International Economics and Policy Reform (CIEPR) (2012) prescriptions. Korea's banking regulators have also re-introduced some norms and rules in order to protect the banking system from volatility, yet some new rules are considered too stringent by the industry.[44] Some of the MPR measures introduced after the GFC might also challenge the OECD code's obligations, in particular those dealing with FX mismatches (Beck et al., 2015).[45] Thus, the Financial Services Commission is interested in transforming sectorial regulation and

44. The latest changes introduced by the regulator involve a restriction on dividend payments, the request for the reduction of fees and interest rates, and a requirement that subsidiaries of foreign financial groups process data in the country instead of relying on regional headquarters ('Foreign Banks Struggle in South Korea', *FT*, 18 September 2013).
45. In particular, the OECD report observes two different measures: (a) a leverage cap on a bank-s FX derivative position and (b) a macro-prudential stability levy (MSL). As noted by the authors, the first of the measures requires banks to limit their FX derivative position at or below a target level. If the measure applies to operations by residents abroad, it has a bearing on liberalization commitments under item XII/B of the OECD code. Even if the measure targets operations among residents, it can be challenging for prior (liberalization) commitments, and, therefore, violate the code. By fixing a levy on FX, the second measure might also be found to contradict the OECD code's obligations: it interferes with the freedom to use foreign currency as a denomination and as a settlement of listed operations between residents and non-residents (Beck et al., 2015, p. 18).

supervision, making it more transparent, but also in encouraging local banks to expand abroad and letting them introduce new financial products.

Korea's Institutionalist Path

The country has been a WTO member since its origin (as a former GATT member after 1967), and an active supporter of multilateralism. Korea's enthusiasm for financial liberalization was established with the ambitious commitments made at the time of the WTO–GATS agreements: guaranteeing foreigners access to local markets (mode 3), although some exceptions remained (Cho, 2010). By virtue of their self-imposed ambitious schedule for financial liberalization, policymakers were left with less policy space – although the balance-of-payments exception remained.

When multilateral negotiations resulted in an impasse, authorities began to consider alternatives. Bilateralism was originally attached to BITs when the first agreement was signed with Germany in 1964, and Korea became an active participant in the BIT scheme –with more than 70 BITs in force.[46] Despite its enthusiasm for BITs, however, Korea remained attached to the multilateral trade system. The 1997 crisis came to challenge this vision, and President Kim Dae-jung transformed into a leading supporter of the new bilateral appraisal. Ten years later, the GFC would push authorities further along this path, as President Lee Myung-bak included an FTA scheme in the 'Global Korea' concept. In between these two mandates, President Roh Moo-Hyun initiated conversations with the US government on an FTA deal. Roh also aimed to transform Korea into a regional financial hub (Cho, 2012). In sum, and as FTA policy remained at the centre of Korea's trade policy (Lee, 2012; Solis, 2013; Park, 2014), further financial liberalization was a natural outcome.

Korea embraced a new trade policy in the nineties, and the government started a new market-opening strategy institutionalized through the signature of PTAs – including FTAs. Initially local negotiators were certainly cautious at meetings with potential partners, limiting market openings in sensitive sectors.[47] This approach could be observed in the first FTA signed in 1999 with Chile, but was also reflected in later agreements: Singapore (2003) or the European Free Trade Association (EFTA) (2004).[48] Political opposition became important, particularly among the sectors which were most affected. As Korea's strategic objective was to become an international trade hub, authorities were aware of

46. Korea signed a total of 77 BITs, of which 68 were finally ratified and became legally binding. A total of 37 agreements were signed in the nineties, but only 16 in the previous years and 15 in the 2000s. Surprisingly, until the recently signed KORUS FTA, Korea and the United States had never agreed to sign an investment agreement. For a list of partners, see United Nations Conference on Trade and Development; UN-UNCTAD International Investment Agreement Database, available at http://investmentpolicyhub.unctad.org/IIA.
47. Agriculture is one the most sensitive sectors in FTAs, particularly for Asian and European countries. Starting with the Chilean FTA, Korean peasants became a leading voice against this type of agreement.
48. Chile became the first country with which Korea had negotiations, as Korea recognized the political experience in its partner and also the complementarities between both economies. The most difficult talks were those dealing with agricultural issues.

the increasing concessions this path required. Internally, FTA agreements were seen as a political tool to promote structural reforms and boost competition – including the financial sector. This objective also forced Korea to expand the FTA net and look for partners everywhere. Negotiators now agreed to sign WTO-plus commitments and also compromised to reduce or eliminate barriers to entry. Consequently, Korean negotiators began talks with different partners, including Peru, Turkey, ASEAN,[49] the United States, the EU) (2011)[50] and India, whereas it continues talks with Japan (Yoon Ja-young, 'Korea to Accelerate FTAs with Mexico, Japan, Korea Times, 26 January 2017),[51] Vietnam, Indonesia, Canada, Mexico, Colombia, Australia, New Zealand, Malaysia, China and MERCOSUR. Later, it would become involved in key multilateral trade negotiations: the RCEP involving 16 different countries, the trilateral China–Japan–Korea (CJK) proposal for an FTA and the US-led TPP comprising 12 different nations from the Americas and Asia (which is now in a limbo, as the United States decided to leave). The next paragraphs analyse some of the latest deals signed by Korea, with special emphasis on the financial front.

The political relationship between Korea and the United States can be considered special and resilient.[52] Nevertheless, the trade relationship between both countries was not exempted from disagreements. Foreign investment, in turn, has always been a sensitive topic in the bilateral economic relationship (Cooper et al., 2010), reflecting the US interest in the Korean market, and the continuing refusal of local authorities to open up their economy.[53] Differences, however, began to be set aside at the late 1980s–early

---

49. The Framework Agreement on Comprehensive Economic Cooperation (the FTA agreement) was negotiated sequentially. The investment chapter was finally signed in June 2009, three years later than the agreement on goods, and two years after the signature for the one dealing with services ('ASEAN–Korea FTA on Investment Signed', Bilaterals.org, posted by Bernama, 2 June 2009).
50. To become effective on 1 July 2011, if ratified by the European Parliament ('EU Signs Free-Trade Deal with South Korea, Its First with an Asian Nation', Reuters, 10 October 2010) and introducing pressure over the US FTA approval (Hwang Doo-hyong, 'Obama Gov't Wants Congress to Approve Korea FTA Before July: Kirk', Yonhap, 14 January 2011, retrieved from bilaterals.org, https://www.bilaterals.org/?obama-gov-t-wants-congress-to&lang=en).
51. Japan is Korea's second trading partner. Discussions were fiercer as political and historical demands added to economic policy questions (Cheong, 2002), while others related to the role of Japan in the early twentieth century. Anti-Japanese sentiment is still present in Korean society, whose inhabitants continue to demand a formal apology from the former colonizer's past misdeeds as well as distortions in Japanese history textbooks, territorial disputes over Tokdo Island and the issue of compensation for comfort women during World War II. From an economic perspective, Korean policymakers were concerned about the possibility of economic subordination and the growing trade deficit with Japan. Nevertheless, Ogura Kazuo, then Japanese ambassador to Korea, officially launched discussions in September 1998. A month later, during President Kim Dae-Jung's visit to Japan, both parties agreed to initiate a joint study on the issue
52. The United States–South Korea military alliance has existed for more than 50 years. Strategically, it not only serves as a buffer against the North Korean dictatorship but also deters China´s increasing power in the region.
53. The disagreement reflected, in part, the Asian prejudice towards American investors' legal demands. Although Asian countries were among the most fervent adherents of BITs, none of

1990s, marking the passing of a new era of market friendly development.[54] In short, talks with the United States were held in Washington in June 2006.[55] On 30 June 2007, the two countries signed the proposed United States–Korea Free Trade Agreement (KORUS FTA). The agreement was finally approved on 15 March 2012, despite prior objections at both sides.

The KORUS FTA structure resembles the structure of other FTAs previously signed by the US administration, including the recently signed Dominican Republic–Central American FTA (DR-CAFTA). The general principles set down in the agreement include a far-reaching definition of investment,[56] the principle of NT and MFN treatment, the minimum standard of treatment. Likewise, the KORUS FTA sets limits on government expropriation of covered investments. It also requires each partner to allow for the free transfer of financial capital pertaining to covered investment both into and out of the country, although it allows some exceptions.[57] Finally, and similar to other agreements, the KORUS FTA establishes procedures for the settlement of investor–state disputes involving investment covered under the agreement. The two countries committed to provide NT and MFN treatment to the services imports from each other; promoted transparency in the development and implementation of regulations in services, providing timely notice of decisions on government permission to sell services; prohibited limits on market access; prohibited FDI requirements, such as export and local content requirement and employment mandates;[58] and, prohibited restrictions on the type of business entities through which a service provider

---

those countries signed a bilateral agreement with the United States (Stanley, 2008). However, South Korea and the United States negotiated an agreement, but it failed due to US opposition to South Korea's so-called screen quota on domestic films and the latter's resistance to lifting or reducing it (Cooper, 2010).

54. The completion of the Uruguay Round in 1995, and Korea's accession to the OECD in 1996 strengthened this trend. Despite commitments assumed at the time of joining the OECD, Korea refused to fully liberalize its capital account (Kim and Yang, 2010) – a pattern to be lifted in 1997.
55. In the late eighties the US government first became interested in Korea's openness. Talks among partners began over Korea's large merchandise trade surplus with the United States favoured by an undervalued won. As for US negotiations, US interest in talks followed Korea's large merchandise trade surplus, originating from an undervalued won – at least from US negotiators (Amsden, 2001, p. 329).
56. Investment includes investment agreements between a government and a foreign firm with respect to natural resources, certain procurement construction activities and more; investment authorizations; enterprises; shares, stock and other forms of equity participation in an enterprise; bonds, debentures, other debt instruments and loans; futures, options and other derivatives; turnkey, construction and management; production, concession, revenue sharing and other similar contracts; intellectual property rights; licenses, authorizations, permits and similar rights conferred pursuant to domestic law; and other tangible and intangible, movable or immovable property, and related property rights, such as leases, mortgages, liens and pledges.
57. Originally Korean negotiators wanted safeguards applicable in case of a foreign exchange crisis, a petition rejected by the United States. In the end, the parties agreed to introduce safeguards at the cost of maintaining financial liberalization (Ahn, 2008).
58. Under chapter 13, neither party can require financial institutions of the other party to hire individuals of a particular nationality as senior managers or other essential personnel, nor can

could provide a service.[59] The agreement allows US companies to supply financial services on a cross-border basis, including management services for investment funds and international transit insurances. Likewise, the two countries agreed to the 'negative list' approach in making commitments in services – a highly valuable principle obtained by US negotiators.

According to the agreement, Korea committed to reducing barriers to trade and investment in its services sector, including the financial one. Furthermore, it guarantees the right to full American ownership of a financial institution in Korea. It might also be the case that Korean prudential regulations can be deemed illegal under the new treaty (Gallagher, 2010b). In addition, the agreement commits partners to refrain from limiting the size of financial institutions (PublicWatch, 2010). Likewise, the commitments are *ratcheted*, meaning that when new services emerge in one of the economies, the FTA automatically covers those services – unless they are identified as an exception (Cooper et al., 2010). Finally, in relation to the capital control issue, the KORUS FTA financial chapter might be read as forbidding any limit to the transfer of capital (PublicWatch, 2010).

The agreement has, without doubt, important diplomatic and security implications (Schott, 2007; Cooper et al., 2010). From an economic perspective, the agreement can reinforce trade and investment flows between partners.[60] For the United States the agreement represents a diplomatic victory, which helps restrict the increasing Chinese influence in Asia (Ahn, 2008; Cooper et al., 2010). Looking at the financial and other services chapters,[61] it becomes evident that the United States obtained a great deal (Cooper et al., 2010), placing it as an international benchmark or a 'model agreement in financial services'.[62] For the financial sector, the agreement 'no better, more sophisticated trade arrangement for financial firms' (William J. Toppeta, president, International MetLife, 6 April 2010). In particular, under the terms of the FTA, Korea's remaining non-tariff impediments to banking services stand at 29 per cent, well below the actual 76 per cent accepted by Korea at the GATS.[63] A similar statement was made by Citigroup's Laure

a party require more than a minority of the board of directors to be nationals or residents of the other party (USITC, 2010, at pp. 4–9)

59. In particular, each party would be required to permit a financial institution of the other party to provide new financial services on the same basis that it permits its own domestic institutions to provide (USITC, 2010, at pp. 4–9).
60. Korea is the seventh-largest trading partner of the United States based on total trade. The US merchandise trade balance with Korea moved from a $ 2.9 billion surplus in 1996 to a $ 13.9 billion deficit in 2006. In 2005, US services exports to Korea were approximately $ 10.3 billion, and US services imports from Korea were $ 6.3 billion. However, the United States holds the largest single-country share of FDI stock in Korea, with 30% (USITC, 2010).
61. Trade in services cut across several chapters of the agreement, among others: chapter 12 (cross-border trade in services); chapter 13 (financial services); chapter 15 (Telecommunications); chapter 11 (foreign investment).
62. The Korea–US Trade Partnership declared it 'a ground-breaking achievement, providing more extensive provisions related to financial services than ever before included in a U.S. FTA' (www.KOREAUSPartnership.org)
63. Non-tariff impediments are synthesized in a single measure: the tariff equivalent (TE), which measures the percentage increase in prices due to trade impediments relative to the price that would exist in the absence of trade restrictions.

Lane, corporate co-chair of the US–Korea FTA Business Coalition: 'the best financial chapter negotiated in a free trade agreement to date'. The KORUS FTA obtained the support of both big trade unions and business associations (US government).[64] As a result, the US service sector is particularly happy with the KORUS FTA approval, as the agreement includes liberalization measures 'in excess of the current General Agreement on Trade in Services (GATS) regime' (USITC, 2010).[65] Surprisingly enough, instead of focusing on the increased access to the US market, South Korean negotiators emphasized 'the medium and long-term gains that would stem from increased allocative efficiency of the South Korean economy, particularly in the services industries'.

Controversies were also observed at the time Korea inaugurated negotiations with the EU, with some among them associated to the financial realm. In particular, in order to remove some of the restrictions imposed on foreign banks, EU negotiators asked Korea to go beyond the GATS commitments (Cho, 2010). Similarly, Europeans were pushing to remove FX limits imposed on foreign banks. Although requirements were made well before the start of the GFC or the European crisis, the EU maintained its posture well beyond 2010. Furthermore, the final agreement included broad liberalization (WTO plus) commitments, affecting all financial sectors. The parties agreed to introduce a negative list approach for the establishment of local subsidiaries or branches, although it maintain a positive list approach for services in general, including the case of cross-border supply. By virtue of the agreement, financial institutions are free to offer services to both European and Korean customers without operating where the customer is based.

A similar ambitious proposal was observed in the FTA recently signed with Australia (KAFTA) and in force since December 2014, which grants full access to investors from both countries. In particular, Australian financial services providers are entitled to establish or acquire institutions in Korea, leaving them free to choose whether to establish under a branch or as a subsidiary form. Surprisingly, the agreement even recognizes Australian firms' right to supply services on a cross-border basis. Finally, KAFTA establishes a negative list regime, which presumes financial services should be allowed unless specifically prohibited. As previously reported, by virtue of this agreement, Australian investors are backed by an international arbitration mechanism.

The proposed agreement with China and the trilateral CJK seems to be less ambitious, at least in considering the proposals on the financial front (Schott and Cimino, 2014). In contrast to deals signed with developed nations, the main purpose of Korean negotiators might be to enhance local banks' access to China's financial market. In contrast to Korea, however, authorities in China do not regard the (FTA) scheme as a vehicle to (financial) market liberalization (Korea Institute of Finance, 2014). A friendlier

64. http://www.whitehouse.gov/the-press-office/2010/12/03/statements-support-us-korea-trade-agreement.
65. Treaty detractors were also found in the United States, among them the NGO Public Citizen's Trade Watch, whose doubts relate to the increasing rights granted to South Korean investors by the treaty, which could end up challenging the autonomy of the US judiciary (www.tradewatch.org).

approach towards financial liberalization might be possible if Chinese authorities remain attached to RMB internationalization (see chapter on China).

Once classified as a developing country, the Korean economy is now actively part of the select OECD club. From a political economy perspective, globalization, which was originally challenged, is now widely supported by local firms and policy circles, as Korean firms are actively involved in global markets. Korea's trade policy remains centred on the active pursuit of FTAs, a scheme that increasingly puts more constraints on authorities' policy space.

The Korean experience demonstrates the challenges imposed by cross-border flows and deregulated financial markets, evidencing the need to advance with financial supervision and prudential controls. By virtue of the guarantees extended in recent agreements, however, investors might be tempted to fulfil a request and, henceforth, be entitled to challenge the latest macro-prudential measures. Despite the latest re-regulation attempts, the ambition of transforming Korea into a financial hub in northeast Asia remains strong.

Part 3

Final Remarks on Financial Globalization and Local Insertion

Chapter Ten

CONCLUSIONS

The founding fathers of Bretton Woods institutions shared a common vision: in order to prevent a new phase of economic instability they intended to create a rule-based multilateral framework, imposing clear obligations on the contracting parties and prohibiting the adoption of protectionist and beggar-thy-neighbour policies. But the post-war economic framework also included clear rules, directed at preventing large capital flow movements. Henceforth, instability was mostly absent, as financial markets remained local. This common vision, however, began to recede 40 years ago when a worldwide liberalization process was initiated and it radically transformed global financial markets. The Keynesian idea of maintaining financial markets as local and stable suddenly vanished, and mainstream economics embraced financial globalization. Thereafter, foreigners would become active players in key financial markets almost everywhere, and local investors would be entitled to invest abroad. In theory, financial integration has been sought as beneficial for both developing countries and EMEs (particularly for those short of funds) and global investors alike (as they would be obtaining higher yields by arbitrating on a global scale). In practice, though, financial globalization pushed emerging markets towards increasing macro volatility and greater financial fragility. Underperformance, certainly, was not necessarily correlated with macro negligence or with the presence of improper institutions (as mainstream advisers have been encouraging in the recent past), but particularly with their excessive exposition to unfettered capital flows (as they actually recognize).

Economic Policy in a World of Pyramids and Triangles

In order to analyse the vast challenges introduced by globalization on open (but small) economies, we have introduced a series of canonical models describing the different (but highly interconnected) constraints binding on the macro, financial and political fronts. Certainly, any of these models cannot describe in detail all the challenges being face by each of the analysed countries, although they help us a lot. Henceforth, and beyond specific geometrical shapes and passionate discussions, we found all of the trilemmas as useful models to describe the basic set of constraints observed in the journey to globalization. In particular, this set might be helpful for policymakers at LDCs and EMEs to realize the vast set of constraints imposed by an excessive or premature globalization. As the previous chapters have shown, internationalizing (opening) the economy is a difficult task, but if properly managed it can bring more benefits than costs.

The assertiveness of the monetary trilemma can be a challenge when governments operate in the middle ground. Why? Because it gives them some room for manoeuvrability (flexibility) in pursuing macro policies. How? As a means of managing exchange rate regimes or any other policy tool having more policy space. Policy space was somewhat neglected in the past, as governments were forced to play at the extremes: either to fix the ER (early nineties) or to maintain an independent monetary policy and flex rates (late nineties). Middle grounds (flexibility) were equalized to more discrete power in rulers' hands. Discretionary power for EMEs or LDCs was seen as a curse. Notwithstanding, after observing that one experience after another was failing and the severity of the crisis mounting, policymakers in EMEs decided to move towards the middle ground. Some were jittery from volatility (fear of floating), and others alarmed by the arrival of capital flow tsunamis (fear of appreciation). Henceforth, the idea of managed ER began to gain more fans (2000s).

The GFC altered all of this. The relevance of more policy space began to be recognized by academics of all schools, and identified as mandatory by policymakers around the world. Regardless of the appropriateness of the liberalization sequence and observed prudence in capital opening management, financial markets are more interconnected nowadays than in 2008. In view of that, some academics are wondering if the original trilemma posed by Robert Mundel in the 1960s remains valid. If the global financial cycle becomes unrelated with macro fundamentals at home, monetary policy is beyond national control. Henceforth, and in order to guarantee financial stability, policymakers are confronted with few options but to (re)introduce capital controls, as suggested by H. Rey (2013). An alternative vision of market instability is offered by M. Obstfield (2014), who suggests it arises through the concurrence of a financial trilemma – not just the simple monetary one. In other words, in order to maintain the effectiveness of the monetary policy, he is suggesting a re-re-regulatory reform aimed at restricting cross-border movements of funds.

Being integrated into global markets, the latest group might argue, represents the most efficient outcome as market participants could profit from pooling funds at a global level. The GFC came to demonstrate the challenges of such a response for EMEs: the less integrated they were, the more stable they remained. Greater autonomy should certainly not imply a ban on foreign banks' entry, though it does imply the importance of regulating them properly: how they are funded, which organizational form adopts them and so on. Otherwise, global banks' presence could seriously disturb the local financial market. Alternatively, the presence of a multinational agreement could do the task. This idea is behind the Basel Committee for Banking Supervision – a supranational agency for dealing with financial stability issues. Unfortunately, as the discussion in the previous paragraphs shows, this sort of agreement is proving difficult to maintain for both the banking industry and the harshly criticized OTC market. In addition, most of the latest regulatory initiatives seem to favour a fragmented financial system. New legislation came to be passed in order to limit cross-border flows and global banks' operations – as observed in the United States and other developed countries. Large EMEs are also aware of these challenges, and most have adopted a tough regulatory stance to avoid a new financial crisis in the future.

Coordination attempts are dwindling. Then, as well, the call for an urgent and necessary reform of the multilateral setting is still valid (international financial institutions). Even global leaders who were part of the G20 were unsuccessful in adopting common reform proposals, nor did they succeed in designing a new international financial architecture. In the meantime, cross-border funds kept increasing and global banks expanded their worldwide presence.

From a policy perspective, the back-to-basics movement seems to be the new normal. Or perhaps it just implies a temporary brake on the hyperglobalization trend experienced in the post–Bretton Woods scenario. This unregulated stage pushed developing countries towards a new dilemma: disregard democracy or abandon any attempt to maintain national sovereignty. The GFC has put stress on the constraints imposed by this type of insertion, although most of the countries (but not all) revisited in this book were already aware of them and, henceforth, avoided being institutionally banned and maintained their policy space.

Some countries decided to adopt extreme solutions, limiting their (policy) options in order to signal their enthusiasm, but in such a case, they are left at the mercy of the constraints dictated by each of the models being described. Aware of the challenges imposed by financial globalization, others preferred to maintain their economies beyond the constraints imposed by a hyperglobalization scenario. A similar preoccupation was observed among policymakers in the North in the aftermath of the Second World War, as they always procured liberal democracy to be maintained. An inclusive multilateralism would not only make (soft) globalization feasible but also simultaneously might prevent a new crisis from erupting. Unfortunately, as proclaimed by H. Minsky, 'The Wall Streets of the world are important; they generate destabilizing forces, and from time to time the financial processes of our economy lead to serious threats of financial and economic instability, that is, the behaviour of the economy becomes incoherent.' (2008, p. 4). We might plead for international coordination, yet nobody can guarantee us that such an arrangement remains feasible. This brings us back to the political arena and the search for a new global era of embedded liberalism. If cooperation and coordination cannot be achieved, we might be condemned to fall into a new deglobalization era whose historical roots can be traced to the early seventies. The future, once again, remains uncertain.

What Is the Comparative Setting Telling Us?

A comparative analysis reconfirms how different the Latin American and Asian countries analysed in this book are. Latin American countries are still working on a trial basis on how to integrate themselves with global financial markets. In a continuous loop, politicians' enthusiasm for playing for the present day is followed by a dismal feeling and distrust in global financial markets. Asians are more cautious, advancing in a piecewise manner and trying to avoid boom and bust cycles – although South Korea embraced a large process of financial deregulation and capital account openness. Autonomy and caution, however, do not mean undertaking a protectionist stance and keeping the economy away from global markets. The experience of Asia helps us understand its proper meaning. Certainly, this message has not appeared out of nowhere. Several developmental economists have written about it, discussing the strategic path adopted by a group of Southeast Asian economies in the past and why Latin America has fallen behind. What is novel in this book is that it presents a broad picture of financial globalization, recommending that we take note of the different and cautious approaches adopted by some countries and why others are just rule-takers.

Argentina and Brazil are still wrangling with inflation trends and exchange rate dynamics. Either backed by a commodity boom or due to the arrival of large capital inflows, both economies seem doomed to remain trapped by the Dutch disease. Therefore, an appreciation bias remains stubbornly in place, affecting economic competitiveness. However, suddenly commodity prices could begin to be dismissed, as occurred during 2013–14 and, consequently, lead to a sudden reversal in capital flows which follows. The external gap reopens. In addition to this gap, both countries have often become exposed to two other gaps (the savings and the fiscal one), whose reappearance follows the outbreak of a new adverse macro cycle.[1] Unfortunately, neither Argentina nor Brazil is capable leaving the triplet behind. Cyclically, it reappears, pushing the macro, which is always subject to sudden movements and threats.

As for Argentina, the new government has managed to bypass the external gap. But the arrival of foreign funds attached to a mounting external debt, has also led to sustaining the peso appreciation bias – a trend initiated by the former administration. The trend is additionally being fuelled by a huge interest rate differential (favouring carry trade operations on a great scale), originating in the tight monetary policy being followed by the BCRA. Given that the peso depreciated by 64 per cent since Macri took office, the multilateral RER was ameliorated by 12 per cent – although by the starting date the peso was 33 per cent below the largest appreciated level observed during the CFK administration (by the end of 2011). Fiscal inheritance is also a huge problem for the new government, as the former administration relied on a highly populist stance. Recognizing this, but trying to avoid mounting social tensions, the actual government decided to undertake new external debt. In other words, as global funds are now available for Argentina, authorities adopted a gradual path to restoring fiscal balance.

Real exchange rate appreciation has also become a highly debated issue in Brazil, basically as it continue to affect the industry' competitiveness. What might shock an impartial observer is the persistence of this trend, which relates to the fact that authorities have been using some of the recommended policy tools to prevent that from happening. As they increased their FX reserves, reserve requirements were limiting the short dollar position of banks or controls to avoid excessive capital inflows (remember the IOF tax). Notwithstanding all these efforts, the Brazilian real remains somewhat overvalued. The government's inability to interrupt the fiscal drainage, and the consumption bias on government spending, might also be collaborating in this observed trend. Additionally, the huge political crisis has pushed authorities towards short-term outcomes – and towards

1. The idea of a triple gap model was introduced by the Brazilian economist Edmar Bacha more than 20 years ago. (E. Bacha, 'A Three-Gap Model of Foreign Transfers and the GDP Growth Rate in Developing Countries', *Journal of Development Economics* 32, no. 2 (1990): 279–96).

engaging in more disputable initiatives. In sum, Argentina's and Brazil's growth rates were blurred in the recent past, although signals of recovery are beginning to be observed.

Asian countries are different in several aspects with respect to Latin American ones, and certainly they differ from a macroeconomic perspective. Like Japan in the past, South Korea first and China two decades later, most of them have followed the export-led growth model. In order to make this model work, a stable and competitive exchange rate remains part of the backbones – often associated with a peg regime, attaching the local currency to the US dollar. But although it has importance for exporters and economic development, authorities have never relied solely on it. Capital controls were always in policymakers' toolkit, and are still in place in countries like China or India. Financial repression plus controls have also been functional to Asians countries' interest in maintaining economic agents' savings at home. Large saving rates, in turn, were permitted to avoid the investment-saving trap (cyclically) observed in Latin America. Obviously this framework could not remain forever; therefore, the main challenge for sovereign states is how to move to a more open and competitive stage without being harmed in the process.

In financial terms, Latin American countries remained practically untouched by the GFC. This does not necessarily respond to the operation of a regulatory framework, at least not only to it. Banks in the region raised money through deposits from retail banking customers, instead of relying on wholesale funding. Nevertheless, foreign claims kept growing and exceeded their pre-crisis levels, although this was later disrupted. Certainly, Argentina remained away from the picture as authorities at the time found unacceptable the Judge Griesa rule – leaving the country beyond the bounds of global financial markets. The picture is more nuanced among Asian countries. More than a third of Chinese banks' total liabilities are now being wholesale funded.[2] Certainly, banking in China continues to be largely local, and cross-border flows' continuity or disruption remains at authorities discretion. In the meantime, China's largest banks are now ranked among the world's biggest. In any case, and right now, monetary authorities are beginning to face a new debt spiral. India has also opted for a sequencing reform, thus avoiding exposure of the financial system to external shocks. What is characteristic of the Indian approach is the consensual path, which is respected by all governments and central bank authorities up to the present, and which was introduced to analyse the system's present weakness and deliberate proper solutions. Finally, the experience of South Korea is quote interesting as authorities, more than 20 years ago, decided to move from repression to financial liberalization. After a boom period, a financial crash followed. Despite this experience, monetary authorities decided not to curb cross-border flows, although several regulations were introduced in order to avoid excessive flows. Notwithstanding all these norms and policies, the global financial crisis pushed the Korean banking system to initiate a profound deleveraging process. A new wave of regulation followed.

2. Alan Smith and Martin Arnold, 'Here Is the Big Reason Banks Are Safer Than a Decade Ago', *FT*, Series Financial Crisis Anniversary, 22 August 2017.

Finally, from an institutional perspective, differences are somehow mixed. On the one hand, there is Argentina's and South Korea's enthusiasm for adopting the *rules of the game*. For one reason or another, both countries adopted this reputational approach during the nineties. Brazil decided to stay away, whereas India adopted a cautious approach to both multilateral and bilateral institutions. China, however, was more enthusiastic about the issue as authorities at the time were searching for international recognition. But at any rate, insertion was not followed. China was ready to negotiate but not to accept being constrained by Washington, DC's rules. This institutional picture was partially altered in the 2000s, as Argentina decided to disregard most of the contracts being signed in the past – although it did not reject them but simply ignored them.

The agenda has recently made another twist. In order to draw investors' attention, the governments of Argentina and Brazil are ready to introduce important institutional change. The Macri administration has already adopted such an approach which was taken during Menem's government, but Brazil has rejected all previous attempts just to preserve its autonomy. Has this stance been adequate or wrong? Why do they not actively engage, as Asian countries have, to favour both investors and the host country together? In the recent past, Itamaraty try to initiate such a path. But, motivated to remain in power and to seduce investors, Temer has become a fierce advocate of strong institutions (i.e. a rule-taker).

China and India, on the other hand, have always maintained a cautious approach towards international institutional insertion. In the case of China, as it has advanced towards becoming the world first economy, it has rapidly adopted more tough rules to protect its investments abroad. India remains attached to its alternative way, as observed in the corresponding chapter. Country size might be backing this stand, but also politicians' awareness of the risks imposed by an unsuitable setting.

A SHORT AFTERWORD

Many changes have been underway since the original draft of this book was sent to the press, and, surprisingly, most of them are showing a deglobalization bias. After the GFC, monetary policy maintained an undisputed role among developed central bankers, although sometimes this setting became disputed by monetary authorities at EMEs as QE was flooding them with capital flows. How should small economies (EMEs) cope with the significant spillovers arising from the QE? But before academics and practitioners agreed on a common answer, a new challenge arrived: the taper tantrum episode in 2013 came to demonstrate, once again, how volatile capital flows could become.

At present, and despite the expansion observed among the most important economies, some risks are still underway and could threaten the sustainability of this trend in the medium term. In particular, we should look for a rise in financial stress as financial cycles mature due to the rise in protectionism. The free flow of capital across borders and currencies exacerbates the build-up of risks. Financial risks, however, can also be endogenously induced, as the Chinese debt-spiral boom seems to suggest.[1] Thus, for EMEs qualifying as commodity exporter countries, the massive arrival of capital flows can lead to an exchange rate appreciation bias. The protectionist surge adds more uncertainty, and, therefore, sudden stops are more likely.

Policymakers as well as economists are no doubt well aware of the questions posed by these huge challenges. Many were always looking beyond commercial benefits and recognizing the formidable costs globalization has impose on civil societies. This has led to some of them to publicly admit the convenience of managing capital flows or even the importance of maintaining a competitive exchange rate for economic development. Messages like this are now being sorted out through the IMF working papers series – both backing the SCRER and supporting capital controls. Other comments, as a renewed defence of the Washington Consensus trying to return to the simplest monetary frameworks, would certainly be inappropriate. Traditional or narrow inflation-targeting schemes are ill-suited; therefore, more complex issues should be taken into account if central bankers want to maintain their legitimacy. EME policymakers should be concerned not only about inflation but also financial stability and competitiveness issues (an SCRER). In short, this calls for the management of capital flows as well as for the idea of a managed exchange rate scheme.

All these events also qualify as a compelling reason to act on the financial front, to advance towards greater global coordination and cooperation. Unfortunately, after

1. See 'China Central Bank Chief Warns of "Minsky Moment"', *FT*, 19 October 2017.

the crisis, transnational (big and too interconnected) banks have kept growing through M&A. Therefore, financial cross-border spillovers might be prone to increasing. And the problems are likely to return. Even the financial press is warning of the likelihood that a *Minsky* moment could occur.[2] Thus, aware of the vulnerabilities of a hand-off scenario, some financial authorities have decided to go back to being local. As Zeti Akhtar Aziz commented, a situation like this happens 'when the global standards are perceived to be incomplete and when the implementation issues are not sufficiently addressed, or when the costs and benefits are not viewed as being balanced, or when a global standard is incompatible with national priorities' (2016, p. 257).

Recent political events (Brexit, Donald Trump's election and so on) have taken market participants by surprise. What the economic implications might be and how policymakers will finally react to these events remain unknown. Would the US actual trend to isolate itself from global institutions be maintained? What role will China play in this new global setting? What about other larger EMEs, such as Brazil or India? Will Argentina's new administration lead the country to a definite take-off stance or it will just bring about another tour in the perpetual cyclical pattern adopted a long time ago? Will South Korea escape from the perpetual threat coming from the North, or will the conflict do nothing but escalate? Obviously, all these questions are beyond the scope of this book, although some of the issues are being revisited, for it might help in delineating the answers. But, in contrast to what has been observed until now, we are entering a new (and unknown) political scenario. In sum, we should add political uncertainty to the previously mentioned financial risks because financial events are difficult to measure. This new political landscape is also beyond the previously commented Rodrik trilemma, but is a new political configuration in which liberal democracy does not remain among rulers' main objectives. In sum, what we all share is a profound sense of confusion. Henceforth, and whatever the shape the future will finally take, the new scenario requires EMEs' governments to gain a policy space.

After all, what is shocking is to observe China's conversion: largely accused for its mercantilist approach, the Middle Kingdom has suddenly become a worldwide Smithian steward. Even more astonishing, however, is to observe how the United States has abandoned liberalism to embrace a tough Colbertian attitude.

2. In the past, mainstream economies but also the specialized press always rebuffed Hyman Minsky's work. The GFC came to rectify that. The following excerpt, from *FT* journalist John Authers, brilliantly explains that 'the phrase "Minsky Moment" coined by the former Pimco economist Paul McCulley, refers to the psychological moment when participants in a market realise that lending has gone too far, and then a crash results. The phrase was never used in the FT until early 2007. It has now appeared more than 80 times. The reason for this is that the Lehman crisis provided us with a perfect, textbook example of a Minsky Moment.'

REFERENCES

Aggarwal, V. K., and R. Mukerji. 2008. 'India's Shifting Trade Policy: South Asia and Beyond'. In *Asia's New Institutional Architecture Evolving Structures for Managing Trade, Financial, and Security Relation*, ed. Vinod K. Aggarwal and Min Gyo Koo editors, 215–58. Berlin; Heidelberg: Springer.

Aghion, P., P. Baccheta, R. Rancière and K. Rogoff. 2009. 'Exchange Rate Volatility and Productivity Growth: The Role of Financial Development', *Journal of Monetary Economics* 56: 494–513.

Ahluwalia, M. S. 2002. 'Economic Reforms in India Since 1991: Has Gradualism Worked?' *Journal of Economic Perspectives* 16, no. 3: 67–88.

Ahn, D. 2010. Legal and Institutional Issues of Korea-EU FTA: New Model for Post-NAFTA FTAs? ScenesPo/GEM Groupe d'Economie Mondial – Policy Brief, October.

Aizenmann, J., M. Chin and H. Ito. 2015. 'The Trilemma Indexes', Portland State University. http://web.pdx.edu/~ito/trilemma_indexes.htm.

Alden, Edward. 2017. 'Trump and the TPP: Giving Away Something for Nothing'. Blog Post by Edward Alden. January 23, 2017 (https://www.cfr.org/blog/trump-and-tpp-giving-away-something-nothing).

Alvarez, J. E., and K. Khamsi. 2009. 'The Argentine Crisis and Foreign Investors: A Glimpse into the Heart of the Investment Regime'. In *The Yearbook on International Investment Law and Policy 2008/09*, edited by Karl P. Savaunt, 379–476. New York: Oxford University Press.

Amsden, A. 2001. *The Rise of the Rest: Challenges to the West for the Latest Industrialized Economies*. Oxford: Oxford University Press.

ANBIMA. 2014. 'The Relevance of Regulatory Harmonization on OTC Derivatives Markets and the Need for Prioritization Of Brazil in International Discussions'. Position Paper. Associacao Brasileira das Entidades dos Mercados Financieros e de Capitais – ANBIMA's International Regulation Working Group.

Anderson, S. 2011. 'Capital Controls and the Trans-Pacific Partnership'. Presentation to the Stakeholder Forum, Chicago, 10 September.

———. 2013. 'The Trans-Pacific Partnership and Capital Account Regulation: An Analysis of the Region's Existing Agreements'. In *Capital Account Regulations and the Trading System: A Compatibility Review*, edited by Kevin Gallagher and Leonardo Stanley, chapter 8. Boston: The Frederik S. Pardee Center for the Study of the Longer-Range Future, Boston University.

Arienti, P. 2007. 'Restruturação e consolidação do sistema bancário privado' brasileiro', *Ensaios FEE. Porto Alegre* 28: 577–600.

Aron, J., G. Farrell, J. Muellbauer and P. Sinclair. 2014. 'Exchange Rate Pass-through to Import Prices, and Monetary Policy in South Africa', *Journal of Development Studies* 50, no. 1: 144–64.

Arora, V., and F. Ohnsorge. 2014. 'Capital Account Liberalization in China: Some Considerations'. In *Capital Account Liberalization in China: The Need for a Balanced Approach*, edited by Kevin P. Gallagher, chapter 1. Boston: The Frederik S. Pardee Centre for the Study of the Longer-Range Future, Boston University.

Aziz, Z. A. 2016. 'Prospects and Challenges for Financial and Macroeconomic Policy Coordination'. In *Progress and Confusion: The State of Macroeconomic Policy*, edited by Olivier J. Blanchard, Raghuram G. Rajan, Kenneth S. Rogoff and Lawrence H. Summers, chapter 25, Cambridge, MA: MIT Press.

Baba, C., and A. Kokenyne. 2011. 'Effectiveness of Capital Controls in Selected Emerging Markets in the 2000s'. International Monetary Fund (IMF) WP/11/281.

Baba, N., and I. Shim. 2011. 'Dislocations in the Won-Dollar Swap Markets during the Crisis of 2007–9'. Bank for International Settlements (BIS) Working Paper no. 344.

Bacha, E. L., M. Holland and F. M. Goncalves. 2007. 'Is Brazil Different? Risk, Dollarization, and Interest Rates in Emerging Markets'. International Monetary Fund (IMF) Working Paper WP/07/294.

Baker. A. 2014. 'The G20 and Monetary Policy Stasis'. *International Organisations Research Journal*, 9, no. 4: 19–31.

Baldwin, R., and S. Evenett. 2009. *The Collapse of Global Trade, Murky Protectionism, and the Crisis: Recommendations for the G20*. London: CEPR, www.voxEU.org.

Bank for International Settlements (BIS). 2014. 'Regulatory Reform of Over-the-counter derivatives: An Assessment of incentives to clear centrality'. A report by the OTC Derivative Assessment Team, established by the OTC Derivatives Coordination Group.

Barbee, I., and S. Lester. 2014. 'Financial Services in the TTIP: Making the Prudential Exception Work', *Georgetown Journal of International Law* 45: 953–70.

Barbosa-Filho, N. H. 2008. 'Inflation Targeting in Brazil: 1999–2006', *International Review of Applied Economics* 22, no. 2: 187–200.

Barroso, R. B., L. A Pereira da Silva and A. Soares Sales. 2013. 'Quantitative Easing and Related Capital Flows into Brazil: Measuring Its Effects and Transmission Channels through a Rigorous Counterfactual Evaluation'. Banco Central do Brasil Working Papers Series no. 313.

Basu, K., B. Eichengreen and P. Gupta. 2014. 'From Tapering to Tightening: Impact of the Fed's Exit on India'. Policy Research Working Paper PRWP 7071.

Bayoumi, T., and F. Ohnsorge. 2013. 'Do Inflows or Outflows Dominate? Global Implications of Capital Account Liberalization in China'. Strategy, Policy, and Review Department (SPR). IMF Working Paper WP/13/189.

BBA. 2011. 'Presence of Foreign Banks in India – Comments from the British Bankers' Association'. Reserve Bank of India Discussion Paper, British Bank Association.

BCB. 1999. 'Monetary Policy Operating Procedures in Brazil'. Central Bank of Brazil – Bank for International Settlements (BIS) Policy Papers no. 5.

Beck, R., J. Beirne, F. Paternò, J. Peeters, J. Ramos-Tallada, C. Rebillard, D. Reinhardt, L. Weissenseel and J. Wörz. 2015. 'The Side Effects of National Financial Sector Policies: Framing the Debate on Financial Protectionism'. European Central Bank Occasional Paper Series no. 166.

Beck, Roland, John Beirne and Francesco Bis. 2010. 'Funding Patterns and Liquidity Management of International Active Banks'. Bank for International Settlements, Committee on the Global Financial System (CGFS) Papers no. 39.

Bell, S. K., and H. Chao. 2010. 'The Financial System in China: Risks and Opportunities following the Global Financial Crisis'. White Paper (Promontory Financial Group, LLC and O'Melveny & Myers, LLP).

Berganza, J. C., and C. Broto. 2012. 'Flexible Inflation Targets, Forex Interventions and Exchange Rate Volatility in Emerging Countries', *Journal of International Money and Finance* 31 no. 2: 428–44.

Bergsten, F. 2014. 'Addressing Currency Manipulation through Trade Agreements'. Peterson Institute for International Economics. Policy Brief, January.

Bhattacharya, K. 2006. 'Monetary Policy Approaches in India'. Bank for International Settlements (BIS) Papers no. 31.

Bickenbach, F., W.-H. Liu and G. Li. 2015. 'The EU–China Bilateral Investment Agreement in Negotiation: Motivation, Conflicts and Perspectives'. Kiel Institute for the World Economy. Policy Brief.

Blanchard, O., and J. Gali. 2005. 'Real Wage Rigidities and the New Keynesian Model'. National Bureau of Economic Research, 2005. NBER Working Paper 11806. http://www.nber.org/papers/w11806.

Blustein, P. 2005. *And the Money Kept Rolling In (and Out): Wall Street, the IMF, and the Bankrupting of Argentina*. New York: Public Affairs.

———. 2012. 'How Global Watchdogs Missed a World of Trouble'. CIGI Papers no. 5.

———. 2013. *OFF-Balance: The Travails of Institutions That Govern the Global Financial System*. Waterloo, Ontario, Canada: CIGI.

Bofinger, P., and T. Wollmershäuer. 2003. 'Managed Floating as a Monetary Policy Strategy'. Mimeo.

BOK. 2009. 'Changes in Foreign Investors' Behaviour in Korean Stock Market in Response to Changes in the International Investment Environment'. Bank of Korea, 31 March. http://www.bok.or.kr/eng/index.jsp.

Borio, C. 2012. 'The Financial Cycle and Macroeconomics: What Have We Learnt?' Bank of International Settlements (BIS) Working Paper no. 395.

———. 2014. 'Monetary Policy and Financial Stability: What Role in Prevention and Recovery?' Bank of International Settlements (BIS) Working Paper no. 440, January.

Borio, C., and P. Disyatat. 2012. 'Global Imbalances and the Financial Crisis: Link or No Link?' Bank for International Settlements (BIS) Working Paper no. 346.

Bouzas, R., and H. Soltz. 2003. 'Argentina and GATS: A Study on the Domestic Determinants of GATS Commitments'. World Trade Organization (WTO). https://www.wto.org/english/res_e/booksp_e/casestudies_e/case2_e.htm.

Branco, R. S., and L. F. Paula. 2015. 'O Impacto da Dívida Pública sobre o Spread Bancário: Uma avaliação empírica (em português)', *Análise Economica* 33, no. 63: 109–38.

Bresser-Pereira, L. C., J. L. Oreiro and N. Marconi. 2015. *Developmental Macroeconomics: New Developmentalism as a Growth Strategy*. New York and Oxfordshide, UK: Routledge.

Bresser-Pereira, L. C. 2008. 'The Dutch Disease and Its Neutralization: A Ricardian Approach', *Brazilian Journal of Political Economy* 28, no. 1: 47–71.

Brummer, C. 2010. 'Why Soft Law Dominates International Finance – and Not Trade', *Journal of International Economic Law* 13, no. 3: 623–43.

———. 2012. 'How International Financial Law Works (and How It Doesn't)'. *Georgetown Law Journal* 99:

Bruno, V., and H. Shin. 2013. 'Capital Flows, Cross-Border Banking and Global Liquidity'. National Bureau of Economic Research (NBER) Working Series WP 19038.

Bruno, V., and H. S. Shin. 2012. 'Assessing Macroprudential Policies: Case of Korea'. Paper prepared for the symposium of the *Scandinavian Journal of Economics* on capital flows.

Buch, C., K. Neugebauer and C. Schroeder. 2013. 'Changing Forces of Gravity: How the Crisis Affected International Banking'. Deutsche Bundesbank Discussion Paper N 48/2013.

Burdisso, T., and L. D'Amato. 1999. 'Prudential Regulations, Restructuring and Competition: The Case of the Argentine Banking Industry'. Central Bank of Argentina (BCRA) Working Paper no. 10.

Bussière, M., G. Cheng, M. Chinn and N. Lisack. 2014. 'For a Few Dollars More: Reserves and Growth in Times of Crises'. National Bureau of Economic Research (NBER) Working Paper Series 19791.

Calvo, G., and C. Reinhart. 2002. 'Fear of Floating', *Quarterly Journal of Economics* 117, no. 2: 379–408

Calvo, G., L. Leiderman and C. Reinhart. 1993. 'Capital Inflows and Real Exchange Rate Appreciation in Latin America: The Role of External Factors'. International Monetary Fund. Staff Papers vol. 40, no. 1.

Calvo, G., L. Leiderman and C. Reinhart. 1996. 'Inflows of Capital to Developing Countries in the 1990s', *Journal of Economic Perspectives* 10, no. 2: 123–39.

Canuto, O., and M. Holland. 2001. 'Ajustamento Externo e Regimes de Taxa de Cambio na America Latina', *Revista Economia Ensaios* 15, no. 2: 95–123.

Cardoso, E., and I. Goldfajn. 1997. 'Capital Flows to Brazil: The Endogeneity of Capital Controls'. International Monetary Fund, Paper no. 115.

Carney, M. 2013. 'Completing The G20 Reform Agenda for Strengthening Over-the-Counter Derivatives Markets; OTC Derivatives: New Rules, New Actors, New Risks', Banque De France, *Financial Stability Review*, no. 17.

Carvalho, F. Cardin de, and F. E. Pires de Souza. 2010. 'Financial Regulation and Macroeconomics Stability in Brazil in the Aftermath of the Russian Crisis'. Initiativa para la Transparencia Financiera. Documentos ITF N 65

CBRC. 2011. *2010 Annual Report*. Beijing: China Banking Regulatory Commission.

Ceballos, F., T. Didier and S. Schmukler. 2012. 'Financial Globalization in Emerging Countries: Diversification vs. Offshoring'. The World Bank. Policy Research Working Paper no. 6105.

Central Bank of Argentina–BCRA. 2008. 'The International Banking Crisis and Its Impact on Argentina'. Bank for International Settlements; BIS. BIS Papers No. 54.

Cervone, E. 2015. 'The Final Volcker Rule and Its Impact Across the Atlantic: The Shaping of Extraterritoriality in a World of Dynamic Structural Banking Reforms'. World Bank, Mimeo, 10 August.

Cetorelli, N., and L. Goldberg. 2010. 'Global Banks and International Shock Transmission: Evidence from the Crisis'. National Bureau of Economic Research (NBER) Working Paper Series 15974.

CGFS. 2010. *Funding Patterns and Liquidity Management of Internationally Active Banks*. Report submitted by a Study Group established by the Committee on the Global Financial System. Basel, Switzerland,

———. 2011. *The MacroFinancial implications of Alternative Configurations for Access to Central Counter-Parties in OTC Derivatives Markets*. Report submitted by a Study Group established by the Committee on the Global Financial System. Basel, Switzerland.

Chandrasekhar, C. P. 2009. 'Financial Liberalization and the New Dynamics of Growth in India'. Published by Third World Network (www.twnside.org.sg)

Chang, H-J. 2007. 'Understanding the Relationship between Institutions and Economic Development – Some Key Theoretical Issues'. In *Institutional Change and Economic Development*, edited by Ha-Joon Chang, chapter 2. Tokyo: United Nations University Press; London: Anthem Press.

Chang, R. 2008. *Inflation Targeting, Reserves Accumulation, and Exchange Rate Management in Latin America*. Direccion de Estudios Economicos, Papers and Proceedings-Inflation Targeting, 233–284 (Department of Planning; Bogota, Colombia).]

Cheikh, N. B., and W. Louchini. 2014. 'Revisiting the Role of Inflation Environment in the Exchange Rate Pass-Through: A Panel Threshold Approach'. FIW Working Paper no. 132.

Cheong, I. 2012. 'Korea's Policy Package for Enhancing its FTA Utilization and Implications for Korea's Policy'. ERIA Discussion Paper Series.

Cheung, Y.-W., and H. Ito. 2008. 'Hoarding of International Reserves: A Comparison of the Asian and Latin American Experiences'. Hong Kong Institute for Monetary Research (HKIMR) Working Paper 7/08.

Chin, M. 2014. 'Central Banking: Perspectives from Emerging Economies'. Mimeo, 29 May.

Cho, H. 2010. *Korea's Experience with Global Financial Crisis*. Ottawa, Canada: The North–South Institute.

Choi, D.-Y., and Y. Lee. 2006. Financial Supervision of Merchant Banking Corporations as a Cause of Korea's Currency Crisis. *Journal of the Korean Economy* 7, no. 1 (Spring): 77–118.

Chopra, A., K. Kang, M. Karasulu, H. Liang, H. Ma and A. Richards. 2001. From Crisis to Recovery in Korea: Strategy, Achievements, and Lessons. IMF Working Paper WP/01/154.

Chwieroth, J. M. 2010. Capital Ideas: The IMF and the Rise of Financial Liberalization. Princeton, NJ: Princeton University Press.

CIEPR. 2012. 'Banks and Cross-Border Capital Flows: Policy Changes and Regulatory Responses'. Committee on International Economic Policy and Reform. September.

Claessens, S., and N. Van Hoeren, 2014. 'Foreign Banks: Trends and Impact', *Journal of Money, Credit and Banking* 46, no. S1: 295–326.

Coelho, A. R. 2014. 'Dodd Frank Act and the Brazilian Capital Market – Extraterritorial Effects of Regulation to the Over-the-Counter Derivatives Market'. Sao Paulo Law School of Fundacao Getulio Vargas – DIREITO GV. Research Paper Series – Legal Studies Paper no. 96.

Coffee Jr., J. C. 2014. 'Extraterritorial Financial Regulation: Why E.T. Can't Come Home', *Cornell Law Review* 99, no. 6 (September): 1259–1302.

Cohen, B. 2012. 'The Yuan Tomorrow? Evaluating China's Currency Internationalization Strategy'. *Journal New Political Economy* 17, no. 3: 361–71.

Coley, A. 2015. 'US Regulation of Cross-Border Banks: Is It Time to Embrace Balkanization in Global Finance?' Draft. 23 September.

Cooper, W., M. Manyin, R. Jurenas and M. Platzer. 2010. *The Proposed U.S.-South Korea Free Trade Agreement (KORUS FTA): Provisions and Implications.* Congressional Research Service (CRS), Report for US Congress. Washington, DC.

Cooper, W., R. Jurenas, M. Platzer and M. Manyin. 2011. *The EU-South Korea Free Trade Agreement and Its Implications for the United States.* Congressional Research Service (CRS) Report for Congress. Washington, DC, www.crs.gov.

Corden, M. 2001. 'Exchange Rate Regimes and Policies: An Overview'. In *Exchange Rate Politics in Latin America*, edited by Carol Wise and Riordan Roett, chapter 2. Washington, DC: Brookings Institution Press.

Costa da Silva, G. J., and M. F. Cunha Resende. 2010. 'Eficácia dos Controles de Capitais no Brasil: Uma Abordagem Teórica e Empirica Alternativa', Estudos Econômicos (São Paulo) 40, no. 3: 617–49.

Crosby, D. 2008. 'Banking on China's WTO Commitments: "Same Bed, Different Dreams" in China's Financial Services Sector'. *Journal of International Economic Law* 11, no. 1: 75–105

D'arista, J., and S. Griffith-Jones. 2011. 'Reforming Financial Regulation: What Needs to Be Done? In *Reforming the International Financial System for Development,* edited by J. K. Sandaram, 143–68. New York: Columbia University Press.

Damill, M., R. Frenkel and M. Rapetti. 2010. 'The Argentinean Debt: History, Default and Restructuring'. In *Overcoming Developing Country Debt Crises,* edited by Barry Herman, José Antonio Ocampo and Shara Spiegel, 179–230. Oxford: Oxford University Press.

———. 2015. 'The New Millenium Argentina Saga: from Crisis to Success and from Success to Failure'. Paper prepared for Jan Kregel's Festschrift.

Das, S. 2011. *Extreme Money: Masters of the Universe and the Cult of Risk.* Upper Saddle River, NJ: FT Press.

De la Torre, A., E. Levy Yeyati and S. Schmukler. 2003. 'Living and Dying With Hard Pegs: The Rise and Fall of Argentina's Currency Board'. Policy Research Working Paper Series 2980, The World Bank.

De Meester, B. 2010. 'The Global Financial Crisis and Government Support for Banks: What Role for the GATS?' *Journal of International Economic Law* 13 no. 1: 27–63.

Delimatisis, P., and P. Sauvé. 2010. 'Financial Services Trade after the Crisis', *Journal of International Economic Law* 13, no. 3: 837–57.

Denae Trasher, R. 2014. 'Leaked TISA Financial Services Text: A Glimpse into the Future of Services Liberalization'. CEGI Exchange – A Global Economic Governance Initiative policy brief, Issue 003.

Diaz Alejandro, C. 1985. 'Good Bye Financial Repression, Hello Financial Crash', *Journal of Developmental Economics* 19, no. 1: 1–24.

Disyatat P., and G. Galati. 2007. 'The Effectiveness of Foreign Exchange Intervention in Emerging Market Countries: Evidence from the Czech Koruna'. *Journal of International Money and Finance* 26, no. 3: 383–402.

Dodd, R. 2002. 'Derivatives, the Shape of International Capital Flows and the Virtues of Prudential Regulation'. United Nations University – World Institute for Development Economic Research (UNU/WIDER) Discussion Paper 93.

———. 2009. 'Exotic Derivatives Losses in Emerging Markets: Questions for Suitability, Concerns for Stability'. International Monetary Fund (IMF) Working Paper Series.

Dodd, R., and S. Griffith-Jones. 2007. 'Brazil's Derivatives Markets: Hedging, Central Bank Intervention and Regulation'. Project research sponsored by ECLAC/CEPAL and Funding from the Ford Foundation.

Dominguez, K., and L. Tesar. 2005. 'International Borrowing and Macroeconomic Performance in Argentina'. National Bureau for Economic Research (NBER) Working Paper no. 11353.

Dooley, M., D. Folkerts-Landau and P. Garber. 2004. 'The Revived Bretton Woods System: The Effects of Periphery Intervention and Reserve Management on Interest Rates & Exchange Rates in Center Countries'. National Bureau for Economic Research (NBER) Working Paper no. 10332.

———. 2009. 'Bretton Woods II Still Defines the International Monetary System'. *Pacific Economic Review* 14, no. 3: 297–311.

Dua P., and R. Rajan. 2012. *Exchange Rate Policy and Modeling in India*. Oxford: Oxford University Press, 2012.

Eatwell, J., and L. Taylor. 2005. *Finanzas Globales en Riesgo: Un Análisis a Favor de la Regulación Internacional*. Buenos Aires: Siglo XXI/CEFID-AR. (Translation from the original English: *Global Finance at Risk: The Case for International Regulation*).

Eichengreen, B. 'International Financial Regulation after the Crisis'. *Dædalus*. Fall 2010.

Eichengreen, B., and R. Haussman. 1999. *Exchange Rates and Financial Fragility: Proceedings*. Economic Policy Symposium, Jackson Hole, WY, Federal Reserve Bank of Kansas City, 329–68.

El-Erian, M. 2016. 'The Chinese Economy's Great Wall'. Project Syndicate, 26 March.

Elliot D., A. Kroeber and Y. Qiao. 2015. 'Shadow Banking in China: A Primer'. Economic Studies at Brookings.

Epstein, G., and E. Yeldan. 2009. 'Beyond Inflation Targeting: Assessing the Impacts and Policy Alternatives'. In *Beyond Inflation Targeting*, edited by Gerald Epstein and A. Erinc Yeldan, chapter 1. Cheltenham, UK; Northampton, MA: Edward Elgar Publishing.

European Commission. 2015a. 'Commission Proposes New Investment Court System for TTIP and Other EU trade and Investment Negotiations'. European Commission – Press release, Europa.eu. 16 September. Accessed: 7 October 2015. http://europa.eu/rapid/press-release_IP-15-5651_en.htm.

———. 2015b. 'Investment In TTIP and Beyond – The Path for Reform: Enhancing the Right to Regulate and Moving from Current Ad Hoc Arbitration towards an Investment Court'. European Commission Concept Paper, May. Accessed: 7 October 2015. http://trade.ec.europa.eu/doclib/docs/2015/may/tradoc_153408.PDF.

European Parliament. 2014. *Financial Services in EU Trade Agreements: Study*. Directorate General for Internal Policies. Document prepared by Policy Department A for the Economic and Monetary Affairs Committee (ECON).

———. 2015a. 'TTIP and Regulation of Financial Markets: Regulatory Autonomy versus Fragmentation: In-Depth Analysis'. European Parliamentary Research Service. 15 June.

———. 2015b. 'Granting Market Economy Status to China: An Analysis of WTO Law and Selected WTO Members' Policy'. European Parliamentary Research Service. 10 October.

Evans, P. 1995. *Embedded Autonomy: States and Industrial Transformation*. Princeton, NJ: Princeton University Press.

Evenett, S., and F. Jenny. 2009. 'Bailouts: How to Discourage a Subsidies War'. In *The Collapse of Global Trade, Murky Protectionism, and the Crisis: Recommendations for the G20*, edited by Richard Baldwin and Simon Evenett, chapter 16. A VoxEU.org publication.

Ewert, I. 2016. 'The EU-China Bilateral Investment Agreement: Between High Hopes and Real Challenges'. Egmont – Security Policy Brief no. 68.

Faia, E., and B. Weder di Mauro. 2015. 'Cross-Border Resolution of Global Banks. Federal Reserve Bank of Dallas'. Globalization and Monetary Policy Institute, Working Paper no. 326.

Farhi, M., and R. A. Zanchetta Borghi. 2009. 'Operations with Financial Derivatives of Corporations from Emerging Economies'. *Estudos Avancados* 23, no. 66: 169–88.

Federico, P., C. A. Vegh and G. Vuletin. 2012. 'Effects and Role of Macro-Prudential Policy: Evidence From Reserve Requirements Based on a Narrative Approach'.Unpublished paper, University of Maryland.

Fietcher, J., I. Otker-Robe, A. Ilyina, M. Hau, A. Santos and J. Surti. 2011. 'Subsidiaries or Branches: Does One Size Fit All?' International Monetary Fund. IMF Staff Discussion Note. 7 March. SDN/11/04.

Fischer, S. 2001. 'Exchange Rate Regimes: Is the Bipolar View Correct?' *Journal of Economic Perspectives* 15, no. 2: 3–24.

Frankel, J. 2015. 'The Chimera of Currency Manipulation'. Project Syndicate, 10 June.

———. 2015b. 'The Plaza Accord, 30 Years Later'. Paper presented at the conference on Currency Policy Then and Now: 30 Anniversary of the Plaza Accord, Baker Institute for Public Policy, Rice University. October.

———. 2015a. 'Congress, China, and Currency Manipulation', China-US Focus, 9 April. https://www.chinausfocus.com/finance-economy/congress-china-and-currency-manipulation/.

Freitas, M. C. P. 2009. 'Internacionalização do sistema bancario: os casos do Brasil, Coreia e Mexico'. *Ciclos en Historia, la Economia y la Sociedad* 5, no. 18: 85–117.

2006. 'An Alternative to Inflation Targeting in Latin America: Macroeconomic Policies Focused on Employment'. *Journal of Post Keynesian Economics* 28, no. 4: 573–91.

———. 2007. 'The Sustainability of Sterilization Policies'. Center for Economic and Policy Research (CEPR), Washington, DC.

Frieden, J. 2006. 'Will Global Capitalism Fall Again?' Bruegel Essay and Lecture Series. 29 June.

FSB. 2014. *Structural Banking Reforms: Cross-Border Consistencies and Global Stability Implications.* Financial Stability Board, Report to G20 Leaders for the November 2014 summit. Basel, Switzerland.

Furcieri, D., S. Guichard and E. Rusticelli. 2011. 'Medium-Term Determinants of International Investment Positions: The Role of Structural Policies'. OECD Economics Department Working Papers 863.

Furman, J., and J. Stiglitz. 1998. 'Economic Crises: Evidence and Insights from East Asia', Brookings Papers on Economic Activity, No. 2.

Gagnon, J. 2015. 'More on TPP and Exchange Rates'. Peterson Institute for International Economics, 1 December.

Galindo, L. M., and J. Ros. 2008. 'Alternatives to Inflation Targeting'. *International Review of Applied Economics*, 22, no. 2: 201–14.

Gallagher, K. and L. Stanley. 2013. *2012 Capital Account Regulations and the Trading System: A Compatibility Review.* Boston: The Frederick S. Pardee Center for the Study of the Longer-Range Future, Boston University.

———. 2015. *Ruling Capital: Emerging Markets and the Re-regulation of Cross-Border Finance.* Ithaca: Cornell University Press.

Gallagher, K. P., J. A. Ocampo, M. Zhang and Y. Yongding. 2014. *Capital Account Liberalization in China: The Need for a Balanced Approach.* Boston: The Frederick S. Pardee Center for the Study of the Longer-Range Future, Boston University.

García-Herrero, A., and D. Santabárbara. 2013. 'An Assessment of China's Banking Reform'. In *Who Will Provide the Next Financial Model? Asia's Financial Muscle and Europe's Financial Maturity*, edited by Kaji S. Ogawa E., 147–75. Osaka: Springer.

García-Herrero, Alicia, Sergio Gaviláy and Daniel Santabarbara. 2006. 'China's Banking Reform: An Assessment of its Evolution and Possible Impact'. *CESifo Economic Studies* 52, no. 2: 304–63. doi:10.1093/cesifo/ifl006.

Glick R., and M. Hutchinson. 2013. 'China's Financial Linkages with Asia and the Global Financial Federal Reserve Bank of San Francisco'. Working Paper Series – WP 2013–12.

Glocker, C., and P. Tobin. 2012. 'Reserve Requirements for Price and Financial Stability – When Are They Effective?' Banque de France. Working Paper 363.

Godement, F., and A. Stanzel. 2015. 'The European Interest in an Investment Treaty with China'. European Council on Foreign Relations (ECFR.EU) Policy Brief.

Gopalan, S., and R. S. Rajan. 2010. 'Financial Sector De-Regulation in Emerging Asia: Focus on Foreign Bank Entry'. *Journal of World Investment & Trade* 11, no. 1: 91–108.

Gorga, E. 2015. 'The Impact of the Financial Crisis on Non-Financial Firms: The Case of Brazilian Corporations and the "Double Circularity" Problem in Transnational Securities Litigation'. *Theoretical Inquiries in Law* 16, no. 1: 131–81.

Gorton, G., and A. Metrick. 2009. 'Securitized Banking and the Run on Repo'. National Bureau of Economic Research (NBER) Working Paper Series WP 15223.

———. 2010. 'Regulating the Shadow Banking System'. Brookings Papers on Economic Activities. Fall.

Gosh, A., M. S. Qureshi and N. Sugawara. 2014. 'Regulating Capital Flows at Both Ends: Does it Work?' International Monetary Fund, IMF Working Paper no. 14/188.

Government of India. 2015. 'Transforming the International Investment Agreement Regime: The Indian Experience'. PPT. Department of Economic Affairs, Ministry of Finance.

Goyal, A. 2011. 'History of Monetary Policy in India since Independence'. Indira Gandhi Institute of Development Research, Mumbai, September. http://www.igidr.ac.in/pdf/publication/WP-2011–018.pdf.

Green, R. 2015. 'The Unfavorable Economics of Currency Manipulation Chapters in Trade Agreements'. Baker Institute for Public Policy, Rice University. Issue Brief 04-27-15.

Greene, E., and I. Potiha. 2013. 'Issues in Extraterritorial Application of Dodd-Frank's Derivatives Rules: Update with Focus on OTC Derivatives and Clearing Requirements'. Mimeo.

Griffith-Jones, S., J. A. Ocampo and K. Gallagher. 2011. *Regulating Global Capital Flows for Long-Run Development.* Boston: The Frederick S. Pardee Center for the Study of the Longer-Range Future, Boston University.

Guillen, M. 2015. 'Will the Trans-Pacific Partnership Deliver on Its Promises?' Knowledge@Wharton. http://knowledge.wharton.upenn.edu/article/will-the-trans-pacific-partnership-deliver-on-its-promises/.

Hadley, K. 2013. 'Do China's BITs Matter? Assessing the Effect of China's Investment Agreements on Foreign Direct Investment Flows, Investor's Rights, and the Rule of Law'. *Georgetown Journal of International Law* 45: 255–321.

Helleiner, E. 1995. 'Great Transformations: A Polanyian Perspective on the Contemporary Global Financial Order'. *Studies in Political Economy* 48: 149–64.

———. 2011. 'The Limits of Incrementalism: The G20, the FSB, and the International Regulatory Agenda', *Journal of Globalization and Developme*nt 2, no. 2. doi: https://doi.org/10.1515/1948-1837.1242.

———. 2014. *The Status Quo Crisis: Global Financial Governance after the 2008 Meltdown.* Oxford: Oxford University Press.

Helleiner, E., and J. Kirshner. 2014. 'The Politics of China's International Monetary Relations'. Introduction to *The Great Wall of Money: Power and Politics in China's International Monetary Relations*, by Eric Helleiner and Jonathan Kirshner. Ithaca, NY: Cornell University Press.

Helleiner, E., and S. Pagliari. 2011. 'The End of an Era in International Financial Regulation? A Post-Crisis Research Agenda'. *International Organization* 65: 169–200.

Heller, H. R. 1966. 'Optimal International Reserves', *Economic Journal* 76: 296–311.

Hermann, J. 2010. 'Liberalização e desenvolvimento financiero: lições da experiencia brasileira no periodo 1990–2006'. *Economia e Sociedade, Campiñas* 19, no. 2 (39): 257–90.

Heyman, M. 2008. 'International Law and the Settlement of Investment Disputes Relating to China'. *Journal of International Economic Law* 11, no. 3: 507–526.

Hoeckman, B. M., and M. M. Kostecki. 2009. *The Political Economy of the World Trading System*. 3rd ed. Oxford: Oxford University Press.

Holanda Barbosa, F. 2006. 'The Contagion Effect of Public Debt on Monetary Policy: The Brazilian Experience'. *Brazilian Journal of Political Economy* 26, no. 2 (102): 231–38.

———. 2011. 'Brazilian Financial Regulation and Governance'. *Revista de Economia Política* 31: 889–92.

IBEF. 2008. 'India: Foreign Direct Investment, the Policy and Regulatory Framework'. India Brand Equity Foundation. https://www.ibef.org/pages/19241.

Igan, D., and H. Kang. 2011. 'Do Loan-to-Value and Debt-to-Income Limits Work? Evidence from Korea'. International Monetary Fund (IMF) Working Paper WP/11/297.

IISD. 2015. 'Side-by-Side Comparison of the Brazil–Mozambique and Brazil–Angola Cooperation and Investment Facilitation Agreements'. International Institute for Sustainable Development. Winnipeg, Manitoba, Canada.

IMF. 2012a. 'From Bail-out to Bail-in: Mandatory Debt Restructuring of Systematic Financial Institutions'. International Monetary Fund. IMF Staff Discussion Notes SDN/12/03. 24 April.

———. 2012b. 'Credit Growth and the Effectiveness of Reserve Requirements and Other Macroprudential Instruments in Latin America'. International Monetary Fund (IMF) Working Paper. June.

———. 2012c. 'The Liberalization and Management of Capital Flows: An Institutional View'. International Monetary Fund (IMF) Working Paper. 14 November.

———. 2013. 'Guidance Note for the Liberalization and Management of Capital Flows'. International Monetary Fund (IMF) Working Paper, April.

———. 2014. *Annual Report on Exchange Arrangements and Exchange Restrictions*. Washington, DC: International Monetary Fund.

Jeanne, O., A. Subramanian and J. Williamson. 2012. *Who Needs to Open the Capital Account?* Washington, DC: Peterson Institute for International Economics.

Jeon, B. N., H. Lim and J. Wu. 2014. 'The Impact of Foreign Banks on Monetary Policy Transmission during the Global Financial Crisis of 2008–2009: Evidence from Korea'. LeBow College of Business, Drexel University School of Economics, Working Paper Series. WP 2014–7.

Johnson, S., and J. Schott. 2014. 'Financial Services in the Transatlantic Trade and Investment Partnership'. Peterson Institute for International Economics. Number PB13–26, 2014.

Kamil, H., and K. Rai. 2010. 'The Global Credit Crunch and Foreign Banks' Lending to Emerging Markets: Why Did Latin America Fare Better?' International Monetary Fund (IMF) Working Paper WP/10/02.

Kawai, M., and M. B. Lamberte. 2010. 'Managing Capital Flows: Emerging Asia's Experiences, Policy Issues and Challenges'. In *Managing Capital Flows: The Search for a Framework*, edited by Masahiro Kawai and Mario B. Lamberte, chapter 1. A joint publication of the Asian Development Bank Institute and Edward Elgar Publishing. Cheltenham, UK; Northampton, MA: Edward Elgar.

Kelsey, J. 2010. 'How the Trans-Pacific Partnership Agreement Could Heighten Financial Instability and Foreclose Government's Regulatory Space'. *New Zealand Yearbook of International Law* 8: 3–43.

Khurana, N. 2007. 'Crisis Prevention and Capital Controls in India: Perspectives from Capital Account in the Current Scenario'. The Hans Böckler Foundation, 1 October.

Kim, Ch. 2013. 'Macroprudential Policies: Korea's Experiences'. Paper presented at the Rethinking Macro Policy II: First Steps and Early Lessons Conference, hosted by the International Monetary Fund, Washington, DC, 16–17 April.

Kim, S., and D. Y. Yang. 2010. 'Managing Capital Flows: The Case of the Republic of Korea'. In *Managing Capital Flows: The Search for a Framework*, edited by Masahiro Kawai and Mario B. Lamberte, chapter 11. A joint publication of the Asian Development Bank Institute and Edward Elgar Publishing. Cheltenham, UK; Northampton, MA: Edward Elgar.

Klein, M. W., and J. C. Shambaugh. 2010. *Exchange Rate Regimes in the Modern Era*. Cambridge, MA: MIT Press.

Koshlscheen, E. 2013. 'Order Flow and the Real: Indirect Evidence of the Effectiveness of Sterilized Interventions'. Bank for International Settlements – BIS Working Papers N 426.

Kumar, N. 1995. 'Industrialization, Liberalization and Two Way Flows of Foreign Direct Investment: The Case of India'. The United Nations University, Institute for New Technologies (INTECH). Discussion Paper Series.

Lan, G. 2015. 'Insights from China for the United States: Shadow Banking, Economic Development, and Financial Systems'. *Berkeley Business Law Journal* 12, no. 1: 144–95.

Lardy, N. 2012. *Sustaining China's Economic Growth after the Global Financial Crisis*. Washington, DC: Peterson Institute for International Economics.

Lavigne, R., and L. Schembri. 2009. 'Strengthening IMF Surveillance: An Assessment of Recent Reforms', Discussion Papers 09–10, Bank of Canada.

Lee, K-K. 2010. 'The Post-Crisis Change in the Financial System in Korea: Problems of Neoliberal Restructuring and Financial Opening after 1997'. Third World Network; TWN, Global Economy Series 20.

Lee, K. J., and H. S. Shin. 2013. 'The Operation of Macro Prudential Policy Measures: The case of Korea in the 2000s'. In *Dealing with the Challenges of Macro Financial Linkages in Emerging Markets*, edited by Otaviano Canuto and Swati R. Gosh, Chapter 7. The World Bank.

Lee, K., G. Kim, H. Kim and H. Song. 2010. 'A New Macro-Financial System for a Stable and Crisis-Resilient Growth in Korea'. *Seoul Journal of Economics* 23 no. 2: 145–86.

Lehmann, M. 2014. 'Volcker Rule, Ring-Fencing or Separation of Bank Activities: Comparison of Structural Reforms Acts around the World'. London School of Economics. Law – Society – Economy Working Papers 25.

Levinson, M. 2010. 'Faulty Basel: Why More Diplomacy Won't Keep the Financial System Safe'. *Foreign Affairs*, May–June.

Levy Yeyati, E., and F. Sturzenneger. 2003. 'To Float or to Fix: Evidence on the Impact of Exchange Rate Regimes on Growth'. *American Economic Review* 93, no. 4: 1173–93.

———. 2007. 'Fear of Appreciation'. Escuela de Negocios – UTDT, Centro de Investigación en Finanzas. Documento de Trabajo 02.

Li, J., and S. Hsu. 2013. 'Shadow Banking in China: Institutional Risks'. University of Massachusetts Amherst – Political Economy Research Institute (PERI). Working Paper Series Number 334.

Liang, Y. 2012. 'China's Banking System in Light of the Global Financial Crisis'. *Chinese Economy* 45, no. 1: 8–27.

Lin, Justin Yifu, and Yan Wang. 2008. 'China's Integration with the World Development as a Process of Learning and Industrial Upgrading'. The World Bank Development Economics Vice Presidency & World Bank Institute Finance & Private Sector Development Division. Policy Research Working Paaper 4799. WPS 4799.

Liu, Y., H.-L. Chang and C-W. Su. 2013. 'Do Real Interest Rates Converge across East Asian Countries Based on China?' *Economic Modelling* 31: 467–73.

Loechel, H., N. Packham and H. X. Li. 2010. 'International Banking Regulation and Supervision after the Crisis: Implications for China'. EU-China BMT. Working Paper Series 13. http://www.frankfurt-school.de/content/en/gcbf/research.html.

Magud, N., and E. Vesperoni. 2014. 'Exchange Rate Flexibility and Credit during Capital Inflow Reversals: Purgatory … Not Paradise'. International Monetary Fund (IMF) Working Paper WP/14/61.

Magud, N., C. Reinhart and E. Vesperoni. 2012. 'Capital Inflows, Exchange Rate Flexibility, and Credit Booms'. International Monetary Fund (IMF) Working Paper WP12/41.

McCauley, R. N. 2003. 'Capital Flows in East Asia since the 1997 Financial Crisis'. *BIS Quarterly Review*, June: 45–59.

McKinnon, R., and G. Schnabl. 2004. 'The Return to Soft Dollar Pegging in East Asia: Mitigating Conflicted Virtue'. *International Finance* 2, no. 7: 169–201.

Mesquita, M., and M. Torós 2010. 'Considerações sobre a Atuação do Banco Central na Crise de 2008'. Banco Central do Brasil, Trabalhos para Discussão 202.

Minikin, R., and K. Lau. 2013. *The Offshore Renminbi: The Rise of the Chinese Currency and Its Global Future*. Singapore: Wiley.

Minsky, H. P. 2008. *Stabilizing an Unstable Economy*. New York: McGraw-Hill.

Mishkin, F. 2009. 'Why We Shouldn't Turn Our Backs on Financial Globalization', International Monetary Fund Staff Papers, 56, 1, 139–170.

Moguillansky, G., R. Studart and S. Vergara. 2004. 'Foreign Banks in Latin America: A Paradoxical Result'. *CEPAL Review* 82 (April): 21–37.

Mohan, R. 2009. *Monetary Policy in a Globalized Economy: A Practitioner's View*. Oxford: Oxford University Press.

Montes, M. F. 2013. 'Capital Controls, Investment Chapters and Asian Development Objectives'. In *Capital Account Regulations and the Trading System: A Compatibility Review*, edited by K. Gallagher and L. Stanley, chapter 8. Boston: The Frederick S. Pardee Center for the Study of the Longer-Range Future, Boston University.

Montoro, C., and R. Moreno. 2011. 'The Use of Reserve Requirements as a Policy Instrument in Latin America'. Bank for International Settlements. *BIS Quarterly Review*, March.

Moreira Cunha, A., D. M. Prates and F. Ferrari-Filho. 2011. 'Brazil Responses to the International Financial Crisis: A Successful Example of Keynesian Policies?' *Panoeconomics* 5, Special Issue: 693–714.

Mortimore, M., and L. Stanley. 2010. 'Standing Tall: BRICs Improve FDI Impacts and Reduce Risks'. TUFTS/GDAE – Working Group on Development and Environment in the Americas. Discussion Paper DP29, January.

Naim, M. 2009. 'Minilateralism: The Magic Number to Get Real International Action'. *Foreign Policy*, 21 June. http://foreignpolicy.com/2009/06/21/minilateralism/.

Naughton, B. 2007. *The Chinese Economy: Transitions and Growth*. Cambridge, MA: MIT Press.

Noland, M. 1996. 'Restructuring Korea's Financial Sector for Greater Competitiveness'. Peterson Institute for International Economics Working Paper 96/14. https://piie.com/publications/working-papers/restructuring-koreas-financial-sector-greater-competitiveness.

Obstfeld, M. 2014. 'Trilemmas and Tradeoffs: Living with Financial Globalization'. Mimeo.

Obstfeld, M., and K. Rogoff. 1995. 'The Mirage of Fixed Exchange Rates', *Journal of Economic Perspectives* 9, no. 4: 73–96.

Obstfeld, M., J. Shambaugh and A. Taylor. 2010. 'The Trilemma in History: Tradeoffs among Exchange Rates, Monetary Policies, and Capital Mobility'. Paper prepared for the conference 'The Political Economy of Globalization: Can the Past Inform the Present?' sponsored by the ISS at Trinity College, Dublin.

Ocampo, J. A., C. Rada and L. Taylor, eds. 2009. *Growth and Policy in Developing Countries: A Structuralist Approach*. New York: Columbia University Press.

Oldani, C. 2015. 'The Risk of OTC Derivatives: Canadian Lessons for Europe and the G20'. The Centre for International Governance Innovation (CIGI) Papers No. 57.

Oreiro, J. L. 2015. 'Desafios do Segundo Mandato da Presidente Dilma Rouseff'. *Brazilian Keynesian Review* 1, no 1: 103–7.

Oreiro, J. L., L. F de Paula, G. J. Costa da Silva and R. Quevedo do Amaral. 2012. 'Por que as taxas de juros são tão elevadas no Brasil? Uma avaliação empírica'. *Revista de Economia Política* 32, no. 4 (129): 557–79.

Panagariya, A. 2004. 'India in the 1980s and 1990s: A Triumph of Reforms'. Paper presented at the NCAER-IMF conference on 'A Tale of Two Giants: India's and China's Experience with Reform and Growth', New Delhi, India, 15–16 November 2003.

Park, S-C. 2014. 'South Korean Trade Strategies in the Post Global Financial Crisis', *Contemporaneous Issues in Business and Government* 20, no. 1: 59–76.

Park, Y-S. 2012. 'Korea's Elections and the KORUS FTA'. National Bureau of Asian Research (NBR) Analysis Brief. http://www.nbr.org/publications/element.aspx?id=594).

Paula, L. F., J. L. Oreiro and G. J. C. Silva. 2003. 'Fluxos e Controles de Capitais: avaliação e proposta de política'. In *Agenda Brasil: políticas econômicas para o crescimento com estabilidade de preços*, edited by and, 65–115. São Paulo: Manole: Fundação Konrad Adenauer.

PBC. 2010. *China Monetary Policy Report Quarter Two, 2010*. Beijing: Monetary Policy Group of the People's Bank of China.

———. *PBC Report*. Beijing: People's Bank of China.

Perrone, N., and G. Rojas de Cerqueira César. 2015. 'Brazil's Bilateral Investment Treaties: More Than a New Investment Treaty Model?' Columbia FDI Perspectives on Topical Foreign Direct Investment Issues No. 159, 26 October.

Pistor, K. 2002. 'The Standardization of Law and Its Effect on Developing Economies', *American Journal of Comparative Law* 50 (Winter): 97–130.

———. 2012. 'Real vs. Imagined Financial Markets: the Regulatory Challenge', Paper prepared for the Third Annual INET Conference, Berlin, 10–12 April.

Prasad, E., and S-J. Wei. 2004. 'The Chinese Approach to Capital Inflows: Patterns and Possible Explanation'. In *Capital Controls and Capital Flows in Emerging Economies: Policies, Practices and Consequences*, edited by Sebastian Edwards, chapter 9. National Bureau of Economic Research; NBER. Chicago: University of Chicago Press. http://www.nber.org/chapters/c0147.

Prasad, E., K. Rogoff, S-J. Wei and A. Kose. 2003. 'Effects of Financial Globalization on Developing Countries: Some New Evidence', International Monetary Fund (IMF) Occasional Paper No. 220.

Prates, D., and B. Fritz. 2013. 'Beyond Capital Controls: The Regulation of Foreign Currency Derivatives Markets in South Korea and Brazil after the Global Financial Crisis'. Berlin Working Papers on Money, Finance, Trade and Development.

Prates, D. M., and M. Farhi. 2015. 'Foreign Exchange Derivatives, Banking Competition and Financial Fragility in Brazil'. Multidisciplinary Institute for Development and Strategies. Discussion Paper no. 3.

Pudwell, C. A. M. 2003. 'Fluxos de Capitais na ALCA: Liberdade ou Controle?' *Indicadores Econômicos FEE, Porto Alegre* 31, no. 2: 131–48.

Radeltt, S., and J. Sachs. 1998. 'The East Asian Financial Crisis: Diagnosis, Remedies, Prospects'. Brookings Paper on Economic Activity.

Raja, K. 2007. 'WTO Discusses China's Financial Services Commitments'. Published at Third World Network (TWN) Info Service on Finance and Development, 15 November.

Rajan, Raghuram G. 2005. 'Has financial development made the world riskier?' Proceedings – Economic Policy Symposium – Jackson Hole, Federal Reserve Bank of Kansas City, August, pp. 313–369.

Rana, S. 2012. 'The Emergence of the New Chinese Banking System: Implications for Global Politics and the Future of Financial Reform', *Maryland Journal of International Law* 27, no. 1: 215–34.

Rapetti, M. 2013. 'The Real Exchange Rate and Economic Growth: Some Observations on the Possible Channels', UMass Amherst Economics Working Papers 2013–11, University of Massachusetts Amherst, Department of Economics.

RBI. 2005. 'RBI Unveils Roadmap for Presence of Foreign Banks in India and Guidelines on Ownership and Governance in Private Banks'. Press Release, 28 February. https://rbidocs.rbi.org.in/rdocs/PressRelease/PDFs/61298.pdf.

———. 2010. *Report on Trend and Progress of Banking in India 2009–10*. Report submitted to the Central Government. Mumbai: Reserve Bank of India.

———. 2013. 'Intervention in Foreign Exchange Markets: The Approach of the Reserve Bank of India'. Reserve Bank of India – Bank for International Settlement (BIS) Papers 73.

Reddy, Y. V. 2010. *India and the Global Financial Crisis: Managing Money and Finance*. London: Anthem Press.

Redrado, M. 2008. 'The Argentine Monetary and Financial Policies and the Crisis'. UCA – Escuela de Negocios. Documento de Trabajo no. 3.

Reinert, E. 2007. 'Institutionalism Ancient, Old, and New: A Historical Perspective on Institutions and Uneven Development'. In *Institutional Change and Economic Development*, edited by Ha-Joon Chang, chapter 4. Tokyo: United Nations University Press; London: Anthem Press.

Reinhart, C. 2000. 'The Mirage of Floating Exchange Rates', *American Economic Review* 90, no. 2: 65–70.

Reinhart, C., and K. Rogoff. 2004. 'The Modern History of Exchange Rate Arrangements: A Reinterpretation', *Quarterly Journal of Economics* 119, no. 1: 1–48.

Rey, H. 2013. 'Dilemma Not Trilemma: The Global Financial Cycle and Monetary Policy Independence'. Federal Reserve Bank of Kansas City Economic Policy Symposium (2013).

———. 2014. 'The International Credit Channel and Monetary Autonomy'. PPT presentation at the IMF Mundell Fleming Lecture, 13 November. https://www.imf.org/external/np/res/seminars/2014/arc/pdf/Mundell.pdf.

Robles Jr, A. C. 2014. 'EU Trade in Financial Services with ASEAN, Policy Coherence for Development and Financial Crisis', *Journal of Common Market Studies* 52, no. 6: 1324–41.

Rodrik, D. 2003. 'Argentina: A Case of Globalization Gone Too Far or Not Far Enough?' In *The Crisis That Was Not Prevented: Lessons for Argentina, the IMF, and Globalization*, edited by Jan Jost Teunissen and Age Ackerman, chapter 2. The Hague. www.fondad.org.

———. 2006. 'The Social Cost of Foreign Exchange Reserves'. National Bureau of Economic Research (NBER) Working Paper Series 11952.

———. 2007. *One Economics, Many Recipes: Globalization, Institutions, and Economic Growth*. Princeton, NJ: Princeton University Press.

———. 2008. 'The Real Exchange Rate and Economic Growth'. Brookings Papers on Economic Activity, Fall, 365–412.

———. 2012. *The Globalization Paradox: Why Global Markets, States and Democracy Can Coexist*. Oxford: Oxford University Press.

———. 2013. 'Who Needs the Nation-State?' Roepke Lecture in Economic Geography delivered to the Association of American Geographers–Economic Geography. *Economic Geography* 89, no. 1: 1–19.

Rogoff, K. S. 2002. 'Rethinking Capital Controls: When Should We Keep an Open Mind?' *Finance and Development* 39 (December): 55–6.

Rooney, K. 2007. 'ICSID and BIT Arbitrations and China', *Journal of International Arbitration* 24, no. 6: 689–712.

Rose A., and T. Wieladek. 2011. 'Financial Protectionism'. VOX CEPR Policy Portal.

Rossi, P. 2015. Política cambial no Brasil: um esquema analítico', *Revista de Economia Política* 35, no. 4 (141) (October–December): 708–27.

Ruggie, J. G. 1988. 'Embedded Liberalism and the Post-war Economic Regimes'. In '*Constructing the World Polity: Essays on International Institutionalization*', edited by John Gerard Ruggie. Routledge. London and New York: Routledge.

Sanford, J. E. 2011. 'Currency Manipulation: The IMF and WTO'. Congressional Research Service (CRS). www.crs.org.

Sauvant, K., and M. Nolan. 2015. 'China's Outward Foreign Direct Investment and International Investment Law', *Journal of International Economic Law* 18, no. 4 (November):1–42.

Schill, S. W. 2007. 'Tearing Down the Great Wall: The New Generation Investment Treaties of the People's Republic of China'. Heidelberg: Max Planck Institute for International Law (Paper 1928).

Schoenmaker, D. 2011. 'The Financial Trilemma'. Duisenberg School of Finance, Tinbergen Institute Discussion Paper TI 11–019/DSF 7, 2011.

———. 2013. *Governance of International Banking: The Financial Trilemma*. Oxford: Oxford University Press.

Schott, J., and C. Cimino. 2014. 'Should Korea Join the Trans-Pacific Partnership?' Peterson Institute for International Economics. Policy Brief PB14–22.

Schwarcz, S. 2014. 'Ring Fencing', *Southern California Law Review* 87: 69–109.

Scott, R. 2015. 'Currency Manipulation and the 896,600 U.S. Jobs Lost Due to the U.S.–Japan Trade Deficit'. Economic Policy Institute, 4 February.

Shah, A., and I. Patnaik 2010. 'Managing Capital Flows: The Case of India'. In *Managing Capital Flows: The Search for a Framework*, edited by Masahiro Kawai and Mario B. Lamberte, chapter 9. A joint publication of the Asian Development Bank Institute and Edward Elgar Publishing. Cheltenham, UK; Northampton, MA: Edward Elgar.

Shambaugh J. 2004. 'Exchange Rate Regime Classification'. Dartmouth University. http://www.dartmouth.edu/~jshambau/.

Sharda, G., N. Swamy and C. Singh. 2014. 'Impact of Foreign Banks on the Indian Economy'. IIMB Working Paper No: 451.

Sheng, A. 2012. *From Asian to Global Financial Crisis: An Asian Regulator's View of Unfettered Finance in the 1990s and 2000s*. Cambridge: Cambridge University Press.

Shin, H. S. 2013. 'Adapting Macro Prudential Approaches to Emerging and Developing Economies'. In *Dealing with the Challenges of Macro Financial Linkages in Emerging Markets*, edited by Ottaviano Canuto and Swati R. Gosh, chapter 1. Washington DC: World Bank.

Silva, A. F. 2010. 'Brazilian Strategy for Managing the Risk of Foreign Exchange Rate Exposure during a Crisis'. Mimeo, Central Bank of Brazil.

Simmons, Beth A. 2001. 'The International Politics of Harmonization: The Case of Capital Market Regulation'. *International Organization* 55, no. 3: 589–620.

Singh, K. 2010. 'Emerging Markets Consider Capital Controls to Regulate Speculative Capital Flows'. VOX Research-based policy analysis and commentary from leading economists, 5 July.

———. 2011. 'India–EU FTA: Rethinking Banking Services Liberalization'. Madhyam Briefing Paper Series, No 1. Madhyam–Delhi, India.

———. 2015a. 'Decoding India's New Model BIT (I)'. Madhyam. www.madhyam.org.in.

———. 2015b. 'Decoding India's New Model BIT (II)'. Madhyam. www.madhyam.org.in.

———. 2015c. 'Decoding India's New Model BIT (III)'. Madhyam. www.madhyam.org.in.

Sobreira, R., and L. F. Paula. 2010. 'The 2008 Financial Crisis and Banking Behavior in Brazil: The Role of Financial Regulation', *Journal of Innovation Economics* 2: 73–93.

Sohiet, E. 2002. 'Índice de controle de capitais: uma análise de legislação e dos deter- minantes ao fluxo de capital no Brasil no período de 1990–2000'. Master's thesis, Escola de Pós-Graduação em Economia, FGV, Rio de Janeiro.

Solis, M. 2013. 'South Korea's Fateful Decision on the Trans-Pacific Partnership'. Foreign Policy at Brookings. Policy Paper no. 31, September.

———. 2014. 'The Answer is Still NO on a Currency Manipulation Clause in the TPP'. Brookings.edu, 15 January. https://www.brookings.edu/blog/up-front/2014/01/15/the-answer-is-still-no-on-a-currency-manipulation-clause-in-the-tpp/.

Stallings, B. 2015. 'Korea's Victory over the Global Financial Crisis'. In *Unexpected Outcomes: How Emerging Economies Survived the Global Financial Crisis*, edited by Carol Wise, Leslie Elliot Armijo and Saori M. Katada, chapter 3. Washington, DC: Brookings Institution Press.

Stanley, L. 2004. *Acuerdos bilaterales de inversión y demandas ante tribunales internacionales: la experiencia argentina reciente*. UN/CEPAL, División de Desarrollo Productivo y Empresarial. Cepal – Santiago de Chile.

———. 2009. 'Resolución de conflictos en material de bonos soberanos: una crítica'. Mirada institucional al papel del CIADI. Nuevos Documentos CEDES No. 58.

———. 2011. '"Smoke But Do Not Inhale": Capital Inflows, Financial Markets and Institutions, a Tale from Three Emerging Giants'. TUTFS/GDAE Working Group on Development and Environment in the Americas. Discussion Paper no. 31.

———. 2013. 'El proceso de internacionalización del RMB y el nuevo protagonismo del sistema financiero chino'. Red Académica América Latina y El Caribe-China/Economía, comercio e inversiones.

———. 2015a. 'RMB Internationalization and Latin America'. Mimeo.

———. 2015b. 'Financial Globalisation and Its Challenges to Economic Sustainability in South Korea'. *Latin American Journal of Management for Sustainable Development* 2, no. 3–4: 264–79.

Stanley, L., and J. M. Fernandez Alonso. 2015. 'Infraestructura y determinantes de la inversión extranjera en América Latina: entre el paradigma de las reglas y los acuerdos (geo)políticos-económicos ad-hoc'. Paper presentado en el Segundo Encuentro del Observatorio Académico Asia Pacífico–América Latina. Santiago de Chile, July.

Steinberg, D. 2014. 'Why Has China Accumulated Such Large Foreign Reserves?' In *The Great Wall of Money: Politics and Power in China's International Monetary Relations*, edited by Eric Helleiner and Jonathan Kirshner, 71–98. Ithaca: Cornell University Press.

Stiglitz, J. 2002. *Globalization and Its Discontents*. New York; London: W. W. Norton.

———. 2002. 'Lessons from Argentina's Debacle', in *Sand in the Wheels*. ATTAC Weekly Newsletter, no. 113, 16 January.

———. 2008. 'The Failure of Inflation Targeting'. Project Syndicate, May.

Su, C-W., H-L. Chang, T. Chang and K. Yin. 2014. 'Monetary Convergence in East Asian Countries Relative to China', *International Review of Economics and Finance* 33: 228–37.

Svensson, L. 2007. 'Inflation Targeting'. CEPS Working Paper no. 144.

Tabak, B., M. T. Latz and D. O. Cajueiro. 2010. 'Financial Stability and Monetary Policy – The Case of Brazil'. Banco Central do Brasil Working Papers Series no. 217.

———. Tarullo, D. 2008. *Banking on Basel: The Future of International Financial Regulation*. Washington, DC: Peterson Institute for International Economics.

Tarullo, D. K. 2014. 'Regulating Large Foreign Banking Organizations'. Remarks at the Harvard Law School Symposium on Building the Financial System of the Twenty-First Century: An Agenda for Europe and the United States. 27 March.

Taylor, J. B. 2000. 'Low Inflation, Pass-Through, and the Pricing Power of Firms', *European Economic Review* 44, no. 7: 1389–1408

Terra, M. C., and E. Sohiet. 2006. 'Índice de Controle de Capitais: Uma Análise da Legislação e seu Impacto Sobre o Fluxo de Capital no Brasil no Período 1990–2000'. *Estudos Econômicos (São Paulo* 36, no. 4 (October–December): 721–45.

Turner, A. 2010. 'After the Crises: Costs and Benefits of Financial Liberalization'. Speech at the 14th Chintaman Deshmukh Memorial Lecture, Reserve Bank of India. fsa.gov. http://www.fsa.gov.uk/pages/Library/Communication/Speeches/2010/0215_at.shtml.

———. 2014. 'Too Much of the Wrong Sort of Capital Flow'. Paper presented at the Conference on Capital Account Management and Macro-Prudential Regulation for Financial Stability and Growth, Centre for Advanced Financial Research and Learning and Reserve Bank of India, New Delhi, 13 January.

UNCTAD. 2015. 'The Investment Policy Hub'. United Nations Conference on Trade and Development. http://investmentpolicyhub.unctad.org.

Van Harten, G. 2014. 'The Canada-China FIPPA: Its Uniqueness and Non- reciprocity'. In *Canadian Yearbook of International Law/ Annuaire Canadien de droit international*, 1–60. Chicago, ssrn.com. http://papers.ssrn.com/sol3/ papers.cfm?abstract_id=2410532.

Vander Stichele, M. 2004. 'Trade in Financial Services: Liberalization in the GATS Agreement and Insufficient Assessment of the Risks'. In *SOMO – Critical Issues in the Financial Sector*, chapter 6. SOMO Sector Report. Amsterdam. https://www.somo.nl.

Vazquez, J. G. 2015. *La forma de las ruinas*. Alfaguara. 1st ed.; English translation *The Shape of the Ruins*, 2016.

Viterbo, A. 2012. *International Economic Law and Monetary Measures: Limitations to State's Sovereignty and Dispute Settlement*. Cheltenham, UK; Northampton, MA: Edward Elgar.

Waibel. M. 2009. 'BIT by BIT, the Silent Liberalization of the Capital Account'. In *International Investment Law for the 21st Century: Essays in Honour of Christoph Schreuer*, edited by Christina Binder, Ursula Kriebaum, August Reinisch, and Stephan Wittich, chapter 26. Oxford: Oxford University Press

Waibel, M. 2011. Sovereign Defaults before International Courts and Tribunals: *Cambridge Studies in International and Comparative Law*. Cambridge: Cambridge University Press.

WEED. 2014. Trade in Services Agreement (TiSA) and Financial Services. WEED. http://www2.weed-online.org/uploads/factsheet_tisa_and_financial_services.pdf.

Whalley, J. 2003. 'Liberalization in China's Key Service Sectors Following WTO Accession: Some Scenarios and Issues of Measurement'. National Bureau of Economic Research (NBER) Working Paper no. 10143.

Williamson, J. 2010. 'Exchange Rate Policy in Brazil'. Peterson Institute for International Economics. Working Paper Series WP10/16.

Wise C., and M. A. Del Tedesco Lins. 2015. 'Macroprudence versus Macroprofligacy: Brazil, Argentina, and the Global Financial Crisis'. In *Unexpected Outcomes: How Emerging Economies Survived the Global Financial Crisis*, edited by Carol Wise, Leslie Elliot Armijo and Saori N. Katana, chapter 7. Washington, DC: Brookings Institution Press.

Wolf, M. 2008. *Fixing Global Finance*. Baltimore: Johns Hopkins University Press.

———. 2015. *The Shifts and the Shocks*. New York: Penguin Press.

Woo, M. J-E. 2007. 'The Rule of Law, Legal Traditions, and Economic Growth: The East Asian Example'. In '*Institutional Change and Economic Development*', edited by Ha-Joon Chang, chapter 9. Tokyo: United Nations University Press; London: Anthem Press.

Woodford, M. 2010. 'Globalization and Monetary Control'. In *International Dimensions of Monetary Policy*, edited by Jordi Galí and Mark Gertler, 13–77. Chicago: University of Chicago Press.

Wouters, J., and D. Coppens. 2008. 'GATS and Domestic Regulations: Balancing the Right to Regulate and Trade Liberalization'. In *The World Trade Organization and Trade in Services*, edited by, 207–63. Leiden: Brill/Nijhof.

Yongzhong, W. 2009. 'An Estimation of the Effectiveness of China's Capital Controls and Sterilizations'. International Trade and Investment Series. Working Paper No. 09008.

Yu, Y. 2010. 'Managing Capital Flows: The Case of the People's Republic of China'. In *Managing Capital Flows: The Search for a Framework*, edited by Masahiro Kawai and Mario B. Lamberte, chapter 8. A joint publication of the Asian Development Bank Institute and Edward Elgar Publishing. Cheltenham, UK; Northampton, MA: Edward Elgar.

Yunling, Z., and Shen M. 2011. 'The Status of East Asian Free Trade Agreements'. ADBI Working Paper Series N 282.

Zeidan, R., and B. Rodrigues. 2013. 'The Failure of Risk Management for Non-Financial Companies in the Context of the Financial Crisis: Lessons from Aracruz Cellulose and Hedging with Derivatives', *Applied Financial Economics* 23 (February): 241–50.

Zeng, K. 2010. 'Multilateral versus Bilateral and Regional Trade Liberalization Explaining China's Pursuit of Free Trade Agreements (FTAs)', *Journal of Contemporary China* 19, no. 66: 635–52.

Zhang, M. 2014. 'Should China Accelerate Capital Account Liberalization Now?' In *Capital Account Liberalization in China: The Need for a Balanced Approach*, edited by Kevin P. Gallagher, chapter 5. Boston: The Frederik S. Pardee Centre for the Study of the Longer-Range Future, Boston University.

Zhang, X. 2015. 'Treading Carefully in the Minefield of the EU-China Investment Treaty'. Europe's World. 1 April. http://www.friendsofeurope.org/global-europe/treading-carefully-minefield-eu-china-investment-treaty.

Zhou, J., V. Rutledge, W. Bossu, M. Dobler, N. Jassaud and M. Moore. 2012. 'From Bail-out to Bail-in: Mandatory Debt Restructuring of Systematic Financial Institutions. International Monetary Fund'. IMF Staff Discussion Note. SDN/12/03.

INDEX

Lightning Source UK Ltd.
Milton Keynes UK
UKHW01n0941310518
323505UK00009B/361/P

9 781783 086740